David and Goliath

David and Goliath

Washington's War
Against Nicaragua

William I. Robinson
and
Kent Norsworthy

Zed Books Ltd.

David and Goliath was first published in the United Kingdom by Zed Books Ltd., 57 Caledonian Road, London N1 9BU, and in the United States by Monthly Review Press, 155 West 23 Street, New York, New York 10011, in 1987.

Cover designed by Andrew Corbett.
Photographs on pages 13 and 355 courtesy of Agencia Nueva Nicaragua; photograph on page 249 courtesy of *Barricada*.

British Library Cataloguing in Publication Data
Robinson, William I.
  David and Goliath : Washington's war against
  Nicaragua.
  1. Nicaragua—Politics and government—
  1979 2. United States—Foreign relations
  —Nicaragua 3. Nicaragua—Foreign relations
  —United States
  I. Title II. Norsworthy, Kent
  972.85′053   F1528

ISBN 0-86232-574-9
ISBN 0-86232-575-7 Pbk

This book is dedicated to the Nicaraguan people,
who are, as a matter of course, its real authors

Contents

Preface: One Goliath, a World of Davids   9

Part 1: The U.S. Strategy

1. Inside Goliath   15
2. The War of the Jackal   39
3. The New Strategy Takes Shape   80
4. Recasting Tactics: Changes in the Battlefields   96
5. Political Warriors and Socioeconomic Attrition   116
6. Casting Long Shadows: The Conflict Environment   156
7. The Internal Front: 1979–1984   193
8. The Counterrevolution: The "Thousand Factors"
   That Did Not Come Together   228

Part 2: The Revolution Defends Itself

9. Total Defense: The Military Theater   251
10. Total Defense: The Nonmilitary Theaters   281
11. Crisis in the Counterrevolution   309

Part 3: Conclusion

12. David's Victory   337

Epilogue: The Chickens Are Coming Home to Roost   353

Notes   357

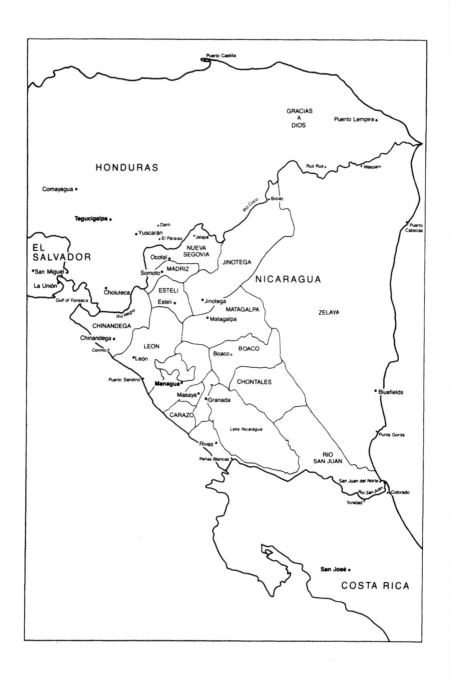

Preface
One Goliath, a World of Davids

Five years ago the song of the roosters and birds
heralded the triumph of the reign of dreams and of
hope. Five years ago the church bells rang out and
rifle and machine gunfire resounded announcing
the news: the birth of the free people of Nicaragua.
And all of Nicaragua began to write the most beau-
tiful poem. . . . But these verses disturbed the
snoring of Goliath, Goliath who had stolen our
voice and shackled our country. These verses an-
noyed Goliath as he saw David standing tall, since
he thought he had killed him when he killed Sandino. Then Goliath hurled himself once again at
David, that is, against the workers, the peasants,
against the young people and women, against children, against the heroic people of Nicaragua.

—Daniel Ortega,
President of Nicaragua, 19 July 1984

The Sandinista government maintains an open door to all foreigners,
who are invited to come and see the reality of the new Nicaragua.

Some months before our arrival in early 1982, the Reagan administration approved a multi-million-dollar program of not-so-covert destabilization against the young Sandinista revolution. As we passed
through customs, workers were discussing a massacre that had taken
place in the north that morning. Fourteen peasants had been tortured
and killed, and another six kidnapped, by the Somocistas. The U.S.
program was already bearing fruit.

As we saw the war grow in intensity, we concluded that the greatest
contribution we could make to opposing the injustice we were witness-
ing was to write what we had seen and learned for people outside
Nicaragua. We therefore decided to stay in Nicaragua and to work as
journalists. The truth is a powerful weapon; we have never lost our faith
that the peoples of the world will act on the truth in defense of justice.

9

In late 1983 the Sandinistas announced the opening of the electoral process, which they had promised in 1979. As the process got under way, we listened to the debates on streetcorners and in restaurants, attended campaign rallies of left, center, and right political parties, and saw peasants and workers for the first time participating in democratic elections with real interest and enthusiasm. Yet according to the Reagan administration these were "Soviet-style sham elections" intended to "legitimize a dictatorship." In September 1984, two months before the U.S. and Nicaraguan elections, we were invited to make a speaking tour in the United States, talking about the Nicaraguan elections and the U.S. effort to undermine them as part of its war strategy.

It was during the tour that we first discussed this book. We met hundreds of people who felt a sense of outrage at what their government was doing in Central America, and we became convinced that documenting the story was necessary so that these people and others could be armed with information to channel their outrage.

Two days after we returned to Nicaragua, the Reagan administration claimed that a shipment of MiG jet fighters was on the way from the Soviet Union and threatened military intervention. It was early November 1984. Of course, U.S. intervention was already several years old by then, but we were nevertheless frightened. Each morning we were shaken by the sonic booms made by U.S. jets flying overhead. Only later did we learn that SR-71 Blackbird high-altitude reconnaissance aircraft were photographing every square inch of Nicaraguan territory, and that these pictures would be used when five thousand contras invaded from Honduras in 1985.

On the one hand, U.S. aggression has become the most determining aspect of reality in Nicaragua; on the other hand, the U.S. "information blockade" has prevented the North American people from learning the truth of what their government is doing in their name. We expect this book to make an important contribution to the process of breaking that blockade.

As journalism students we were told that reporters do not take sides, they take notes. This, of course, cannot apply to the real world, where journalists are important social actors, and where journalism has a vital impact on shaping society. With regard to Nicaragua, the line between right and wrong, justice and injustice, is clearly drawn, as are the responsibilities of a journalist. In all our journalistic work, and throughout this book, we are *objective*; we relay historical facts truthfully and accurately. But we are not, and do not pretend to be, *neutral*. We have taken sides. If we may quote Nicaraguan Vice-president Dr. Sergio Ramírez, "We are part of that historic wave of poor and exploited peoples who are struggling for the avalanche of humanity toward peace and justice, and *we will not cede that place.*"

Nevertheless, interpreting reality can be a risky undertaking, since it is easy to bend reality to fit one's interpretations. We hope we have done reality justice, and take full responsibility for the interpretations and analysis, as well as any weaknesses and shortcomings—of which there are undoubtedly many. For one thing, we have had to severely limit our scope, and we do not pretend to analyze the internal dynamic of the Nicaraguan revolutionary process or the contradictions particular to it, except insofar as they relate to our main theme, the United States–Nicaraguan contradiction.

This book was written under wartime conditions, which put great constraints and pressures, not just on ourselves, but on all those involved in the project. Therefore the support and assistance of many friends and colleagues is especially appreciated. We owe particular thanks to the Coordinadora Regional de Investigaciones Económicas y Sociales (CRIES) and the Agencía Nueva Nicaragua (ANN): they paid our salaries while giving us leaves of absence and provided important institutional backing for the project. We are also especially indebted to Judy Butler, without whose editorial skills, critical suggestions, and time set aside to work with us (even while maintaining two other jobs), this manuscript would never have materialized. And we would like to thank Roger Burbach of CENSA for his input and constant encouragement from the very beginning, Sarah Miles of Nicaragua Exchange (especially for her contributions to Chapter 1), and Deborah Barry from CRIES, who deserves recognition for her pioneering research on low-intensity conflict. In addition, we would like to thank Ellen Kaiser and *Frontline* newspaper, Carlos Fernando Chamorro from DAP, Richard Stahler Sholk, Beverly and Mike Winchell, Rosa Maria Castillo, Kevin Robinson, Cecilia Cabieses, Ruth Spinola, Roberto Bardini, Allan Frankovich, David Sweet, Tony Cavin, José Lobo, Roberto Larios and Ana Patricia Lacayo from DAP, Maria Flores, Aldo Espinoza, Anabell Zepeda, Larry Boyd, and the staff at Monthly Review Press for their contributions. Finally, special appreciation to Yolanda Chávez and Gioconda Espinoza for their patience and support.

War is a dialectical process. We chose the image of David and Goliath because it reflects the dialectic of the U.S. war against Nicaragua. The Nicaraguan people are not only defending themselves against the U.S. aggression, but are deepening and strengthening their revolution even in the midst of—indeed *in response to*—the war. The weaker part of the contradiction—revolution—is growing in strength, overcoming its antagonist—counterrevolution—and realizing itself in the process of resolving the contradiction. The way we have chosen to demonstrate this is by first making a theoretical presentation of the U.S. strategy (in Chapter 1), then discussing its emergence and consolidation *as intent* (in Chapters 2 and 3), the extent to which the United States has been able to *implement* the strategy (in Chapters 4 through 8), and finally Nicaragua's *response*, which sets in motion a *tendency* toward the resolution of the contradiction in favor of revolution (in Chapters 9 through 11).

Chapter 1 analyzes the Reagan Doctrine and the strategy of low-intensity warfare, presenting the framework necessary for understanding the context in which the war is taking place. Although this chapter may appear somewhat removed from the nitty-gritty of the book's central discussion—the U.S. war against Nicaragua—it is worth following closely in order to acquire the historical and analytical perspective necessary to appreciate the rest of the book. Chapter 2 begins with 1979 and ends with late 1983, when the strategy of low-intensity warfare crystallized. Chapter 3 backtracks, taking us behind the scenes to look at the emergence of this strategy as it was applied to Central America; it also examines several key U.S. actors in this conflict. Some of the most well-known events of this stage of the war are discussed in Chapter 4. In Chapters 5 and 6 we take a closer look at the complex inner workings of the U.S. strategy. The time frame for these three chapters is 1984 through 1985. Chapter 7 introduces a new component to the war—the counterrevolution's internal front—and reviews its formation and development from 1979 through 1984. Chapter 8 then shows how, by 1985, all the elements were coming together. In Chapters 9 through 11, we turn to the Sandinista revolution as protagonist, examining its evolving response to the war from 1979 through 1986. We have combined analysis with journalistic chronicle, so as to endow the skeleton of analysis with the flesh and blood of reality.

The work of a journalist constantly demands renewal in consonance with day-by-day developments. The war against Nicaragua is a burning issue and the heat of battle does not give the journalist the opportunity to "finish" a work; the vital importance of getting timely information out means that a book such as this is never complete. In the meantime, history continues to unfold.

—Managua, Nicaragua
September 1986

Part 1
The U.S. Strategy

1
Inside Goliath

The Reagan Doctrine

Nations exist only in relation to each other. Foreign policy is the instrument by which peoples seek to assure their survival in a hostile world. War, not peace, is the norm in international affairs.

—The Committee of Santa Fe[1]

In its 200 years as an independent nation, the United States has waged some 150 declared and undeclared wars around the world and has sent troops across other countries' borders on an average of once a year. Since World War II, it has employed military force more than 200 times;[2] carried out up to 20,000 covert operations; overthrown countless govenments; and killed hundreds of thousands of people. It has initiated a major military conflict approximately once every ten years.

By the mid-1980s, a decade had passed since the end of the nation's last major military adventure, the Vietnam war. In terms of historic continuity, therefore, with the war on Central America the United States has not gone to war, it has gone *back* to war.

"World War Three has already begun," declared the Committee of Santa Fe, Ronald Reagan's policy team for Latin America, in 1980, sounding the battle cry of the incoming administration.[3] In this war, which is being waged on a global basis, Central America has emerged as the primary theater of operations. Since 1978, more than 120,000 of the region's inhabitants have died as a result of the U.S. war. One out of every five Central Americans has been uprooted. A considerable proportion of the region's 20 million people has grown accustomed to facing aerial bombardment, white phosphorus and napalm, chemical and biological warfare, supersonic overflights, U.S. naval exercises off their countries' coasts, mass torture and kidnappings, and refugee camps that have come increasingly to resemble concentration camps. Since 1982, over 90,000 U.S. soldiers have participated in the Central American war.

15

It is unlikely that we will see any large-scale deployment of U.S. troops in Nicaragua; jungle warfare will not be televised in living rooms across North America. The conflict is escalating and expanding daily, yet the United States shows none of the characteristics of a nation at war. Commentators and analysts hotly debate when and how the "invasion" will take place, when "war" will be declared. Meanwhile the *real* invasion has long since begun; *real* war is being waged. The U.S. military has made this quite clear: in the words of one high-level Department of Defense (DOD) official, "If we ever reach the point of shooting it out with conventional . . . formations, we already will have lost. What we are talking about here is the real war."[4]

What distinguishes this war is that it is not a military contest but a political struggle. The United States has learned a key lesson from recent history: military supremacy does not necessarily lead to victory. In the wake of its disastrous defeat in Southeast Asia, U.S. imperialism is experimenting with a new doctrine: *low-intensity warfare* (LIW). It grows out of U.S. military doctrine but is a radical departure from it. LIW involves maintaining a multiplicity of pressures—political, economic, diplomatic, psychological, and ideological—against the enemy, and synchronizing those pressures with permanent but low-key military aggression. At its heart is the political invalidation, rather than the military defeat, of the enemy. LIW is a twentieth-century version of nineteenth-century Prussian military theorist Carl von Clausewitz's axiom that "War is the extension of politics by other means."

As the site of the first full-scale low-intensity war waged by the United States, Central America is both a symbol and a testing ground. But while the Central American war is a regional one, the *strategic core* of the U.S. objective in the region is the destruction of the Sandinista revolution in Nicaragua.

Revolution breeds counterrevolution. Social revolution in today's world is a process whereby a new socioeconomic project is constructed in opposition to the old. The two projects, old and new, correspond to the interests of distinct classes and sectors of the society concerned, and the class in power will defend its project against that of the competing class. The first step in any revolution is the seizure of power by the formerly dispossessed classes, followed by the consolidation of that power and the construction of a new socioeconomic order that will serve their own interests. Just as the British government sent troops to the United States in 1776 in an attempt to regain its former colonies, so the displaced inevitably set out to recapture power and reconstruct the old order. Thus is *counterrevolution* born out of revolution.

Every revolution in modern history has faced counterrevolution. The hostility shown by successive U.S. governments to every revolution that has taken place in the present century reflects the United States' unflagging determination to maintain its authority over countries that have claimed, or seek to claim, their independence and sovereignty.

From the moment that the Sandinista revolution triumphed in Nicaragua, the forces of counterrevolution were set in motion. But what started out as the spontaneous reaction of those most immediately displaced from power—Somoza and his clique—rapidly became a comprehensive project conceived and designed by, and directed from the United States. While this is not the first time the United States has directed a counterrevolution in the third world, it has become the most advanced project of a new doctrine whose aim is to guide the U.S. empire in the latter part of the twentieth century.

Stated simply, this doctrine, known as the Reagan Doctrine, signifies global counterrevolution. It is a *radical response* to the long-term decline of U.S. imperialism in the face of successful wars of national liberation. The Reagan Doctrine represents a qualitative break with the doctrines of previous administrations in that it seeks not to *maintain* but to *alter* the world correlation of forces in its favor. "Preservation of the status quo is not enough. The United States must seek to improve its relative position," declared the Committee of Santa Fe, which was charged in the summer of 1980 with drawing up the general contours of the Reagan administration's foreign policy, particularly with regard to Latin America.[5]

The Postwar Years

The Reagan Doctrine is deeply rooted in recent U.S. history. In the thirty years between the two world wars, the United States moved from being a regional capitalist power to being the overlord of a vast and powerful empire. Yet during this same period, the Russian Revolution of 1917 gave birth to the first socialist state in the world. The contradiction between the Soviet Union, as the center of world socialism, and the United States, as the center of world capitalism, has been at the heart of U.S. foreign policy since 1945. This contradication has played itself out not in *direct* confrontation between the two "superpowers," but in the struggle between the peoples of the third world—striving for independence and sovereignty—and the United States, which has sought to maintain its domination over these peoples.

The U.S. search for supremacy has been expressed in various versions of the "containment" doctrine, formalized by President Truman in 1950 in National Security Council (NSC) Memorandum NSC-68.

One of the key foreign policy statements of the postwar period, the Truman Doctrine proposed that, to contain the Soviet Union, the perimeters of U.S. power must be defended militarily. NSC-68 asserted that the United States must "foster a fundamental change in the nature of the Soviet system [by using] any means, covert or overt, violent or non-violent" to achieve its global objectives; only on this basis can "a successfully functioning political and economic system be created."[6]

The synthesis of the U.S.-sponsored counterrevolution around the globe with U.S. hostility toward the Soviet Union was expressed in the reduction of a complex and diverse world into a rigid, bipolar one, which then becomes the terrain of the "East-West" conflict. When considered from this particular ideological viewpoint, any country that is attempting to map out a nominally independent or nationally oriented road to socioeconomic development—much less to develop an alternative political system that may challenge U.S. hegemony—becomes by definition a "pawn of Soviet expansionism." The convergence of the threat posed to imperialism by socialism and that posed by national liberation is the driving force behind the containment policy.

Twenty years after its formulation, however, containment was on the ropes. Vietnam had become the front line for the defense of the imperial system, the symbol of U.S. resolve to hold back the tide of history. And it was rapidly becoming clear that containment was failing.

The United States had entered the Southeast Asian morass in the 1950s as the undisputed leader of the world capitalist system, enjoying virtually unchallenged hegemony. It emerged from its defeat by the Vietnamese people with its interventionist capacity severely eroded and its internal post-World War II foreign policy consensus shattered. While U.S. troops were battling in the jungles of Southeast Asia, in Washington the Nixon administration was reevaluting the limits of empire. The last U.S. forces were withdrawn in 1974, and the Nixon policy of détente became the new form of containment—an acceptable means of defending U.S. interests in the face of the new correlation of forces.

More than any other event of the postwar period, the Vietnam war had a profound effect on U.S. society and on the redefinition of international relations. The Vietnamese victory cast doubt upon the efficacy of the U.S. bourgeoisie and emboldened peoples all over the world who were struggling for freedom. The post-World War II foreign policy consensus was replaced with a generalized and semi-spontaneous opposition to military intervention abroad on the part of the U.S. public; this became known as the "Vietnam syndrome," and was to act as a powerful check against any further attempts to intervene overseas.

Following the U.S. withdrawal from Vietnam, a period of ideological flux and redefinition of policies and strategies ensued, a time when what some Reaganites now call "low politics" (their term for economic concerns) dominated over "high politics" (their term for security concerns). Presided over by the Carter administration, this period of redefinition, with its emphasis on human rights, trade, and economic cooperation with the third world, was a necessary step in the refurbishing of imperialism.[7]

The United States may have been taking a respite from intervention abroad, but in the third world popular struggles for liberation continued unabated. Liberation movements in Africa, Asia, and Latin America took advantage of the historic opening afforded by the U.S. weakness. Between 1975 and 1980, revolutionary forces in Angola, Mozambique, Zimbabwe, Kampuchea, Grenada, Nicaragua, and elsewhere came to power, and the United States found itself unable to halt this process. During these six years, fourteen new revolutionary and progressive states emerged in the third world.[8]

Thus from World War II to the commencement of Reagan's first term, the global correlation of forces had altered radically. By the time the Republicans assumed office, the unprecedented economic crisis and the gradual deterioration of relations among the Western powers contributed to a near-generalized crisis of imperialism. The 1980 Republican party platform moaned: "The American experiment, so marvelously successful for 200 years, has come to a dismal end." Thus, although the initial Republican program may have appeared insurgent, it was devised *in response* to the substantial weakening of U.S. imperialism over a twenty-year period. Right-wing counterrevolutions have flourished in the mid-1980s precisely because a whole series of left-led revolutions succeeded.

The Roots of Reaganism

Containment of the Soviet Union is not enough. Détente is dead. Survival demands a new U.S. foreign policy. America must seize the initiative or perish. For World War Three is almost over. America is everywhere in the retreat . . . *an integrated global foreign policy is essential . . . a worldwide counter-projection of American power* is in the offing. The hour of decision can no longer be postponed.

—The Committee of Santa Fe[9]

The immediate roots of Reaganism can be traced back to 1976 and the formation of the Committee on the Present Danger (CPD) by rightist forces that had been organizing since the U.S. withdrawal from Vietnam two years earlier. The CPD attracted elements of the traditional U.S. ruling elite tied to finance capital in the Northeast, so-called neoconservatives, the new right-wing organizations in the southern and western states, and factions of the "old right." All these groups eventually merged in a coalition that came to be known as the New Right. In the 1978 congressional elections the New Right managed to make significant inroads into Congress, and in 1980 swept Ronald Reagan into the White House.[10]

Characterized by some as "cowboy style," Reagan's foreign policy in fact represents forces and interests deeply embedded in the power structures of the United States. An examination of the full spectrum of administration policymakers shows that behind the New Right stands a major cross-section of monopoly capital.[11] With only a few exceptions, Reagan's first cabinet was composed of conservative millionaires tightly enmeshed in the military-industrial complex, men who had an important stake in the remilitarization essential to the implementation of the Reagan Doctrine.[12] Essentially the program envisioned by the doctrine is undertaken on behalf of these power structures. Indeed, the Reagan Doctrine is Reagan's in name only.

The new administration immediately set out to restore U.S. hegemony in the world by any means available—political, economic, social, and military. The most critical aspects of administration thinking were the determination to achieve strategic nuclear superiority over the Soviet Union; to embark on the greatest peacetime military buildup in U.S. history;[13] to "roll back" the advance of "communism" around the world; and to transfer wealth on a massive scale from the working class to the war machine and the ruling classes through drastic cuts in social spending, corporate tax breaks, reductions in real wages, etc.

To implement such a program without the support of the majority of the population is a difficult enough task; it proved much more so in a nation where, following Vietnam, there was widespread sentiment against the military and against intervention abroad. The New Right's counteroffensive therefore needed an ideological component capable of creating a climate of public acceptance for its program.

> The first challenge for the future is to create a new
> vested-interest attitude and sense of patriotism and
> urgency throughout the body politic of this nation.
>
> —Maj. Gen. Michael J. Healy,
> U.S. Army, ret.[14]

During its first two years, the Reagan administration successfully moved the entire spectrum of "acceptable" U.S. politics to the right. It sought to stake out a new political center and then construct a new consensus around it. The administration's initial concern was to eradicate the Vietnam syndrome, a job that required the permanent ideological bombardment of the populace: any and every challenge to U.S. hegemony abroad became an excuse for whipping up a siege mentality. Vociferous anticommunism, such as had not been witnessed since the McCarthy era, characterized every administration utterance. The Reaganites portrayed the confrontataion between East and West in quasi-theological terms, as a struggle between the forces of democracy and the "evil empire," while the president's chauvinistic nationalism expressed itself in such phrases as "America is back" and "standing tall." Soviet troops were suddenly "discovered" in Cuba after having been there—as the Department of Defense knew perfectly well—for seventeen years, and mythical Libyan hit squads were invented to maintain the momentum of the Reaganite disinformation campaign. By early 1983 a highly placed Pentagon official was able to boast: "Now, after a decade of near isolationism, when even the hint of military action brought denunciations of 'planning for another Vietnam,' we can realistically think about the use of force again."[15]

The next stage in the implementation of the Reagan program—moving from planning to testing—came with the invasion of Grenada in October 1983. Eliminating a revolutionary regime that had committed suicide before U.S. forces arrived, in a tiny Caribbean island-nation of some 100,000 inhabitants, was certainly no great feat. Its symbolic significance far exceeded its actual accomplishment, however: the invasion demonstrated that the United States was once again prepared to use military force to impose its will abroad. It also showed that the ideological offensive had succeeded in eroding (although by no means erasing) the Vietnam syndrome: the invasion had sufficient domestic support to demonstrate to the administration that its doctrine of reversing revolutions could be put into practice. In the words of the right-wing ideologues of the Heritage Foundation, "the intervention in Grenada . . . shattered spreading notions that communist advances are irreversible. It thereby encouraged democratic forces resisting Soviet domination elsewhere in the world."[16]

But enthusiasm alone was not enough, as the United States was learning in Lebanon, where political complexities and risk made decisive U.S. action impossible. The killing of 241 Marines in Lebanon just days before the invasion of Grenada taught the administration that there was still a price to be paid for intervention. Associated risks and the real prospects for success would have to be carefully analyzed before a final decision was reached regarding the selection of the front lines of the global counteroffensive.

Anatomy of the Reagan Doctrine

A political doctrine is not merely an abstraction from policy; nor is it simply the ideological legitimization of that policy. A political doctrine is a comprehensive and cohesive *framework* that guides policy. By mid-1984, the Reagan Doctrine had matured considerably: it now amounted to a great deal more than sporadic sponsorship of counter-revolution and renewed interventionism conducted under the general rubric of virulent anticommunism and the enhancement of "national security."

In the summer of 1984 the Heritage Foundation released a report entitled *Mandate for Leadershp II: Continuing the Conservative Revolution*, a blueprint for the second Reagan term (the Santa Fe document was considered the foreign policy blueprint for the first term) and synopsis of the intellectual and programmatic underpinnings of the emerging Reagan Doctrine. Its essentials were later outlined by Secretary of State George Shultz in a speech given at the Commonwealth Club in San Francisco on 22 February 1985: (1) support for "peaceful democratic change" throughout the world, including in noncommunist, pro-Western countries; (2) support for "democratic governments by providing economic and security assistance against a variety of threats"; (3) support for "the forces of freedom in Communist totalitarian states"; (4) support for "those struggling against the imposition of Communist tyranny." In sum, the whole world was a battleground and the Reagan Doctrine a "prudent strategy combining different elements suited to different circumstances."

The four programmatic planks described by Shultz constitute an integrated framework for foreign policy. The first reflects the administration's conviction that the latent instability of right-wing dictatorships poses a threat to imperial interests and, accordingly, that "peaceful democratic change"—or reforming fascist states into bourgeois democracies—is necessary if a worldwide counteroffensive is to be launched. Such change should not, however, go so far as to provide an opening for the forces of revolution.[17] The second plank represents a general reaffirmation that those "pro-Western" countries that enjoy moderate stability will not be abandoned should they come under revolutionary threat in the future, and that those countries already facing a major revolutionary challenge (e.g., El Salvador), and those that play key geopolitical roles (e.g., Honduras) against young revolutionary governments will be given special attention. The third plank indicates that covert harassment of socialist countries is to become official U.S. policy.

The fourth plank is, without doubt, the crux of the doctrine. While the destabilization of revolutions is not a novel aspect of U.S. foreign policy, here it assumes new features and undergoes both a *quantitative* expansion and—more significantly—a *qualitative* transformation. It is this qualitative transformation that constitutes the very core of the strategy to reverse the global correlation of forces. It is the principal means by which the United States seeks to confront the Soviet Union. Vernon Asparturian, a commentator who is associated with the Rand Corporation, has put it like this: "There is an old Russian folk-proverb that 'the cloth unravels at its edges,' and in the case of the Soviet empire, the unravelling process is most easily initiated at its margins."[18]

In the vocabulary of the Reagan Doctrine, revolutionaries become "terrorists," terrorists become "freedom fighters," and counterrevolution becomes "revolution." But the language of the Reagan Doctrine is not mere double-talk; it is one of the most important structured elements in the entire ideological edifice. Beyond language, Washington seeks to legitimize the U.S. counterrevolution as a form of self-defense sanctioned in international law. "Support for freedom fighters is self-defense, and totally consistent with the OAS [Organization of American States] and UN charters," said Reagan.[19]

While ambitious in its goals, the Reagan Doctrine is also realistic: it recognizes that the U.S. government has neither the resources nor the capacity to organize or direct full-blown counterrevolutions in any and every country whose politics it abhors. The selection of the countries where efforts and resources are to be concentrated is based on the careful appraisal of the prospects for success. Such appraisals entail evaluating the *stage of consolidation* of the revolutionary target, assessing the potential for creating "anti-Marxist insurgencies" by establishing proxy armies composed of reactionary elements and modeled after authentic national liberation movements (a strategy that offers technical, political, and economic advantages over the deployment of U.S. troops), and judging the economic and geopolitical importance of the country concerned. The selection process also considers such criteria as cost effectiveness and the potential benefits to be derived from each counterrevolutionary project.

The Heritage Foundation report also recommends that the U.S. government "employ paramilitary assets to weaken those Communist and non-Communist regimes that may already be facing the early stages of insurgency within their borders and which threaten U.S. interests," listing Kampuchea, Laos, Vietnam, Angola, Ethiopia, Afghanistan, Iran, and Libya.[20] In a highly revealing passage, the report states that "it may not be possible to reverse each of these situations. But it should be possible, at the very least, to *use them for leverage in a larger strategic approach* emphasizing that the U.S. no longer will countenance the subversion or overthrow of friendly governments within the developing world."[21] In other words, while the destruction of a revolution may be preeminently desirable, *any* counterrevolutionary action will serve the greater strategic objective of scoring points in the larger global context. And, of course, the anticommunist insurgencies will send a signal to those struggling for national liberation that they will have to pay a high price for their national democratic aspirations.

Although it is beyond the scope of this book to analyze the extent to which Reaganism enjoys the full support of the U.S. bourgeoisie, there can be little doubt that its general premises have been accepted by the class as a whole: it is clearly recognized that if U.S. imperialism is to survive, it must wage an aggressive struggle on a world scale. The political disagreements that have surfaced within the United States concerning the counteroffensive relate to its configuration, not to its advisability.[22]

In sum, with the launching of the Reagan Doctrine, the United States has initiated World War III against the third world.

Central America: The Cutting Edge of the Reagan Doctrine

In the eyes of the Reagan administration, Nicaragua met the doctrine's "optimum criteria": the geopolitical stakes were extremely high, organizing the counterrevolution would be a low-cost operation, and the chances of success were considered good. Not only was the Sandinista revolution still undergoing consolidation, but it also faced numerous obstacles that the seizure of state power had failed to eliminate.[23]

The United States has long considered Central America and the Caribbean to be of paramount importance, both politically and economically, to U.S. preeminence in the Western hemisphere. In 1823 President James Monroe staked out the U.S. claim in his annual message to Congress: "As a principle in which the rights and interests of the United States are involved, [we] will not tolerate [foreign] influence in the affairs of the Western hemisphere countries." Originally designed to dissuade the European powers from challenging nascent U.S. hegemony over its natural domain, the Monroe Doctrine was to become the basis for over 150 years of intervention. Every attempt by the peoples of Latin America to win their independence ran up against the "principle" of the Monroe Doctrine. And then, 157 years after Monroe's historic address, the Committee of Santa Fe put out the cry for the Reagan administration to breathe new life into the fifth president's words.

U.S. economic interests in the Caribbean Basin include corporate holdings—productive investments as well as banking and financial operations—exceeding $23 billion, and another $30 billion in Mexico, together comprising over 20 percent of U.S. investment abroad.[24] Caribbean Basin regional debt to U.S. banks surpasses $130 billion; virtually every major corporate sector in the United States has a stake in this investment. It should also be noted that approximately 75 percent of the petroleum consumed in the United States or handled by U.S. oil companies passes through the Caribbean, as do most of the nation's imported raw materials.

Even more significant than this direct economic stake is the region's geopolitical importance.[25] It was here that the United States first consolidated its empire, and further imperial adventures around the globe have been predicated on absolute domination of the Caribbean and Central American "backyard." Thus any challenge to U.S. hegemony in this region—the "soft underbelly"—strikes at the underpinnings of the entire imperial system. The Committee of Santa Fe stressed: "For a balancing state like the United States, there is no possibility of flexible global action if its power [in the Caribbean Basin region] is immobilized or checked."[26]

The Central American and Caribbean region is where U.S. capitalism's internal and external domains meet, the bridge between imperial intent and world hegemony. *It is also the site of the most advanced challenge to that hegemony in the 1980s.* It is not surprising, then, that the Committee of Santa Fe targeted Central America as the number one U.S. foreign policy concern.[27] As Reagan declared in 1983, "If we cannot defend ourselves there, we cannot expect to prevail elsewhere. Our credibility would collapse, our alliances would crumble and the safety of our homeland would be put in jeopardy."[28] Months later, the Kissinger Commission made similar claims, asserting that the region "is in the geostrategic crossroads of a world with global dimensions, [and] for this reason Central America is a test for American credibility."

At the core of the Central American challenge to U.S. hegemony is the Sandinista revolution in Nicaragua. On 19 July 1979 Nicaragua ceased being just another of Uncle Sam's banana republics. The Sandinista victory shattered U.S. pretensions to regional supremacy and, in the eyes of some, signified the beginning of the end of U.S. domination in the region. For the Reagan administration, defeating the insurgencies in El Salvador and Guatemala and maintaining U.S. control over Honduras and Costa Rica hinge on the destruction of the Sandinista revolution. One Reaganite ideologue spelled out this position even before the Republicans came to power: "As long as [revolution] exists in any great strength in any one of [the countries of Central America], the others will be in danger. Thus, the security of El Salvador requires the removal of the government in Managua."[29] In the global equation, the Sandinista revolution, and the U.S. efforts to destroy it, constitute the front line in the battle between revolution and counterrevolution, the conflict on which the Reagan Doctrine is predicated. The revolution in Nicaragua has many implications for the countries beyond its borders. And it is only in light of this fact that the fanatical obsession of the rulers of the most powerful country in the world with a nation that is smaller than the state of New York and has a population of barely 3 million people can be understood. "There has possibly never been another moment in the history of the United States in which a country so tiny and underdeveloped has been treated with such aggressiveness," pointed out Sandinista leader Bayardo Arce.[30]

Low-Intensity Warfare

Our political and military decision-makers, like the shrewd buyer in the marketplace, should select the model that will suffice for the purpose at the least cost. Low-intensity conflict is an economical option which we must, as a result of Vietnam, recognize as a legitimate form of conflict at least for the next twenty years. The last quarter of the twentieth century is going to call for measured national initiatives which combine economic, psychological, and military ingredients. We cannot afford a military which provides only a sledgehammer in situations which demand the surgeon's scalpel.

—Former U.S. Army officer,
a veteran of the war in
Southeast Asia[31]

The Emergence of Low-Intensity Warfare

Following the defeat of U.S. forces in Vietnam, bewildered U.S. military and political analysts undertook a systematic evaluation of the reasons for that failure. Concluding that the United States had experienced a *tactical* victory but a *strategic* defeat, they argued that a new strategy for waging counterrevolution in the third world would have to be devised if the United States was to succeed in such conflicts in the future.[32] And it was low-intensity warfare which draws on the work of theorists both classical (von Clausewitz) and modern (Mao Zedong, Vo Nguyen Giap, and Che Guevara), as well as on the lessons of British, French, and other counterinsurgency operations in the third world—that eventually provided the conceptual framework within which the new strategy has developed. Representing a radical alternative to traditional counterinsurgency strategy, LIW recasts the strategic military concepts that constituted the intellectual underpinnings of the U.S. aggression against Vietnam in a form that reflects the lesson learned there.[33]

Many of the people who were directly involved in the design and execution of the war against Vietnam, and who later participated in the critique of the U.S. defeat, have since assumed positions of influence within the institutions of the Reagan administration and those of the New Right. From these institutions, which range from think tanks that provide strategic guidelines for the administration to key posts in the Pentagon, the State Department, the Central Intelligence Agency, and U.S. missions abroad, LIW proponents are directing the executive apparatus's implementation of the LIW strategy.

At the heart of the LIW strategy is the reconceptualization of wars against national liberation movements as *political* rather than *military* undertakings: the military apparatus thus becomes a means of achieving political ends, and the ultimate objective of engagement becomes the political defeat of the enemy. This shift of emphasis, from military annihilation to political invalidation, entails reducing the military element to only one of many means for attaining the newly defined objective. The military element therefore moves from a strategic to a tactical role. But its form is also redefined: as Col. John D. Waghelstein, former head of the U.S. team of military advisers to El Salvador, has put it, LIW is "revolutionary and counterrevolutionary warfare. It is *total war* at the grassroots level—one that uses *all* of the weapons of total war, including political, economic and psychological warfare, with the military aspect being a distant fourth in many cases."[34]

War is thus redefined as the struggle for supremacy between antagonistic alternatives (revolution and counterrevolution), and the battlefield is no longer viewed in terms of territory, much less as the site where military forces engage in combat. Rather, it is *everywhere* that the antagonistic alternatives confront each other. LIW knows no borders, geographic or otherwise: it is waged in the mountains of Nicaragua and El Salvador, in international lending agencies, in diplomatic forums, and in the realm of ideas (in the media and elsewhere). "In conventional war, where you have an identifiable opponent, you just occupy critical terrain while also destroying the opponent's will to fight," asserts Waghelstin. "In [LIW] . . . the only territory you want to hold is the six inches between the ears of the peasant."[35]

In the LIW framework, the distinction between war and peace is obscured. Because LIW is total war, many of its aspects can seem invisible. Thus the term itself is misleading. Taken from the language of traditional military conflict, which assumes a gradual broadening of the spectrum of conflict—from sanctions to terrorism, to full-scale insurgency, to conventional war, to tactical and finally strategic nuclear war—the term "low intensity" is derived from the low level of sophistication of the weaponry used and the low numerical magnitude of the forces deployed, all relative to conventional warfare. But LIW is not simply a stage in warfare—a precursor of conventional war—but an *alternative strategy*, one that operates with its own dynamic. The distinctive nature of LIW relates more to the character of the conflict than to its level of intensity or to the scale of forces involved.

Moreover, even in military terms there is nothing "low intensity" about this type of warfare from its victims' point of view.[36] For a small country like Nicaragua, for instance, mining harbors, bombing airports, and terrorizing the population means that every man, woman, and child feels the intensity of war. LIW penetrates all aspects of life: the fact that the military component is often the most visible aspect of a low-intensity war can conceal the larger political battle.

As a strategy, LIW entails cracking the logic of a revolution, learning what holds it together, understanding the tactics it employs to advance its interests—and then using this knowledge to warp that logic, to destroy the revolution's internal cohesion, and to render its tactics ineffective. One advocate of LIW has explained this aspect of the strategy thus: "The most effective strategy for successful counterrevolution is the creation of a 'revolution' against the revolutionary system."[37] And LIW is extremely flexible: tactics can be adapted to the specific conditions of each conflict. Unless considered from the perspective afforded by LIW, the logic and coherence of the U.S. war against Nicaragua cannot be properly understood.

The concept of LIW also redefines victory. As one military strategist put it, "In low-intensity wars victory is normally obtained by altering the political variables to the point where the enemy becomes ineffectual, and not by actually defeating enemies in battle."[38] LIW campaigns are thus aimed at delegitimizing, isolating, and suffocating a revolution until it is no longer considered a viable political alternative in the eyes of the population, or of other populations that are inspired by it. Once this has been accomplished, the counterrevolution has triumphed. All that remains is determining the way in which state power is to be transferred from the revolutionaries to the counterrevolution.

LIW is the principal vehicle for implementing the Reagan Doctrine in the third world. Its proponents recognize that the need to wage global counterrevolution makes large-scale intervention in any one place risky: such intervention could weaken the United States' capacity to act elsewhere and could generate both a domestic backlash and a chorus of international condemnation, thus creating a combination of circumstances that would threaten the entire counteroffensive.

Direct Intervention in Low-Intensity Conflicts

LIW is a "long-haul, low-cost" strategy. Its political costs are relatively low, while the permanent aggression at every level builds toward either of two possibilities: a political victory (which might include a military element) over the revolutionary forces, or, should conditions seem favorable, large-scale intervention.[39] In either context, direct intervention becomes a "mopping up" operation, merely formalizing a victory that has already been attained.

The strategy of LIW is diametrically opposed to the strategy of direct intervention. Although its proponents consider invasion a legitimate option, they view the threat of intervention as a much more effective means of realizing their objectives. The Reagan administration, for instance, has used calculated "leaks," disinformation, verbal insinuations, and military movements in and around Central America to give the impression that an invasion of Nicaragua was imminent.[40] "A calculated aspect of the covert action against Nicaragua [is] the bluff of imminent intervention," explained one Reagan official.[41] In the case of Nicaragua, this tactic has served numerous objectives, as we shall see in later chapters. Indeed, low-intensity warfare involves a strong psychological component, in which the gap between appearance and reality is an intentional aspect of the war. For this reason, surface phenomena cannot simply be interpreted literally.

A literal interpretation of the invasionist threat has led many to adopt the direct interventionist framework in their analyses of the U.S. war against Nicaragua. On this basis, a dichotomy is drawn between the "current aggression" and the "future invasion," in the belief that the former is simply building toward the latter. Those who warn that U.S. policy in Central America is setting the stage for "another Vietnam" have failed to grasp the fact that the proponents of LIW are devising their strategy in Central America precisely on the basis of the lessons they drew from Vietnam.

The Defeat in Vietnam and the Seeds of Low-Intensity Warfare[42]

"You know you never defeated us on the battlefield," said the American colonel.

The North Vietnamese colonel pondered this remark a moment. "That may be so," he replied, "but is is also irrelevant."

—Conversation in Hanoi,
April 1975[43]

The U.S. war against Vietnam was fought within the framework of traditional counterinsurgency doctrine, which had been elaborated by the Kennedy administration and first tested in Latin America in the early 1960s. In the case of Vietnam, U.S. aggression involved a massive outlay of human and material resources, and the strategy centered on a concentrated application of firepower that was, by every historical standard, incomprehensible in relation to the size of the country. During the peak years of U.S. intervention—1965-74—more than 6.5 million Vietnamese were killed or injured. All told, more than 3.3 million U.S. troops were deployed, while U.S. bombers dropped more than 7 million tons of bombs, nearly three times the total dropped during World War II and the Korean war combined.[44] Yet these efforts were to no avail.

Five key conclusions emerged from the critique of the errors and misconceptions of this debacle. These formed the basis for the articulation of LIW as the new strategy for U.S. military involvement in the third world.

1. The first conclusion was that of the two alternative approaches used in Vietnam—the attrition strategy and pacification—the latter was far more successful relative to the objectives set, even though it was quickly overshadowed by the former with the arrival of U.S. combat troops in 1965.[45]

The strategy of attrition—often referred to as "search and destroy" or the "big-unit war"—used the same approach that the United States had used in conventional wars, relying on superior firepower and troop mobility. U.S. units repeatedly attempted to seize the military initiative and inflict heavy casualties. Yet in the end, every escalation inflicted little damage on the revolutionary forces, further isolating the counter-revolution from the people. Massive military force was not simply ineffective; it was inimical to the war effort.[46]

In contrast, pacification or the "hearts and minds" program, involved a sophisticated combination of civic action and repression, including propaganda campaigns, psychological operations, and selective terrorism. The Green Berets and Marines who conducted the programs often spent more time on public works projects than they did on killing revolutionaries (although they did plenty of that too). The principal objective of the program was to win the support of the local population and turn them into active agents of the counterrevolution. "The program sensed almost from the beginning that the Vietnamese peasant, rather than the Viet Cong (VC), was the genuine goal of the war," noted one official involved in the program. "An analysis of statistics . . . showed that the number of villages under VC control in Vietnam had increased everywhere except where [pacification programs] operated."[47]

The critique of attrition and pacification concluded that the people would have to be the target of the new counterrevolutionary strategy, and that diversity and flexibility of forces are more important than their size, brute strength, or technological capacity.[48] In this new strategy, gains are not measured in terms of "body counts" or battlefield victories; political and psychological factors are often more important indicators of success than military ones, and firepower is subordinated to "manpower" (which is not measured in numbers but in quality).

2. The second conclusion was that the culture and sensibilities of the people, as well as the historic particularities of the situation, had not been adequately taken into account in Vietnam. Even the pacification program, which targeted the people and coordinated military operations with a host of nonmilitary types of aggression, did not consider an understanding of the culture and worldview of the population vital to its chances of success. The architects and agents of pacification failed to understand how the revolutionary forces operated from within the population, keeping the initiative in the face of each new twist introduced by the United States.

The lesson that LIW's proponents have drawn from this evaluation is that future U.S. conflicts must be predicated on a careful study of the political, social, and geographic terrain of the target country.[49] Moreover, a full understanding of the tactics and strategy of the revolutionary forces was essential in order to combat them. "The substantive dimensions of low-intensity conflicts [must be] directly linked to the political-social milieu of the indigenous area," explained one LIW proponent. "Effective operations [are] aimed at the political-social system with all its nuances [and require] skillful political organizers who have penetrated deeply into the fabric of the indigenous system."[50]

3. The third conclusion was that not enough had been done to build a viable political community and stable government in South Vietnam. Even if pacificiation had become the centerpiece of the war effort, this would not have been enough, since, as a strategy, it did not take into account the weaknesses of the South Vietnamese government—the rampant corruption, the absence of a responsible political community committed to national goals, and the lack of any direction, particularly in the realm of socioeconomic development. The conclusion was that the counterrevolutionary alternative must be legitimized and stabilized, and that it must develop an internal cohesion. Invalidating a revolution is only part of the road to victory: that revolution's antithesis must also be validated. The Pentagon now calls the effort to stabilize the alternative to revolution "nation building." As part of its low-intensity campaign, the United States is promoting this process, both where revolutionary forces are fighting for state power (e.g., El Salvador) and where they have already seized it (e.g., Nicaragua).

4. The fourth conclusion was that in Vietnam the principal impediment to pacification had been the military establishment's resistance to breaking with traditional military doctrine, as well as the lack of cooperation and coordination between civilian and military authorities. Even though pacification was demonstrably more cost effective and superior, it was considered of secondary importance by the planners in the Pentegon and received only one-tenth of the total resources dedicated to the war. The conclusion was that if low-intensity war is to be waged, the bureaucratic inertia and resistance to change that characterize the majority of U.S. military institutions must be overcome.[51] New forms of political and military organization, as well as more flexible coordination between and among civilian and military institutions, are necessary; and this in turn necessitates the reorganization of those institutions involved in the planning of foreign policy.

"For both doctrinal and organizational reasons, revolutionary warfare goes deeply against the grain of the U.S. military," notes Ernest Evans, an LIW advocate from the New Right's American Enterprise Institute.

"The doctrinal problem is that there has always been a widely shared belief that military issues are and should be kept separate from political issues. The organizational problem is that the U.S. military is a big-unit, high-technology military."[52] Even though these changes clash sharply with traditional U.S. military doctrine, the proponents of LIW within and outside of government structures are actively pursuing the reorganization necessary for the new type of warfare, and have made significant headway in recent years.

5. The fifth and final conclusion was that large-scale military conflicts fought in accordance with the strategy of attrition need domestic support and tend to generate domestic opposition unless an early victory is achieved. Such opposition can be a major impediment to a nation's ability to wage war. But if a "long-haul, low-cost" strategy had been put into effect in Vietnam, it would have reduced the opposition, particularly since casualties would have been lower, while evidence of success would have disarmed opponents of the war.[53]

None of these conclusions was arrived at, or implemented, in the immediate aftermath of the Vietnam war. But as the United States became involved in the conflict in Central America, and even while the debate was in progress, the Reagan administration began to reorganize the instruments of the U.S. state so as to wage low-intensity war.

Reorganizing the U.S. War Apparatus for LIW

The high priority we have assigned to Special Operations Forces reflects our recognition that low-level conflict—for which SOF are uniquely suited—will pose the threat we are most likely to encounter throughout the end of this century.

—Secretary of Defense Caspar Weinberger,
report to Congress, February 1984[54]

The key formations that carry out low-intensity warfare are the Special Operations Forces (SOF) and the CIA, with several so-called civilian institutions (not publicly associated with war) playing essential adjunct roles.[55] Conventional military units are assigned back-up functions or relegated to future contingencies. This new mode of warfare requires armed forces that function within a political rather than a military framework and use operational methods that are coordinated with the often dominant nonmilitary forms of aggression. The armed forces involved in LIW are thus "demilitarized" to the point where they become *militarized political units.*

The unconventional units known as Special Operations Forces—seven in all, distributed among the four branches of the armed services—constitute the raw material for this new role. With extensive specialized training in every imaginable situation, the small and versatile SOF detachments are tailor-made for low-intensity operations. Experts define these units "as 'parapolitical' rather than paramilitary. The ultimate objective is political . . . but the intermediate objectives and the chosen instruments range from the political, into the military and paramilitary fields . . . they represent diplomacy conducted by other means."[56]

Following the U.S. withdrawal from Vietnam, the SOF deteriorated to the point where they virtually disappeared. Their restoration was launched with the advent of the Reagan administration in 1980. The Department of Defense announced a "revitalization" of the armed forces, including major budget and manpower increases, new weapons systems, and the beginning of an ongoing reorganization of military institutions to provide for more efffective integration of the reconstituted SOF and their operational requirements and activities.[57] The reorganization program also involved making structural changes at the level of command and administration in each of the military services. Just two days before the Grenada invasion, the Joint Special Operations Agency (JSOA) was established as an interservice planning agency for special operations.[58] In May 1985 Secretary of Defense Caspar Weinberger's office ordered an exhaustive inquiry into the requirements for training and reorienting U.S. military forces for low-intensity conflict.

At the same time, however, the proponents of LIW were calling for a more radical reorganization. Many continued to insist that the SOF should become an autonomous fifth branch of the services. Edward N. Luttwak, a Reagan administration adviser and vociferous champion of LIW, argued that "low-intensity wars should belong to the Special Operations Forces unambiguously and fully."[59] Yet even this drastic proposal was but a part of what such far-sighted strategists viewed as the necessary sweeping overhaul of the civilian and military institutions involved in foreign policy.

Although technically not a "Special Operations Force," the CIA—sometimes referred to as the "fifth service"—is an essential particiant in LIW, coordinating its multiple elements. The CIA is able to take on many functions simultaneously, including intelligence gathering, logistics and planning, and overt and covert political and paramilitary activity spanning whole continents and involving relations from the village level right up to the citadels of foreign governments.[60]

The 1980 Republican campaign promised to rebuild and expand the U.S. intelligence agencies. CIA covert actions increased fivefold during Reagan's first term. Within six weeks of the inauguration, CIA director William Casey presented the NSC with ambitious plans to refurbish the agency. Shortly thereafter, new covert operations programs were approved for Afghanistan, Kampuchea, Grenada, Guatemala, Iran, Laos, and Nicaragua.[61]

The Reagan Doctrine (particularly with respect to the execution of LIW) requires the rapid implementation of decisions and quick coordination between government entities, and thus has necessitated the reorganization of policy-making and decision-making processes at the highest levels. Such coordination can only be achieved through a centralized body that oversees the entire gamut of LIW operations from conception to elaboration to implementation. This body is the National Security Council (NSC), the highest organ of the imperial state.[62] The proponents of LIW, both in and out of government, are virtually unanimous in calling for the concentration of policy-making and decision-making authority regarding LIW in the NSC, as well as for the reorganization of existing bodies (and the creation of new ones) throughout government in a hierarcy from the NSC down.[63] *Mandate for Leadership II* proposes creating a "special group for low-intensity conflict" within the NSC,[64] and asserts that "changes in the role of the National Security Council should boost the chances of the Reagan [Doctrine] succeeding."[65]

Composed of the president, vice-president, and the chiefs of the principal executive organs of government, the NSC has become the real center of power in Washington, and its operation is free from congressional and public scrutiny.

LIW and the War of Ideas

The United States must seize the ideological initiative. . . . The war is for the minds of mankind.

—The Committee of Santa Fe[66]

The success of LIW is closely tied to the U.S. political process. Although the full relationship between the internal and external processes is beyond the scope of this discussion, it must be remembered that LIW is waged everywhere that the two antagonistic alternatives face each other, and that U.S. society itself is also a theater of operations. Those in solidarity with national liberation movements, or those who simply oppose U.S. aggression against other countries, become actual and potential targets of the U.S. government's counteroffensive. What concerns us here is the closely intertwined effort by the U.S. government to win over the populations in the target countries and to build a consensus within the U.S. population in favor of the Reagan Doctrine.

Conducting LIW involves a multiplicity of generalized ideological and psychological operations, both against the people of the United States and those abroad. Carpet-bombing the public with anticommunist propaganda, creating a national security psychosis, and whipping up a chauvinistic patriotism are only the beginning. Controlling the *perception* that the U.S. public has of counterrevolutionary wars abroad is the central effort from which flows endless disinformation campaigns and propaganda blitzkriegs against such revolutionary forces as the Sandinistas in Nicaragua and the Farabundo Martí Liberation Front (FMLN) in El Salvador. By molding public perception of these issues, support can be garnered for the war effort and then transformed into active participation—be it in donations to "anti-Marxist insurgencies" or participation in activities in solidarity with a so-called counter-revolutionary government in exile. In the words of one LIW proponent from the Rand Corporation, "Our most pressing problem is not in the Third World, but here at home in the struggle for the minds of the people. . . . That is the most important thing there is. If we lose our own citizens, we will not have much going for us."[67]

Mass psychological operations aimed at controlling public perceptions are a systematic aspect of LIW, and are known as *perception management*. A secret Pentagon document, drafted in 1983 and leaked to the U.S. press a year later, for the first time discussed the existence of a "program of perception management" in Central America. According to the document, entitled "Central American Initiatives," the Defense Department, along with the State Department and the CIA, was to have the principal responsibility for carrying out this program in Central America. Domestic perception management, however, was entrusted to another agency.

In 1984 the Reagan administration upgraded the White House Office of Public Liaison (which had, according to one official, been created a year earlier to carry out "a bit of psychological warfare here"),[68] renaming it the Office of Public Diplomacy and providing it with direct access to the Oval Office. With Otto J. Reich, State Department coordinator for public policy on Latin America and an important figure from the New Right community at its helm, the Office of Public Diplomacy is charged with organizing these perception management operations.[69] It has concentrated its attention on Central America, and particularly Nicaragua. To quote one Washington source, "Nearly everything saying the Sandinistas are bad guys comes out of Reich's office."[70]

Among the tools in the war of ideas are disinformation, misinformation, the selective use of facts, the manipulation of public sentiment, and deliberate "leaks" of information—which can be authentic or created for the purpose—all with the element of opportune timing in accordance with events. Perception management is ground out of Washington on a daily basis. While the intended perceptions gradually seep into the collective consciousness of the population, exceptional efforts are stage-managed, in coordination with the war effort and with political events on the ground in Central America and elsewhere.

Perception management has two sides. The strategists in Washington also attempt to mold the perception of the people in the target country with regard to the aggression against them—creating a different perception from that imposed on the U.S. public, and with different purposes. For instance, giving the Nicaraguan people the impression that an invasion is imminent raises tensions inside the country to a peak, forces intensified national mobilization, and disrupts normal social and economic activity. The United States wants to impose upon Nicaragua a war psychosis that penetrates the collective consciousness and—it is hoped—breaks down the will of the Nicaraguan people to resist.

Intent and Ability

In what follows, it must always be remembered that the Reagan Doctrine is not an initiative but a *response* to sustained initiatives taken by peoples around the world who are struggling for their liberation. So, too, LIW, as a key instrument of that doctrine, is *reactive*: it attempts to seize the initiative from peoples and their revolutions, and then to turn revolutionary processes against themselves. But if this is what makes LIW different from its predecessor doctrines, it is also its ultimate weakness.

Despite its apparent perspicacity, the fallacy of the critique of the Vietnam war is its overall conclusion: that the United States defeated itself, that it could have won had it done things differently. The fact is that the *Vietnamese defeated the United States*, and no amount of rewriting history can change that truth. The critique sees revolution as ahistoric, static—as something that can be placed in a test tube and studied. Yet revolution is, by its very nature, a *protagonist*. Because it is based on an understanding of historic forces, and because these forces are operating in its favor, it can understand imperialism better than imperialism can understand it. It is above all active, not reactive. And revolutionaries understood long before the U.S. proponents of LIW that the essence of the struggle is political, not military.

Moreover, there is an enormous gap between intent and ability in the Reagan Doctrine; it is fraught with internal and external contradictions. The doctrine seeks to implement a socioeconomic system based on market values at a time when the capitalist world economy is in deep crisis. U.S.-sponsored counterrevolution offers no realistic long-term solution to the problems of people in developing countries. Revolutionary and counterrevolutionary projects compete for support, yet the latter's offer amounts to little more than a bribe. LIW is a cunning attempt to skirt this reality. But while it seeks to exploit the weaknesses of the revolution, it does not have the capacity to exploit the revolution's ultimate strength: that the revolutionary project offers the only realistic solution to the impoverished majorities in the nations of the third world. This is why it is no cliché to assert that, despite the newfound sophistication of the U.S. counterrevolution, history is on the side of revolution.

The Sandinista revolution was born at a moment of profound international crisis, a moment when imperialism was moving from the defensive to the offensive. The revolution's attempt to resolve the most fundamental issues of food, clothing, shelter, and democracy for the poor majority has had the sad fate of being singled out, for historic and geopolitical reasons, as a test case for the U.S. empire's new global counteroffensive. Recognizing that the lives of billions of human beings are ultimately tied to this quest, Nicaragua has accepted the challenge. Sandinista leaders are correct when they assert, "In Nicaragua, the destiny of humanity is at stake."

We now turn to the subject of this book, the U.S. war against the Sandinista revolution in Nicaragua.

2
The War of the Jackal

Everything in war is very simple, but the simplest thing is difficult. The difficulties accumulate and end by producing a kind of friction that is inconceivable unless one has experienced war. Friction is the only concept that more or less corresponds to the factors that distinguish real war from war on paper.

—Carl von Clausewitz[1]

Defending revolutionary power is much more difficult than winning it.

—Comandante Carlos Núñez,
member of the FSLN
National Directorate

By the final days of the 1979 insurrection, the National Guard was deserting en masse. With Somoza's departure on 17 July, it literally disintegrated. It was not uncommon to find heaps of National Guard uniforms and helmets tossed in empty lots on streetcorners. Some of the fleeing guardsmen were captured, others turned themselves in, but most sought asylum in the nearest friendly embassy or headed for the Honduran border. Several CIA operatives reportedly entered Nicaragua under cover, posing as diplomats or International Red Cross workers, in order to smuggle out National Guard officers identified as valuable to U.S. interests.[2] All told, between five thousand and seven thousand guardsmen found their way out of the country, along with between three thousand and five thousand Somocista politicians and businessmen. Within days of the Sandinista triumph, the U.S. intelligence services had established regular contact with these exiles.[3]

Carter's strategy during the Nicaraguan war of liberation had been to try to replace Somoza with representatives from the conservative opposition and to preserve the National Guard as an institution in order to prevent a victory of the revolutionary forces—to create, in effect, a "Somocismo sin Somoza." Despite U.S. pressure, however, Somoza refused to step down, and the Carter administration was faced with the *fait accompli* of a Sandinista victory.

The Sandinistas' successes temporarily weakened the position of those U.S. officials who had favored standing by Somoza until the end. Although Stansfield Turner, who was then director of the CIA, admitted several years later that in 1980 the administration had drawn up contingency plans for the overthrow of the Sandinistas,[4] the idea of using former National Guardsmen to achieve this objective was only a peripheral element of administration thinking. Instead, Carter's initial strategy was one of economic pressure and political manipulation. The administration hoped to minimize the FSLN's influence on Nicaraguan political life and thus to reroute the revolutionary project onto a reformist path that would preserve U.S. interests in Nicaragua. This was the policy of "neutralization."

Central to this policy was an effort to bolster, with injections of U.S. aid, the position of the conservative business and political organizations that had worked desperately with the United States to prevent the revolutionary triumph. Alongside this official aid, the CIA expanded its program of covert assistance to internal right-wing elements, which had begun in 1978.[5] In addition, diplomatic and political pressure was put on the Sandinista government to turn over a greater share of power to these groups.

Due to the havoc wrought upon Nicaragua by fifty years of Somocista plunder and underdevelopment and a war of liberation, national reconstruction required massive amounts of international aid. This permitted the United States to engage in economic blackmail. The Carter administration responded to the Sandinista government's call for outside assistance with various loans and grants, including a proposal for a $75 million aid package—$70 million in credits to buy U.S. goods and a $5 million direct grant—as part of the Fiscal Year (FY) 1981 foreign aid bill, which was submitted to Congress in late 1979. After a heated battle in Congress, the package was approved. Its disbursement, however, was subject to several conditions: 60 percent was to go to the private business sector, the government was to meet "overall human rights performance" and hold elections within a "reasonable period of time," it was not to support "international terrorism," and it could not use the funds on facilities that had Cuban personnel.[6] This final condition meant that no money could go to the literacy campaign, to the construction of schools, or to teacher training, since Cuban pedagogic volunteers and technicians were working in all these areas.

Nicaragua needed the U.S. aid package because international banks were holding up $500 million in requests until its approval, which would be a "signal of U.S. confidence in the stability of Nicaragua."[7] The international banks were also pushing for the aid since they had $1.6 billion in debts accumulated under Somoza tied up in Nicaragua, including some $620 million due by the end of 1979. They did not want to see U.S.-Nicaraguan relations sour before they had secured repayment commitments from the Sandinistas. Nicaragua accepted the conditions.

The final years of the Carter administration served as an important intelligence-gathering period, one that laid the groundwork for later destabilization efforts. In September 1979 former CIA agent Philip Agee had outlined the CIA's objectives for Nicaragua at that time:

> The CIA needs to know the precise power structure within and between the elements of the Sandinista political organization, the government, the military and security services, [etc.]. The CIA must seek to identify potential friends and foes. . . . What are the media organizations and opinion-makers who can be counted upon to oppose [the revolution]? . . . What are the main vulnerabilities of the government and political leadership? Who are the leaders of other countries who could be enlisted secretly to denounce Nicaragua?[8]

Meanwhile, the structure of power in Washington was undergoing major changes, with dramatic implications for Nicaragua. The policy of neutralization was coming to an abrupt end, and the revolution was not prepared for what was to come.

Reagan and the Birth of the Destabilization Program

The 1980 Republican platform established the goal of overthrowing the Sandinista government as the core of its strategy toward Nicaragua. A Heritage Foundation report released that year, which is widely viewed as the original intellectual blueprint for Reagan administration policy toward Nicaragua, recommended:

> A well-orchestrated program targeted against the Marxist Sandinista government. . . . The longer that government remains in power, the stronger its security apparatus will become, and the more difficult it will be to dislodge it. . . . [The Sandinista] government is still weak and could be dislodged through a determined, coordinated, and targeted effort.[9]

This "determined, coordinated, and targeted effort" became the CIA destabilization program. Destabilization is a word that entered world currency when former CIA director William Colby used it to describe what the CIA had done in Chile. It means studying the myriad factors that constitute the basis of a society's cohesion and then using that knowledge to pull that society apart, through overt programs of socio-economic and diplomatic harassment and through covert programs of paramilitary and psychological terror.

The destabilization program against the elected government of Salvador Allende in Chile had proven effective (relative to its objectives), as had that employed against the social-democratic administration of Michael Manley in Jamaica. The CIA's program of destabilization against Nicaragua, however, was not to resemble those it had conducted in Chile and Jamaica. This was because there were two aspects of the situation in postrevolutionary Nicaragua that had not applied in those two countries. First, the former government power structure in Nicaragua had been dislodged economically, politically, and militarily. Its remnants could not effectively threaten the revolution from within. Secondly, revolutionary power in Nicaragua was defended by a *popular army* and an *armed population*. Nicaragua's armed forces could not, therefore, be turned against the revolution, as had happened in Chile. For these reasons, the Heritage Foundation report asserted, "It will not be possible to dislodge the current communist government of Nicaragua except through military action."[10] The report added that discontented Nicaraguans could be brought to support armed operations by former members of the National Guard.

On 9 March 1981, six weeks after the new administration took office, Reagan endorsed CIA Director William Casey's proposal for an embryonic destabilization program, sending a "finding" to congressional intelligence committees which stated that the United States needed to expand its "intelligence" capacity in the region. CIA agents soon notified ex-National Guard groups in Miami and Honduras that government funds would be forthcoming, and between March and November some 150 paramilitary experts were rehired by the CIA and sent to Central America to lay the logistical groundwork for the program.[11] In the Panama Canal Zone, Green Berets began training three companies of former National Guardsmen in paratroop-airdrop techniques, guerrilla tactics, and the use of explosives.[12]

On 1 December Reagan authorized a ten-point plan of covert operations. At the core of the plan, according to press reports, was the formation of a 500-man, U.S.-supervised force on the Honduran border, as well as covert U.S. assistance to a larger paramilitary force of ex-National Guardsmen.[13] The rationale for the program was the need to interdict an alleged flow of arms from Nicaragua to El Salvador. Endless press space and debate has been devoted to ascertaining the accuracy of this White House charge, which though never substantiated, certainly served its purpose. For over three years it drew attention away from the real aim of U.S. policy, which was to overthrow the Sandinista government.[14]

Resurrecting the National Guard

Following their flight from Nicaragua, the former National Guardsmen and Somocista collaborators dispersed throughout Central America and the United States. While some integrated into civilian life, others joined security forces and death squads in Honduras, El Salvador, and Guatemala, or simply headed street gangs in Central American capitals; still others clustered together into some fifteen to twenty roving bands in southern Honduras, each with its own power cliques, infighting, and personal vendettas. At first these were anarchic groups of thirty to forty poorly armed bandits who roamed the border region, stealing cattle, committing numerous atrocities against local civilians, and occasionally clashing with Sandinista patrols. They carried out a reported forty-nine attacks from Honduran territory in 1980, the most brutal of which was the murder of literacy *brigadista* Georgino Andrade in the northern village of El Mancital on 21 May 1980. The Somocistas dragged the young man into a cornfield and tortured him for several hours before finally bayoneting and then shooting him. The attack sent a shiver throughout Nicaragua, reviving memories of the bloody days of the National Guard's rampages under Somoza.

Among the most important of these groups was the "15th of September Legion," headed by Enrique Bermúdez Varela, Somoza's military attaché at the Nicaraguan embassy in Washington and representative to the Inter-American Defense Board. A long-time agent in the pay of the CIA, Bermúdez had led the Nicaraguan contingent in the 1965 invasion of the Dominican Republic and had had many years to cultivate relationships in U.S. military and intelligence circles. In 1979 he headed the list of officers whom the Carter administration hoped would assume command of the National Guard after Somoza's departure. Well-known and trusted by the Reagan White House, Bermúdez became the most powerful contra figure. His associates in the 15th of September Legion comprised the majority of the former high command of Somoza's army. Perhaps the most notorious member of Bermúdez's force was Ricardo "El Chino" Lau, the Nicaraguan intelligence officer who in 1980 assassinated Salvadoran Archbishop Oscar Arnulfo Romero, for which the Salvadoran fascist Roberto D'Aubuisson paid him $120,000.[15]

The CIA also kept a close watch on Somocistas other than ex-National Guardsmen, hoping that they too could be brought under its direction. These included Edmundo and Fernando "El Negro" Chamorro Rapaccioli, conservative businessmen who had left shortly after the Sandinista victory and linked up with Somocistas in Honduras and Miami and with right-wing elements in Costa Rica, Venezuela, and Argentina. The brothers formed the Nicaraguan Revolutionary Armed Forces (UDN-FARN), which was initially headquartered in Tegucigalpa. By mid-1981, the group had been brought under the supervision of the CIA and Argentine intelligence.

Another important group was the National Liberation Army (ELN), composed of non-ranking former National Guardsmen and led by Spanish-born Nicaraguan Pedro Ortega, a business partner of Somoza. Other Somocista formations included the Nicaraguan Democratic Revolutionary Alliance (ADREN), led by Somoza's son "Chiguín"; the Anti-Communist Army; the Anti-Communist Revolutionary Armed Forces; the Nicaraguan Democratic Armed Forces (FADN); and a splinter group from the 15th of September Legion that went by the same name. Other groups maintained no formal structure, often making up or changing their names and composition as they went along. Although estimates of the total numbers involved in these groups vary widely, the most probable figure is around three thousand.

In late 1980, even before Reagan took office, the CIA had arranged for the military regime in Argentina to provide advisers and trainers for the contras.[16] The Argentine intelligence network, one of the most aggressive in Latin America, had previously been installed in Central America to carry out surveillance of Argentine expatriates. The CIA's use of Argentine intelligence operatives as proxies reduced costs and provided other advantages—they already spoke Spanish, knew Latin American culture, and deflected attention from the U.S. role. The initial arrangements were worked out by Gen. Vernon Walters, then roving ambassador to Latin America. In late 1981, CIA director William Casey met with Gen. Leopoldo F. Galtieri, chief of staff of the Argentine military junta, to synchronize the already extensive Argentine intelligence operation with the CIA program, which by then had been officially approved.[17]

Following Reagan's inauguration, the United States steadily inten-

sified the stream of threats and propaganda against Nicaragua, concentrating on portraying that country as a militarized "Soviet-Cuban
satellite." The Reagan administration effectively integrated the military
and diplomatic offensives on 11 August 1981, when Assistant Secretary
of State for Inter-American Affairs Thomas Enders visited Managua.
"He brought a message from President Reagan outlining the United
States' points of interest . . . arms build-up, relations with Cuba and the
Soviet Union [etc.]," recalled Sandinista People's Army (EPS) Brig.
Commander Julio Ramos, who attended the meeting. "Enders also
brought with him the threat of developing the armed counterrevolution,
warning that we couldn't confront a major power like the United
States."[18]

On the same day that Enders was busy explaining Reagan-style
blackmail in Managua, a meeting was being held in Miami under the
auspices of the CIA. There, the 15th of September Legion, the UDN-
FARN, the ELN, and the ADREN joined together to form the Nicaraguan Democratic Force (FDN). The timing was no coincidence.
The Enders maneuver was the prototype of what would become a
systematic tactic in the U.S. war: the coordination of diplomatic and
military aggression, in which military pressure, and not just the threat
of it, was used as an "incentive" to force Nicaragua to make concessions.

Following the December 1981 directive, the CIA stepped up its
efforts to organize the contra army. One secret Defense Intelligence
Agency (DIA) report noted that "whether [the paramilitary program]
will succeed eventually in overthrowing the government will depend
largely on successful unification efforts, the extent of popular support
received both from within and outside of Nicaragua, and the effectiveness of Sandinista counterinsurgency operations."[19] The bulk of the
funding over the next months—released in strategic doses—was aimed
principally at financing the regrouping of the numerous Somocista
groups under the FDN umbrella organization and turning them into a
professional armed force. This task was made easier by the fact that all
these groups were made up of former National Guardsmen and led by
ex-officers or political associates of the former dictator.

The FDN was the Washington-sponsored resurrection of the military
instrument the United States had created in 1927 and relied on to
protect its interests during fifty years of dictatorship. As late as April
1985—by which time the contra army had managed to expand its ranks
to include many Nicaraguan peasants—a congressional report still concluded that "the army is organized and commanded by former National
Guardsmen . . . 46 of the 48 positions in the FDN command structure

are held by the Guard."[20] The National Guard was the United States' only remaining "Nicaraguan" possession, and the only entity Washington had ever really trusted.

Throughout 1981, ex-National Guardsmen were trained in weapons skills, sabotage techniques, terrorist tactics, intelligence and counterintelligence, explosives, ground combat, and light artillery. The U.S. advisers created platoon and squad leaders, training the commanders in leadership development. The most promising candidates were sent to Argentina for specialized training, while the majority went to one of at least a dozen camps set up in southern Honduras or to the several others that had been established in the United States. The latter ranged across the country, from the Florida Everglades, southern Louisiana, and Texas to the Mojave Desert in California, where former U.S. Army Rangers, Green Berets, Vietnam veterans, and Cuban exiles ran the training programs.[21] The CIA coordinated the entire affair, contacting former National Guardsmen and other Somocistas throughout Central America and the United States, putting them on the payroll, and sending them to one or another of the locations. The hundreds of Argentine, Cuban, and Honduran officials, along with other instructors and collaborators and the contra commanders themselves, received salaries from the CIA that averaged between $1500 and $2000 a month. Argentine operatives, according to Hector Francés, one of those involved, were charged with effecting daily transfers of tens of thousands of dollars for "working expenses."

Francés, who had been carrying out assignments for the counterrevolution under the joint supervision of the Argentine military and the CIA since late 1980, shocked journalists in December 1982 when he revealed elaborate details of the contra network. The Latin American Journalists Federation (FELAP) aired his hour-long testimony—filmed in secret to protect him—on Mexican television. Originally, according to Francés, a three-tier contra command structure had been set up in Honduras, with the top tier composed exclusively of U.S. officers and CIA agents, the second made up of high-ranking Honduran military officers (led by Honduran strongman Gen. Gustavo Alvarez Martínez), and the third comprising the FDN high command itself, which was headed by Bermúdez and another former National Guard colonel, Emilio Echeverry.[22]

By the time counterrevolutionary terrorist actions began in earnest in mid-1982, the FDN was a force of six thousand men with a modern military structure and better weaponry than they had had under Somoza. "Without the aid and the 'green light' from Washington," UDN spokesman in Tegucigalpa Raúl Arana admitted in 1982, "we'd have little possibility" of any operational capacity.[23] Although Nicaragua repeatedly denounced U.S. involvement in the contra campaign, the Reagan administration was still refusing to admit that a state of war existed.

The National Guard Returns to Nicaragua

In the beginning, the United States envisioned a rapid military victory over the Sandinistas. In an inverted version of the 1960s *foco* theory of revolution in Latin America, the contras would throw the Sandinista revolution into turmoil, spark a right-wing insurrection, advance on Managua, and seize power. Exactly how the final overthrow of the government was to be effected was never clear to those in Washington; the details would be worked out as victory approached. Perhaps limited military back-up from the United States and its Central American allies, including tactical air support, would provide the edge that the contras, once they were close to Managua and had sparked an insurrection, would need to seize power.* There could, on the other hand, be direct U.S. troop deployment if necessary. Secretary of State Alexander Haig had commissioned studies of U.S. military options for this purpose.[24]

The CIA drew up a timetable for victory. "The timetable," said one agency official, "was about a half-dozen pages long and set out the projected month-by-month growth of the CIA-backed army up to the end of 1983, when the anti-Sandinista rebels were to march into Managua and seize power."[25] A former member of the FDN directorate, Edgar Chamorro, recalled in 1985 that "they didn't want this to be a prolonged war . . . [and] always said, 'the President of the United States wants you to go to Managua.' "[26] These assessments were based on the assumption that the Sandinista revolution's popular support could easily be broken down, and that the contras could in turn win backing.

There were many in Washington who never fully agreed with this

---

*It is important to remember that in analyzing war, the key indicators are not events but rather the strategy and the objectives under which events take place. U.S. military actions, ranging from covert operations to naval blockades, surgical strikes, and full-scale invasion can take the same *forms* under conventional warfare (in this case the direct-interventionist line against Nicaragua) as they do in low-intensity warfare. The distinguishing factor is the *strategic* context in which these events take place and the objectives they pursue.

strategy, but since these critics were not in a position to articulate an alternative, the direct-interventionist line predominated. This line, grounded in conventional military doctrine, followed the logic of linear escalation in pursuit of purely military objectives, the last of which was a direct U.S. invasion.

The Sandinista revolution was still young and unconsolidated in 1982, with weak military defense structures. This important factor allowed those who advocated the direct-interventionist line to argue that it could succeed. "We did not have the experience in constructing an army, a consolidated officer corps or massive popular organization [in defense]," Nicaraguan Defense Minister Humberto Ortega told us in 1986. "They saw us as guerrillas who knew nothing about military [doctrine] and wouldn't be able to face a contra offensive, and on this basis attempted to remove us from power [through a strategy] based on a short-term vision."[27]

One road to Managua involved terrorist actions and sabotage. "In Brazil, Chile, Jamaica, etc., the creation of economic chaos has been the first step in economic destabilization," Nicaraguan Interior Minister Tomás Borge told journalists at a 12 January 1982 Managua press conference during which the full details of a conspiracy to blow up Nicaragua's only oil refinery and a major cement factory were made public. Both installations were crucial to national reconstruction.

In mid-1981, the CIA assigned the Chamorro brothers (of the UDN-FARN) to organize this operation, and channeled several hundred thousand dollars to them through the Argentine military and FDN committees in Miami. Among those recruited inside Nicaragua were José Esteban González, head of the right-wing Nicaraguan Permanent Human Rights Commission, Vicente Rapaccioli, and William Baltodano Herrera, who went by the alias "Comandante Romulo."

According to Baltodano, who was arrested by the Sandinistas before the plot could be consummated, he and the Chamorro brothers were summoned to Washington, where they met with Enders and other administration officials to plan the operation. With a passport purchased by Esteban González, Baltodano linked up with the Chamorro brothers in San José and they all shuttled between the United States and the capitals of Honduras, El Salvador, Venezuela, Argentina, and Chile, working out details of financial support and the supply and infiltration of arms and explosives.

By December, the weapons had arrived in Tegucigalpa, ostensibly for the use of the Honduran military. Baltodano returned to Managua to firm up the final details, but as he passed through a border post he was recognized by Nicaraguan customs officials. Nicaraguan State Security was then able to penetrate the entire network and crack the conspiracy. Seventeen conspirators—all of whom were either members of right-wing Nicaraguan political parties or former National Guardsmen pardoned in 1980—were arrested. Various others managed to escape the country.

A more successful action that same December was the placing of an explosive device aboard an Aeronica jet at Mexico's international airport. The bomb was apparently intended to go off once the plane was airborne, but the flight had been delayed and the plane was destroyed just moments before the 100 passengers were to board. The FDN claimed responsibility for the act.

In February 1982 terrorism hit the Nicaraguan capital. On the morning of 20 February, customs workers at Managua's Sandino International Airport were unloading baggage from a recently arrived flight when a powerful explosive device hidden in a suitcase detonated, causing an explosion that ripped through the customs lounge, killing four airport workers, seriously injuring another three, and inflicting major damage on the terminal. According to Hector Francés, the explosives were placed in the aircraft in Miami by the FDN. The timing was not accidental: hundreds of delegates to a meeting of the Permanent Conference of Latin American Political Parties were already arriving in Managua. Moreover, Mexican President José López Portillo was scheduled to begin an official state visit to Nicaragua later that week.

The culmination of this three-month spate of attacks came on 14 March. The CIA had assembled special groups for high-risk sabotage missions, selecting those former National Guardsmen who had received advanced training in Argentina, Guatemala, and Honduras. A young former private in the National Guard, Efraín Mondragón, was put in charge of one of these groups, a 15-man demolition unit assigned to blow up the 400-foot-long Río Negro Bridge, near the town of Somotillo, in Chinandega Province. For several months the commando unit rehearsed the operation in the Honduran camps, and Mondragon infiltrated Nicaraguan territory to take photographs of the target. On the evening of 14 March, Mandragón's team, organized into several commando units and accompanied by Honduran and Argentine advisers, slipped across the border with twenty-two pounds of C-4, a powerful plastic explosive produced exclusively by the CIA and twice as powerful as TNT.[28] At exactly 11:00 P.M., the commando units set ten C-4 charges under the girders of the bridge, took cover, and watched as the immense structure collapsed into the river. At the same time, another commando unit executed a smiliar operation, bringing down the Río Coco Bridge, some fifty kilometers downriver, near Ocotal.

"After the charges were placed," Mondragón recounted to journalists in Managua after his 1985 defection from the FDN, "I was withdrawing when one of the others cried out 'Who lives?' The others shouted back, 'Somoza!' Seconds later, the explosives went off."[29] Only the day before, in Washington, CIA director Casey had boasted: "It is much easier and much less expensive to support an insurgency than it is for us and our friends to resist one. It takes relatively few people and little support to disrupt the internal peace and economic stability of a small country."[30]

To confront this escalation of aggression, the Sandinista government declared a state of emergency the day after the bridges were destroyed. The Reagan administration quickly condemned the measure, claiming that it demonstrated a "totalitarian tendency" and constituted a violation of human rights. Despite the airport bombings in Managua and Mexico City, the destruction of the Río Negro and Río Coco bridges, the urban conspiracies, and the training of thousands of ex-National Guardsmen in neighboring countries, U.S. Ambassador to the UN Jeane Kirkpatrick, speaking at a session of the Security Council on 25 March, insisted that the emergency measures were a result of Sandinista "paranoia." In fact, trade unions, peasant associations, and grassroots organizations had been pressuring the Sandinistas for several months to take stricter measures to confront the internal and external provocations. Following the emergency decree, thousands of people demonstrated in support of the measure in the cities throughout the country—many of them claimed that the Sandinistas' response to the crisis was insufficiently tough.

While the invocation of the state of emergency legally suspended many rights, in practice its application was highly flexible. Rights and guarantees—such as freedom of expression, freedom to hold indoor meetings, freedom of movement, etc.—remained in force, and, in contrast with past practice in other countries facing similar situations, there was no imposition of martial law, and, consequently, no subjection of the populace to invasions of privacy or restrictions of movement. For the vast majority, life went on as usual. The emergency did, however, reduce the space in which conspirators who were headquartered abroad (such as those involved in the attempt to blow up the refinery and cement factory) had to plan their terrorist actions.

During the next several months, the contra groups were expanded to some two hundred men each, armed with U.S.-made M-16s, Belgian FAL automatic rifles, M-79 grenade launchers, mortars, and machine guns. In April an NSC "summary paper" on the destabilization program reported that "in Nicaragua, the Sandinistas are under growing pressure thanks to our covert efforts."[31] At least twenty-six civilians were killed between January and mid-July of 1982.

Red Christmas: Washington Targets the Miskitos[32]

At the time of the Sandinista victory in 1979, Nicaragua's Pacific Coast region had been through years of popular struggle and a mass insurrection, but little of this had reached the Atlantic Coast region. Many Miskito Indians and other isolated ethnic communities only learned of the revolution after the FSLN arrived to establish the new administration. Now, just two years after the overthrow of Somoza, it was the eastern region of the country that became the most intensely engulfed in war.

Colonized by rival powers (England and Spain), the two halves of Nicaragua had been pitted against each other for several hundred years. Following the final departure of the British from the Atlantic Coast in 1894, U.S. mining, lumber, banana, and fish-processing companies successively invaded the ethnically diverse coastal province of Zelaya and set up classic enclave economies. Boom-bust cycles ravaged the Atlantic Coast's resources, disrupted social life, and left virtually nothing in the way of a productive infrastructure. The companies and U.S. missionaries, operating with little interference from Managua, did, however, bequeath a strong pro-U.S. and anticommunist ideology, which was now to be turned against the Sandinistas—as was the aspiration of the dominant Miskitos and English-speaking black Creoles to recover the relative positions of power they had once enjoyed, the former as the junior trading and military partner of the British and the latter as the self-professedly civilized administrator of the U.S. companies and of Atlantic Coast social life in general. Deep mistrust of those whom the people of the Atlantic Coast even today categorize, somewhat dismissively, as "Spanish" from the Pacific Coast, overshadowed all relations between the two groups.

The FSLN arrived on the Atlantic Coast eager to implement its program, developed in 1979, to reverse the economic and social isolation of the region, introduce special economic development projects, end discrimination, and integrate the Atlantic Coast population into the life of the nation. In its post-victory exuberance, however, the government in Managua made several erroneous assumptions. These included the idea that revolutionary development in the western part of the country could be transplanted to the Atlantic Coast, and that the population of the region would welcome such initiatives. Reflected in these assumptions was a serious failure to understand ethnic oppression in general and the distinguished characteristics of the six cultures of the Atlantic Coast in particular. The Atlantic Coast population's rejection of the revolutionary initiatives was further aggravated by the attitude of inexperienced young FSLN cadres who had not yet overcome their own enthusiasm.

The always self-critical Sandinista leadership later recognized their errors, but in 1981 enough damage had been done for the counter-revolution to be able to establish itself on the Atlantic Coast. It was aided by the Reagan administration, which manipulated the tensions between the two regions while disguising its own ambitions. The Sandinistas were at that point unable to differentiate between legitimate ethnic claims and those that were the product of U.S. manipulation, and, when tensions suddenly erupted into large-scale military activity, they failed to grasp the difference between those who were deliberate participants in the U.S. war and those who collaborated because they believed they were defending their indigenous rights and aspirations. As a result, the Sandinistas ended up mistreating people who considered themselves innocent of any wrongdoing.

In November 1979 seven hundred Miskito delegates, with a sprinkling of representatives from the two other Indian peoples in the region, had formed MISURASATA (Miskito, Sumu, Rama, and Sandinista United), which was granted a representative in the Council of State (the Nicaraguan parliament); its charismatic Miskito leader, Steadman Fagoth, was elected to the post. The Miskitos, who mainly inhabited Zelaya Norte, the vulnerable northern border zone with Honduras, and constitute the largest of the six ethnic groups on the Atlantic Coast, offered the best opportunity for the counterrevolution.

Fagoth, who was later discovered to have been an informer for the Somoza regime, quickly proved more interested in developing his own power base in order to confront the nascent revolutionary state than in representing legitimate Indian demands. He also brazenly exploited the Sandinistas' miscalculations and the deep-rooted apolitical and religious views in the region.

In concert with the mounting disinformation campaign being waged against the Sandinista revolution from Washington, Fagoth began preaching in the Miskito communities of Zelaya Norte, sermonizing to the effect that the Sandinistas were "atheist Communists" who would outlaw their church and confiscate their land. Frightened by the prospect, Miskito lay pastors, all but a handful of whom were members of the Moravian church, added their weight to the message. The growing unrest in the area broke into open conflict in February 1981, shortly after Reagan took office. The Sandinistas had information that Fagoth was promoting a separatist movement and that he planned, during the closing ceremony of the literacy campaign (which had been carried out in the native languages), to demand as a first step that the Sandinistas turn over one-third of Nicaraguan territory to MISURASATA. The government responded promptly, arresting Fagoth and a number of other MISURASATA leaders.

All but Fagoth were quickly released, and pressure from the Miskito communities forced the Sandinistas to parole him after two months. Within days, he had crossed the border into Honduras and linked up with the 15th of September Legion. With the help of the Honduran military and the CIA, he began setting up bases and training camps for the several thousand young Miskitos who had joined him. Calling his organization MISURA (Miskitos, Sumus, and Ramas together), he made it an indigenous adjunct to the legion. Fagoth broadcast into Nicaragua in Miskito on the contra group's radio transmitter, condemning the Sandinistas and urging the Miskitos to rise up against the revolution.

Washington was watching Fagoth's progress carefully. Conservative U.S. columnist Georgie Anne Geyer, known for her intelligence connections, wrote in July 1981 that "Fagoth is beginning to represent to some important people a real chance to overthrow the Sandinista regime in his country."[33]

By late 1981, Washington was ready to launch its "Miskito Offensive," dubbed "Operation Red Christmas." The plan involved an invasion of Zelaya Norte by MISURA and Somocista formations in order to spark an uprising, take Puerto Cabezas, and declare the Atlantic Coast "liberated Miskito territory." According to the plan, the United States would bring in air support and a blockade if the counterrevolution could maintain control of the zone.

At least eighty-five Nicaraguans were killed in scattered clashes during the three months of the offensive. Fagoth repeatedly threatened the Miskitos, telling them that when the attack came, anyone who failed to join MISURA would be considered a Sandinista and killed. His forces followed through with this threat: on 14 December they attacked the town of San Carlos on the Río Coco (which had not heeded their call), kidnapped twelve villagers, and later murdered them on the other side of the border. During the most intense fighting, between 12 December and 25 December, Fagoth broadcast that Sandinista aircraft were coming to bomb Miskito villages, and that the Sandinistas considered all Miskitos their enemies. He told them to cross the river and come to the Honduran refugee camp at Mokorón.

In response to these attacks—which were among the most intense yet conducted by the contras up to that time—the Sandinista government made the strategic decision to move the Zelaya Norte communities away from the Río Coco and further into the interior. This was done both because the EPS could not guarantee the safety of the civilian population in the contested border zone, and because resisting the counter-revolution required militarizing the border strip and preventing the contras from using existing village infrastructures. Responding to Fagoth's call, some 10,000 inhabitants from the Río Coco communities had fled across the river in the midst of the chaos. The refugees had then become a recruiting pool for MISURA and an excuse for millions of dollars in international refugee aid, which was used to finance both MISURA and the FDN.

With the evacuation of the Río Coco villages and the destruction of abandoned buildings and crops, the Red Christmas plan collapsed, although ground fighting continued. Nicaragua protested Honduran complicity with the contras in diplomatic notes to the Honduran government and the secretary general of the United Nations, and reiterated its appeal for joint border patrols. Honduras responded by charging the EPS with crossing the border and massacring two hundred Miskitos in the refugee camps. The accusation was later rejected as "totally false" by delegates from the Honduran College of Education, who visited the site, as well as by two Honduran army colonels in the zone.[34] But the disinformation campaign nevertheless continued to escalate. Ambassador Kirkpatrick unblinkingly claimed that "some 250,000 Mestizo [sic] Indians are being so badly repressed that concentration camps are being built on the coast of Nicaragua to try to imprison them."[35] Reagan called Nicaragua the worst human rights violator in all of Central America, and Secretary of State Haig, tears in his eyes, waved a photograph of "burning bodies"—purported to be Miskitos—before television cameras in Washington. A few days later, it was revealed that the photograph (which came from the Paris newspaper *Le Figaro*) had been taken by the Red Cross in Estelí in 1978 and showed bodies burning after a Somoza air bombardment.[36]

The much-publicized relocation, which involved thirty-nine villages, was extremely painful for the Miskitos, who were forced to leave their beloved Río Coco, which had become synonymous with their historic identity. But contrary to Fagoth's accusations, which were repeated by Reagan and other U.S. officials, none among the five thousand who made the long trek to the relocation site was killed, and pregnant women, children, and the elderly were flown by helicopter. The communities were relocated at Tasba Pri, a settlement to the west of Puerto Cabezas, where modern houses, schools, and health clinics were soon built and electricity and running water installed. The families were given farmland and agricultural assistance. Tasba Pri was not in any sense a "concentration camp," and the only restriction was that people could not return to the war zone.

Americas Watch, a highly respected human rights organization, sent a high-level delegation to Nicaragua in April 1982 which reported that the government's justification for the relocation was "not unreasonable," and found no basis for press reports of a "widespread massacre." An International Indian Treaty Council (IITC) delegation reached a similar conclusion.[37]

The propaganda tactics employed by the United States during the Red Christmas offensive were not without precedent. They represented the calculated application of the "Big Lie," a "black propaganda" (disinformation) technique first developed by Joseph Goebbels, Hitler's minister for propaganda and national enlightenment. According to Goebbels, "The important thing is to repeat. . . . A lie, when it is repeatedly said, is transformed into the truth."[38] The Big Lie has become a favorite weapon of the Reagan administration in the war against Nicaragua.

Reshuffling the Somocistas

The Argentine role in the war had proved useful, but dramatic events in the Southern Cone forced modifications in the arrangement. In March 1982 Argentine forces occupied the Malvinas (Falkland) Islands, a British territory lying off the Argentine coast. When the British government responded by dispatching a task force to recapture the islands, the Latin American nations called on the U.S. government to honor the commitment enshrined in the OAS charter and the Inter-American Reciprocal Defense Treaty—known as the Rio Treaty—to defend any country in the hemisphere attacked by a foreign power. The United States, however, ignored this commitment—which had served as an effective smokescreen for U.S. intervention for so many years—in favor of standing by its British ally. The angry Argentine government quietly reduced its involvement in the U.S. war in Central America. Even the most cynical military advisers and intelligence personnel were antagonized, including Hector Francés. "The same satellites that took photographs of the bridges in Nicaragua before they were blown up by the counterrevolutionaries were used to aid the English pirates in massacring Argentines in the Malvinas," said the embittered Francés.

As British shells and missiles rained on the Malvinas, the CIA took greater control of the U.S. war against Nicaragua. Following the failure of the UDN-FARN sabotage actions, full-scale contra campaigns in northern Nicaragua became the focus of activity. The contras began to target rural population and production centers, going beyond the previous hit-and-run ambushes and border-post attacks.

The new operational methods were tested for the first time on 24 July 1982, when a heavily armed force of over one hundred contras swooped down from the Honduran base of Las Minas onto the town of San Francisco del Norte, in Chinandega Province. This town, of no strategic importance, was far west of the border strips and tiny mountain villages that had until then been the scene of contra activity. The contras indiscriminately fired on the inhabitants, killing fourteen and injuring another four. The local militia leader, Victorio Centeno, was captured by the contras, dragged down the main street, and ordered to shout "Long live Somoza!" When Centeno defiantly replied with revolutionary slogans, the contras beat him to death in the presence of the townspeople. The invading force kidnapped eight residents and took them back to Honduras; two escaped and told of how the other six had been brutally murdered.

Such attacks now became a daily occurrence, and the "secret war" could no longer be kept out of the public spotlight. Testimony on contra antrocities by the Nicaraguan victims made headlines around the world. "When the contras came to our village, they took my daughter away. She'd given birth one month before and they gang-raped her," recounted one traumatized woman following a FDN raid in the Segovian Mountains in late 1982. "My son tried to resist, so they killed him, pulling out his intestines and filling them with stones. Then they busted up his head and his legs and left his body, along with others, on the other side of the ravine." Another woman in the same village recalled how "they cut my aunt's and uncle's throats and then cut out their intestines too. They filled them with paper and dirt, and then they went and cut out their eyes. They also took one woman's seven-year-old daughter, raped her, and then killed her."[39]

These were neither wanton nor accidental terrorist acts, as the FDN leadership would later claim. Rather, as former CIA agent John Stockwell has pointed out, "Encouraging techniques of raping women and executing men and children is a coordinated policy of the destabilization program."[40] Later the United States would make a concerted—although unsuccessful—effort to transform this generalized terror into selective terror, but in 1982 such methods were employed with the official approval of the U.S. government.

The Honduran Connection

The defeat of Somocismo had sparked a U.S. resolve to defend the rest of Central America from popular revolution. In late 1979, the Carter administration had initiated emergency military support to the governing military junta in El Salvador. In Guatemala, where although the insurgency was steadily advancing, legislative restrictions (enacted in the early Carter years) prevented overt security assistance, the United States orchestrated a coup in March 1982, bringing to power Efraín Ríos Montt, a diehard anticommunist who was also a fanatical Protestant fundamentalist. With covert U.S. assistance, Ríos Montt promptly launched one of the most vicious counterinsurgency campaigns in modern history, temporarily checking the advance of the revolutionary forces.

Honduras, meanwhile, was the only country in the "northern triangle" which did not face a major revolutionary challenge; it was also strategically located between Nicaragua, El Salvador, and Guatemala. Thus the process began of converting this once-classic banana republic into the epicenter of the regional counterrevolution. This involved a two-pronged strategy: to remove the military from the government and to transform it into a modern force capable of serving U.S. designs. Despite the democratic veneer provided by the fact that the country's president, Robert Suazo Córdova (who was elected in late 1981), was a civilian, power was to remain with the military, which was headed by General Alvarez; his task was to oversee the implementation of the Reagan administration's ambitious designs for Honduras.

Part of the Honduran role with regard to Nicaragua included securing a Somocista rearbase in Honduran territory. The Honduran armed forces, a backwater force traditionally in the pay of the local oligarchy and the U.S. fruit companies, shared a historic identity with the Nicaraguan National Guard, many of whom quickly reformed old friendships when they arrived from Nicaragua.

But this was only part of the Honduran role in the war against Nicaragua. As early as 1981, Honduran aircraft regularly violated Nicaraguan airspace, and ground soldiers and artillery provided back-ups for the contra raids. Honduran aggression had two specific objectives in addition to bolstering the contra effort. First, the border incidents provided fuel for the diplomatic campaign to present the Sandinistas as "aggressors" against their neighbors. Each of Nicaragua's formal protests to the Honduran government over aggression was met with the accusation of "Sandinista attacks against Honduran sovereignty," duly repeated and amplified by the Reagan administration. Despite extensive efforts, however, arguments to prove "Sandinista aggression" collapsed under the weight of evidence in Managua's favor, while Honduras never responded to irrefutable proof of its own aggression against Nicaragua, including the downed Honduran army helicopters and the Honduran soldiers captured miles inside Nicaraguan territory.

The second objective was to provoke Nicaragua into launching a retaliatory attack on Honduras. David McMichael, a former CIA agent, testified before the World Court in 1985 that the contras were directed to carry out terrorist acts in Nicaragua specifically for that purpose. "It was a program to destabilize not just the Nicaraguan government, but the entire zone, so that the United States could justify a direct military intervention," reported McMichael. Washington, he added, assumed that "the Sandinista army would penetrate neighboring countries," since the CIA chiefs had concluded that the Nicaraguans "lack maturity, behave impulsively, and have a guerrilla mentality."[41]

The strategy of the U.S. military intervention under the smokescreen of a Honduran-Nicaraguan war provoked by Managua's "aggression" was gradually phased out, but remained a possibility throughout the period 1981–83. A U.S. military officer in Honduras admitted: "If such an attack occurs and if the aggressor—in this case, probably Nicaragua—is clearly the aggressor in the eyes of the world and the international press, you bet we'll come in [to Nicaragua]."[42]

Tensions between Nicaragua and its neighbors—which had peaked with the Red Christmas offensive and then subsided—flared up again in July 1982, when joint U.S.-Honduran military maneuvers began in eastern Honduras. During the maneuvers, new airfields were constructed twenty-five miles north of the border with Nicaragua, capable of handling the full range of U.S. jet fighters and even the gigantic C-5 Galaxy transport planes. C-130 aircraft from the U.S. Southern Command (SOUTHCOM) in the Panama Canal Zone flew a battalion of Honduran troops and their equipment into Puerto Lempira, about fifteen miles north of the Nicaraguan border on the Atlantic Coast, where they served to confine the Miskito "refugees," back the FDN and MISURA on their return from incursions into Nicaragua and act as the transmission belt for weapons supplies to these groups.

In Washington, Lt. Col. John H. Buchanan, USMC, ret., a former field officer in Vietnam, following an extensive fact-finding trip to Central America, testified before Congress that "General Alvarez seems to be under personal pressure—from some of the Honduran military and the U.S. government—to engage in a war with Nicaragua in the near future. . . . The information I have coming out of Central America is that a war between these two countries will start in December."[43] War between Nicaragua and Honduras did not start in December in a definable sense, but Honduras was nevertheless turning into a country at war. The U.S. military was installing its facilities and personnel across the nation, the contras would roam freely, and the Honduran army was seeing battle alongside them.

Military spending in Honduras, which is the second poorest country in the hemisphere, consumes one-third of the national budget, while health and education combined amount to less than 7 percent. According to the Ministry of Health, 70 percent of the population suffers from malnutrition and nearly the same number have no permanent employment. More than 50 percent of the peasantry is landless, while 5 percent of the population monopolizes 60 percent of the country's arable land and 80 percent of the national income. It is no wonder that President Suazo Córdova, who was never a proponent of egalitarianism, once moaned that Nicaragua is "like a cancer [whose] only cure is to cut it out."[44] The stark social and economic inequalities that characterize Honduran society have been steadily disappearing in neighboring Nicaragua as a result of agrarian reform, income redistribution, and social programs.

Plan C

Throughout the summer and fall of 1982, the CIA set up contra camps in isolated mountain regions of Nicaragua and established supply lines from the Honduran rearbase. The DOD ordered the transfer to these camps of some four thousand tons of military equipment, which had been sent to Honduras during the joint maneuvers. By November 1982, the EPS had broken up several of these encampments, which contained sleeping quarters, rudimentary first aid facilities, and even crude prison cells to hold abducted peasants.

The contras were now talking about a major operation being imminent. The counterrevolution was ready to open a new phase in the war, organized by the CIA and to be initiated with a project dubbed "Plan

C." Up to four thousand contras were to invade the Nicaraguan provinces of Chinandega, Madriz, and Nueva Segovia, sabotaging roads, bridges, and other economic installations. In tandem with this assault, urban commando groups were to be established in the north-western cities of León and Chinandega. The centerpiece of the plan was a concentrated siege of Jalapa, a fertile valley with a population of some 25,000 nestled in the Segovian Mountains, which are bounded on three sides by Honduran territory. The objective was to capture the Jalapa Valley and declare a provisional government which would be recognized and supported by the United States and its Central American allies.

A provisional government, however, would need a modicum of legit-imacy, and the Somocistas' bloody image was a hindrance to the plan. The FDN therefore concluded that it needed to create a civilian lead-ership which could garner international support. On 8 December 1982, at a flashy press conference in Miami's Hilton Conference Center, seven prominent Nicaraguan exiles announced the formation of an FDN "Political Directorate."

Nearly three years later, one of the seven, Edgar Chamorro, de-scribed in detail how the CIA had worked behind the scenes for weeks to make the announcement a public relations success.[45] Chamorro, an ex-Jesuit, former vice-dean of the Central American University (UCA) in Managua, and Democratic Conservative party (PCD) activist, had left Nicaragua in late 1979 and settled in Miami, where he participated in anti-Sandinista political activities. In November 1982 he received a call from a man who called himself Steve Davis. "I am speaking in the name of the government of the United States," Davis told Chamorro, explaining that the United States wanted to give the contras a "respect-able" political leadership. He and the other six were told that "we would march into Managua by July 1983," or the end of the year at the latest.

Heading the group as the FDN's new "commander in chief" was Adolfo Calero Portocarrero, formerly owner of the Nicaraguan Coca-Cola franchise and general manager of the company's bottling plant in Managua, president of the Nicaraguan Chamber of Commerce, leader of the PCD, and long-time CIA agent. Calero had been implicated in gun-running for the contras and had left Nicaragua in late 1981. He had been a favorite candidate of the U. S. embassy in Managua in the days when the Carter administration was endeavoring to find a suitable substitute for Somoza. Calero and Bermúdez—who remained chief of the FDN military high command—enjoyed a close relationship and were the real powers in the FDN.

The CIA appointed Alfonso Callejas, a long-time Somoza associate and one-time vice-president of Nicaragua, as head of international relations for the FDN. Marco Zeledón, a former Managua businessman who had served in the U.S. Army, was named communications chief. Lucía Salazar, widow of Jorge Salazar, a "martyr" of the right-wing Nicaraguan business community, was strategically placed to enhance the contras' image. Indalecio Rodríguez, ex-rector of UCA, was put in charge of "military-civilian" relations. Finally, Chamorro was appointed head of public relations.

The CIA put them all on its payroll, with salaries of $2,000 a month plus expenses. Once the press conference (which was dubbed "90 percent propaganda" by the CIA agent who rehearsed it) was over, Bermúdez and Chamorro returned to Honduras, while the other five were dispatched to Europe and Latin America to win support for the revamped FDN.

With the political groundwork laid, Plan C could be launched. Starting mid-December, some four thousand contras, organized in groups of about thirty men each, crossed the border into Nicaragua. Former National Guard sergeant Pedro Pablo Ortiz Centeno, who went by the alias "El Suicida," led the principal attack force of about seven hundred men. The Sandinista government had already declared a state of military emergency in the northern municipalities closest to the border, giving local EPS commanders greater authority in operations against the invaders.

While clashes engulfed the northern region, the urban component of Plan C, called "Bitter Christmas," was attempting to sow terror in the cities. C-4 plastic explosive, supplied by the CIA, had been "packaged" in flashlights and childrens' lunch boxes. Each container held one half-pound of C-4. Presenting the confiscated materials and captured individuals to journalists on 23 December, Interior Minister Borge said the plan, uncovered by Nicaraguan State Security while still in the preparation stage, had been to detonate the charges in supermarkets, movie theaters, and buses on Christmas Eve.

In the north, Plan C fared little better. Despite several weeks of heavy fighting, the invaders were pushed back without reaching the city of Jalapa. According to Defense Ministry figures, a total of 476 contras were killed, 159 wounded, and 113 captured during December 1982 and January 1983. The FDN military leadership would later complain that Ortiz Centeno had jumped the gun, attacking Jalapa before conditions were ready in the Pacific region and on the Atlantic Coast.

In Nicaragua, Jalapa became a symbol of national resistance to contra aggression. Even before the offensive, the campesinos of the valley and surrounding mountains had suffered more than those in other regions. Jalapa is the only densely populated area in the border region, and its exposed geography meant that the contras could penetrate anywhere along the eastern and western sides of the triangle from their Honduran sanctuary.

Following the November 1982 declaration of a state of military emergency in the war zones, the campesino communities began to organize themselves for civil defense. In December 1982, when we visited Jalapa during the middle of Plan C, a local farmer told us: "We're building bomb shelters to protect ourselves against mortar attacks and organizing civil-defense brigades. We're also working out a system of warning signals to alert the communities when the enemy approaches, and setting up 'vigilance' teams that do guard duty both day and night."

When Plan C failed, the contras regrouped in Honduras, and the CIA worked out a new plan for taking Jalapa. This required reorganizing the FDN troops into *task forces*, or flexible units of some two hundred to two hundred-fifty men each. The name and organizational structure was that used by U.S. Army SOF formations during the Vietnam War. By March 1983, "Plan Siembra" was ready. This time, seven task forces were to penetrate deep into the interior of the country—into Jinotega Province in the east and Madriz and Estelí in the west and south. These forces would be used to distract Sandinista troops, for Jalapa would be the principal target. This time, however, supplies would be airlifted to the contras from U.S. and Honduran military bases across the border, allowing them to maintain a prolonged presence deep inside the country.

During Plan Siembra, two task forces attempted to take Jalapa in a pincer move. The attackers saturated the town and surrounding communities with mortar shells and automatic rifle fire. They managed to take the surrounding hills and outlying settlements, and came dangerously close to the town. But the nearer they approached, the fiercer was the resistance of the townspeople, who defended the town from trenches dug around its perimeter. The push slowed to a standstill, and the task forces withdrew. The two sides had been so close that they could see each other.

By May 1983, the second major FDN offensive had been defeated and the contras had begun to retreat toward Honduras, amid pitched battles in Nueva Segovia and with heavy losses on both sides. The CIA had still not abandoned the idea of a contra military victory that year, although it was now clear that the contras would need greater back-up from the Honduran forces.

Late in the afternoon of 3 June, a burst of artillery fire shattered the temporary tranquility of the Jalapa area, which was still recovering from the March–April offensive. Three Honduran artillery battalions pounded the town of Teotecacinte—literally a stone's throw from the border at the northern point of the triangle—with mortar and cannon fire. The town's one thousand men, women, and children ran frantically into underground shelters, which had been built following the Plan C invasion. The siege lasted three hours and provided back-up for the six hundred Somocistas who crossed the border in order to attack selected targets.

"We could see the support the Hondurans provided for the contras: there were even trucks and ambulances on the border, for their wounded," reported a member of a Teotecacinte tobacco cooperative. "They destroyed about twenty tobacco sheds. The population was in danger. When we saw the extent of the attack, we realized that we were only prepared to defend ourselves against the contras, not against attacks like that one by the Honduran army."[46]

Tensions flared between the two countries. "The systematic defeat of the counterrevolutionaries by Nicaragua has forced the Honduran military to play a greater role," said Daniel Ortega. "The situation is developing so rapidly that war with Honduras cannot be ruled out. We are ready for the worst."[47]

The contras promised an offensive to disrupt the 19 July anniversary celebrations, but Nicaraguan's defense systems had been sharply upgraded since Plan C. Under the fourth anniversary slogan of "All the Arms to the People," thousands of peasants in the northern war zones had organized themselves into defense and production cooperatives. While some cooperative members worked the fields, others would stand guard. Villagers organized elaborate civil defense systems—air raid shelters, militia depots, and round-the-clock watches. Thousands of volunteers had come forward in the preceding months, overflowing the ranks of the Sandinista People's Militias (MPS), and new battalions were patrolling the north. Despite what Defense Minister Ortega described as a "larger, better organized, and better equipped" contra force, little headway was made against the newly armed and trained civilian population. In many instances, the civilian defense organizations were repelling the contras on their own.

Despite contra threats, Nicaraguans celebrated the fourth anniversary of the triumph of the Sandinista revolution without major incident. On 19 July, the Pentagon dispatched nineteen war ships, carrying sixteen thousand U.S. Marines, to sit off Nicaragua's coasts. The Sandinistas interpreted this dramatic escalation in the U.S. military presence, coming as it did at the same time as the dangerously high tensions on the Honduran border, as signaling the imminence of direct U.S. military intervention.

"They are not going to find resistance in the ocean because we don't have battleships, cruisers, or aircraft carriers, but if they dare to disembark, they'll find an armed people that is not just going to resist, but is going to win," Defense Minister Ortega told an assembly of thousands of newly organized MPS members in Managua's Plaza of the Revolution on 27 July. Repeating the slogan that had been a byword among revolutionaries since the Spanish Civil War, the militia members shook the plaza with a thunderous chorus: "*No Pasarán!*" they roared—"They Shall Not Pass!"

The Costa Rican Connection

Converting Honduras into the epicenter of the regional counter-revolution was time-consuming but presented few political difficulties. With the principal contra rearbase secured, the United States turned to Nicaragua's southern neighbor, Costa Rica, which had historically been a close political ally.

Wedged between Nicaragua and the Panama Canal Zone, which is the principal U.S. military complex in the region and the headquarters of SOUTHCOM, Costa Rica offered important advantages as another strategic rearguard in the war against Nicaragua. The northern province of Guanacaste provided direct access to Nicaragua's densely populated Pacific Coast, which is not within reach from Honduras. Moreover, Costa Rica stands out among Central American countries as the only one to have maintained a stable civilian form of government and bourgeois democratic parliamentary structures since World War II, attributes which had earned it the title of the "Switzerland of Central America." Over several decades, the social-democratic administrations of the ruling National Liberation party (PLN) had cultivated important audiences and contacts in Europe and Latin America. Costa Rica's prestige gave Washington a lever in international forums in its diplomatic assaults on Nicaragua.

On the other hand, in turning Costa Rica into another strategic rearguard for the counterrevolution, the United States ran up against obstacles it had not faced in Honduras. The army had been abolished in 1949, and in the absence of an indigenous military institution that could be developed and made part of the counterrevolution, the United States was forced to start from scratch. Moreover, the abolition of the army had reinforced the antimilitarist, antidictatorial, and isolationist traditions of the population.

In Costa Rica, U.S. brokers, who were accustomed to dealing with reliable oligarchies and armies, could not count on consistent and powerful internal allies capable of aiding U.S. endeavors to bring about the economic, political, and military changes necessary for a regional counterrevolution. Unlike that of Honduras, the Costa Rican party political system involved a diffusion of power among ruling groups, a situation that the United States found difficult to understand and, as a result, even more difficult to exploit to its advantage. The way around these obstacles came with Costa Rica's economic crisis, as contradictions inherent in Costa Rica's welfare state began coming to the surface.

Tied to the dollar and dominated by U.S. capital, Costa Rica is a classic example of dependent capitalism. The rapid growth of exports in the first three decades following World War II provided the capital base for internal development and for the expansion of social services. But dependency had its price tag, and by the early 1970s the economy had reached the limits inherent in its dependent structures. The government turned to massive foreign borrowing from international lending agencies and from consortiums of commercial banks, many of them American. By 1981, Costa Rica had a debt of over $4 billion, one of the highest per capita debts in the world. Payments were falling due and President Rodrigo Carazo admitted that the country was virtually bankrupt.

Economic blackmail was the first lever used to move Costa Rica into action. In June 1982 Luis Alberto Monge, the newly inaugurated president, made a well-publicized visit to the United States. His spokesmen openly acknowledged that his mission was to seek additional U.S. aid and assistance in renegotiating the foreign debt. In his meeting with President Reagan and Secretary of State Haig, Monge was promised help in exchange for adopting a firm anti-Sandinista position. Following the meeting, Monge announced to the Washington press corps that economic salvation was on the way, and that "Marxist-Leninist encirclement directed from Nicaragua" was now the principal danger to Costa Rica.[48] In the following months, Costa Rica's formerly cordial relations with Nicaragua deteriorated rapidly. In July, Monge expelled three Nicaraguan diplomats on dubious charges of involvement in a bombing incident in San José.

Nicaragua's own diplomatic offensives acted as a counterweight to U.S. and right-wing Costa Rican pressure on Monge. Managua consistently pointed out that toeing the U.S. line would only serve to drag

Costa Rica into a conflict that was inimical to the national interests of both countries. The Sandinistas urged Costa Rica to seek a bilateral solution to their differences. The conflict between considerations of national interest and U.S. economic and political pressure produced an ambiguous "seesaw diplomacy" in San José.

Edén Pastora and the Southern Front

While building the Somocista army, the United States continued to look for alternatives that could broaden the counterrevolutionary base, win it international legitimacy, and at the same time provoke divisions inside Nicaragua and within the international community that was supporting the Sandinista government. One alternative became apparent when Edén Pastora finally defected to the counterrevolution in 1982.

Pastora has been billed as a Sandinista hero who played a major role in the struggle against Somoza and only became disaffected when the revolution was "betrayed." The reality of Pastora's checkered history, vacillations, inflated ego, and erratic personality reveals a very different picture of the man and of his role in the revolution. The son of a Conservative party leader, Pastora first became involved in the anti-Somoza struggle when his father was killed by the National Guard following a personal business dispute with the dictator over land holdings. But rather than become involved in the FSLN's arduous, patient accumulative of forces against the dictatorship, Pastora opted for a spate of poorly planned and ill-fated adventures that were backed by the right-wing opposition parties, which hoped to force Somoza out of power and replace him with a conservative leader.

In 1970 Pastora was approached by Daniel Ortega and agreed to join the guerrilla struggle in the northern mountains, but he soon left again, believing that victory would not be attained in the near future. In October 1977 the FSLN began its uninterrupted offensive, and Pastora, sensing that victory was now within sight, approached the FSLN and asked to take part again. In August 1978, when FSLN founder Germán Pomares fell ill, Pastora was assigned command of the National Palace takeover.[49] Humberto Ortega, who directed the armed struggle at a national level in its last two years, recalls that this was "a show of confidence and a stimulus for Pastora in our efforts to cultivate in him a revolutionary attitude."[50]

As the triumphant Sandinista commando unit boarded its getaway planes at the airport after seizing the National Palace and securing the release of several important members of the FSLN, Pastora—who was known as "Comandante Cero" ("Commander Zero")—was the last man to board. Before hundreds of foreign reporters, photographers, and television crews, he ripped off the red and black handkerchief that he wore as a mask and allowed the world its first glimpse of the newly proclaimed "Sandinista hero."

From that moment on, Pastora had captured the interest of the U.S. State Department, and the CIA began the arduous process of building up his image.[51] Because of his military capabilities and his ability to win the confidence of right-wing anti-Somoza circles, the FSLN appointed Pastora military commander of the Southern Front forces, which operated out of northern Costa Rica during the insurrection. From his headquarters in the northern Costa Rican town of Liberia, Pastora continued to charm reporters from all over the world. In the final month of the insurrection, the Carter administration pushed desperately to have Somoza approve a replacement government dominated by the consevative opposition. Those mentioned by the State Department included Alfonso Robelo (a prominent industrialist and right-wing politician), Adolfo Calero, and Edén Pastora, but none of the "more radical Sandinistas."[52] Pastora sent a message up to Washington during the insurrection: "If [the U.S.] wants to prevent a victory by radicals, it should convince Somoza to pull the National Gaurd back from the south and give [me] a chance to get to Managua."[53]

Following the triumph, Pastora was appointed vice-minister of defense and put in charge of the MPS. But he was not satisfied with his quota of power. In June 1981 he resigned and left Nicaragua, leaving behind a note to Defense Minister Ortega: "I'm going to the trenches where the duty of an internationalist combatant leads me. . . . I'm going after the smell of gunpowder."[54] The FSLN leadership publicly criticized his decision.

Pastora spent part of the following year being rejected by one revolutionary organization after another due, in the words of the Guatemalan National Revolutionary Unity (URNG), the country's main revolutionary coalition, to his "immaturity, political and ideological inconsistencies, and his permanent lack of revolutionary commitment."[55] Then in early 1982, he met secretly with Duane Clarridge (who went by the pseudonym "Dewey Maroni"), head of the CIA's Directorate of Operations for Latin America. Maroni reported back to the Reagan administration that the United States should bolster Pastora's position because he could play a strategic role in the counterrevolution. Pastora insisted that he would accept his role on the condition that he have "absolute deniability," so as to maintain his image. As a result, an elaborate network of Latin American and European intermediaries smuggled the hardware and laundered the money that began flowing to Pastora and his followers. Only about four or five people in the Reagan administration knew of this connection, rather than the thirty or so officials who are normally informed of all aspects of a covert operation.[56]

Pastora resurfaced on 14 April 1982, at a press conference in the lush Los Portales Hotel in San José. "The nine are going to have to kill me," he declared. "If not, I'll send them to their graves. They have betrayed the ideals of the popular revolution and I'm going to remove them by bullets from their mansions and Mercedes Benz." He then announced the formation of the Revolutionary Front of Sandino (FRS) and presented a seven-point plan "to remove Nicaragua from its state of bitterness, sadness, insecurity, and fear." The points included a mixed economy, ideological pluralism, the holding of elections in the medium run, respect "at all costs" for individual rights, "strict" freedom of worship, "total" press freedom, and a "statute of guarantees" for all Nicaraguans. Pastora's authoritarian rhetoric was virtually indistinguishable from that of the Reagan administration, and was aimed at blurring the fact that most of these "revolutionary proposals" were already in effect.

The day after Pastora's appearance in San José, thousands of enraged MPS members filled Managua's Plaza of the Revolution. They lit huge bonfires and, one by one, burned their MPS identity cards, which Pastora had signed when he was still head of the organization. In Managua, Estelí, Matagalpa, León, Granada, and other cities, people took to the streets to repudiate "Cero," and walls were quickly covered with graffiti: "Traitor Pastora," "Death to the traitor," and "Pastora, a zero of history."

During his San José press conference, Pastora had described as "criminal slander" Managua's charges that he was conspiring with Alfonso Robelo, who had gone into self-imposed exile just before Pastora, to join the counterrevolution. Eight months later, on the same day that Plan C was launched, the Democratic Revolutionary Alliance (ARDE) was formed out of Pastora's FRS, Robelo's Nicaraguan Democratic Movement (MDN), the UDN-FARN of the Chamorro brothers (who had squabbled with Bermúdez earlier in 1982 and moved their operation to Costa Rica), and the forces around Brooklyn Rivera, a Miskito leader who had broken with Fagoth over personal differences and created his own armed organization, reclaiming the name MISURASATA.

Typical of the extent to which the international press mimicked the line that Pastora wanted nothing to do with either the Somocistas or the United States was *Newsweek*'s November 1982 cover story, "A Secret War for Nicaragua": "The United States tried to cultivate Edén Pastora after he resigned from the government in July 1981. That effort failed. 'Pastora is a man who would not accept a penny from the CIA,' swears one associate. After [U.S. Ambassador to Honduras John] Negroponte began to deal with the Somocistas, any chance of recruiting Pastora probably was lost." Yet according to Hector Francés, who first met Pastora in 1982, "The CIA was supporting Pastora not just with advice but also with a major flow of capital that allowed him to pay salaries to his mercenaries and to buy all the material necessary to maintain approximately 1000 men in Costa Rica."

By maintaining two separate contra organizations, reactionaries who still had qualms about associating with former National Guardsmen could be attracted to the contra fold, and it was also possible to project the counterrevolution as a growing grassroots movement against Sandinismo. This policy, however, not only required disguising Pastora's subordination to the CIA, but also maintaining the stance that ARDE was a "third way," an alternative between the extremes of Sandinismo and Somocismo. An assistant to Pastora even called several congressional aides in Washington to explain that they should "ignore the anti-U.S. statements made [by Pastora] because they're only for public consumption."[57]

Despite the rhetoric, the two contra factions were in communication and collaboration throughout this period. Shortly after his meeting with Maroni, Pastora traveled to Honduras for a joint strategy planning session with U.S. officials, Honduran army commanders, and the FDN. The mid-March meeting was picked up by the local papers in Honduras, but received scant coverage in the international press. Nevertheless, one angry FDN spokesman said Pastora had "an uncontrollable mouth" for talking to Honduran reporters about the meeting.[58]

Pastora's other task was to try "to provoke divisions" over Nicaragua within the Socialist International. The pro-Nicaragua stance of the social-democratic parties and governments in Western Europe and Latin America irked the Reagan administration, particularly in those first years when it hoped that the rapid diplomatic and economic isolation of Nicaragua would create favorable conditions for a quick contra victory.

Within a month of his San José press conference, Pastora was off to visit Portugal, Spain, Italy, Belgium, and West Germany—all of which had social-democratic governments at that time—and from there made a tour of the Latin American social-democratic and Christian Democratic governments. The United States hoped that Pastora's relations with important social-democratic governments would win their support for the counterrevolution, but despite these efforts, Pastora was unable to bring the Socialist International into the counterrevolution.

The ARDE forces, which Pastora had commanded since the coalition's formation, filled a major gap in the military aggression by opening the Southern Front—thus bringing fighting to both of Nicaragua's land borders. Coordinated actions between north and south forced the Sandinistas to disperse their forces and fostered the deterioration of relations between Nicaragua and Costa Rica.

Even before the ARDE operation had gotten off the ground, Somocista elements had established a limited infrastructure in Costa Rica. At least twenty-four contra attacks were registered from Costa Rican territory in 1981. Throughout 1982 and early 1983, ARDE built up its political-military infrastructure. Starting in May 1982, U.S. air shipments of everything from boots to antiaircraft guns began to arrive at Costa Rican farms after dark. "We'd unload the ships in five or ten minutes—they never turned their engines off," one CIA agent stationed in northern Costa Rica reported.[59] The agent, Bruce Jones, estimated that between May 1982 and May 1984 there were 100 such CIA-supervised deliveries. The elaborate supply network stretched from New Orleans to Miami to Tegucigalpa, with San Salvador's military airport, Ilopango, often serving as the final loading site for shipments to Costa Rica. During this period, Jones, as one of the agency's chief coordinators of the Southern Front operation, organized support teams of CIA and mercenary operatives. "We helped with transportation and camp emplacements, and coordinated logistics requests. We even bulldozed jeep trails right into Nicaragua." Ten assaults in rapid succession in April 1983 marked the inauguration of the ARDE's Southern Front. In just months, the sparsely populated border zone had been rapidly militarized. At least a dozen camps were spread out along the length of the border.

In opening the Southern Front, the United States relied heavily on the community of right-wing American expatriates who had purchased thousands of acres in the northern zone of Costa Rica during the 1960s and 1970s, evicting local campesinos and setting up modern export-crop plantations. Along with Jones, Indiana-born John Hull, the best known of these landowners, played an important role in organizing the northern zone, which local Costa Ricans began calling the "zona norteamericana." During his two decades in Costa Rica, Hull had established a personal empire, and in 1982 he was installed in a fortress-like compound a few miles from the city of Quezada, complete with security guards, an electronic fence, guard dogs, floodlights, and a double roof to protect the manor house from grenades. With its far-flung holdings and hidden airstrips, Hull's domain proved indispensable to the establishment and consolidation of the Southern Front. In August 1982 the Mexican daily *Excelsior* reported that Hull, "accompanied by other men, takes off from his small plane and penetrates Nicaraguan territory to strafe villages. On returning [they] disperse throughout the farms and resume their work."[60]

Large-scale fighting soon broke out in southern Nicaragua. By the end of May 1983, according to the Defense Ministry, the Sandinistas had killed fifty ARDE contras in combat and taken forty prisoners, and Sandinista forces were also suffering serious losses. With the presence of the contra apparatus, an atmosphere of terror and repression gripped northern Costa Rica. "The Somocistas, openly or disguised, have forged a power structure in this region of Costa Rica that includes pressure mechanisms, name lists, blackmail, and reprisals against those who do not accept submission to their activities," one Costa Rican reporter from the zone told the authors.[61]

Black September

In the eight months from December 1982 to July 1983, the contras had launched three large-scale offensives, each more brutal and sustained than the last. Yet they had failed to capture any Nicaraguan territory, to mount urban terrorist operations, to occupy the Atlantic Coast, or to move toward Managua. The Reagan administration was becoming impatient. In early August, CIA director William Casey gathered his principal officers in charge of Central American operations in his conference room at CIA headquarters in Langley, Virginia. The day before, he had reported on his June trip to the contra camps in Honduras to the NSC, and had received guidelines for proceeding with the agency's resources. President Reagan, angered by the House vote to reject further contra funding, wanted visible results. "We have made enormous progress in organizing the freedom fighters," Casey told the group, but

> until we can show real damage to the Sandinistas we will lose. . . . We
> have our orders. I want the economic infrastructure hit, particularly the
> ports, and I want as many thousands of the ground troops as possible
> moving across the border in the coming months, and this includes the

Miskitos . . . but if they can't get a particular job done, we'll use our own people and the Pentagon detachment. We have to get some high-visibility successes.[62]

The CIA dubbed the escalation "Black September," the title given the coup that had overthrown the Allende government in Chile a decade earlier. Within weeks, new task forces were sweeping across the northern border to shore up the scattered groups that were still roaming the mountains, spreading terror among the rural population. This offensive, which was known as "Plan Marathon," was directed against Ocotol in Madriz and Somoto in neighboring Nueva Segovia. The contra forces advanced to within two kilometers of Ocotal, but Sandinista reinforcements pushed them back in several days of fierce fighting.

While gunfire and mortar explosions echoed through the northern mountains, Managua residents were awakened on 8 September by the sound of exploding bombs. The counterrevolution was opening the air war. Shortly before dawn, a twin-engine light plane, in an apparent diversionary action, flew over the southwestern section of Managua, dropped two bombs near the home of Nicaraguan Foreign Minister Miguel D'Escoto, and headed south toward Costa Rica. The bombs exploded on the grounds of a nearby elementary school. Moments later, at 5:30 A.M., a second plane—a Cessna 404—flew in low over Lake Managua and apprached Sandino International Airport. Passengers waiting to board the day's first commercial flight were suddenly shaken by the explosion of two 500-pound bombs. One hit a commercial airline hangar, while the other fell near installations of the Sandinista Air Force (FAS). Within seconds, antiaircraft batteries brought the airplane crashing down into the control tower. Miraculously, only one airport worker was killed and three wounded. The attack caused an estimated quarter of a million dollars in damage. Identity documents and flight plans recovered from the wreckage indicated that the plane had taken off from a small airport outside the Costa Rican capital. That same morning, ARDE released a communiqué in San José claiming responsibility for the attack.

The very next day, two T-28 jet fighter-bombers assaulted Corinto, Nicaragua's principal commercial and petroleum port. Taking off from one of the U.S. naval vessels stationed 50 kilometers off the Pacific Coast and flying in at an altitude of less than 100 meters to avoid radar detection, the planes aimed their bombs at the port's major bridge, a Soviet merchant vessel, and a pair of petroleum storage tanks. Under heavy fire from Sandinista antiaircraft units, the jets fled back toward the armada without hitting their targets.

The abortive raid was an omen of what was to come, and nerves were on edge in Nicaragua that week. Further air raids were conducted in different parts of the country: a small plane coming from the south launched three rockets near the city of Estelí; Honduran naval units and aircraft fired on Sandinista Coast Guard patrols in Nicaraguan Atlantic Coast waters; Sandinista antiaircraft missiles brought down a Cessna TU-206G near El Castillo in Río San Juan Province as it was operating in support of contra ground forces.

The incursions demonstrated a far greater coordination between the ARDE and the FDN than had previously existed. On 26 September the two organizations launched back-to-back attacks against the El Espino and Peñas Blancas border posts. The two customs stations, linked by the modern Pan-American Highway, are the main points through which overland transport enters and leaves Nicaragua. Combined with the attacks against Corinto, the plan was to cut Nicaragua off from the outside world. The DOD and the CIA were taking greater control over the entire gamut of war operations.

Heavy ground fighting continued into October but the temporary lull in air and sea attacks came to a dramatic end on 10 October. At 11:30 P.M., a U.S. aircraft flew over Corinto, distracting the attention of the city's defense forces, as U.S. Navy Sea Air and Land Units (SEALs)—the naval branch of the SOF—slipped into the harbor in a sophisticated, artillery-equipped speedboat, launching rockets and firing machine-guns at port installations. Within seconds, a storage tank containing 1.6 million gallons of diesel fuel burst into flames. The explosion literally shook the city; a 48-hour nightmare had begun.

While the dockworkers took up combat posts, the local militia and mass organizations went into action, evacuating nearby residents and battling the blaze, which spread to an adjacent fuel tank. Firefighters were brought in from cities around the country, and volunteers helped erect sand-bag walls to contain the flames and remove goods awaiting shipment in port warehouses. By afternoon, U.S. television crews were sending pictures of a city in flames into U.S. living rooms; newscasters read communiqués issued by the FDN claiming responsibility for the terrorist attack.

That evening, the intense heat ignited a third fuel tank. Cuban, Mexican, and Columbian firefighting experts were brought in. Fearing an explosion in nearby tanks containing jet fuel and gases, the authorities ordered the evacuation of the entire city. The combined efforts of the Nicaraguans and the international experts prevented the further spread of the blaze, and by noon of the third day it had been brought under control. "If all this had exploded, not one soul would have been left in Corinto to tell about it," one weary Mexican technician told us. Four storage tanks, 660 tons of foodstuffs, and 40 tons of medical supplies donated by the UN were lost, while pipe and pump systems, cranes, and warehouses were damaged. "This is going to strike at every Nicaraguan home. The country will necessarily have to change its pace of life and place itself on a war economy," declared one government report.[63]

While the ashes were still smoldering, another commando unit blew up the underwater oil pipelines at Puerto Sandino, directly south of Corinto, for the second time in less than a month. On the Atlantic Coast, mortars lobbed from a *piraña* (a type of armored speedboat) missed the oil storage tanks in Puerto Cabezas but hit two in Puerto Benjamín Zeledón. The loss of oil threatened to force the closure of the mines and agroindustrial projects in the region and did temporarily stop production in smaller industries.

Shortly after the Corinto attack, its real perpetrators were revealed. Former National Guardsman Emerson Uriel Navarrete, an FDN member who had been captured by the Sandinistas in September, described how he and nine others had been trained by the CIA in speedboat operations and underwater sabotage. After an intensive three week course, the group was shown photographs of the pier at Corinto, Paso Caballos (the bridge linking Corinto to the mainland), and Puerto Sandino, and briefed on the operation. "Four days later, they told us the plan was off . . . the CIA felt that we weren't competent enough for the operation," said Navarrete. The commando unit was deactivated and its members distributed among several task forces; the CIA proceeded to call in Pentagon detachments to execute the plan.

Then, on 3 October, a DC-3 given to the FDN by the CIA was shot down over Matagalpa Province, and its three Nicaraguan crew members were captured. They declared that the CIA had brought its own experts into Honduras, eliminating any FDN participation in the more sophisticated operations. According to the pilots, who were presented to journalists later that month, a U.S. Army colonel, who went by the alias "Raymond" and said he was from the CIA, was in charge of all contra operations, transmitting orders in English to a select group of CIA, DOD, and contra intermediaries in charge of implementing the plans.[64] At a press conference in Managua on 5 October, Defense Minister Ortega said the United States had supplied the contras with at least ten aircraft for Black September and had set aside the U.S. military's El Aguacate airbase in Honduras for FDN use. Pastora's aircraft were traced back to mysterious CIA-linked companies in the United States.[65]

The Failure of the Direct-Interventionist Line

If the forces available for [the U.S. invasion] are not available, if the costs of such an action are seen to be militarily prohibitive, and if the political consequences are seen to outweigh the political gains that would be associated with a successful intervention, *then an intervention ought not to take place at all.* We have had enough of well-orchestrated interventions in which we won most of the battles and lost the war.

—Richard H. Shultz and
Alan Ned Zablosky[66]

The Black September operation temporarily put the initiative in Washington. Meanwhile, FDN leaders, Honduran military officers, and CIA representatives held a series of meetings in Tegucigalpa between July and September to reevaluate the strategy of the war against Nicaragua. As the effort sagged, the most vociferous proponents of the direct-interventionist line intensified their search for ways to change the original equation and bring about the military defeat of the Sandinistas by the end of 1983. They doggedly reassessed the contingency plans first drawn up during Haig's tenure at the State Department.

One alternative—sending the Honduran army against Nicaragua—would not only be difficult to justify politically, but the Honduran forces would be no match for the battle-hardened Nicaraguan population in any protracted conflict. The United States now attempted to assemble other proxy forces by reactivating the Central American Defense Council (CONDECA), which could join the Central American militaries with U.S. forces in a direct action against Nicaragua. This reactionary military bloc had been founded in 1963 during the heyday of Kennedy's Alliance for Progress, but had deteriorated following the three-day "Soccer War" between El Salvador and Honduras in 1969, and disintegrated completely with the demise of the Somoza regime—whose National Guard had spearheaded the council. Following the Sandinista victory, Carter had tried to rebuild the alliance, and the Reagan administration accelerated these efforts. (The traditional mechanism for U.S. intervention—the Rio Treaty—was no longer viable in the wake of the nationalist reaction to the U.S. role in the Malvinas conflict.) A flurry of meetings between Central American and U.S. military officials culminated on 1 October with a secret summit of the defense ministers of El Salvador, Guatemala, Honduras, and Panama, held under the auspices of Gen. Paul Gorman, head of SOUTHCOM, during which CONDECA was formally reactivated.

On 25 October 1983 Nicaraguans awoke to the news that U.S. troops had invaded the tiny Caribbean island nation of Grenada. The Sandinista National Directorate met in an emergency session for the entire day and the national radio network called on the population to be prepared for the possibility that a similar action might be taken against Nicaragua. Daniel Ortega addressed hundreds of thousands of Managua residents at a demonstration repudiating the invasion, telling them "alongside the invasion of Grenada, the United States has convened a special meeting of the military chiefs of Guatemala, El Salvador, and Honduras for the purpose of working out concrete plans of aggression against Nicaragua."[67]

Indeed, to the Nicaraguans all the pieces appeared to be in place for a U.S.-CONDECA invasion. For several months U.S. naval formations had been stationed off Nicaragua's Atlantic and Pacific coasts, led by the aircraft carriers *Coral Sea* and USS *Ranger* and the battleship USS *New Jersey*. The Big Pine II military maneuvers in Honduras, which had begun in August, were to culminate in mid-November with the arrival of over five thousand U.S. Marines and SOF troops, transported in yet a third naval armada. "We are positioned to block, invade, or interdict [Nicaragua]," confirmed one administration official.[68]

On 28 October Washington ordered a fresh wave of air, sea, and land attacks by the contras, the Honduran army, and the secret U.S. commandos. These were interpreted by Managua as "softening-up operations." Days later, a fleet of fifteen Honduran jet fighters swept over Nicaragua's northern provinces, retreating under fire from antiaircraft batteries, while Honduran artillery initiated four days of uninterrupted bombardment along the length of the border. In Costa Rica, U.S. soldiers were supervising the rapid construction of an immense, secret runway in the strategic northern zone. In mid-October, heavy machinery had been introduced into the area. Warehouses, barracks, and other buildings were erected almost overnight, all heavily guarded by watch-tower machine guns.[69]

Nicaragua was living its most tense moments since the 1979 insurrection. "All the signs, all the military intelligence reports available to us, and the recent events indicate that a large-scale aggression against Nicaragua is already in the works," warned Interior Minister Borge.[70] In Tegucigalpa, FDN leader Adolfo Calero brazenly declared: "A plan exists for the U.S. to invade Nicaragua with the backing of CONDECA."[71] In Washington, the Council on Hemispheric Affairs

(COHA), citing the same administration source that had leaked the details of the Grenada invasion six days before it took place, said that the DOD's code name for the plan was "Operation Pegasus." According to COHA, the plan was now in motion and included massive air strikes, a naval blockade, and a land invasion by CONDECA troops.[72]

The deployment of offensive forces reached its height with the arrival of U.S. troops in Honduras on 18 November. Nicaragua was now surrounded: 25 U.S. warships carrying nearly 25,000 soldiers and 150 fighter bombers were cruising off the country's two coasts; an additional 20,000 Honduran, U.S., and contra troops were poised on the northern border. The firepower carried on the three armadas exceeded any maritime deployment during the entire course of the Vietnam war.[73]

Inside Nicaragua, defense preparations, which had already been put into high gear following the arrival of the first war flotilla in July, reached a feverish pitch. Every *barrio* was stockpiling food and water. Hospitals and schools ran emergency evacuation drills. Block by block, each neighborhood organized its own medical, firefighting, child care, and rubble-clearing brigades. The first sight facing any visitor to Managua in those tense days was that of young and old, men and women, shovels in hand, digging trenches and air raid shelters everywhere—in backyards, empty fields, and along roadsides.

Virtually everyone in Nicaragua was organized into one or another of these military and civil defense structures, a reality depicted most graphically by the sight of upper-class families in Managua's wealthiest neighborhoods supervising the digging of air raid shelters by their servants. No one asked whether U.S. bombers could or would distinguish between supporters of the revolution and those who were against it.

The combative spirit that accompanied these "preparations for a popular war of national resistance" was comparable only to that demonstrated during the final months of the war of liberation. Workers in the country's principal production centers worked out plans to defend their installations. Stockpiles of raw materials and spare parts were transferred from warehouses to factories in order to guarantee decentralized wartime production. Tens of thousands of people enrolled in intensive evening and weekend military training courses, and thirty-six new militia centers were set up in Managua alone. Reports from the U.S. embassy to Washington could only have warned that direct intervention would mushroom into a prolonged conflict within unforeseeable consequences.

In mid-November, paralleling internal defense preparations, Managua launched an ambitious diplomatic "peace offensive," an attempt to reduce the international political terrain in which Washington could carry out an invasion. The objective was to alert the world to the consequences of U.S. intervention for international peace and security, and to bolster support for the peace negotiations that were then being conducted by the Contadora Group, which had been formed in January 1983. Nicaraguan leaders began whirlwind tours of Western Europe and the Contadora nations (Mexico, Panama, Colombia, and Vene-zuela), and convoked emergency sessions of the UN Security Council and the Coordinating Bureau of the Non-Aligned Movement.

The massive deployment around Nicaragua had obviously been planned many months earlier, probably when it still appeared that the direct-interventionist line could succeed. By the time of the actual deployment, however, it was not clear who in Washington was com-manding it, and whether its objective was actually to launch a direct invasion.

(The massive and costly deployment of U.S. and Central American forces undoubtedly served to test Nicaragua's capacity to defend itself. Even though the deployment did not result in an invasion, it gave the Reagan administration and the U.S. military a valuable opportunity to gather information on Nicaraguan capabilities. The deployment was also of assistance to the proponents of LIW. As we shall see later, such operations serve as multidimensional pressure mechanisms against Nic-aragua so long as they do not result in a hasty invasion, which would be highly counterproductive in the context of LIW.)

Managua's peace "offensive" demonstrated to Wshington that the United States would be internationally isolated in the event of a direct intervention,[74] which certainly raised the costs. This fallout could be weathered for a short period, but its accumulation over time would make the cost/benefit tradeoff unacceptable. Since it was already clear that an invasion could not secure rapid victory, as in Grenada, this additional factor added to the argument that the direct-interventionist approach was not a realistic option. By this time, a debate was well under way about the viability of the objective itself, and those articulat-ing an alternative strategy were gaining the upper hand. The interna-tional and Nicaraguan response to the deployment of U.S. forces further bolstered the position of those pushing the alternative to the direct-interventionist strategy.

The scenario in late 1983 thus had major ramifications for the course and nature of the war. The direct-interventionist line was replaced by a strategy endorsed by so-called moderates in the administration, those who favored a political over a military solution. The strategic differences between proponents of invasion and proponents of LIW were resolved in favor of the latter.

Perhaps inadvertently, then-FDN leader Edgar Chamorro expressed this transition:

> In October and November 1983, we saw the possibility of getting diplomatic or military backing from CONDECA for a provisional government, and we thought that the United States might lend a hand. Now this is changed a lot, and the tendency seems to be to seek a political solution.[75]

From now on, the strategic objective of the U.S. war was the *political defeat* of Sandinismo. Military aggression was no longer a means of achieving victory for the counterrevolution, but was the tactical hub which would catalyze the numerous nonmilitary spokes of aggression. This did not mean that an invasion would never take place, however, only that the character of such an event would be radically different.

3
The New Strategy Takes Shape

The Anglo-American is currently incapable of conducting a protracted war. Anglo-Americans are essentially poker players. Yankees play each hand as it is dealt them. Reacting to the cards in hand and trusting it to the luck of the draw, Northamericans tend, therefore, not to plan or initiate action, but to counter. Moreover, as poker players, they have limited vision, since they play from deal to deal and are, thus, short term in their thinking. Based on the business theory of the "exception principle," U.S. leaders confront situations as they arise. Consequently, U.S. military and foreign policy is a series of unintegrated, isolated acts without continuity or apparent purpose.

—Lewis A. Tambs and Frank Aker[1]

The U.S. strategy had mapped out the relatively rapid overthrow of the revolutionary government through a military front of mercenary forces. If the war has now been prolonged, it is not because the United States planned this in the beginning. The "quick victory plans" have failed due above all to the strength of, and popular support for, the revolutionary government.

—Humberto Ortega[2]

In the summer of 1980, Lewis Tambs participated in the Committee of Santa Fe which drew up the guidelines for the Reagan's administration's Latin America policy. Shortly after the election he was appointed ambassador to Colombia. Like many of the New Right ideologues close to the conflict in Central America, Tambs followed the unfolding U.S. policy with concern. As the pieces began to be assembled, Tambs and others saw the shortcomings of the emerging picture and did not hesitate to criticize what they saw. Middle-level officials like Tambs were joined by "theoreticians" from right-wing think tanks and by such important officials as Undersecretary of Defense for Policy Fred C. Iklé and Deputy Assistant Secretary of Defense for Inter-American Affairs Nestor Sánchez, by Constantine Menges from the NSC, and by others from the CIA. By mid-1983, even prominent Pentagon figures were expressing their reservations over the direct-interventionist strategy, further eroding the position of its advocates.[3]

By 1983, U.S. policy toward Central America had reached a crisis point. This was the essence of Jeane Kirkpatrick's report to the NSC following her well-publicized visit to Central America in February.[4] The Salvadoran revolutionaries were continuing to advance, the Sandinista revolution was consolidating, and a majority of the U.S. public, fearful of "another Vietnam," opposed further U.S. involvement. It had become apparent to policymakers in Washington that their approach lacked coherence, longe-range vision, and, above all, thorough *integration* of military, economic, political, psychological, and diplomatic activities.

The key people responsible for policy implementation in Central America, particularly Gen. Wallace Nutting of SOUTHCOM and, later, his successor as SOUTHCOM chief, Gen. Paul Gorman, felt Washington's weaknesses on the ground. The war was dragging on because of the tenacity of the revolutionary forces, with their ability to respond and overcome each U.S. escalation. Washington was reacting to the cards dealt in a poker game on a short-term, deal-by-deal basis. As early as 1982, SOUTHCOM officials had sounded a warning and hinted at another way forward: "The solution will not be the destruction of the [enemy] in the physical sense," cautioned Nutting. "Somehow, they have to be persuaded that they can't win. But I don't think we have made a commitment that is sufficient. . . . We are not acting yet like we're serious."[5]

Those who endorsed the low-intensity approach had never subscribed to the quick military victory strategy. Nevertheless, they had considered the destabilization program a satisfactory beginning, and the contras a useful pressure mechanism. "Some people around here and in Washington really thought that they could incite an insurrection and overthrow the Sandinistas," commented one U.S. diplomat in Honduras. "I always thought that was a lot of crap, but in any event the contras are [a good] instrument of pressure."[6] Now, however, the direct-interventionist strategy began increasingly to be displaced as the proponents of LIW pushed their alternative stragegy through the citadels of power in Washington.

Assessments of the poor performance of U.S. policy over the previous two-year period obviated the need to make what Nutting referred to as a "serious commitment," which meant waging a *prolonged, holistic regional war*. Prolongation went from being a de facto reality forced on Washington by circumstances to becoming a policy objective. If the enemy was waging a prolonged popular war, the empire decided that it must wage a prolonged *antipopular* war, wedded to the postulates of low-intensity warfare.

U.S. policy thus entered a period of redefinition. The transition was not an event, but rather a lengthy and uneven process. Following Kirkpatrick's report, the administration convened a series of NSC and interagency meetings to rechart its strategy for the entire region. Reagan took the lead on the public front. Between February and April, he delivered six major speeches on the U.S. commitment to Central America, culminating in an unprecedented nationally televised address to a joint session of Congress on 27 April. "The national security of all the Americas is at stake in Central America," he said. "If we cannot defend ourselves there, we cannot expect to prevail elsewhere. Our credibility would collapse, our alliances would crumble and the safety of our homeland would be put at jeopardy."[7]

The interagency meetings culminated on 8 July, with a NSC "summit" attended by all the principal White House, Department of State, DOD, and CIA officials in charge of Central America policy. "The situation in Central America is nearing a critical point," stated one of the summit's secret working papers. "It is still possible to accomplish U.S. objectives, provided that the U.S. takes timely and effective action . . . . [We must look] beyond incremental improvements; we need to develop a long-term strategy."[8] The summit gathered together the diverse ideas and proposals that had taken shape in preceding months and drew up the general contours of the new approach. The new framework would provide the context for the articulation of piecemeal tactical and policy elements into a coherent strategy. And this process would have to be accompanied by organizational changes in Washington to facilitate coordination between strategic conception, planning, and implementation.

Several immediate steps were approved, among them:

—A concerted program to achieve domestic support for the new policy within ruling circles and the general population.

—Consolidation of the program of ongoing military maneuvers throughout the Caribbean Basin, and particularly in Honduras.

—Expanded long-range economic development and security programs for Central American allies, and deeper penetration of these societies by U.S. institutions.

—The establishment of a "bipartisan commission" to map out detailed proposals for the new long-term strategy.

—A major expansion of the war against Nicaragua, including the reorganization of the contras and the pursuit of a diplomatic strategy to isolate Nicaragua.[9]

The transition to the new strategy was not so much a matter of introducing novel practices as refining and recombining old elements into a new framework. Since 1981, the United States had been employing diverse military, economic, psychological, political, and diplomatic tactics, some of which were already more sophisticated than those that had been employed in earlier U.S. destablization programs. These provided fertile ground upon which to consolidate prolonged antipopular warfare. U.S. policy would not be simply the sum of its parts, but rather a synergistic whole in which each element would complement the others, all in the context of long-term regional objectives.

These conceptual changes were defined during the summer of 1983. Nevertheless, they were only the first steps in a lengthy and conflict-ridden process of reorienting practice in Central America and reorganizing roles and functions in Washington. Over the next six months, the pieces were gradually put into place. The Kissinger Commission was established in July, and the massive Big Pine II military maneuvers were in full swing by early August. In October, the DOD created the Joint Special Operations Agency (JSOA) to take charge of special operations around the globe, but with a particular focus on Central America. The White House set up the Office of Public Diplomacy to spearhead perception-management programs in the United States and to build a popular constituency for the war effort. It also established the Central America Outreach Group to provide an institutional link between the U.S. government and its constituency in grassroots New Right organizations.

Meanwhile, sweeping changes were underway in SOUTHCOM. The smallest of six U.S. regional military command centers around the globe, SOUTHCOM had been a low-priority, backwater post responsible for defending the Panama Canal Zone. Now the DOD quietly rewrote the command's "Mission Statement," officially changing its priority from defense of the Panama Canal Zone to defense of Central America, with a particular emphasis on Nicaragua.[10]

The SOUTHCOM men played an important role in overhauling the regional war effort. General Gorman, who replaced General Nutting in May 1983, was a decorated hero of the Korean and Vietnam wars and one of the foremost DOD proponents of LIW."[11] His first move was to bring down dozens of DOD experts in intelligence, communications, aviation, civic action, and psychological operations. Under his leadership, SOUTHCOM quickly moved to center stage in both the planning and the execution of the war against Nicaragua. Gorman orchestrated more effective coordination between the CIA, the contras, and the DOD, including the use of SEAL units in the fall of 1983, deploying Green Berets to train the contras, and the organization of direct operations by other SOF formations.

The process that took place—from conceptualizing the new strategy in Washington to implementing changes in Central America—was inevitably uneven and contradictory, beset by interdepartmental rivalries and fierce debates within and between government agencies—as reflected in the November 1983 invasion scenario, for instance. Even as the new strategy was coming into focus in the corridors of Washington, the Salvadoran army, the contras, and CIA operatives in Honduras continued to fight a war that was quickly going out of style in the nerve centers of the U.S. empire.

In January 1984 the Kissinger Commission released its report,[12] which endorsed the conclusions already reached in the administration and SOUTHCOM. It expressed the view that the "military option" would not work in Central America, and argued that the only alternative was a prolonged effort based on the careful integration of various policy instruments. The report laid out concrete region-wide proposals on how to take advantage of economic aid programs, "humanitarian assistance," and ideological and military initiatives, and made numerous recommendations regarding the difficult task of coordinating the work of the myriad U.S. government agencies.

Meanwhile, the DOD and the CIA accelerated a process, begun in 1981, of bringing hundreds of retired political warfare specialists and paramilitary operatives to advise the administration on the nuts and bolts of the unfolding low-intensity warfare strategy, and to become directly involved in operations in Central America. One month after Kissinger had handed his report to the president, the DOD convened a two-day conference on "new tactics to use against the Sandinista government," the culmination of special panels that had been held since April of the year before.[13] The conference, which was organized by Undersecretary of Defense Iklé's office, brought together some of the most experienced individuals in unconventional warfare both in and out of active service, among them Edward Lansdale, a veteran of counterinsurgency and covert operations programs in the Philippines and Vietnam. John Singlaub, a retired U.S. Army general who would go on to play an important role in the war, was the moderator.[14] The experts hammered out the details of putting the war against Nicaragua on a low-intensity footing. The destruction of the Sandinista revolution would now be sought through a political victory over the Sandinistas, and all the tactics of unconventional warfare, military and otherwise, were to be employed to this end.

The Role of the CIA

The prominent role that the CIA has played in the war against Nicaragua has contributed to its being perceived as the CIA's "dirty war." But while the agency laid the necessary groundwork for the evolution of the war, it was never "Casey's War." "Looking at the war against Nicaragua in its political context, many people misconstrue the CIA as an executive agency responsible for every phase," one leading authority on the CIA told us, in explaining the relation of the agency to overall U.S. policy.[15] "The CIA does not really *run* anything; it coordinates all the elements, tries to put all the pieces in place," he said. For instance, the CIA had to "evaluate assets—psychological profiles of everyone from Pastora to Bermúdez, to see how reliable they were, how to use them, what they would have to be given, what they could do—that's the agency." Rather than holding all the reins, the CIA is more the additive in the battery that activates the diverse working parts of U.S. foreign policy. Two prominent Reaganite academics have noted that "CIA paramilitary experts made significant contributions to prior U.S. counterinsurgency and guerrilla efforts, especially in recruiting, training, logistics and planning."[16] As an agency whose functions span the gamut of intelligence, paramilitary operations, psychological warfare, and a host of "dirty tricks," the CIA is an institution ideally suited to meet the needs of low-intensity campaigns, which are often designed and built up on the basis of pervasive and high-quality intelligence, in the gathering of which the agency plays a paramount role.

The real nerve center of the U.S. war, however, is the National Security Council. In the first days of the Reagan administration, a Restricted Interagency Group (RIG) was set up to direct and supervise policy toward Nicaragua. According to some specialists, the RIG is a continuation of an NSC working group that had been established under Carter.[17] The RIG was made up of key officials from the top echelons of the administration: Thomas Enders, and later Langhorne Motley, from the State Department; General Gorman (representing the Joint Chiefs of Staff) from the DOD; Nestor Sánchez; NSC staff member Lt. Col. Oliver North, USMC; and Undersecretary of Defense for Policy Iklé, originally from the Hoover Institute.[18]

The RIG also included Duane R. Clarridge, head of the CIA's Directorate of Operations for Latin America. In the initial stages of the war, Clarridge had been the key liaison between the RIG and on-the-ground operations. Several other NSC members worked closely with the RIG, including Clarridge's boss, CIA Director William Casey, National Security Adviser William Clark, and Ambassador to the UN Kirkpatrick. The RIG reported back to, and was directed by, the NSC, which includes the secretaries of state and defense and the president and is the highest organ of the U.S. state. Casey and the CIA leadership received their guidelines directly from the NSC. As the war progressed and the CIA infrastructure consolidated, the DOD replaced the CIA in many key functions, and the NSC moved to take ever greater control over the planning and execution of the war.

Only when this pyramidal structure, on whose commanding heights sits the executive apparatus, is understood as the real nerve center of the war can all of the actors on the ground and the events over half a decade be seen in context. Diverse and carefully timed war tactics, carried out in a coordinated way on numerous fronts—i.e., ranking U.S. diplomats visit Nicaragua to "dialogue" on the same day that thousands of contras invade the country, the Costa Rican press carries anti-Sandinista headlines, and major U.S. military maneuvers begin in Honduras—are directed from the citadels of the U.S. state, not by CIA operatives in Tegucigalpa or Miami.

It is in this context that the Nicaraguan leadership accuses the United States of "state terrorism."

The Role of the U.S. Congress

The Reagan administration's annual campaigns to obtain congressional funding for the contras have been viewed as being of primarily financial significance. This is a misinterpretation, however: Washington has little trouble coming up with the resources needed by the contras, with or without congressional endorsement, while the enormous amounts of money channeled to the contras through the CIA and other state organs far transcend the amounts publicly approved by Congress. From the almost $20 million announced by the president in December 1981 to the allocation of $27 million in "humanitarian aid," in June

1985, the contras have officially received approximately $107 million. This does not include the use of contingency funds, which the CIA is not required to report, or interdepartmental transfers, which run into hundreds of millions of dollars.[19] Neither do they include spending by the DOD and other government agencies and departments, whose general budget categories amount to billions, or private contributions and transfers through third countries.[20] FDN sources confirm that they have received laundered funds through governments and organizations in Western Europe and elsewhere, as well as financial and material donations from Israel, Taiwan, Guatemala, and Argentina, among others.[21] The Nicaraguan government's estimates that the United States spent at least $1 billion on the counterrevolution between 1983 and 1985 alone are certainly plausible.[22]

However, the importance of congressional funding for the contras is not financial but political. The United States seeks to corral its own and the world's resources into the war effort, to make the war *national* policy and not merely administration policy. "Only official aid from the United States," said President Reagan during his 1985 campaign for new congressional funds, "can make the all-important symbolic point that we stand behind the [contra] forces."[23] Presenting the government and public as being fully united around the administration's strategy is a key component of pursuing the war's objectives on the diplomatic and political fronts, provides Washington with greater flexibility on the military front.

"Privatization" or "Publicization"?

The twilight battlefield of low-intensity conflicts
. . . *is an enormous area in which private-sector resources can be used.* We must find a way to *incorporate into a grand strategy the total resources of our
society,* so as to address those needs essential to our
security beyond the limitations of our current defense structure.

—Secretary of the Army John O. Marsh[24]

It was mid-morning on 1 September 1984. The Hughes 500 helicopter gunship, with its crew of three, took off from Tegucigalpa's Toncontín airport, heading toward the U.S. base at El Aguacate in the southeast for refueling by U.S. military technicians. Flight patterns and mission instructions were reviewed. Shortly before 2:00 P.M., the chopper lifted off and headed south to rendezvous with three Cessna 02A counterinsurgency aircraft, which had taken off from the Jamastrán military airfield to the southwest. After meeting up, the four aircraft crossed the Segovia Mountains into Nicaragua and headed in combat formation toward the town of Santa Clara, some fifteen miles inside the border. Circling over the military training school on the town's outskirts, at exactly 2:15 P.M. the Cessnas fired a dozen air-to-ground missiles as the helicopter opened up with machine-gun and cannon fire. Five civilians were killed, including two children selling refreshments to soldiers and a man gathering fruit nearby. As the Cessnas circled around and headed back toward Honduras, the helicoptor swooped down to attack the town's electrical substation. By this time, Sandinista antiaircraft batteries were in action: at 2:20 P.M. the chopper was hit and went down in flames.[25]

Two of the three crew members were subsequently identified as Dana Parker, an Alabama policeman and captain in the Special Forces Group of the U.S. National Guard, and James Powell, a former U.S. Air Force pilot from Tennessee; both were Vietnam veterans. The third body was too charred to be identified. All three were part of a fifteen-man training team that had been sent by Civilian Military Assistance (CMA) to work with the contras. CMA is a right-wing paramilitary group, composed mainly of Vietnam veterans, that was set up in 1983 to provide aid and training to the contras and to the Salvadoran army.

In a note to Secretary of State Shultz the following day, Nicaragua protested U.S. government involvement in the attack, a charge immediately denied by Washington. But the facts surfaced quickly over the next several days, exposing the elaborate connection between the mercenaries and the Reagan administration. The State Department admitted that the U.S. embassies in San Salvador and Tegucigalpa had facilitated the arrival of the CMA mercenaries and their equipment.[26] The Cessnas used in the attack were part of a twenty-plane fleet that had belonged to the New York State National Guard and had been declared "surplus" in 1983; it had then been channeled to the CIA through Summit Aviation, Inc., a CIA front company. (Documents recovered from the ARDE plane brought down over Managua's Sandino International Airport in September 1983 also traced it back to Summit Aviation.) The CIA then brought the aircraft to El Salvador and Honduras for use by the contras, the Salvadorans, and in U.S. paramilitary operations. The project went by the codename "Elephant Herd," and reached all the way up to the Joint Chiefs of Staff.[27]

The scandal over U.S. involvement with the mercenaries, which was in violation of both U.S. and international law, for the first time thrust into public view the extensive three-way network that had been developing between the contras, private right-wing paramilitary and civilian organizations in the United States, and the U.S. government. The Reagan administration claimed that private "contributions" to the counterrevolution were necessary because of the suspension of congressional funding in mid-1984.[28] This line was quickly picked up by the press and served to obscure the real significance of what came to be known as the "privatization" of the war against Nicaragua.

The private contribution is certainly significant: estimates run as high as $80 to $100 million since 1983. One CMA member reported that his organization alone supplies "at least one million a month."[29] The financial contribution is far from the most important aspect of the privatization process, however. More important, the administration's "private wing" plays a key role both in executing the war in Central America and in developing the necessary political conditions inside the United States and around the world for the regional counterrevolution. Behind privatization is the growing fusion of the right wing in and out of government, a process closely tied up with the reconfiguration of U.S. society and the imperial state to wage low-intensity warfare. A closer examination of privatization reveals that there is such an extensive overlapping in the design and execution of policy toward Central America that the distinction between private and public is disappearing altogether.

Through a combination of congressional support and the extensive direct participation of private groups in the war, Washington has tried to turn the war against Nicaragua into a *national* project.[30] If the war was to be prolonged, popular backing in the United States would be necessary to sustain the effort. Public approval was important, but not enough: support for the war effort had to be qualitatively transformed into active participation. With Nicaragua as the test case of the Reagan Doctrine, popular support for the worldwide counteroffensive would be predicated on garnering support for the anti-Sandinista campaign. The fanatical sense of urgency behind the anti-Sandinista propaganda campaign, aimed at whipping up mass agitation, comes as much from the "private wing" of the administration as from the White House itself. In fact, bringing the U.S. public into the war is a task largely assigned to the privatization network. Thus, what appears to be a "privatization" process is in reality part of a "publicization" process—turning what began as a "private" administration war into a "public" project at the grassroots level.

Selling the contras to the U.S. public has required giving them broad public exposure, and the private organizations have helped in that by sponsoring speaking tours for FDN representatives. Wearing elegant suits and ties, with mastery of English and speeches peppered with phrases about "freedom," "justice," and "democracy," Calero, Bermúdez, and other contra leaders are presented in slick, stage-managed appearances organized by experienced public relations experts of the New Right. They thus become divorced in the eyes of the U.S. public from the murder and mayhem perpetrated by their forces inside Nicaragua.

One solicitation from this private network urged contributors to help "send 20,000 'Christmas bags' to guerrillas at the front and their families in remote camps." The group said that it was "organizing luncheons and soliciting donations from supermarkets, toymakers and other sympathetic individuals. A $3.50 contribution will buy a bag filled with candy, a T-shirt, a coloring book, crayons, balloons and a small toy for the child of a rebel."[31] Soliciting contributions from millions of U.S. taxpayers for gifts, food, and medicine for "downtrodden refugees"—rather than for the guns and bullets with which to assassinate Nicaraguans—is part of the war of images, aimed at convincing the population that the United States is doing "good things" in Central America. In turn, no matter what the nature of the "contribution," donors and participants are left with a vested interest in the fate of the counterrevolutionary project.

The Veterans of Foreign Wars (VFW) was one of the first groups to try and tap into its mass base and attach it to the war effort. In August 1983, during the VFW's annual convention, delegates set up the Humanitarian/Truth Fund for Nicaraguan "freedom fighters," with the goal of "providing food, clothing and medical supplies" to the contras and of carrying out public relations compaigns for the FDN in the United States. Soon, 2 million U.S. war veterans were receiving brochures soliciting participation in the "fund."[32]

The private groups are linked together in an informal, syndicated network, and have interlocking boards and umbrella organizations. The list of their leaders constitutes a veritable "who's who" of the New Right. Such a structure multiplies individual constituencies and makes it possible to coordinate their work. The VFW fund, for instance, was administered by the American Security Council (ASC), on whose board Reagan served before his election. The ASC is a New Right clearinghouse that groups together sixty-five organizations, among them the Teamsters' Union, the Reserve Officers' Association, and the National Coalition for Peace Through Strength. It was quickly able to boast that the 10 million U.S. citizens who belong to one or another of its member organizations were participating in the Nicaraguan counterrevolution.[33]

Another important part of the private network is made up of such prominent corporate leaders as Joseph Coors, who was a major contributor to Reagan's first presidential campaign, and millionaire industrialist J. Peter Grace. Grace heads the U.S. division of the Knights of Malta, whose membership includes William Casey, Alexander Haig, and Zbigniew Brzezinski (who served as national security adviser from 1977 to 1981). The Council for National Policy, which has sixty of the country's most prominent corporate executives on its board, plays a leading role in bringing corporate resources into the privatization process.[34]

The network is three-tiered. The first tier is composed of right-wing "grassroots organizations," such as the Christian Broadcasting Network (CBN) of the reactionary evangelical minister Pat Robertson, the VFW, and the Knights of Malta. The second is made up of New Right political organizations, many of which trace their roots to the conservative insurgency of the 1970s. This tier includes the ASC, the National Defense Council, the Confederation of the Associations for the Unification of the Societies of the Americas (CAUSA), which is the political arm of the Reverend Sun Myung Moon's Unification Church, and others, and functions as the gears of the network. The third tier consists of such paramilitary groups as CMA, Soldier of Fortune, and the Air Commando Association. These groups, considered the lunatic fringe only a few years before, were by 1983 organizing hundreds of scattered veterans and mercenaries for military-related work on the ground in Central America. On *their* fringes are fascist organizations ranging from the Ku Klux Klan and the American Nazi party to survivalist groups. The network has set up dozens of front organizations that offer direct support to the counterrevolution, among them the Nicaraguan Refugee Fund, Friends of the Americas, the Nicaraguan Freedom Fund, the Americares Foundation, and the Pro-America Education Foundation.

Extensive private operations in Central America itself fill in many of the missing gaps in the war. Many of the private crusaders trace their roots back to active service in the Special Operations Forces, the Vietnam War, and in U.S. paramilitary and psychological operations around the globe. They carry out functions that range from training and advising the Somocistas, to winning the "hearts and minds" of the refugee populations that the war has generated, to supervising the arrival, distribution, and use of material resources for the contras, to high-risk commando missions in situations that are too complicated for the contras and where their participation is more expedient than the use of official DOD operatives.

As far back as 1980, the Committee of Santa Fe noted that private groups can carry out work like this far more efficiently than can U.S. government agencies. "Innovative and adaptable personnel working and living with these indigenous people, not enormous sums of money, is the key [to winning them over]," said the committee's document. "The existing [U.S. government] delivery system is not appropriate . . . because it either operates through public institutional structures which are remote, overly sophisticated and impersonal, or because [they can't] win the locals' confidence; whereas a long-term, localized and highly personalized approach is necessary."[35] Privatization makes this possible.

Equally important, the hundreds of war veterans and out-of-service special operations experts are a mine of accumulated experience in unconventional warfare that can only be tapped through privatization. In other words, until the Pentagon can produce a whole new generaton of its own cadres trained in low-intensity warfare, privatization provides the means to harness these dormant resources.

CMA "is capable of providing military advisement and hardware as well as all kinds of support functions very efficiently," the CMA's Bill Johnson reported.[36] It is more common to see "private" individuals in Honduran contra camps and "refugee" centers than U.S. government officials. According to Johnson, war material collected by CMA is stored in a central warehouse that the FDN leases in New Orleans and then shuttled to Honduras on weekly flights. In 1984 Congress approved the Denton Amendment, which authorizes the Pentagon to transport so-called humanitarian assistance collected by the private groups to Central America.[37]

At the top of the privatization network sit officials of the Reagan administration, together with a handful of private individuals who are some of the best unconventional warfare experts the nation has to offer. Many of these men, including Singlaub and Lansdale, participated in the 1983 Pentagon and NSC panels on recharting U.S. Central America policy. Conversely, many administration officials sit on the boards of these private groups. For example, Lewis Tambs and Roger Fontaine, who served on the NSC staff after participating in the Committee of Santa Fe, are both officers of the Council on Inter-American Security (CIS), as is Lt. Gen. Gordon Sumner, U.S. Army, ret., who is also a special consultant to the State Department.[38]

In early 1984, President Reagan approved a secret plan for White House coordination of the privatization effort. The NSC's Col. North was appointed to execute the plan,[39] and the NSC became the highest coordinating body of the privatization network. By this point the distinction between "public" and "private" had all but disappeared. Singlaub was selected as the principal liaison between the government and the private groups. He was to have direct access to the offices of Iklé and Sánchez, and was to then transmit NSC directives to the private network.

Singlaub is chairman of the World Anti-Communist League (WACL), a coalition of far right and fascist groups and political parties from some one hundred countries. Founded in 1967, WACL is often referred to as the "Fascist International," and numbers among its members the leaders of Latin America's notorious death squads, government officials from South Korea, Taiwan, Saudi Arabia, and Israel, and some of the most hawkish military men in the NATO alliance.[40] It was considered a pariah organization by previous U.S. administrations, but President Reagan sent a warm message of greeting to its 1982 meeting in Tokyo.[41] Through the WACL, the United States has thus been able to harness a powerful global network of reactionary forces to the Nicaraguan counterrevolution. According to Singlaub, for instance, Israel agreed to supply captured PLO weapons to the FDN, while he personally arranged for private businessmen and local WACL chapters in several other countries to channel resources to the contras.[42] The WACL has also mounted propaganda campaigns around the globe in favor of the counterrevolution, while its U.S. chapter, the United States Council for World Freedom (also headed by Singlaub), links international efforts to the internal U.S. effort.

As part of the privatization plan, administration officials readily lend their names to private groups. President Reagan was the keynote speaker at a fund raising dinner held in April 1985 in Washington by the Nicaraguan Freedom Fund (NFF) and attended by some seven hundred wealthy conservatives. NFF board member Jeane Kirkpatrick sent a highly publicized $20,000 contribution to the "freedom fighters."[43]

The public association between the Reagan administration and the NFF underscores just how far the project has come in a few short years. The NFF was launched by the *Washington Times*, a reactionary newspaper owned by CAUSA. The "Moonies" have been working in Central America since at least 1982, when CAUSA developed direct contacts with Honduran strongman Gustavo Alvarez and his inner circle and established relations with the Somocistas. At first the lunatic image of the Unification Church and the Reverend Moon's tax evasion scandals led the White House to distance itself from CAUSA,[44] but by the time of the NFF dinner all such qualms had disappeared. In effect, the fascist ideology and paramilitary extremism of WACL, the Unification Church, and Soldier of Fortune had much in common with the New Right forces behind the Reagan administration, expressed in the common thread of fanatical anticommunism. The "pro-freedom" image given to violent anticommunism as part of the Reagan Doctrine dissolved the differences of appearance. In September 1985 WACL held a grandiose public meeting in Dallas.[45] Among the keynote speakers was Singlaub, who read Reagan's personal greetings, and the FDN's Adolfo Calero. The full spectrum of New Right personalities, international mercenaries of various shades, and representatives of "freedom fighters" in Angola, Afghanistan, Mozambique, and Southeast Asia was in attendance.*

By 1986, it had become all but impossible to distinguish U.S. government officials from those in "private" groups when they were speaking about Central America. In early 1986, speeches by Reagan urging Congress to approve new funding for the contras were broadcast virtually back-to-back with privately funded television commercials which featured Singlaub standing in front of the White House and urging the U.S. public to support the Somocistas.[46]

The Contras' New Role

The new stage of war against Nicaragua meant a redefined role for the contras. The armed counterrevolution had to move beyond naked military force and transform itself into a contender in the Nicaraguan national social and political equation, in which military aggression was to be reduced to a means of achieving broader social and political goals. Washington assigned the FDN and the ARDE to carry out multidimensional operations that would grind away at the Nicaraguan social and economic infrastructure. Combined with aggression on other war fronts, the contras would play an important role in undermining the

---

*Although it started out as an aspect of the Central American counterrevolution, by 1985 the privatization network was coalescing into a solid political and material foundation for the Reagan Doctrine around the world. Privatization is part of a deeper process: the merger of the corporate representatives of monopoly capital, the most reactionary sectors of the U.S. bourgeoisie, political and grassroots activists, and the violent fringe groups (Soldier of Fortune, the Ku Klux Klan, etc.), all of whom share the aim of carrying through worldwide counterrevolution, regenerating U.S. capital accumulation through the military-industrial complex, and subjugating the U.S. working class to this purpose. These are the building blocks of a fascist project in the United States.

defensive capacity of the revolution and building a base of support for the counterrevolutionary project.

No longer were the Sandinista armed forces to be the target of contra aggression. The new strategy meant that the FDN and ARDE bands were to *avoid* direct clashes with EPS troops,[47] instead targeting health clinics, schools, peasant cooperation, agricultural and construction machinery, and any installation that symbolized the progress and development brought about by the revolution. "We have instructions from the U.S. government to attack the most important centers of production and then retreat into the mountains," said Adolfo Calero.[48] Key objectives were the disruption of agricultural production and, complemented by political activities in areas where there was a contra presence, the whittling away of support for the revolution among the peasantry. At the same time the contra forces sought to expand the zones of military conflict to include large stretches of the northern and southern border regions, the Atlantic Coast, and the central highlands. This, it was hoped, would force intensified military mobilization and greater diversion of resources from social and economic development to the defense effort, and put the contras in direct contact with broader sectors of the population. Calero described this redefined role: "The objective now is to wear them down. We don't believe that a military solution is any longer possible."[49]

The contras' redefined role was part of *the specific Nicaraguan variant of low-intensity warfare, the war of attrition*.* This new strategy "will seek to tire us, exasperate us and demoralize us with a prolonged war," said Deputy Interior Minister Luis Carrión Cruz.[50] Each sphere in which revolution and counterrevolution meet—diplomatic/international, political, ideological, military, and economic—was to become a battlefield. International diplomacy was to be a weapon to diminish the Sandinistas' legitimacy and validate the counterrevolution. The revolution's process of socioeconomic transformation was to be made unworkable through military and other types of aggression. Above all, Nicaragua's civilian population was to be the ultimate target of these activities. The attrition process was designed to breed discontent and to delegitimize the revolution, and this in turn would open the way for the counterrevolution to develop a social base and present itself as an alternative. The principal indicator for success would be the extent to which the counterrevolution—in which the armed contras would be but a detachment—was able to influence and win over the people.

---

*The term "attrition" is used here in a very different sense than in Chapter 1, where it described a military doctrine that means the physical extermination of enemy forces through the massive application of firepower.

4
Recasting Tactics: Changes in the Battlefields

> If the quick destruction of the enemy is not possible, then one should concentrate on "wastage" of the enemy—making the war more costly to him through laying waste to the enemy's territory, increasing the enemy's suffering, and wearing the enemy down in order to bring about a gradual exhaustion of his physical and moral position . . . to destroy his will by operations that have direct political repercussions.
>
> —Carl von Clausewitz, as quoted
> by Col. Harry G. Summers, Jr.[1]

> The enemy has upped the ante; the war has qualitatively changed.
>
> —Sandinista leader Dora María Téllez[2]

Throughout January and February 1984, the Somocistas in Tegucigalpa were discussing a major operation. In late February it came: over eight thousand FDN contras and numerous ARDE columns invaded Nicaragua simultaneously in what the counterrevolution dubbed its "General Offensive." Heavy fighting soon engulfed three major regions of the country: the north and the northern Pacific Coast border with Honduras, the southeastern border with Costa Rica, and the Atlantic Coast. The sheer magnitude of the offensive—previously no more than three thousand contras had entered the country at one time—as well as the extensive logistic support from U.S. and Honduran forces, allowed the contras to penetrate into the interior of the vast mountainous provinces of Jinotega, Estelí, Matagalpa, and Boaco, which had thus far been unaffected by the war. Continuous resupply flights arrived from Honduras in three stages. Supplies arriving from the United States, the Panama Canal Zone, El Salvador, or Tegucigalpa were first shuttled to the El Aguacate military base in the Honduran Department of Olancho, which was run by U.S. forces and had been virtually turned over to the FDN after the Big Pine II maneuvers. From El Aguacate they were airlifted to supply bases along the border, and then airdropped to the contra forces deep in Nicaraguan territory. At the same time, U.S.-piloted electronic surveillance flights over the combat zones gathered precise information on Sandinista troop movements in order to guide the Somocistas and coordinate the resupply missions. As Comandante Joaquín Cuadra, chief of the EPS high command, charged at 12 April press conference in Managua, "The U.S. has provided its mercenary army with a level of logistical support never seen before—almost inexhaustible."

The new supply structure was a qualitative upgrading of the earlier system, in which supplies had been concentrated on the border and either carried in overland or stockpiled until the FDN forces returned to Honduras. Now the contras could remain inside Nicaragua for an indefinite period—in fact, according to Cuadra, the CIA had given specific orders for the contras to remain inside at all costs. The United States had also supplied them with light artillery, sophisticated communications systems, new aircraft, and *pirañas*.

In order to achieve this new level of operational capacity, the CIA had reorganized the FDN forces into hierarchically structured "regional commands"—large-scale units comprising at least three task forces of between 250 and 300 contras each. "This allows the U.S. to exercise greater and more direct control over its mercenary army in Honduras," said Cuadra. The contras united under this structure formed the principal invasion force, but there were also several other independent task forces that were sent across the border on specific distraction and sabotage missions, and still others that were stationed along the border to act as relief and logistical service units.

In the sparsely populated south, the ARDE was deployed in order to force the EPS to spread itself thin, and also to carry out pincer actions on the Atlantic Coast, in coordination with FDN troops descending from the north and MISURA and MISURASATA forces already operating in the region. As in the north, CIA penetration of Costa Rica and its control over the ARDE were greatly increased in the first few months of 1984. The London *Sunday Times* reported that dozens of CIA agents and Pentagon operatives under the cover of the U.S. embassy or private U.S. companies had arrived in Costa Rica between January and March in order to take direct control of all ARDE activities.[3] With vast stretches of northern Costa Rica virtually turned over to Pastora's men, and thick jungle and swamp terrain dominating the south of Nicaragua, a less elaborate resupply structure was required. The Pentagon had already carried out intensive night flights from bases in El Salvador and Honduras, transferring arms, munitions, and other supplies to ARDE forces on the ground. One of these planes, a DC-3, crashed on 24 March 1984 near the Nicaraguan border, on property owned by John Hull, a key CIA liaison in northern Costa Rica. The four U.S. and three Salvadoran crewmen were killed instantly. Hull had the bodies buried and the wreckage quietly removed so as not to attract attention.[4]

In early April, Washington attempted to launch a propaganda campaign to complement the fighting on the ground. Most of the ARDE's troops were concentrated to the extreme northeastern corner of Costa Rica, on the banks of the Río San Juan, which divides the two countries (the river itself is part of Nicaraguan territory). The target was San Juan del Norte, a small Atlantic Coast port town at the mouth of the river. Early in the last century it had been known as Greytown, and was used by the British pirate Henry Morgan, among others, as a base for incursions up the river into Lake Nicaragua in order to sack the cities on the Pacific Coast. Later, the U.S. tycoon Cornelius Vanderbilt had made the town a transit point for adventurers crossing the Pacific during the California gold rush, and in 1848 it was razed to the ground by U.S. naval forces during one of Nicaragua's civil wars. Despite this colorful history, in 1984 San Juan del Norte and the surrounding region had no military or economic significance whatsoever. The zone was deserted, surrounded by dense jungle and swamp, and only accessible by air or sea. The town's inhabitants had been evacuated to safer areas in mid-1983, when ARDE attacks had begun in the south, and only a small EPS garrison of nearly eighty men was left behind to defend it. San Juan del Norte's isolation led the United States to believe that it would be an easy target.

On the evening of 6 April more than five hundred ARDE troops began a prolonged siege of the town. They had inexhaustible supplies, reinforcements, and other forms of support from their bases in Costa Rica, including constant artillery fire, sea-based attacks from the *pirañas* supplied by the CIA, and the unrestricted use of Costa Rica's highways, airports, and harbors. Outnumbered by more than six to one, post commander 2d Lt. Lino Mendoza Chávez and his soldiers held off the onslaught for seven days. On 13 April the U.S. battleship USS *McKinley,* which had arrived off the coast as the attack began, opened fire, giving the ARDE troops the final edge they needed to move in on the town. "It was understood that [the Americans] were in charge of the naval actions," an ARDE spokesman in San José explained.[5]

The publicity show was worked out well in advance: within hours of the occupation, foreign journalists were shuttled in and a "triumphant" Edén Pastora declared that he was establishing a "beachhead" inside Nicaragua, that he would form a "provisional government," and that he was ready to march on to Managua.[6] Yet no sooner had the journalists left than the Sandinista counteroffensive began. As the ARDE troops retreated, they left behind stockpiles of U.S.-manufactured weapons, including rocket launchers, grenades, automatic rifles, and even U.S. Army maps. By 17 April EPS detachments had regained control of the town and had expelled the contras from Nicaraguan territory. ARDE's "occupation" of San Juan del Norte came to a quick end. Journalists flown in by EPS helicopter on 22 April saw a desolate town, with only five or six wooden houses still standing amid the ashes and the stench of death. The bodies of the seventy-eight Sandinista defenders lay half-buried in their trenches. "The *compañeros* fought from their trenches, and when someone fell, right then and there they buried him, writing his name on a piece of paper and sticking it in his clothing," an EPS officer told the authors.

In the north, the rural communities were taking a beating. Because of the contras' hit-and-run tactics, it was difficult for the EPS to pin them down, and the brunt of the defense fell on the peasant militias and self-defense cooperatives, which declared themselves on a "war footing" and organized counteroffensives region by region, using the mobile EPS units as back up. By May, the contras' momentum had been broken, and the regional commands were dispersing into the mountains. Nevertheless, heavy fighting continued, and both sides suffered numerous casualties.

Throughout 1984, the United States continued to reorganize the counterrevolution in the mirror image of its own armed forces, particularly the SOF. Having first been transformed from roving bands into task forces and then into regional commands, in late 1984 the contras were again restructured into operational commands, even larger conglomerations which allowed for better coordination and flexibility. Within each operational command the U.S. advisers created specialized units in order to allow for greater tactical diversity. These ranged from Tactical Operations Commands, Special Operations Commands (COE), Psychological Operations Units, and TESONs (Troops Trained in Jungle and Nighttime Operations), among others. These units, modeled on the U.S. SOF formations, show the extent to which the contras were the local extension of the Pentagon. Many contras even wore patches with triple lightning bolts, the insignia of the SOF. The strategy of low-intensity warfare includes the substitution of indigenous for U.S. forces, organized, trained, and directed by small SOF contingents and linked to command centers in Honduras, SOUTHCOM, and the United States. This is not a war between Nicaraguans, but a war between the United States and Nicaragua.

The Mining Fiasco

In the final months of 1983 Washington planned an action which finally showed the world the degree to which this was a U.S. war: the mining of Nicaragua's harbors.

Between February and April 1984, U.S. forces placed at least six hundred aquatic mines in Nicaragua's principal harbors, Corinto and Sandino on the Pacific Coast and El Bluff on the Atlantic Coast. This sophisticated operation involved three different types of underwater explosive devices, designed by the CIA Weapons Group in Langley and the Mine Warfare Division of the Naval Surface Weapons Center in White Oaks, Maryland.[7] The mines were emplaced by SEAL commando units "loaned" by the U.S. Navy to the CIA. The SEAL units arrived in armored speedboats deployed from the U.S. frigate USS *Gallery*, which was stationed some forty miles off the Pacific Coast. It was the first time since the Vietnam war that any country's ports had been mined.

Daniel Ortega first denounced the mining on 26 February, after two Nicaraguan fishing boats hit the devices.[8] Ten days later, a freighter flying the Panamanian flag hit a mine in Corinto and sustained moderate damage. The Sandinistas accused the United States of directly planning and executing the action, a charge to which the Western press responded with skepticism. Instead, broad coverage was given to a communiqué that Pastora issued on 1 March attributing the mining to ARDE.[9] The next day, Edgar Chamorro, the FDN's chief of public relations, issued a statement claiming that his organization was responsible. Several weeks later, congressional and administration sources leaked the truth to U.S. newspapers.[10] As Chamorro explained nearly two years later: "The [CIA] deputy station chief wrote our statement on the mining. He woke me up in the middle of the night and told me to issue it. It was the first I knew of it."[11]

Deactivating the mines was a very costly process for the Nicaraguans.

Dozens of lobster fishermen joined Sandinista Coast Guard divers in deactivating the devices and in sweeping the ports. The surface mines, which are detonated by direct contact, were the easiest to remove. Two other types—those placed on the harbor floor and set off either by movement or by sonic waves—proved more risky, and some thirty people were injured. Between February and April, nine foreign vessels were damaged, including Japanese, British, Dutch, and Soviet ships, and fifteen seamen of different nationalities injured. At least two dozen Nicaraguan fishing boats were damaged or destroyed.

Nevertheless, the mining was essentially a psychological operation. It was intended to frighten off foreign ships that wanted to enter Nicaraguan ports, thus creating a "de facto blockade," as the Nicaraguans put it. The Reagan administration expected that, once the first ship ran into a mine, Nicaragua would be "off limits" to international maritime trade." About a dozen vessels did make a detour into Costa Rican ports, where merchandise was unloaded and sent overland. Nicaragua also set up an escort system, deploying its fishing fleet and Coast Guard units to steer foreign ships into port. Despite these efforts, the mining took a high economic toll. Nicaragua reported losses of over $10 million, including lost seafood exports, delays in other exports, damage to Nicaraguan vessels, loss of merchandise, and increased insurance costs.[12]

The contradictions created by the mining operation showed the complexities of the new strategy of attrition. On the one hand, the Reagan administration saw the mining as a good way to achieve important objectives. By preventing ships from entering or leaving Nicaraguan ports, it could quickly cut off Nicaragua's foreign trade: paralyzing imports and exports would virtually asphyxiate the economy. The timing was carefully chosen with this in mind: November to April is harvest season for Nicaragua's principal export crops, for which speedy shipment is essential. The socioeconomic dislocation provoked by a cutoff in foreign trade would generate the ideal internal conditions for whittling away at the revolution. In addition, the mining operation was an effective adjunct to the contras' General Offensive, which involved disrupting export crops at the point of production.

On the other hand, mining a nation's ports is tantamount to an act of war, and is indefensible by any international juridical standard. Nicaragua quickly mobilized the international community to censure the mining. The UN Security Council, the OAS, and governments around the world condemned the United States. The Reagan administration emerged in the eyes of the world as an ugly Goliath and Nicaragua as a valiant David. Even the United States' staunchest allies, such as the conservative British and West German governments, distanced themselves from the mining. The Reagan administration had underestimated the intensity of the international fallout, which far exceeded any benefits accrued—particularly since, far from disrupting the internal cohesion of Nicaraguan society, the mining in fact strengthened the nation's unity, and even right-wing opposition sectors came out against it.

The uproar in U.S. ruling circles, and inside the administration itself, was partly because critics felt the mining had been a strategic blunder, one that underscored internal differences over the interrelation of LIW. Those within the executive who opposed the action did so precisely because it undercut the aims of the political battle against Nicaragua. As one administration official put it, "It was neither illegal nor immoral, but it was incredibly destructive. . . . It couldn't have been better designed to undermine our policy."[13]

On the domestic front, a majority of Congress questioned the expediency of continuing the war in the face of the increased political costs. Such reservations were expressed in the congressional cutoff of official government funding for the contras in the summer of 1984. Although this had little material effect on the contras' ability to operate, it did constitute a significant political setback for the administration.

The Changing of the Guard in Honduras

While the debate over the mining of the harbors raged in Washington, tensions within the Honduran military, which had been simmering for some time, came to a boil. The possibility of war with Nicaragua in late 1983 and the conflicting signals coming from Washington had intensified existing internal divisions. For its part, the U.S. embassy in Tegucigalpa had been contemplating a reorganization of the Honduran rearguard in accordance with the new U.S. strategy. Pressures and behind-the-scenes maneuvering by embassy officials converged with tensions within the Honduran armed forces to produce a de facto coup d'état that ousted Gen. Alvarez on 30 March 1984.

The general was arrested that morning while attending a meeting of the Association for the Progress of Honduras (APROH) in the northern industrial city of San Pedro Sula. APROH, a grouping of the most reactionary business and professional interests and military men in Honduras, was created in late 1982 under the auspices of the Unification Church. Following a visit to Honduras by the Reverend Sun

Muyng Moon's right-hand man, Korean army colonel and CIA agent Bo Hi Pak, Alvarez had been named president of the group, which he used as a base for accumulating power and organizing his inner circle of cohorts.

Following his arrest, Alvarez was taken in handcuffs to Tegucigalpa and brought before President Suazo Córdova and Honduran air force commander Gen. Walter López, who ordered his immediate expulsion to Costa Rica. But the changing of the guard went further, digging deep into the fabric of the Honduran power structure. Those removed included the heads of the Honduran joint chiefs of staff, the navy, and the draconian Public Security Force (FUSEP), as well as about thirty additional high-level military officers.

Alvarez was bewildered. In a brief press conference in San José on 4 April, he described his removal as the result of a "conspiracy" by "a group of disloyal and ambitious military officers."[14] But in fact the coup had little to do with the personal ambitions of those who carried it out and much to do with U.S. plans. Alvarez had served U.S. strategy well since U.S. Ambassador John Negroponte had masterminded his rise to power three years earlier. The Honduran military had been transformed into a professional fighting force, the country converted into a U.S. base, the nascent popular movement crushed, and the contras installed. But he was increasingly a threat to a prolonged, regional counterrevolutionary strategy, which required *avoiding* a full-scale military conflict between Honduras and Nicaragua while continuing to create the impression that such a situation might arise. His reckless behavior and his apparent thirst to test his troops' capacity against Nicaragua put U.S. plans in jeopardy.

In addition, the United States believed that the process of "nation building" in Honduras required "clean" government: a civilian image, no corruption, social control through highly selective repression, and efficient institutions rather than strongman tactics. The fact that Alvarez had been centralizing power, both in and out of the military, in his own hands, was making it difficult for the United States to control Honduran life. Only weeks before his removal, Alvarez had put about rumors that he was planning, with the support of APROH, to secure nomination as a candidate in the 1985 elections, or to replace Suazo Córdova some other way. Swindling, corruption, and arbitrary repression was the norm for APROH, and in March Alvarez had been publicly accused of embezzling $30 million in government funds, a charge quickly seized upon by foreign journalists and one that tarnished the regime's image. Alvarez had also launched Honduras into an era of death squads and clandestine cemeteries at a time when the United

States was scrapping these forms of social control as antiquated and counterproductive.[15] Despite the fact that he had successfully decapitated the nascent popular movement between 1981 and 1983, he had clearly outlived his usefulness, as had APROH, which was effectively removed from the political equation with Alvarez's fall.

Negroponte's only comment during the coup was that Washington was "aware of the situation." At the very least, however, the U.S. embassy—which shared the same concerns as those who ousted Alvarez—undoubtedly knew of the coup *beforehand*, even if it did not orchestrate his removal from beginning to end.[16] The Granadero I joint military maneuvers began as scheduled, literally within hours of Alvarez's fall. Given that the entire high command of the Honduran armed forces (with the exception of López) was removed, it is difficult to imagine how thousands of Honduran troops could participate in military exercises without total confusion unless the affair had been worked out with the Honduran army's U.S. sponsors.

Similarly, the shakeup did not stop the Honduran armed forces from acting as the rearguard for the contra General Offensive. In fact, the changes helped discipline the contras and forced them to wage war more efficiently. "Before [Alvarez's removal] it was like Vietnam: three-fourths of our forces were in reserve and one-forth in Nicaragua," said one FDN commander. He also asserted that those who replaced Alvarez "made it so that we put our activists more and more in Nicaragua. Before there were too many who strolled around and too few who fought: now we can't go to Tegucigalpa as often to get drunk and feel under women's skirts."[17] The Sandinista government, however, was not deceived by the changes: "These changes do not mean that there is going to be any change in U.S. policy. We have to be clear about this; we can't lower our guard," said Nicaraguan vice-president Sergio Ramírez.[18]

Alvarez's replacement was the forty-three-year-old Walter López, who told the Honduran press the day after the National Assembly appointed him as the new commander in chief of the armed forces that Alvarez had been "overthrown" in order to save "the nation's democratic institutions." The López group was depicted in the press as a "reformist young officer corps," which was partially true. These officers did resent the U.S. military and intelligence domination of their "turf," which was taking away the autonomy of the Honduran military. They also wanted more in return for the country's subjugation to the United States, including increased economic aid. Their pragmatic approach to the changes taking place in Honduras dovetailed with U.S. plans and necessitated avoiding the exacerbation of social tensions and the monopolization of power by individual strongmen. However, the López group was open to the long-term regional counterrevolutionary strategy, which also pleased the United States.

Diplomacy as Warfare

Border provocations against Nicaragua by the Honduran armed forces, which had continued virtually uninterrupted since the Reagan administration came to office, did not diminish with the changing of the guard. In late April, the army initiated a fresh wave of mortar attacks and incursions into Nicaraguan territory. Then, on 8 May, Sandinista antiaircraft batteries brought down a Honduran air force helicopter after it penetrated more than ten miles into Nicaraguan airspace on what was apparently an espionage mission over the military installations in the Consigüina Peninsula of Chinandega. All eight Honduran crew members were killed.

The Hondurans claimed that the helicopter had been fired at while it was over Honduran territory; they then changed the story and declared that "heavy winds" had forced it off course. Finally, they maintained that the Sandinistas had forced the craft to the ground in the border zone and then destroyed it.[19] Despite the absurdity of the Honduran claims (the helicopter went down ten miles inside Nicaraguan territory), the incident gave the Honduran authorities another pretext for whipping up tensions between the two countries. Three days after the downing of the helicopter, Honduras expelled Nicaraguan Ambassador Edwin Zablah and recalled its ambassador to Managua as a "reprisal."

"Diplomatic" aggression against Nicaragua increased. Provocations by Nicaragua's neighbors were hardly novel, but now they became events with which to feed the anti-Sandinista campaign internationally and to heighten the isolation of Nicaragua regionally. They were used to portray Nicaragua as an aggressor against its neighbors and, thus, as the source of regional instability and conflict.

Nowhere could the fabrication of diplomatic incidents be seen more clearly than in Costa Rica. An internal NSC memorandum leaked to the press in April had stated that the tension between the two countries "provides us with the possibility of helping to tilt the political balance in our favor on Nicaragua's southern flank. . . . It could provoke a significant change in the neutralist balancing act, pushing the country more publicly and explicitly to the anti-Sandinista camp." The document continued, "It is vital to portray Nicaragua as an aggressor . . .

for public relations efforts, it is impossible to neutralize the 'ARDE factor.' *The story must be Nicaragua against Costa Rica, not Nicaragua against its armed opposition.*"[20]

As efforts intensified to "Honduranize" Costa Rica and to make Nicaragua's southern flank a secure political and military rearguard for the counterrevolution, the simmering "border dispute" flared with ever greater frequency. Pastora's abortive seizure of San Juan del Norte in April set the stage for the further deterioration of relations. On 3 May Costa Rica accused the Nicaraguan government of sending two thousand EPS troops into the Pocosol River zone of Costa Rica. Col. Oscar Vidal, head of the Costa Rican Rural Guard, who had apparently not been told by his civilian superiors that he should stick to this story, sent an investigative team into the zone and concluded that "there is a lot of speculation going on, and we have confirmed that there are no Nicaraguan soldiers here."[21] Despite this swift and clumsy collapse of the accusation, Costa Rica followed the Honduran example and expelled Nicaraguan Embassy Secretary Francisco Gutierrez. U.S. Ambassador to Costa Rica Curtin Winsor stated that the border incidents "prove once and for all that the Sandinistas are a threat to Costa Rican democracy."[22]

During this period, Washington's skill in combining actual contra military aggression with its own threats and diplomacy also progressed. According to Secretary of State Shultz, "Diplomacy is unlikely to work unless there is effective resistance . . . that is the relation between power and diplomacy."[23] In this equation, the contras would provide the military pressure—the "resistance"—to back up the diplomatic maneuvering. Shultz himself demonstrated how this worked on 2 June, when he paid a surprise visit to Managua, claiming that "President Reagan sent me on a peace mission to initiate direct conversations in order to seek regional solutions in Central America."[24] Just as his jet was touching down, six hundred contras launched a lightning attack on the northern border town of Ocotal. "It was an attack planned to coincide with the arrival of Shultz in order to pressure us," said Defense Minister Ortega.

Another part of the U.S. strategy was to "multilateralize" the diplomatic front of the war. "[We must] adopt more active diplomatic campaigns to turn around Mexico and social democrats in Europe [with regard to Nicaragua]," counseled a National Security Council document back in April 1982. "In the meantime, keep [Nicaragua] isolated on Central American issues."[25] By isolating Nicaragua regionally and internationally, the United States believed it would lay the groundwork for corralling international forces into supporting its war effort.

Particularly important in this regard was Latin America. "We must maintain a high level of pressure on the Sandinista government [to make sure] that it pays a price for its aggression," explained Assistant Secretary of State for Inter-American Affairs Elliott Abrams the following year, expressing what the United States had been trying to do since the beginning of the war. "In this, the Latin American governments play an essential role . . . we need the other democratic countries to join us publicly in pressuring the Nicaraguan government."[26]

The first step, begun much earlier, was to bring the United States' regional allies together in an anti-Sandinista diplomatic bloc. In February 1982 the outgoing Carazo administration in Costa Rica had hosted the foreign ministers of El Salvador and Honduras at the founding of the Central American Democratic Community, the first of several such forums designed to institutionalize this bloc. The effort won little international repsect, despite its stated intention of seeking "peaceful democratic solutions" to the regional crisis. The "Forum for Peace and Democracy," held in Costa Rica in October, to which Panama, Colombia, and several other Caribbean Basin countries were also invited, suffered the same fate. The heavy hand of the United States—this event became known in diplomatic circles as the "Enders Forum"—and the absence of Nicaragua made it clear that this was not a genuine effort in the search for peace.* Nonetheless, by 1983 these efforts had achieved their main objective, the consolidation of a pliable anti-Sandinista diplomatic bloc, comprising the "democratic" countries of Costa Rica, Honduras, and El Salvador. This bloc was to be the essential component of subsequent diplomatic stragegy.

The next step, which entailed bringing the rest of Latin America into the fold, proved much more difficult. In early January 1983, the heads of state of Mexico, Panama, Colombia, and Venezuela met on the Panamanian resort island of Contadora. The four presidents initiated a diplomatic effort—unprecedented in Latin American history—to work out a negotiated solution to the Central American crisis. Unlike the earlier U.S.-sponsored efforts, the new group—which became known as

---

*Guatemala's military junta was not invited to either of the meetings. This gave the United States the pretext for claiming that it was not "anti-Nicaragua" but rather "anti-totalitarian" or simply "pro-democratic." (Nicaragua was "totalitarian" from the left and Guatemala from the right, went Washington's line.) Yet there was another important dynamic with regard to Guatemala. The Guatemalan regime had decided to maintain regional neutrality, believing that participation in Washington's regional counterrevolution would heighten its internal problems, particularly the revolutionary challenge it faced inside its own borders. This Guatemalan neutrality became an important factor as the war against Nicaragua progressed.

the Contadora Group—achieved immediate international recognition. The United States gave it a cool reception, as did Costa Rica, which was blocked from joining by Mexico, which considered Costa Rica too closely aligned with the United States.[27] Despite this, the broad international support, which included Washington's European allies, acted as a powerful force to contain the extremes of U.S. aggression, especially in late 1983.

The Contadora Group emerged out of the preoccupation of the Latin American bourgeois democracies with the consequences of a possible U.S. invasion of Nicaragua and/or a regional conflagration in Central America. The essential difference between the Contadora Group and other forums was precisely that it came into existence without the United States; it was an authentic *Latin American* political initiative to deal with the regional crisis from the standpoint of Latin American interests. It was felt that continental anti-imperialist sentiment, political upheaval, the disruption of regional economic relations, and the spread of military conflict in the wake of a direct U.S. intervention in Central America would seriously affect the precarious internal stability of many Latin American regimes. The Contadora countries believed that U.S. policies threatened their future more than did the revolutionary forces in the small Central American nations.

By mid-1985, Argentina, Brazil, Uruguay, and Peru had formed a Contadora Support Group (known as the Lima Group) to join the four Contadora nations. This additional support reflected contradictions that were emerging between U.S. imperialism and Latin America, currently played out most sharply in the drama of the debt crisis. In effect, the 1960s alliance between U.S. imperialism and Latin American bourgeois reformism has given way to a more complex political situation in which nationalist alternatives that are attempting to address pressing social and economic problems are also demanding more independence from—and even confrontation with—the United States. This contradiction has led to a renewed sense of Latin American nationalism, often referred to as the new "Bolivarianism."

Popular democratic movements surged in Latin America through the late 1970s and early 1980s, resulting in the replacement of military dictatorships in Argentina, Brazil, and Uruguay by elected civilian governments committed to democratization. More independent-minded and even anti-imperialist governments emerged in Peru and Venezuela, and democratic forces were strengthened across the continent. All this was the product of social pressures intimately tied to the revolutionary enthusiasm sparked by the Nicaraguan revolution and to Sandinismo's continental political and ideological influence. As Tomás

Borge has noted, "Without the existence of the Nicaraguan revolution these changes would not have taken place. It is in the interests of [the democratic upsurge] that the Nicaraguan revolution not be destroyed [since this would result in] a return to the kingdom of the Latin American gorillas."[28]

Daniel Ortega's visit to Uruguay for the inauguration of Julio María Sanguinetti in February 1985 brought hundreds of thousands of Uruguayans into the streets of Montevideo shouting "Viva Nicaragua Libre!" This was eloquent testimony to the influence of Sandinismo, which had come to symbolize Latin American aspirations for sovereignty and self-determination. The combination of popular pressure on governing regimes and the contradictions between those regimes and the United States made "Bolivarian nationalism" into a hefty counterweight to the U.S. war against Nicaragua.

Nicaragua's foreign policy has consistently stressed nonalignment, peaceful coexistence, broad political and economic relations with all countries and regions, and the constant mobilization of international opinion into an anti-interventionist front, both through bilateral relations and through multilateral organizations (UN, OAS, Non-Aligned Movement, etc.).[29] Sandinista diplomacy seeks not only to contain but also to isolate the U.S. war policy.

With its inception, Contadora quickly became the principle battleground for the diplomatic dimension of the U.S. war. Managua, which viewed its diplomatic strategy as the "first ring" of defense, energetically supported Contadora as a "shield of containment" against direct intervention. Nicaragua sought to emphasize the differences between Latin America and the United States with regard to Central America, but it also demonstrated a remarkable flexibility and willingness to make concessions. In the words of Tomás Borge, "We are willing to negotiate everything but the revolution itself."

In addition to supporting Contadora, Nicaragua had made—and continues to make—numerous peace initiatives of its own. On 19 October 1983 Nicaragua presented the United States with three draft treaties, encapsulating several earlier proposals, of a comprehensive bilateral settlement. The drafts addressed the Reagan administration's publicly expressed concern about Nicaragua's "threat to U.S. national security." First, although Washington had never come up with any evidence for its charge that Nicaragua was "exporting" its revolution, the proposed treaties committed Nicaragua to nonintervention in the internal affairs of neighboring countries and proposed joint border patrols to guarantee that there would be no "flow of arms" out of Nicaraguan territory. Second, the treaties proposed the withdrawal of *all* foreign military advisers from Nicaragua, El Salvador, and Honduras. Third, they proposed a region-wide inventory of troops and weapons stocks, with a view toward achieving regional balance, and proposed concrete mechanisms for verification.[30] The White House paid little attention to these Nicaraguan gestures.

Although the United States expressed verbal support for Contadora, it acted to undermine the group's efforts by blocking the signing of any peace treaty that would stand in the way of its regional counterrevolution. It also sought to transfer Latin American-sponsored negotiations to the OAS, where it exercises strong influence. At each OAS gathering, U.S. representatives urged the Latin American nations to bring the Central American case before the OAS as the "appropriate forum."[31] The United States also appointed special Central American/Contadora ambassadors to push its position—first Richard B. Stone, then Harry Schlaudeman, and later Philip Habib.

As the U.S. strategy consolidated around a program of prolonged antipopular warfare, "negotiations" and a "political solution" were no longer necessarily obstacles to this end. By 1984 U.S. diplomacy had gone well beyond isolating Nicaragua commercially and politically, regionally and internationally; its intent was now to wring concessions, legitimizing the counterrevolution and providing the Sandinista revolution with an "outlet" for its eventual surrender.

Contadora thus moved from being a "diplomatic thorn" in the Reagan administration's plan to being a potential instrument for achieving its objectives. Nicaragua's flexibility could now be turned against the revolution; the concessions it was willing to make could be exploited. The new approach was summarized by State Department special adviser Lt. Gen. Gordon Sumner: "I think Mr. Reagan's thrust on this is: we will take this process [Contadora] and shape it to what *we* want, not what *they* want, and we will keep pressure on them to force them to do this. It is going to be a long, painful process."[32] Managua had drawn up a diplomatic strategy pegged to the United States' direct-interventionist strategy, and now its efforts were thrown off balance, especially with regards to Contadora.

Back in September 1983, after nine months of Contadora negotiations, all five Central American governments had signed the "Document of 21 Points," which was to serve as the framework for the elaboration of a comprehensive peace treaty. The document's thrust was that there were to be multilateral commitments among the five nations on such issues as military parity, withdrawal of all foreign military advisers, mutual nonaggression pacts, noninterference in the internal affairs of other countries, and the termination of all support for "irregular forces" (the contras and revolutionary guerrilla movements).[33] The negotiating group presented its first draft treaty in June 1984, and in September delivered a "Revised Contadora Treaty," which was the version that was to be signed and then implemented.

During the tense months of negotiations, from September 1983 to September 1984, the United States prefected its new tactics. On the eve of each meeting of the negotiating group, the United States would launch an attack on Nicaragua, either a major assault by the contras, a Honduran army border "provocation," or the announcement of U.S. "war games" in Central American territory. Meanwhile, U.S. officials traveled back and forth between Washington and the Central American capitals for "consultations," both before and after the Contadora meetings. The administration also never failed to express its "complete" support for the negotiations. This was not only an integral part of the war of images, but was a way of putting pressure on Nicaragua by holding a match close to the bomb that it had placed under the negotiating table.

Using its Central American surrogates, the United States was able substantially to modify the treaty document. Instead of regional commitments, there were clauses that could mean major concessions on Nicaragua's part.[34] These "refinements" referred to Nicaragua's internal political process in clauses that dealt with "political pluralism," "human rights," "internationally supervised elections," etc. If allowed, they would clearly have provided mechanisms for the dismantling of the revolutionary state and popular power.

The treaty also included clauses that would severely constrain the United States in its prosecution of the war, such as the prohibition on foreign maneuvers and military bases in the region. But the United States presumed that the concessions Nicaragua was being asked to make would lead it to reject the treaty, thus becoming the intransigent enemy of peace. The United States would then not have to sign the treaty at all.

Nicaragua, however, took the United States and its allies by surprise, opting to "accept it in its totality, and sign the Revised Contadora Treaty immediately and without any modification whatsoever." The Sandinistas believed they could live with the concessions as long as the United States also complied with the treaty.

Nicaragua's acceptance forced the United States into a corner: with foreign military maneuvers, advisers, and support by outside powers for irregular forces proscribed, the United States would have had to suspend its war against Nicaragua. The White House began a flurry of diplomatic activity; it claimed that the treaty was "biased" in favor of

Nicaragua and quickly dispatched high-level officials to Central America. Within weeks, Costa Rica had reversed its earlier decision to approve the treaty, and Honduras and El Salvador then followed suit. In early October, the three met in Honduras and released the "Tegucigalpa Document," which reproduced the U.S. position that the treaty needed additional modification.[35] These changes, if incorporated, would place unilateral restrictions on Nicaragua's ability to defend itself, while allowing the United States to continue its military activities in the region. The State Department was then able to announce the U.S. rejection of the treaty without appearing as an obstacle to peace.

In an internal document that was leaked to the press in late October, the NSC boasted: "We have effectively blocked Contadora Group efforts to impose [the] Revised Contadora Act. Following intensive U.S. consultations with El Salvador, Honduras and Costa Rica, the Central America [states] submitted a counter draft to the Contadora states . . . [that] shifts concern within Contadora to a document broadly consistent with U.S. interests."[36]

It took nearly a year for the United States to consolidate this "shift," but constant pressure and diplomatic maneuvering finally paid off. On 11 September 1985, the four Contadora countries presented still another revised version of the peace treaty to the Central American governments at a meeting in Panama City. The most essential elements of the treaty had been modified in the new draft.

The Fusion of the Contras Moves into High Gear

By 1984, the counterrevolutionary project had matured to the point where the original reasons for maintaining ARDE and the FDN as separate organizations with distinct political images had become obsolete. The United States was attempting to remove the image of Somocismo from the FDN and present it as the legitimate expression of the Nicaraguan people. It was felt that a unified counterrevolution was needed which could be the nucleus around which to accumulate the forces outside the sway of Sandinismo: the consolidation of the revolution, as well as polarization inside Nicaragua, made two choices unnecessary in the efforts to bring people into the U.S. fold. The contras had to move from being an assortment of military groups to being a political organization and finally to being a "government in exile," with structures paralleling those of the revolutionary government. This could only be done with a unified organization.

In December 1983 roving U.S. Ambassador to Central America Richard Stone had met in Panama City with the leaders of all the contra groups in order to move the unification forward. "The fusion is difficult, but not impossible," Stone told a press conference after the meeting.[37] Following the defeat of the ARDE forces in San Juan del Norte, the CIA decided that the fusion could no longer be postponed. Using its material support for ARDE as a pressure mechanism, the CIA told Robelo in Washington on 30 April 1984 that he and Pastora "had thirty days" to announce their unification with the FDN "or they would cut off funding."[38]

Pastora, who had never had any objection in principle to aligning his organization with the FDN, reiterated his long-standing condition that he be appointed "supreme commander" of any united group. This was unacceptable to the United States, which was distrustful of the ex-Sandinista's personal idiosyncracies and unwillingness to submit to discipline. The CIA remained adamant that overall contra leadership had to be in the hands of Bermúdez and Calero, its two most trusted men.

Washington's ultimatum sparked a flurry of activity in the contra ranks. On 15 May ARDE representatives and their FDN counterparts drew up a draft unity pact which was accepted by everyone present but Pastora. On 21 May FDN leader Alfonso Callejas traveled to San José to hammer out the final details. All that remained was a press conference to formally announce the unification. But Pastora, although he expressed his support in principle, released a communiqué from the FRS complaining that "dark forces are trying to impose pressures with manipulations and false expectations."[39]

Throughout the following week, Pastora shuttled back and forth to Tegucigalpa and in and out of meetings with FDN, ARDE, and CIA officials in an effort to win appointment as supreme leader of the counterrevolution. But the Reagan administration would not change its position. In a final meeting of all ARDE-affiliated groups, held in San José, Robelo warned Pastora to agree and declared that unification would be consummated "with or without your cooperation." After the meeting, Pastora's men told reporters that the FRS leader "constantly fears for his life at this time."[40]

Immediately before the "thirty days" were up, Pastora spokesmen in San José announced that on 30 May their leader would hold a press conference in La Penca, on the banks of the Río San Juan, just inside Nicaraguan territory, to make an "important announcement." Several dozen journalists flocked to northern Costa Rica. But Pastora had not begun his presentation to the gathered journalists before a powerful blast ripped through the wooden building that served as his headquarters, killing eight people instantly and injuring another twenty-eight, almost all reporters. Pastora was himself seriously wounded. Thus began one of the conflict's most bizarre intrigues.

All the initial evidence, as well as the logic of the incident, suggested that it was a CIA operation and it was carried out by either an agent or a hired professional. Subsequent investigations by Costa Rican State Security indicated that an unidentified Latin man operating under cover as a journalist and carrying a stolen Danish passport bearing the name Per Anker Hansen, had planted a C-4 bomb in the building. Immigration authorities reported that he left the country for the United States a few hours after the incident. For their part, Pastora's men reported that the "important announcement" was to have been that Pastora's organization, the FRS, was leaving the ARDE alliance; Pastora was also going to expose the inner details of the contra unification process, which might have embarrassed a great many people, especially in Washington.[41]

On 4 June ABC News reported that, according to U.S. "intelligence sources," the suspect was a member of the Spanish separatist organization ETA, and that he then went with five others from Costa Rica to Cuba, and from there sought refuge in Managua. Mysteriously, Costa Rican immigration authorities could not produce departure records for the original suspect, and after a visit to Washington on 7 June, Costa Rican State Security chief Minor Calvo changed San José's original line to fit the administration's. The right-wing Costa Rican press and the Western media joined in.

Two Costa Rica-based U.S. journalists, Martha Honey and Tony Avirgan, one of whom suffered minor injuries in the explosion, began an intensive fifteen-month investigation of the incident. By the summer of 1985, they had collected a broad array of information which pointed to the CIA as the architect of the bombing. Although several questions remained, they concluded that the bomb had been planted by a right-wing Libyan exile named Amac Galil, a professional terrorist, recruited in Chile in 1984 by FDN and CIA agents, who posed as the Danish photographer. According to "David," one member of a "dirty tricks squad" that Honey and Avirgan uncovered, "The bombing was planned at meetings in Honduras attended by FDN leader Adolfo Calero Portocarrero; two Miami Cubans; John Hull; and a North American citizen who was identified to David's group as being from the CIA." Galil was considered ideal for the job because if his identity became known, people would assume he was working for Libyan leader Col. Muammar

Qaddafi. For his part, "David" was murdered after it was discovered that he was talking to the press.[42]

But why would the CIA have wanted to eliminate Pastora?

"Traitors can be utilized, in fact they are always utilized by imperialism," Sandinista guerrilla heroine Dora María Téllez—Comandante Dos, who led the 1978 palace raid at Pastora's side—had declared in 1982, a few days after Pastora's defection from the revolution, "But imperialism will never fully trust them. And finally it is going to do what it always does with a traitor: toss him aside like an old rag that is thrown out."[43] Pastora was learning a lesson that had come home to the Honduran Gustavo Alvarez only a month earlier: he had served imperialism well but had become more of a hindrance than an asset.

The La Penca incident momentarily postponed the unification of the FDN and ARDE, but it was finally announced on 25 July in Panama City. A central plank in the strategy for winning political victory over the revolution is the construction of a viable alternative to Sandinismo, and the unification of the FDN and ARDE was an important step in this direction. Much remained to be done, however. Above all, the counterrevolution still had to develop a coherent political substance with which to present itself to the Nicaraguan population and the world. This process would take another year to mature.

5

Political Warriors
and Socioeconomic Attrition

The tactical effort in guerrilla warfare is directed at the weaknesses of the enemy and at destroying their military resistance capacity, and should be parallel to a psychological effort to weaken and destroy their socio-political capacity at the same time.

—*Psychological Operations in Guerrilla Warfare*[1]

We can't lose sight of the fact that, despite the profound effects of the war, this continues to be a revolutionary process. But it is a process [whose development] has been hampered by the aggression.

—Daniel Ortega,
speaking in November 1984[2]

In October 1984 the Associated Press broke the story that the CIA had supplied the contras with a manual instructing them to hire criminals and "neutralize" Nicaraguan government officials. Self-righteous congressmen condemned U.S. "involvement" in producing the manual and dispatched experts to determine its "legality." Press headlines raised the "spector" of a return to the era of "dirty tricks." Yet the contras had been "neutralizing"—murdering—Nicaraguans on the U.S. government's explicit orders since 1982, and if they were not hired criminals, then the term loses all meaning. Lost amid the headlines was the real significance of the manual.

Entitled *Psychological Operations in Guerrilla Warfare*, the ninety-page booklet was a primer for training the contras in the tactics of prolonged antipopular warfare, a practical guide for transforming them into motivated political warriors capable of winning the support of the Nicaraguan peasantry. The manual's essential content was taken from the guerrilla warfare handbooks developed by the CIA and Pentagon for the

Special Operations Forces involved in the pacification program during the Vietnam war.[3] The prolongation of the conflict in Nicaragua meant that the contras would have to operate in the mountains for much longer than anticipated, which required redefining their relation to the population. If in El Salvador the United States had to *destroy* the popular sanctuaries of the revolutionary insurgency, in Nicaragua it had to *create* them for the counterrevolution. The war of attrition needed a "sea" for the contra "fish" to move in.

Since the essence of low-intensity warfare is the political struggle, with the military element an adjunct, the contras had to learn to subordinate military force, turning it into a tactical instrument. "In this type of conflict," declared Col. John D. Waghelstein, former head of the U.S. military advisers team in El Salvador, "the only territory that you want to hold is the six inches between the peasants' ears."[4]

The peasants' heads are the focus of the manual.[5] The introduction states:

> Guerrilla warfare is essentially a political war. Therefore, its area of operations exceeds the territorial limits of conventional warfare, to penetrate the political entity itself: the "political animal" that Aristotle defined. . . . Once his mind has been reached, the "political animal" has been defeated, without necessarily receiving bullets. . . . Our target, then, is the minds of the population, all the population: our troops, the enemy troops and the civilian population.[6]

The manual explains the general techniques and practice of psychological warfare, and tells how to form special units within each contingent specifically dedicated to this work. Such units are to complement the military actions of the "regular" FDN forces, in the same way that Psyops (Psychological Operations) units and Civic Action units in the U.S. armed forces reinforce U.S. military action.

"Psyops are conducted to exploit grievances and raised expectations, to influence the populace and to promote the loyalty of insurgent members," states the U.S. Army's *Field Manual 100–20*. In the same way, the contra psyops units, called "armed propaganda teams," are instructed on how to coordinate with military actions to win over the population: how to "soften up" a zone *before* a contra military operation, participate *during* the operation in order to make the people perceive it as being in their interests, and identify the elements to be incorporated into a support network *following* an attack. The armed propaganda teams were to enter villages and establish "fifth columns," much as the Nazis did in the countries they occupied during World War II.

Such psychological operations are to employ the *form* of "face-to-face persuasion" rather than coercion: the Socratic method, body language, folk songs, and variations in tone of voice ("a happy tone for a happy subject, a sad tone for a sad subject, an animated voice to describe a heroic or brave act"), complex oratorical techniques, and so on.[7] The *content* of the psychological operation is a series of word-associations and themes, specifically relating to the Nicaraguan reality and selected with the peasants' fears and grievances in mind—fears and grievances produced by historic circumstances, anticommunist propaganda (the Sandinistas will take away your land, close your churches, bring in Cubans, etc.), and the socioeconomic hardship that has resulted from military aggression. The end goal is to instill in the minds of the peasants a fundamental dichotomy between themselves and their world, on the one hand, and the Sandinistas on the other:

> The armed propaganda team can use this principle in its activities, so that it is obvious that the "exterior" groups ("false" groups) are those of the Sandinista regime, and that the "interior" groups ("true" groups) that fight for the people are the freedom commandos.
>
> We should inculcate this in the people in a subtle manner so that these feelings seem to be born of themselves, spontaneously.[8]

The manual recommends that the contras engage in civic action programs:

> Putting aside weapons and working side by side with the peasants in the countryside: building, fishing, repairing roofs, transporting water, etc. . . . teaching the people environmental hygiene, to read, etc., in order to win their trust . . . [will] . . . establish a strong tie between [the people] and the guerrillas, and at the same time a popular support for our movement is generated.[9]

Little distinction is made between winning popular support and winning *control* over the population. These tactics must be employed to "maintain control of [the people's] activities."[10] The manual emphasizes the need for *selective* terror, rather than the generalized terror tactics of the past. The crude application of indiscriminate military terror against the civilian population served the objectives of the original destabilization program, but the prolonged war necessitated a well-planned combination of selective terror and psychological persuasion. On the one hand, therefore, the manual stresses "showing each guerrilla the need for good behavior to win the support of the population," and even urges "respect for human rights" when dealing with civilians not identified with the Sandinistas. But another section is dedicated to the "selective use of violence" and contains almost twenty references to the use of terror and violence against Sandinista officials, including such words as "kidnap," "remove," "neutralize," "eliminate," and using "tribunals" to try them. Repression is therefore to be limited to those the counterrevolution considers to have been irreversibly won over to the revolution. Thus, when the contras enter a locale they will no longer go on a rampage, stabbing and shooting indiscriminately. Now they will round up only those people associated with the Sandinistas, going beyond local government officials and civil servants, members of the mass organizations, and militia personnel to include teachers, health, agricultural, and construction workers, and others working on social projects.

The manual attempts to mimic the art of revolutionary struggle—expose the source of oppression, turn the people into protagonists of their own liberation. The guerrilla, according to the booklet's guidelines, must be a selfless individual buttressed with political consciousness, devoted to a cause, and therefore imbued with a discipline that goes beyond the military realm. In short, the political warrior envisioned by the manual must be endowed with the attributes of a *revolutionary* fighting for a popular cause. But these are *antipopular* counterrevolutionaries, and their "art" is divorced from the original aim of creating a new society free from exploitation. The tactics which, under the leadership of a revolutionary movement, aim at *conscientization* here become a process of *manipulation*. This contradiction is expressed in the enormous gap between the program envisioned in the manual and the real prospects for its translation into practice. This would become increasingly apparent as the war unfolded.

The significance of the CIA manual transcends the boundaries of Central America. A central aim of the Reagan Doctrine is to create right-wing insurgent armies modeled after authentic national liberation movements, and the manual provides a blueprint for reorganizing armed counterrevolutionaries into guerrilla movements composed of political combatants versed in the art of low-intensity warfare. Since Nicaragua is the front line of a worldwide counteroffensive, it is no wonder that the contras are the first group that the U.S. government attempted to transform along these lines.

The Fight for the Peasantry

By 1984, the FDN and the ARDE had managed, through a combination of repression, family ties, psychological warfare, and exploitation of the mistakes made by the Sandinistas, to win significant influence among the peasantry in certain zones.

Those regions where the bulk of the peasantry lives were chosen as the principal military theater. Developing a contra support-base was a complex process. To help understand it, it is useful to divide Nicaragua into three zones (see map at beginning of book):

• The center and center-west of the country, a vast mountain and plateau region that runs from the Segovian Mountains on the border with Honduras, to the semi-arid plains of Boaco and Chontales in the center, to the marshland and jungles of the Río San Juan region, north of the Costa Rican border and east of Lake Nicaragua. With about one-third of the total population, the region is dominated by the peasantry. This is the region of military conflict. It is the "first war theater."

• The Atlantic Coast. Sparsely populated tropical lowland where the ethnic question is the key issue. The character of the war here shares little with that in the rest of the country. It is the "second war theater."

• The Pacific Coast. Comprising the westernmost third of the country, with over one-half of the total population. The major cities and industries, modern export agriculture, and international trading points are located here, as are the working and professional classes and the rural proletariat. This relatively populated zone has seen little overt military conflict; the war here is principally political and ideological. It is the "third war theater."

The first war theater can in turn be divided into two subregions. Zone 1 includes much of the departments of Nueva Segovia, Madriz, Estelí, and the western parts of Jinotega, Matagalpa, and Boaco. It is historically the land of the peasantry. The gradual penetration of capitalist relations of production into the countryside throughout the twentieth century, and particularly between 1950 and 1975, pushed many peasants out of this area toward the remote mountains and toward the east and south into Zone 2. Forced to open up virgin land for primitive agricultural exploitation, these uprooted peasants had little access to roads, communications, social services, and other infrastructure. Encompassing vast tracts of Jinotega, Matagalpa, Boaco, Chontales, and western Zelaya, the area became known as the "agricultural frontier" and is extremely underdeveloped.

Initially the war strategy was to put the contras in Zone 1, both because of its proximity to the FDN's Honduran sanctuary and as part of the effort to seize population centers and highways in a thrust toward Managua. What support the contras had in this region—apart from that of the land barons, who still had extensive property despite the Sandinistas' agrarian reform program—was mainly the product of terror: in the absence of a strong EPS presence, the peasants feared reprisals if they did not collaborate.

The testimony of numerous peasants who did collaborate in one way or another with the contras in Zone 1 corroborates this. Lucio Madariaga, a middle-aged farmer from El Tizo, a community outside of the Segovian city of Ocotal, told of his encounters with the FDN, which repeatedly coerced him into collaborating:

> [Finally, one day] they arrived and, pointing a gun at me, told me they'd come to take me off. What else could I do? When we reached El Hato, they forced me to carry a heavy backpack full of bullets. Not far from El Hato they let me free and continued on their way. From then on my family and I were uneasy. It's tough when they're after you. All of this was happening at the end of 1983. Another time, I was home in the afternoon when a friend arrived and told me that the contras were coming. I took off so that they wouldn't grab me, but in La Rastra we ran into an ambush; they made us all get out of the truck. Then they stuck another one of those heavy packs with bullets on my back. It had the same tag from the United States. We walked all day until reaching the base in Honduras. When we arrived, they started to interrogate me, threatening to kill me with a knife, and at the same time trying to convince me to take up a rifle and join them.[11]

Madariaga was held for several weeks. He was able to escape while he was being transferred to the FDN's La Lodosa training camp. He concluded: "We're always afraid now because there is a constant threat. Some people have left because the contras have told them that, if they don't go to Honduras with them, they'll kill them. They get scared, and they go."

But the contra support was extremely limited. Sandinismo has deep roots in Zone 1: Sandino's rag-tag army had been based in the Segovias, while the FSLN's rural guerrilla struggle decades later focused on the same area. The relatively developed infrastructure helped the revolution to move in with social services, new administrative structures, commercial infrastructure, and political cadre familiar with the particularities of the region.

By late 1983, the infrastructure developed by the United States in Honduras had greatly improved the FDN's logistical and operational capacity, allowing it to push deep into the interior of Nicaragua. By 1984, it had an extensive presence in Zone 2. At the same time, its transition from a conventional military force to a guerrilla army meant that it was now consciously targeting the backward and isolated peasantry of the agricultural frontier as the social group that was to constitute its base of influence. It was here, therefore, that they were able to create their "sanctuary" inside the country. As EPS chief of operations Javier Carrión put it, "The FDN, logically, has achieved a social base in the most marginalized zones of the agricultural frontier, where the Revolution has not reached due to the economic and social limitations that we face."[12]

The contras initially developed support networks by taking advantage of family ties with the local population, focusing on relatives of National Guard members and FDN recruits, as well as on large landowners who felt threatened by the revolution. Beyond this, the contra sanctuary was forged by systematically exploiting the objective limitations faced by the revolution and the mistakes the Sandinistas made. All this was in accordance with the procedures set out in the CIA manual, which notes that support among the population "is achieved through the exploitation of the social and political weaknesses of the target society."[13]

The government faced real material limitations in bringing the revolution's social and political programs to the agricultural frontier. Nicaragua is one of the poorest and most underdeveloped countries in Latin America, and while the revolution brought about a fundamental reorientation of national priorities toward meeting the social needs of an impoverished population, raised expectations nevertheless far outstripped economic resources and the ability to satisfy needs with sufficient rapidity. These limitations were felt particularly severely in isolated rural communities. In certain areas, for instance, teachers, doctors, and Sandinista political organizers often had to travel for days by mule just to arrive at the community to which they had been assigned. This meant that in many communities there was no tangible material and political presence on the part of the revolution—a vacuum easily filled by the contras. In fact, there is a direct correlation between the degree to which the revolution had penetrated an area and the extent of FDN influence within that area.

At the same time, the contras consciously directed their military attacks toward preventing any further penetration by the revolution, as well as destroying whatever presence it had. This included razing physical installations (health clinics, schools, silos, etc.) and assassinating people working in these installations or identified with the Sandinistas' social and political programs. As the EPS chief of operations noted:

> They arrived at a community with the message that we are to blame for the lack of health services or education. In other cases, where we have been able to bring in these services, they assassinate such representatives of the

Revolution, doctors, technicians, educators. They destroy banks, agrarian reform projects, etc. They tell the local population that [those working on government projects] are communists and are against the people. The contras blame all the difficulties on the Revolution as a way to win over the peasantry.

They have had success in certain places, precisely those places where we have not been side by side with the population, explaining our reality, our problems, and the objectives of the Revolution. Wherever they have a presence, it's because we have not yet arrived there.[14]

Exploiting Weaknesses and Grievances

Beyond the revolution's objective difficulties, the counterrevolution adroitly exploited legitimate grievances and Sandinista mistakes. The inevitable dislocations caused by the dismantling of the socioeconomic system of the dictatorship and the difficulties in constructing a new one gave them further room for maneuver.

With the overthrow of Somoza, the FSLN turned to the infinitely more difficult task of constructing a new society on the ashes of the old. The government drew up a program for democratizing the country and addressing the problems of poverty, backwardness, and injustice. This program was constructed on three basic pillars: a mixed economy, political pluralism, and nonalignment.[15] On this basis, the government pursued a policy of national unity which sought to transform the multi-class antidictatorial alliance achieved during the struggle against Somoza into an anti-imperialist alliance that would form a shield against aggression.

But this model for social transformation had clear limitations, and these could be seen most concretely in the countryside. The initial terms of national unity necessitated maintaining an alliance with the large private landowners, and this in turn meant limiting the extent of agrarian reform. When this was combined with the full weight of the war, portions of the peasantry were inevitably shortchanged. Essentially, the terms of national unity restricted the ability of the state to meet the most basic historical demand of the peasantry—land.

Like most of Latin America, the Nicaraguan countryside was characterized by the classic *latifundismo-minifundismo* pattern: an extreme concentration of land in the hands of giant land barons alongside masses of poor peasants owning tiny plots that often did not even suffice for subsistence. Many peasants were therefore forced into seasonal wage labor, sharecropping or indentured servitude. In 1978, for instance, barely 2,500 out of some 156,000 property holders monopolized nearly half of the agricultural land. At the other end of the spectrum 50,000 peasant families lived on subsistence parcels, while another 70,000 did not even own that much—the two groups together had less than 15 percent of the agricultural land. Further, the conditions endured by these poor peasants were among the worst in Latin America: widespread malnutrition, illiteracy, disease, domination by the oligarchy, and persecution by the National Guard.[16]

The new government made improving this situation a top priority. It drew up an ambitious agrarian reform program which it hoped would democratize land tenure *without* affecting most large landowners. First, in 1979 properties owned by Somoza and his clique—some 20 percent of all agricultural land—were expropriated and transferred to the state. Since this modern sector could not be broken down into smaller parcels without affecting production, it was to remain in state hands and form the nucleus of a developing agroindustry.

Then, in 1981, the Agrarian Reform Law was passed. As part of the alliance with the private sector, the law placed no limits on the amount of land an individual could possess, so that expropriation was possible under only two conditions: when land exceeded 1,234 acres in the Pacific region and 2,470 in the rest of the country and was abandoned or left idle. This type of agrarian reform was more conservative than similar programs in El Salvador, Peru, or Chile. Its aim was to stimulate production and curb decapitalization in the private sector, not to create a vehicle for massive expropriation; the Sandinista government hoped that the abandoned and idle land would be sufficient to meet the needs of the land-hungry peasantry. As it turned out, this expectation was based in part on faulty (and insufficient) statistics; under Somoza, land tenure was more often than not a dirty business, which made a realistic assessment of who owned what virtually impossible.

Nevertheless, from 1981 to 1984 the new law provided thousands of peasant families with sufficient land for their needs. By the end of 1984, 1.235 million acres had been handed out to over 30,000 peasants, both as individuals and as members of cooperatives. At the same time, the "titles program," which began in early 1984 and involved giving legal title to thousands of families who had been farming as squatters or who had opened up virgin land whose status under law had not been defined, encompassed 2.47 million acres and helped stabilize many peasant households. All told, the plight of between 50,000 and 60,000 peasant families was resolved—and over 50 percent of the country's rural tenure system was affected.[17]

By mid-1984, however, agrarian reform had begun to reach its limits and one-half of the poor peasants remained subject to the old *latifundismo* system: only 490 landowners had been forced to turn over even part of their property. "Five years after its introduction, the [agrarian reform] law was exhausted," explained Agriculture Minister Jamie Wheelock. "Why was this? Because our laws were born as part of the principles that the Revolution had been establishing, and this meant protecting private property by limiting the law's effect. The original law was motivated more by political factors than by economic or technical considerations. It left us with a relatively small pool of land" to give out to the peasants.[18]

The sector of the peasantry least affected by agrarian reform was in the agricultural frontier—the second of the two zones of military conflict—where some 60 percent of the remaining *latifundios* were concentrated. The three largest families in the departments of Boaco and Chontales owned over 1 million acres. At the other extreme, fifteen thousand peasant households there were still scratching out a living on plots insufficient even for subsistence.[19] The desperate situation of these families provided fertile ground for the contras to seek a base of support.[20] "The campesinos should be made to see that they do not have land," says the CIA manual.[21]

The initial program of national unity was in part a response to the military threat from the north. In the first years of the conflict, when direct U.S. intervention was very much on the agenda, this policy galvanized internal and external forces into an anti-interventionary shield. But even after the United States redefined its agenda, the Sandinistas continued to maintain a program for national unity whose first priority was to improve the country's capacity to resist invasion. The internal tradeoffs necessitated by this policy actually worked in favor of the counterrevolution to the extent that the character of national unity as defined and promoted by the Sandinistas drove a wedge between the revolution and a vital part of its social base—the peasantry—which was in turn exploited by the counterrevolution to advance the formation of its own social base.

This situation was further exacerbated by adjunct agricultural policies that the FSLN tried to implement, as well as by poor administration in the countryside. Agrarian policy was based on the premise that agricultural production could be transformed through the intensive use of modern technology, and efforts were therefore concentrated on the state sector and on land under collective ownership (i.e., the cooperatives). The peasants' demand for land was often addressed by making land grants and essential state services conditional on the formation of cooperatives.[22] The revolutionary government saw cooperative production as a superior form of organization, in which modern technology and economies of scale could be introduced and absorbed, while it feared that granting individual land titles would stimulate a wave of land takeovers, which might have jeopardized the fragile alliance with the private sector. It also feared that granting thousands of individual parcels would further erode the scant labor force available for the large export-oriented estates.[23]

At first, many peasants did join cooperatives. But as the cooperative sector became heavily dependent for technical assistance on the state apparatus, whose ability to attend to its needs was reduced by the economic constraints caused by the war, peasants were increasingly loathe to join. Moreover, by 1984 the contras were consciously targeting the cooperatives, which scared many peasants away. The result was a growing resistance to cooperativization, and increasing numbers of land-hungry peasants found themselves marginalized from the agrarian reform. As the contra strategy took root, the government had still not revised its policies, which were feeding the deterioration of its social base among parts of the peasantry.

At the same time, the dismantling of the Somocista system led to a breakdown of traditional marketing and supply systems in the countryside, which had been controlled by a small and unscrupulous class of middlemen who were closely tied to, and often overlapped with, the *latifundistas* and the Somoza clique. They bought crops from the peasants at low prices, and supplied them with overpriced consumer goods. In many cases they also gave the peasants usury credit, subjugating them to a vicious cycle of debt. The middlemen amassed great wealth from the labor of the peasants, but they also played a key role as intermediaries in rural-urban exchange networks and in the commercialization of peasant production.

In its effort to eradicate peasant exploitation, the revolutionary government planned to replace these middlemen with state structures. But creating the necessary institutions and networks proved more difficult than anticipated, and was made all the more problematic by the war conditions in the countryside. In many areas, the war situation led to the rupture of rural-urban exchange relations, which meant that the peasants could no longer market their produce or receive essential manufactured goods, such as boots, machetes, fertilizers, and household items. Again, this rupture particularly affected the peasants of the agricultural frontier. As a document circulated within the Ministry of Agricultural Development and Agrarian Reform (MIDINRA) in early 1985 noted:

Diverse measures adopted by the Revolution, although they were in pursuit of just objectives, had the effect of violently rupturing the intricate commercial exchange networks that articulated the varied and complex relations structured by the big traders–land barons, who provided usury credit, bought up future crops, and brought in supplies at speculative prices. The Revolution's measures to control this speculative trade, reduced *latifundismo,* etc., affected these networks, through which economic activity in the countryside was organized, and it was not possible to effectively offer substitute mechanisms.[24]

The problem was exacerbated by administrative disorder. One ministry was charged with buying peasant crops, another with attempting to set fair prices, a third with supplying consumer goods, a fourth with selling production implements, a fifth with supplying state credits, etc. Each institution developed its own policies, which often clashed with those of the others; the result was inconsistency and contradictions in the countryside. The problems were as much due to the government's having elaborated policies without having a clear enough understanding of how they would function in practice as they were the result of the kind of dislocations a revolution inevitably confronts when trying to build a new system.

The Reagan administration's political warriors were intent on exploiting these weaknesses; the contras penetrated the countryside carrying the ideological banner of the agrarian bourgeoisie, which was well received by many peasants. The counterrevolution was able to turn the problems associated with the disintegration of Somocismo—the system that had dispossessed the peasantry in the first place—into problems brought about by *Sandinismo.* "Once the needs and frustrations of the target group [i.e., the peasants] have been determined, [they] will be made to see that when [Sandinismo] has been eliminated, the cause of their frustration will be eliminated and they will be able to fulfill their desires," states the CIA manual.[25]

Meanwhile, the threat of intervention and the invasionist character of the contras in the first period led the Nicaraguans to build a conventional army as part of an urban-oriented system of defense. This did not mean that Sandinista soldiers were confined to urban barracks, but the thrust of the defense program was to protect major population centers and installations. In the first period this worked well in all the war zones because it was the cities and major socioeconomic installations (highways, bridges, etc.) that were the targets of the counterrevolution. But as the contras moved from being an invasion force toward becoming a guerrilla army, the Sandinista defense system gave them considerable room for maneuver in the countryside. The contras could be chased from urban peripheries, highways, and major installations, but could find refuge if they retreated into the rural areas.

As the situation developed, the United States sought to provoke a repressive response from the government to the incipient polarization between the revolution and significant sectors of the peasantry. If the Sandinistas could be made to *overreact*, the mistakes they then made would contribute to their destruction. But although they did sometimes overreact against peasant communities under contra influence those involved were punished, and such cases were isolated. In perhaps the most severe example, the local FSLN secretary and his assistant killed several Somocista collaborators following a contra raid on the northern farming community of Pantasma in late 1983, in which forty-three civilians were slaughtered by Somocistas. The two Sandinistas were tried and sentenced to long jail terms. Nevertheless, as Interior Minister Borge noted in the fall of 1984, the neutralization of contra influence "has been limited by a dynamic that became a vicious circle: the violence of the war led to an excessive violence [on our part] that, despite the intent of our revolutionary leadership, was not sufficiently controlled."[26]

Throughout 1984 the contras took advantage of all these factors to apply the tactics outlined in the CIA manual. As the MIDINRA document cited above noted:

> In many rural zones, the presence and consolidation of FSLN structures was only incipient and we did not have a clear orientation regarding treatment of the different sectors of the peasantry. At the same time, with the initiation of aggression we were busy forming an army that could face armed aggression coming from outside, and were thus not prepared for an enemy adopting irregular tactical modalities. This allowed the counter-revolution to establish military hegemony in certain territories in the interior of the country. This hegemony was combined with [the enemy's] powerful means of communication, its taking advantage of traditional ties and of the economic and cultural backwardness of the countryside, and its capitalizing on our difficulties and limitations. In this way the counter-revolution was able to attract a growing number of peasants in the center and interior of the country and to begin a process of undermining our social base.[27]

The contras' establishment of a sanctuary in Zone 2 of the peasant region was a major strategic advance. Although it contained at most twenty-five thousand peasant households, it covered a vast area and gave the FDN room to maneuver. Indeed, pro-FDN Canadian journalist Pete Bertle, traveling with the contras during this period, gleefully bragged that "if it weren't for the campesinos' support [the

FDN] would be nothing . . . [it] wouldn't even exist."[28] The sanctuary also provided a staging ground for operations in Zone 1, an internal rearguard for incursions into other areas, and a psychological stimulus for the entire counterrevolutionary project. It was thus the first step in winning over the peasantry and using it against the revolutionary government—in concert with discontent in the cities and semi-urban zones of the Pacific Coast and rebellions on the Atlantic Coast. The United States hoped that the growing polarization between the peasantry and the revolution would accelerate to the point where foreign aggression could be converted into a peasant war against the Sandinistas.

Nevertheless, this sanctuary had very little in common with the *popular social base* forged by authentic national liberation movements. There were no areas where the FDN exercised uncontested control—much less "liberated zones" where it could erect parallel administrative and power structures or organize the civilian population, regulate production and distribution, and establish social programs. The contra sanctuary was solely a base for recruiting combatants and for providing its army with food, intelligence, and other logistical support.

Expanding the Contra Ranks

The armed counterrevolution was originally composed almost exclusively of former Somocista National Guardsmen, but by 1984 combat casualties had whittled down the original core of some six thousand men, and the United States had begun to rely on a rank and file of poor Nicaraguan peasants (under the command of the guardsmen). "The source of basic recruitment for guerrilla cadres will be the same social group of Nicaraguans to whom the psychological campaign is directed . . . the campesinos," states the CIA manual.[29] At its peak in late 1984, following a year-long recruiting campaign, the contras' troop strength approached twenty thousand. This figure is based on an estimated maximum of fourteen thousand FDN troops, four thousand armed Miskitos, and two thousand ARDE personnel.[30]

The United States has tried to use the peasant composition of the FDN's "foot soldiers" to claim that the counterrevolution is a popular movement representative of the Nicaraguan people—a peasant army—but the recruitment methods make this a dubious claim. They range from forced recruitment (terror, threats, and mass kidnappings), to offers of lucrative salaries (bribes), to a host of political-ideological manipulations. Thus, in late 1983, when CIA advisers in Honduras ordered a massive recruitment campaign, the first step, according to one former FDN commander involved in the campaign, was to round up all those Nicaraguans in Honduras who, for whatever reason, were not then involved with the contras.[31] Thousands of dollars were used to buy recruits and to pay Honduran immigration police to cancel the resident status of exiled Nicaraguans who refused to join.

Inside Nicaragua, the easiest method was also the outright bribe, and the CIA supplied millions of *cordobas* (Nicaraguan currency) for this purpose. Another widely used method—one promoted by the CIA manual—was to blackmail a peasant by implicating him in contra activities: "The initial recruitment will be carried out through several private consultations with a cadre," according to the manual. "Then the recruit will be informed that he or she is already inside the movement, and will be exposed to the police of the regime if he or she does not cooperate. The target, then, is faced with the fact of his participation in the struggle."[32] The manual even told how to send clandestine letters to the Sandinista authorities framing those who still refused to join, so that their cases could be used as examples for others who showed resistence to recruitment. And of course, once a recruit participates in murder or other contra crimes, his commitment is sealed with the blood of his victims. Numerous peasants who have deserted the FDN have explained how they were forced to kill prisoners so as to harden their sense of irreversible commitment.

Another important recruitment method was to create a belief in the contras' military superiority. By projecting themselves as a powerful force and the FSLN as weak, the contras persuaded many peasants, caught up in a war in which neutrality was not an option, to choose the contras because they were the "winning side." This was made easier because in 1984 the Sandinista armed forces were still oriented toward the urban areas: "If the government [forces] cannot put an end to the guerrilla activities, the population will lose confidence in the government, which has the inherent mission of guaranteeing the safety of citizens," says the CIA manual.[33] The lack of a strong Sandinista military presence increased the sense of contra superiority, even if this did not correspond to reality at the national level—for few peasants does reality extend beyond the local community. And constant broadcasts by the contras in Honduras announcing that the Somocistas were advancing across the country further reinforced the illusion. Local communities had no way of knowing that they were being deceived.

The CIA manual emphasizes that the modern weapons supplied by the United States should be made as visible as possible to the civilian population. This is the context in which it distinguishes between "implicit and explicit terror": explicit terror (i.e., murder) is to be used against those identified with the revolution; implicit terror, on the other hand, is a low-key psychological tactic to be used to manipulate the population into supporting the counterrevolution. "A guerrilla armed force always involves implicit terror because the population, without saying it aloud, feels terror that the weapons may be used against them. However, if the terror does not become explicit, positive results can be expected."[34]

Moreover, the backwardness of many isolated peasant communities, the illiteracy, deep religious sentiments, and the absence of a Sandinista presence provided fertile ground for all types of crude ideological manipulation. "When they came into our village," recalled a woman from Boaco, "they warned everyone that the Sandino-communists would kill the pregnant women and eat the children. I didn't believe that, but there were many who did."[35]

Forcing the peasantry to take up arms against its historic, and in many cases even immediate, interests is not a new phenomenon in Nicaragua. The extreme poverty that was part of life under Somoza forced many peasants to see the National Guard as the only means of employment—just as the U.S. armed forces today are disproportionally filled with poor minority and working-class youth who cannot find other jobs. Vice-president Sergio Ramírez eloquently expressed this reality:

> What popular war would we have to wage in Nicaragua if those who have taken up arms were only a handful of pro-Yankee ideologues, expropriated landlords, and select officers from the EEBI [the Somoza regime's Basic Infantry Training School]? The soldiers of the old Somocista Guard were from among the people; poor peasants were taught to kill, mutilate, torture. The Guard uniform was forced upon the unemployed, upon those expelled by the laws of the market from the consumer society. . . . Ideological mechanisms were always employed in order to convince and force the poor to take up arms against their own interests. [These mechanisms] continue against the peasants, pressured by the same Guard as before, who imbue them with the idea that they must rise up against those who want to expropriate their cows and chickens, close their churches, steal their children, enslave their women, and send them in chains to Russia.[36]

Another sector of the population that was open to contra recruitment was those youth fleeing the country to escape the military draft (initiated in late 1983). Although they included only a small percentage of the draftees, they nevertheless numbered in the thousands, and the counterrevolution had been able to establish elaborate networks inside Nicaragua that facilitated the flight of these resisters into Honduras—

where they are then forced to join the FDN. The network includes reactionary elements in the cities, who identify and encourage possible resisters; large landowners in the countryside, who offer their farms as havens in the contra "underground railroad"; and roving FDN bands which have the specific task of providing military escorts to the contra bases in Honduras. The youth are invariably told that upon their arrival in Honduras, the counterrevolution—acting out of concern for their "freedom"—will get them jobs in Tegucigalpa or send them on to "paradise" in the United States. But once in southern Honduras, the resisters find that they are virtual prisoners of the FDN, terrorized with threats and blackmail. Those who resist are tortured and often killed.

The story of César Blandón Rodríguez, from Matagalpa, is typical. At age twenty-three, Blandón was convinced by a local reactionary to make the trip and was then sold a "ticket" on the underground railroad. His odyssey began with a stay on a farm north of Matagalpa, where more youth were continually arriving from around the country. Within a week, a band of forty FDN troops arrived to take the group to the "Managua" contra camp on the other side of the Río Coco.

"I still thought that they would send me to Tegucigalpa, find me a job, and later get me to the United States where my aunt lives," Blandón reported later. "I decided to talk to the contra chief, but he cut me off in mid-sentence, saying: 'Anyone who comes here does so to get training and kick ass on the communists, and those who don't like it we'll kill right here on the spot.'" The boy's nightmare had only begun. He tried to escape, but was recaptured by the contras, stripped, tied up, and tortured for several days before finally giving in and agreeing to go into training. But when he was sent into Nicaragua on his first mission, the irony of his situation overcame him: "I didn't even know where we were going; I kept thinking of death and how stupid I was because I was about to fight, doing exactly what I was trying to escape from, and even worse, without any purpose." More fortunate than others, he managed to escape and turn himself into the Sandinista authorities before entering combat.[37]

Outright kidnapping has been by far the most common means of contra recruitment. Once in Honduras, the victims are completely at the mercy of their abductors. They are forced into training, and then combat, by bribes, by separating the men from the women and children and holding the latter hostage, by torture, and by death threats. They "are often sent to firing squads if they refuse to fight, [a policy handed down] directly from the FDN high command," reported one former FDN officer. "Hundreds have been killed like that."[38]

Fear of being killed if caught prevents many kidnap victims from attempting to escape. And although those finally persuaded or coerced into fighting may start shooting at Sandinista soldiers or attacking civilian communities against their will, they invariably end up feeling a commitment to the counterrevolution once they have taken part in its crimes.

Refugee Generation

One of the most pronounced features of the Central American conflict is the dislocation and displacement of large populations: one in every five Central Americans has been uprooted at one time or another since 1979. In many cases this may appear as an inadvertent by-product of the conflict, but in a war in which the civilian population is the target, the forced movement of populations is clearly intentional. One U.S. analyst of the U.S. war against Vietnam noted the *"implicit policy of refugee generation* through compulsory relocations, combat operations, and crop destruction. . . . Over 20 percent of the [Vietnamese] population had been refugees at one time or another."[39]

The objective of this practice has always been to generate refugees. But whereas in Vietnam the aim was to separate the civilian population from the revolutionary army, so as to facilitate the extermination of the guerrillas through the massive application of firepower, in Central America it is the civilian population itself that is the target. Thus entire communities are moved from one location to another by such varied means as military terror, mass kidnappings, psychological operations, civic action, political manipulation, and economic coercion, all with the twofold purpose of neutralizing the human rearguard of the revolutionary forces and building up the rearguard of the counterrevolutionary forces. Refugee generation in the war against Nicaragua is part and parcel of the counterrevolution's objective of building a support-base, recruiting combatants, and wearing down the revolution.

There have been three types of refugee generation in the war against Nicaragua: the transfer of thousands of Nicaraguans from the Pacific and central regions to southern Honduras and northern Costa Rica; the creation of internal refugees, those who have been forced to flee their homes but remain inside Nicaragua; and the massive migration of Miskito Indians to the Honduran *Mosquitia:* (the zone inhabited by Honduran Miskitos, in the southeastern department of Gracias a Dios).

For the first, thousands of Nicaraguan civilians have been kidnapped and taken to Honduras, while thousands of others have migrated "voluntarily" after intense political manipulation on the part of contras inside Nicaragua. The "refugees" in Honduras number in the tens of thousands, and include all types of people—including FDN combatants. CMA mercenary Bill Johnson explained that the equipment CMA brings down for the contras "comes officially as refugee aid, which is allowed [by U.S. law], but we can't separate the FDN from the refugees."[40] Part of the Nicaraguan refugee population in Honduras ends up in United Nations High Commission for Refugees (UNHCR) or International Red Cross camps, while part is confined to "refugee centers" set up and administered by the FDN, various private U.S. groups, and the U.S. Agency for International Development (AID).

"Refugee assistance" has become an important element of the U.S. war effort: the contras are responsible for generating the refugees, while U.S. money and experts, both private and public, work on the refugee populations in order to turn them into agents—willing or not—of the counterrevolution. The private U.S. groups are able to bolster the counterrevolutionary rearguard through their "refugee relief work." One such activist in Washington explained: "The best strategy for countering [the revolution] lies in undermining its objectives through positive action such as providing food and medicine, rather than in trying to defeat them through conventional military means. . . . [Our] efforts are aimed at immediate humanitarian needs through refugee relief."[41]

In July 1985 we visited two camps administered by UNHCR, both of which were outside Danli, in the southern Honduran Department of El Paraíso. The two camps, Jacaleapa and Teupasenti, together housed about 5,500 Nicaraguans. About one-fifth of those in Teupasenti are youth between the ages of fifteen and twenty-five who have fled Nicaragua to evade military service. The rest are older peasants, the majority abducted from northern Nicaragua.

UNHCR's resources and personnel are limited; the best it can do is to maintain a modicum of supervision and assure the delivery of food and supplies. It is clear that the FDN controls the life of the settlement. For instance, before we could conduct our first interview, we were greeted by a young man named Germán López, who identified himself as the "elected coordinator" of the refugees and told us that he would accompany us. We later learned that López was a former officer at the Somoza dictatorship's dreaded Basic Infantry Training School and one of the founders of the 15th of September Legion. He had been injured in combat inside Nicaragua and had been assigned to "supervise" the refugee camp.

Of the dozen or so people we interviewed, all but two were kidnapped from different parts of Nueva Segovia and Madriz. Pedro Rodríguez and his wife Luisa Elena, an elderly couple from La Mulla, a municipality in Nueva Segovia that saw heavy fighting in 1983, used to work on the property of a local land baron. "Our problems began in 1983, when we sought out the help of the Association of Rural Workers [ATC—the Nicaraguan farmworkers' union] following abuses by our boss. As soon as the landlord got wind of our complaints, he 'invited' an [FDN] task force to take us to Honduras," the elderly man told us. The couple's son, Alejandro Rodríguez, was bribed into fighting with the contras in 1984, but later managed to desert and make his way back to Teupasenti. "They had promised me $300 a month, but I never got a penny," he recalled. We heard similar stories from others we interviewed.

One exception to the kidnap victims was a middle-aged woman named Montoya Delgadillo, who had arrived at Teupasenti with her five children a few weeks earlier. She had spent the previous six months traveling "underground" from Managua to the Honduran border, trying to get her one draft-age son out of the country. Friends of her husband, a former National Guardsman captured and imprisoned in July 1979, had put her in touch with an urban network that sent youth out of the country: "We were moved slowly to the north through the safe houses [the contras] have on big farms and in cities, and finally made it to the shores of the Gulf of Fonseca." An FDN motor-boat picked them up at a spot on the shore and turned them over to the Honduran navy, which took them to Honduran immigration authorities, who promptly delivered them to the camp. She looked worried as she said, "They have already come from the FDN looking for my sons to fight, but I don't want them involved in that." Obviously, her contra contacts in Managua had given her another version of what to expect in Honduras.

Those in the UNHCR and International Red Cross camps are relatively protected from counterrevolutionary pressures. But the camps run directly by the FDN and by right-wing U.S. organizations are indistinguishable from military bases. These "refugee camps" are located closer to the border, in a militarized zone where the Somocistas are the sole authority: anyone who wants to enter the area needs special permission from FDN officials in Tegucigalpa. We were denied such permission, but one FDN commander did tell us that "a refugee is held almost as a prisoner—bad food, terrible living conditions. But if he joins the FDN he'll eat well. The choice is to go to our refugee centers or join our struggle."[42]

One of the objectives of refugee generation is to harness the refugees as a labor force. A peasant from Ciudad Sandino, in the Segovias, who was kidnapped in April 1985, told us that the FDN had sent him and other abducted peasants to work as day laborers on the farms of Honduran land barons and then used the money for the war. And another abducted agricultural worker, who had escaped back to Nicaragua in 1984, recounted: "We had to repair the roads they used to bring in food and weapons. We leveled out gullies and built houses for them to store their supplies in. Sometimes, we saw foreigners arrive; I think they were North Americans."[43] In February 1986 two hundred peasants escaped en masse from the Honduran camps and returned to Nicaragua, taking advantage of the government's amnesty. They were kidnap victims, and they explained that most of the men had been integrated into FDN task forces, while the women and children had been forced to grow food for the contras.[44]

Refugee generation also involves clearing out civilians from those rearguard areas in Costa Rica and Honduras that have been allocated exclusively for military purposes. During the Big Pine II maneuvers, for instance, U.S. soldiers forcibly relocated nine hundred Honduran civilians from the border strips in El Paraíso and Choluteca, under the guise of protecting them from being in "dangerous border areas."[45] Similarly, hundreds of peasants have been cleared out of the Costa Rican border region to make way for the ARDE. Thus, when Pastora's forces launched a massive assault on the Costa Rican border town of Upala in 1983, the town was nearly destroyed and many families were forced to flee to refugee camps set up by the government. "It's what they want, to make an open area for the war against Nicaragua," said one Costa Rican peasant organizer from the area.[46]

Meanwhile, war conditions in the Nicaraguan countryside were creating the second kind of refugee, the *internal refugee*. Between 1981 and the end of 1984, over 120,000 peasants were uprooted; many fled the contra terror—some after their houses and farms had been destroyed—while others were so intimidated by contra threats and the potential for attack that they decided to seek safer areas and migrated toward more populated zones. Wartime economic conditions meant that still others found themselves unable even to subsist: cutting off a local highway, for instance, could suddenly render a whole community unable to market its produce or obtain supplies. Many chose to leave.

One U.S. nun who worked in Jalapa described the flow of internal refugees generated by contra activity at one point in 1983: "For two days refugees had been pouring into Jalapa from the mountain villages from the north and west. They came with their children and anything else they could carry in their arms or on their backs. They came both day and night, and in the mornings you could see them making their way in long lines down the mountain trails. They were all over the streets. They had no place to go. . . . Some were wounded, mainly from shrapnel."[47]

The practice of internal refugee generation was not generalized, but was applied to specific zones according to an overall counterrevolutionary strategy. Disrupting productive activity through the dislocation of entire farming communities furthers the aims of the war of attrition by accentuating food shortages in the cities and reducing agricultural export revenues. Similarly, the influx of peasants into the urban areas increases the strain on already overtaxed urban social services, and exacerbates the rural-urban structural imbalances inherited from Somocismo. But while the aim was to create refugees in certain areas, in others—those where a sanctuary was to be created—the aim was to *stabilize* the peasant communities in order to assure food supplies, intelligence sources, and a pool of recruits for the army.

Honduras: The Miskitos' Promised Land?

The transfer of large numbers of Miskitos to the Honduran side of the border was the key tactical achievement that allowed the counterrevolution to carry the war to the Atlantic Coast. By late 1983, the contras were relying heavily on mass kidnappings of Miskitos to maintain their rearguard in Honduras, and to secure reserves of manpower. "When we need more combatants," said a former National Guardsman assigned by the FDN to advise MISURA, "we go into the refugee camps and select candidates for the next training course."[48] And the statistics on forced migration to Honduras back this up: in April 1984, 497 were forced to go, in May 700, in June 200, in July 300, etc.[49]

This practice went largely unnoticed outside Nicaragua until late 1983, when the United States decided to combine one of these operations with a major anti-Sandinista propaganda maneuver. Early on the morning of 20 December, three hundred heavily armed MISURA contras attacked the remote northern Atlantic Coast town of Francia Sirpi and kidnapped all one thousand residents. The conservative bishop of the Atlantic Coast, Salvador Schlaffer, a sixty-three-year-old U.S. citizen who had worked in Nicaragua since 1947, was in the town at the time of the attack and joined the trek.[50] The government announced that the residents had been abducted and were headed toward

Honduras. The next day, U.S. Ambassador Anthony Quainton phoned the Nicaraguan Foreign Ministry with a message from the State Department: the population of Francia Sirpi had not been kidnapped but had left voluntarily for Honduras, and the bishop was leading the march. The ambassador reiterated unsubstantiated charges—made by MISURA spokesmen in Honduras—that the Sandinista Air Force was bombing the "fleeing civilians" to prevent their "escape from Nicaragua" and "requested" that they be allowed peaceful passage.[51]

"How could the U.S. government claim to know what is happening with a group deep in the Nicaraguan jungle?" asked Daniel Ortega. "Does the U.S. embassy in Managua have consulates in Francia Sirpi or scattered throughout the jungles of the Atlantic Coast?" The Nicaraguan Foreign Ministry released a communiqué stating: "The information transmitted by the U.S. ambassador and the declarations by the mercenary forces make it evident that there is a clear system of communication and coordination between the two that is only possible when there are plans and actions directed from a single central command."[52]

The propaganada stunt was well planned. On 23 December Schlaffer and the kidnap victims reached Honduran territory, where U.S. officials, the Honduran army, MISURA leaders, and foreign journalists were waiting. The bishop and the MISURA leaders were then flown to Tegucigalpa, where the bishop announced that the Francia Sirpi residents had marched willingly to Honduras, and charged that the Nicaraguan Miskito population was rebelling against "the current government's tendencies toward Marxism and Communism." The next day, Schlaffer returned to the United States; on Christmas morning he received a telephone call from President Reagan wishing him well. In Managua, Archbishop Miguel Obando y Bravo, an outspoken critic of the Sandinistas, compared Schlaffer to a "new Moses" leading the oppressed to the "promised land."[53]

The exodus made headlines throughout the world. Unreported, however, was the contradictory testimony of others involved in the episode. Five Miskitos who managed to escape the attack reported that their journey had been a forced march. Even Schlaffer admitted that no bombings had taken place, although he did not offer an opinion as to why this had been reported in the first place. But while the bishop and the MISURA leaders had been flown to Tegucigalpa, the one thousand Francia Sirpi residents had been corralled into "refugee camps"; several months later a number of them escaped back to Nicaragua, where they described the ordeal as a kidnapping. Some had gone willingly, but the community as a whole had been forced to march at gunpoint. According to one of these reports:

The contras went into each house and hauled the people out with kicks and rifle butts. We could take only what we could carry. They bound me with a rope since I work for the government as a teacher. Everyone who is paid by the government was tied up, the social workers and the teachers. They murdered two health workers, shot them. A guard with an M-60 was supposed to watch over us. The other contras stole everything they could take with them. They completely emptied José Zuñiga's grocery story. The contras began to get drunk from the booze they stole and got crazier and crazier, firing their guns into the air. The children and women cried. The contras ran around the whole time and fired shots without any apparent reason.[54]

Meanwhile, the thousands of Miskitos who had been manipulated or coerced into migrating to Honduras were now discovering that the "promised land" had nothing in common with Moses' Israel. Between April and August of 1984, we made several trips to Zelaya Norte and carried out extensive interviews with dozens of civilians who had been marched to Honduras at gunpoint and had managed to return. Orlando Wayland, one of those taken from Francia Sirpi, had spent three months in MISURA's hands before finally escaping. During an hour-long interview, he described the elaborate military and "refugee" structures set up by U.S. forces, the Hondurans, and MISURA in Gracias a Dios.

He and the other kidnap victims were put into the Mokorón refugee settlement, which he described as a concentration camp. Shortly afterward, the young men from Francia Sirpi, including Wayland, were taken to various military training camps, while the women and children were left behind in Mokorón, where MISURA exercises heavy influence. Wayland was sent to the Center for Miskito Military Instruction (CIMM), where he was accused of being a Sandinista spy—since he taught in a government school—tortured, imprisoned, and finally offered the alternative of fighting with MISURA.

"Three gringos were there in CIMM and said they were Vietnam veterans. Olive green U.S. Army helicopters arrived each day bringing arms and equipment, and twin-engine planes also came bringing special food for the gringos," he told us. According to his account, the three North Americans supervised Honduran soldiers and Somocistas, who gave direct military training to the kidnap victims. In CIMM he learned basic military tactics—handling arms, attack methods, and formation. He was then taken to the "China Base," run by "Orientals who said they were Vietnamese and South Koreans." They wore black uniforms and spoke a language that "nobody understood." This base specialized in sabotage and commando tactics. "They taught us how to handle explosives, burn installations, place mines, and other tactics." Finally, he was transferred to the Elite Troops (TE) base, "run directly by Northamericans and dedicated exclusively to advanced training in the use of artillery, antipersonnel, antitank and other heavy weapons." Wayland's training in TE was cut short "because we received orders to enter Nicaragua and kidnap the population at Sumbila."

In late March, Wayland crossed the Río Coco with five hundred contras, among whom there were several other victims of the Francia Sirpi kidnapping. Once inside Nicaragua, a group of two hundred split off and went to blow up the Salto Grande Dam—which they did on 27 March—while the other three hundred headed toward Tasba Pri, the group of settlements constructed for those who had been moved from the Río Coco during the Red Christmas fighting. Wayland got permission to fill his canteen in a river near the village of Wisconsin and managed to escape and flee in the direction of Puerto Cabezas. The rest of the group attacked Sumubila on 17 April.

In Tegucigalpa we interviewed top-level UNHCR officials about the twenty-five Miskito settlements that the organization administers in Gracias a Dios.[55] Some 12,550 Miskito and Sumu refugees were in the camps, or about one-half of the indigenous Nicaraguans who are in Honduras. These settlements are located about fifty miles from the Nicaraguan border, as part of a UNHCR policy of removing refugees from conflict areas.

MISURA maintains a heavily armed presence throughout Gracias a Dios, which creates an atmosphere of fear and coercion even in the UNHCR camps. Louise Drake, the UNHCR director in Honduras at the time of our visit and a German citizen, told us that "hundreds had expressed their desire to return" to Nicaragua. "There are many more who have subtly indicated their desire, [because] to say so openly is a risk; a refugee is exposed to all types of pressures and dangers," she said. Stories abound of Miskitos, individuals and families, who have attempted the trek back to Nicaragua on their own. Many have been killed by the contra forces, while others have been sent back to the camps. "The problem of protection is very grave; there's clear evidence of harassment and kidnapping of refugees who have voiced their desire to return," Drake told us.[56]

Meanwhile, MISURA forces and private U.S. "humanitarian" organizations make every effort to remove the refugees from UN supervision. Numerous private U.S. organizations, from CMA and Soldier of Fortune to CAUSA, the WACL and the Knights of Malta have invaded Gracias a Dios. One of the most important of these organizations is Friends of the Americas, formed in April 1984 to work with Miskito refugees and run by Woody Jenkins, archconservative Louisiana state representative and a personal friend of Ronald Reagan. "I'm all for the freedom fighters. I want the Sandinistas kicked out of Nicaragua. That's the main motivation for my work," Jenkins says.[57]

Drake told us that Friends of the Americas tries to persuade the refugees in the UNHCR camps to move to settlements that it and similar organizations have established along the border, offering money, better conditions, and so on. A 1985 congressional report on the contras confirmed that "aid from Friends of the Americas and other [right-wing private groups] has the effect of keeping the refugees directly on the border, rather than north of the border where the United Nations has bona fide refugee camps, and thus of sustaining MISURA base camps."[58]

Transforming the Miskito Rebellion

From the beginning of the war, the United States needed a climate of conflict on the Atlantic Coast, and creating a "Miskito problem" was therefore essential to the counterrevolutionary project since its inception. Yet in the new, more sophisticated stage of the war, it was necessary to transform crude resistance to the "Sandinista Communists" into the "progressive" cause of a national liberation movement among Nicaraguan Miskitos. Raising the banner of national liberation as the ideology of counterrevolution on the Atlantic Coast was a key component of the war of attrition there.

By breaking down the traditional system of domination and repression, the revolution created the possibility among the coastal peoples that they could now demand their historic rights. When the Indians asked for their land, for example, they were demanding the return of territory that previous governments had seized from them and given to foreign companies. When they demanded recognition of their languages, it was because that recognition had been officially denied by earlier governments, which had decreed that all schools must teach in Spanish.

It was the U.S. goal to hijack this struggle and turn it into a military confrontation against the "national oppression and ethnocide" practiced by the new government. The irony is that in any other country in Latin America the United States would have *helped* put down an Indian struggle for liberation; in Nicaragua, however, rather than destroy the Indians' newfound perception of themselves as protagonists in this struggle, U.S. strategists sought to manipulate this authentic perception and make it an instrument to use against the revolution. Thus, it was the counterrevolution that channeled the indigenous awakening onto a military path. And once the conflict flared, the military actions of many MISURA and MISURASATA combatants, as well as civilian support for these actions, became, for them, a legitimate way to win their historic demands.

Some of the Indian forces—such as Steadman Fagoth and his followers in MISURA (under the direction of the FDN)—concentrated on brutal pillaging. Others—particularly Brooklyn Rivera and MISURASATA—were more adept at raising the banner of "indigenous liberation." Thus, even while MISURASATA fought alongisde Pastora's forces in the ARDE, Rivera was developing contacts with organizations in the United States and Europe that were allegedly concerned with Indian oppression, and raising the "indigenous liberation" banner over Nicaragua. Yet the most important of these organizations, the Washington-based Indian Law Resource Center (ILRC), had repeatedly been accused of being a CIA front,[59] and by late 1984 Rivera had surrounded himself with advisers from these organizations, including ILRC associate Bernard Neitschmann, a University of California geographer.

Nietschmann had spent several years before the revolution doing research on the Atlantic Coast, financed in part by Somoza's Central Bank, and he had developed an interest in the Miskitos. In late 1983, he became one of the Reagan administration's favorite "experts" on indigenous oppression in Nicaragua.[60] The ILRC, particularly through Miskito staff member Armstrong Wiggins, became a mouthpiece for MISURASATA ideology, while the New Right privatization organizations shuffled Nietschmann from one public stage to another. They even arranged for him to be interviewed on CBN's "The 700 Club" (the network's most high-profile program) and by the *Washington Times*, which is owned by the Unification Church. And while MISURASATA's original demand was for title to communal lands, by 1984 a MISURASATA publication reported what this meant in practice: "The objective of the indigenous war is to throw out the Sandinistas from our lands . . . and obtain external recognition, the right to sovereignty and the inalienability of our nation."[61] This was a banner that could be raised in the coastal communities, in the refugee camps, and in international forums, particularly those dealing with indigenous concerns, and which provided another front for the U.S. effort to have the world see the Sandinistas as antagonistic to the interests of the Nicaraguans.

This brand of "indigenous liberation" is increasingly referred to as the "fourth world" ideology.[62] According to this construct, Indian peoples are in permanent conflict with the rest of the world (capitalist, socialist, and the third world); uncontaminated by any political tendency, from either the "left" or the "right," or by any internal social or class divisions, they are simply defending their age-old struggle against "outside" powers for control over their land and resources—in the case of Nicaragua, against the Sandinista government.

But the "fourth world" ideology can only lead to the reproduction and intensification of Indian oppression, not to its termination. Its logical extension is the notion of the "Indian reserve," in which indigenous communities are confined to reservations (whether or not this is what they are called) where they are easier to control and exploit—resulting in further ethnic disintegration and generally precluding any prospect of socioeconomic development. In the Nicaraguan context, the "fourth world" ideology views the Atlantic Coast as a "paradise" that has been "lost" as a result of the revolution, ignoring the fact that this was a "paradise" of poverty and disease, of the disruption of indigenous forms of social organization, a "paradise" subjected to the exigencies of the enclave economy (at certain times, U.S. capital *did* bring prosperity—albeit short-lived—whose memory the counterrevolution exploited).

The "fourth world" ideology gained a certain legitimacy in and out of the Nicaraguan Atlantic Coast, including among some who oppose U.S. policy toward Nicaragua, because it *appeared* to address the needs of authentic liberation. But while it may be an understandable reaction to centuries of Indian oppression, it ignores the fact that the Sandinista revolution is a popular movement *against* the forces of colonialism and imperialism that have exploited the Indian populations of Latin America. It also ignores all the Sandinistas' efforts to correct their early limited understanding of Indian aspirations and to find a means of enhancing ethnic identity within a multi-ethnic nation-state (see section on the autonomy project in Chapter 10). The United States has been able to use the "fourth world" ideology to separate the indigenous struggle from the revolutionary movement and then harness that struggle into the counterrevolutionary project—as a demand for independence from the Nicaraguan nation.

By the end of 1983, the Sandinistas had already taken the preliminary step toward the rectification of their earlier mistakes with regard to the peoples of the Atlantic Coast. In December of that year, the government declared an amnesty for those hundreds of Miskitos who had been imprisoned for participating in contra operations. The measure was well received in Zelaya, although a chill was cast when MISURA made several pre-dawn raids on the homes of former prisoners, shooting the families in cold blood—a message not to cooperate with the government. The population thus experienced the death and destruction committed by the contras in its name. Former National Guardsmen and Ladino recruits from the FDN, along with foreign mercenaries, were often leading the military expeditions. Those Miskitos who had originally viewed Fagoth as their leader began to withdraw their support. This in turn led Fagoth to resort to increasingly desperate tactics, and MISURA began to attack Miskito villages in order to destroy the social and economic infrastructure, assassinate known Sandinista supporters, and abduct the community to Honduras.

The tactics of the war of attrition were actually initiated on the Atlantic Coast before they were employed on the Pacific Coast. By mid-1983, the armed bands had abandoned their earlier tactics of seeking out EPS patrols. In April, MISURA attacked a reforestation project in Sumalili (ironically, reforestation had been a major Indian demand), and in October it attacked a community sawmill in Sukatpin, as well as a school and health clinic; over one hundred Miskito families were put out of work. The destruction of oil depots in Puerto Benjamín Zeledón that same month, along with a generalized escalation of the war, finalized the transition to a war of attrition on the Atlantic Coast.

By the time of the attack on Sumubila in April 1984 and on Columbus in June, the population was becoming increasingly disaffected. Several hundred MISURA and FDN members poured into these communities in the early morning hours, destroying health centers, generating stations, warehouses, schools, and recreational facilities. Ten Miskito civilians were killed, thirty injured, and seventy-nine kidnapped. The contras failed, however, to achieve their principal objective: to transfer the communities en masse to Honduras.

There were no EPS units present at the time of the attacks—the only defense was provided by Miskito self-defense militia units that had been set up months earlier. For the first time, Miskito civilians faced and repelled contra sieges on their own, underscoring another tragic reality of the conflict on the Atlantic Coast: Miskitos defending their communities were forced to turn their guns against those among their own people who had been manipulated by the counterrevolution. One of the Miskitos' most important values is the sense of community and shared identity, expressed in the term "Miskito family," which many Miskitos use to describe their ethnic group. The division of entire families and communities into the two sides in the conflict, and the physical division between the communities in Nicaragua and the refugees in Honduras, was a painful and deeply felt consequence of the U.S. war.

Just days after the July attack on Columbus, representatives from virtually every Miskito community in Zelaya Norte (sixty-five in all) came to Puerto Cabezas for a two-day conference to hammer out the details of a new organization, Miskito Aslatakanka Nicaraguara, or the Nicaraguan Miskito Organization (MISATAN). It differed from its predecessors in several respects. The most important was that, although it was highly critical of some of the government's actions, it recognized that the revolution was the only historic hope for the people of the Atlantic Coast in the struggle for their rights.

In the days preceding the conference, the contra radio stations— including MISURA's "Miskut," the FDN's "Radio 15 de Septiembre," ARDE's "Radio Impacto," and the Voice of America—broadcast continuous threats that those who participated would be killed. They tried to depict MISATAN as a "ploy" of the FSLN that would break the "unity" of the Miskito people around the aims of the counterrevolution. MISATAN was undeterred: "Reagan's war has set back our possibilities of organization and participation. We Nicaraguan Miskitos affirm that we have an important role to play in the struggle of the Nicaraguan people to continue forward with the Revolution," stated MISATAN's founding constitution.[63] "Our organization intends to struggle for the full rights of the Nicaraguan Miskitos to participate in the construction of the new Nicaraguan society, on the basis of our own historic experience and our culture." The new organization approved a six-point plan of struggle, including "reunification of the Miskito family" (the repatriation of those in Honduras), an end to the military conflict, and a solution to the problematic question of local control over indigenous land and resources within the context of national unity.

The highly polarized situation that had prevailed in 1982 had given way to a much more complex and multidimensional reality. The "Miskito family" was deeply divided, not only physically, but ideologically as well, between those who sought to solve the indigenous problem within the revolutionary process, and those who, embittered by the Sandinistas' early approach to the indigenous question and heavily influenced by counterrevolutionary propaganda, continued to work within MISURA or MISURASATA. Many others stood between or outside these two positions. There was, however, one sentiment that all Miskitos shared: the desire for peace. Over the next year, the seeds for the resolution of the Atlantic Coast conflict germinated. In the meantime, revolution and counterrevolution fought it out.

Socioeconomic Attrition: The War's Pivot Point

The war imposed on us extracts a price from the entire people; the counterrevolution seeks to alter the logic of the economy's rational functioning and provoke catastrophic social effects that throw the country's stability, and therefore revolutionary power itself, into crisis.

—Vice-president Sergio Ramírez,
speaking in 1985[64]

It was early in the morning of 4 December 1984. Thirty-one Nicaraguan civilians, most of them communications workers from Managua, were riding in a flat-bed truck through the rolling mountains between Matagalpa and Estelí. The truck rounded a bend in the dirt road and descended between two steep inclines. At that moment, two hundred heavily armed contras, laying in wait, opened up with automatic rifles, grenade launchers, and rockets. They then descended from the roadside slopes and, upon reaching the truck, poured gasoline on the defenseless victims as they lay wounded, and, amid terrified shrieks and moans, set fire to the vehicle itself. Nearly all were killed.

"The contras, wearing olive green, came up to the truck and, hearing the groans, bayoneted the people before setting fire to the vehicle," Jorge Luis Briones, one of the few survivors, told us from his hospital bed in La Trinidad. The young communications worker lowered his voice, as if his account of the atrocity should not be heard, and continued: "There was a little boy with his mother in that truck, and peasants who had asked for a ride. How is it possible that they burned them alive?"

Briones's incredulity was natural for someone who had been through such a horrifying experience. But the FDN atrocity was anything but arbitrary: the majority of the victims were on their way to begin volunteer harvesting at the El Pericón state coffee farm in Estelí, part of a national effort described as the "coffee battle."

Coffee plays a vital role in the Nicaraguan economy, and the coffee bean—like sugarcane in Cuba—has come full turn, from symbolizing oligarchic rule to epitomizing the struggle of the revolution to break out of centuries of underdevelopment and economic dependence. Now tens of thousands of students and urban workers volunteer to spend the November-March harvest picking coffee in order to compensate for the critical labor shortage brought about by the agrarian reform (most of the pickers during the Somoza dictatorship were landless peasants who have since been given plots and no longer need to seek seasonal work). And each year, the counterrevolution attempts to undermine production and harvesting. The 4 December 1984 massacre was thus intended to send an unequivocal message to all those preparing to participate in the harvest. "They were trying to instill fear, hoping to discourage pickers from participating with the warning that their lives would be in danger if they did so," Miguel Barrios, Matagalpa regional director of MIDINRA, told us after the attack.

If military aggression is the *spearhead* of the war, socioeconomic attrition is the *pivot* through which the United States attempts to inflict a political defeat on the revolution. By throwing Nicaragua into economic crisis, the United States hopes to pervert the people's consciousness and to foment social unrest, organize this unrest into opposition, and delegitimize the revolutionary project. This strategy makes the economic front perhaps the most complex one; it is also the only theater in which the United States has scored significant successes, and the one that is the most difficult for the revolution to confront.

Economic destabilization is not a novel instrument of U.S. foreign policy. In certain cases, such as Allende's Chile, it was the cutting edge of the U.S. effort. The mechanisms—ranging from using bilateral aid as a pressure mechanism, to blocking international loans, to sanctions, to direct economic sabotage—have not changed. But the new strategy has redefined both framework and objectives: the purpose of *economic destabilization* was to weaken governments—whether they were revolutionary or merely not in U.S. interests—and thus enhance the conditions for their removal, be it through a coup d'état (Chile), an electoral defeat (Jamaica), or a foreign invasion (Angola). *Socioeconomic attrition,* on the other hand, aims at warping the project of transformation that is at the heart of revolutionary change, invalidating the entire project in the eyes of the people, and turning those people into protagonists of the counterrevolution. "The Reagan administration refuses to give up its hope [of bringing about] Nicaragua's economic and social collapse," said Vice-president Ramírez. "It hopes that, under the weight of the difficulties and limitations imposed by the war . . . the people will turn their rifles against the Revolution and thus against their own historic project of change and transformation."[65]

Five hundred years of foreign domination and fifty years of Somocista pillaging left Nicaragua one of the poorest and most backward countries in Latin America. With its economy devoted to the export of raw materials to the capitalist world market (principally the United States), extreme sectoral disarticulation, superexploitation of the working classes, and abject poverty among the masses—side by side with sumptuous lifestyles for a tiny minority—Nicaragua faced external dependence, chronic underdevelopment, and stark inequalities. The damage wrought by the war of liberation (the GNP fell by 30 percent in 1979) literally shattered the country's productive infrastructure, compound-

ing inherited economic problems. The fragile and disarticulated economy constituted the soft underbelly of the revolution.

Economic destabilization was part of Carter's "neutralization" policy,
and the Reagan administration used Carter's "economic assistance" as
part of its propaganda effort, arguing that the United States had been
"financing totalitarian consolidation" in Nicaragua. But Carter nevertheless laid the groundwork for Reagan's socioeconomic attrition, and
the strategists of the incoming Republican administration stressed the
importance of undermining Nicaragua's economy even before Reagan
was inaugurated. In October 1980 the Heritage Foundation pointed out:

> Nicaraguan workers continue to have an emotional attachment to the
> revolutionary movement. This attachment can be expected to weaken as
> the economy deteriorates. . . . There are some indications of growing
> support to take arms to overthrow the Sandinista government, and this
> support could increase as further problems develop. . . . Economic short-
> comings might provoke at least limited civilian unrest by the end of the
> current harvest season.[66]

The Reagan White House shifted from exerting pressure by making
U.S. loans and credits conditional upon the Sandinistas compliance
with various U.S. demands to direct economic sabotage—by blocking
external financing. Shortly after he took office, Reagan suspended the
last $15 million of a $75 million loan approved by Carter and cut off
wheat exports to Nicaragua. A few months later, he cancelled all
bilateral U.S. aid and began exerting pressure on multilateral lending
agencies. In the World Bank and the Inter-American Development
Bank (IDB), the United States vetoed numerous loans that had been
approved on technical grounds by the banks' officers. The World Bank,
in an oft-cited 1981 report on the Nicaraguan economy,[67] identified the
projects that it and the IDB planned to finance as being essential for the
development of the economy, especially the rural sector and related
social infrastructure. Many of these projects were in the private agricultural sector (which in 1985 still accounted for nearly 70 percent of
the country's agricultural output). Nevertheless, by early 1985 the
World Bank was declaring Nicaragua "ineligible" for any further assistance, formalizing its de facto embargo. That same year, the United
States took its campaign to unprecedented heights, threatening to cut
off U.S. contributions to the IDB's reserves if that institution disbursed
an already approved $58 million loan to Nicaragua. (Until then, IDB
funds had gone to Nicaragua through the bank's "special window"
category, in which funding is approved by a simple majority vote,
undercutting the U.S. veto power.[68]) In total, more than $400 million in
loans and credits approved as bi- and multilateral aid between 1981 and
1985 were blocked by the United States.[69]

The Reagan administration capped the four-year "creeping" economic blockade in May 1985 with the imposition of a total commercial embargo. This had major repercussions for the entire process of production and circulation in Nicaragua, given the historic dependence of the economy on the U.S. market. The Sandinistas, however, had been anticipating such a move for several years, having learned from the Cuban experience. In 1981, following Reagan's inauguration, they had greatly expanded an early program of market diversification as the centerpiece of an effort to broaden relations with the international community. As a result, new markets were opened in Western Europe, the socialist nations, Asia, Latin America, and other developing countries. The idea was to eliminate or at least diminish, Nicaragua's dependence on the United States ("diversification of dependence"). And indeed, the structure of the country's foreign trade altered radically between 1981 and 1985: exports to the United States decreased from about 35 percent to less than 15 percent, and imports dropped from 30 percent to a little over 15 percent.[70] This reduction was important in mitigating the embargo's effects on exports, and these effects were limited to the initial dislocations resulting from the development and consolidation of new markets and to the greater costs involved in transporting goods to more distant ports.

The United States' suspension of exports to Nicaragua presented a more complex problem, however, since much of the country's agricultural equipment and industrial plant depended on U.S. machinery, spare parts, and technology.[71] The abrupt cutoff therefore had a shattering impact, in the short term, on virtually every sector and subsector of the economy. This can be seen by the ripple effects caused when just one economic activity was paralyzed. Managua's Polycasa factory is the country's principal producer of raw plastics, which are used in dozens of other industrial enterprises, as well as in health, commerce, agriculture, communications, etc. At the time of the imposition of the embargo, 80 percent of Polycasa's machinery came from the United States, and the lack of a spare part for *one* machine paralyzed the entire factory for several weeks following the embargo.

The diversification policy, however, helped ameliorate the damage.[72] Industrial raw materials imported directly from the United States had already dropped from nearly 50 percent to approximately 30 percent. Within months of the embargo, U.S. subsidiaries in third countries had begun providing some of the machinery and equipment previously imported directly from the United States. Moreover, the importation of capital goods from the United States had dropped to next to nothing by 1983, and the government had begun to install new lines from other countries, particularly the socialist nations, which also offered reliable and stable markets. The technological and industrial dependence that remained by 1985 was thus reduced to the maintenance of existing plant and machinery.

Beyond the objective of blocking Nicaragua's access to much-needed credits, U.S. financial aggression has been aimed at strangling the country by cutting it off from international economic intercourse. Central American, Latin American, and European governments are constantly pressured by the United States to reduce their trade with Nicaragua. The 1985 AID annual report "recommended" that AID's funding to Central America be used to pressure these countries to reduce trade with Nicaragua.[73] The United States has also used military force, such as the mining of Nicaragua's ports, to achieve this aim, and in September 1983 the FDN threatened the Mexican government with blowing up its tankers if it continued deliveries of crude oil to Nicaragua.[74]

That same year, the CIA drew up its *Freedom Fighters' Manual*, a comic-book-style pamphlet meant for mass clandestine distribution inside Nicaragua by the contras and by reactionary elements in the cities.[75] The manual, described in its introduction as a "practical guide to liberate Nicaragua from oppression and misery by paralyzing the military-industrial complex of the traitorous Marxist state," consisted of twenty-one pages of illustrations, accompanied by demagogic slogans, of simple sabotage actions that the "ordinary freedom-loving Nicaraguan" could carry out. The actions included calling in sick, damaging equipment in the workplace, wasting water and electricity, opening corrals on state farms so that livestock can escape, dropping typewriters in government offices, smashing windows and lightbulbs, blocking public toilets, cutting telephone cables, painting anti-Sandinista slogans in public spaces, disrupting traffic by placing rocks on the highways, and sabotaging vehicles by pouring sand into the gas tanks or cutting distributor wires. "There is an essential economic infrastructure that any government needs to function, which can easily be disabled and even paralyzed without the use of armaments or costly and advanced equipment, with a small investment of resources and time," states the handbook.

Unlike *Psychological Operations in Guerrilla Warfare*, the *Freedom Fighters' Manual* was not for use by the contras, but was intended to reach the population at large. It represented a crude attempt at bringing the civilian population into the counterrevolution through small-scale, local sabotage activities—at having the people participate in their own socioeconomic attrition.

The handbook was quickly discovered, and in many neighborhoods and production centers copies were confiscated by the workers themselves. Trade unions and other mass organizations convened *barrio* and factory assemblies to expose the manual. Many of them ended up on union and neighborhood bulletin boards, where they became objects of popular ridicule as the people saw for themselves the crude machinations of the counterrevolution and were thus educated in guarding against local sabotage.

The shift from a strategy of military victory to one of a prolonged war of attrition necessitated linking military and economic aggression more closely. The contras' new role was to use military force to grind away at the country's socioeconomic infrastructure and undermine the revolution's social base. Although the economy had been feeling the effects of financial aggression since 1981, it was in late 1983 that the economic effects of the war began to take a real toll. Although the strategy has not resulted in the economic collapse or widespread social unrest that the United States expected, it *has* had a devastating effect on the country, with repercussions in every aspect of life. It affects every social and economic indicator, and is the principal—although certainly not the only—cause of the economic crisis that began in 1983.*

The Nicaraguan government estimates that military aggression led to direct and indirect losses of over $1.3 billion between 1981 and 1985—more than three times the amount the country earns in foreign exchange every year and more than one-half of the Gross Domestic Product.[76] (The comparable figure for destruction of the U.S. economy would be about $1 trillion.) This includes looses from the destruction of existing capital stock and infrastructure, such as dams, bridges, silos, fishing boats, power stations, farm and construction machinery, etc.; the concomitant losses of production; the decline, and in some cases the complete paralysis, of production in war zones; the reduction in agricultural and industrial output resulting from drops in imports of spare parts and raw materials, etc.

Even this figure may be a gross underestimation, since the chain from primary to secondary and tertiary repercussions is, in a practical sense, endless.[77] To take just one example, the lumber industry had virtually

---

*Obviously, the effects of the international economic crisis, the backward economic structures inherited from Somocismo, mistakes in Sandinista management and planning (e.g., fiscal policies), and the inevitable dislocations that any economic system experiences in the initial stages of its transformation also contribute to Nicaragua's crisis. But in most of these respects Nicaragua's crisis is no different from the crisis afflicting all Latin American countries; the fact that Nicaragua is also having to deal with a war that is targeting the socioeconomic foundations of society distinguishes the country's predicament.

ceased to function by 1983, since the timber extraction and lumber yards are all located in the Atlantic Coast and central regions, where the conflict is intense. The ripple effects include the cutoff of dollar earnings on wood exports, the drop in production in other sectors due to decreased foreign exchange earnings, the closing of furniture, pulp, and related factories in Managua, shortages of paper products and printed products, the bankruptcy of commercial enterprises dealing in wood-related items, prolonged unemployment for thousands of artisans, and a drop in wood-based construction.

Comparing real economic performance and that which might take place if there were no aggression reveals the profundity of the war's economic effects. The World Bank report cited above noted the short-term problems Nicaragua was bound to face (balance of payments deficit, for example), but gave a bright forecast for the future. It estimated that national production would increase by 38.9 percent between 1980 and 1985; real growth was only 9 percent. It calculated a stable 6 percent growth rate between 1985 and 1990, compared to the 1985 projection, taking the war into consideration, of only 1 percent. A 1984 UN Economic Commission on Latin America (ECLA) report on the Nicaraguan economy broke traditional practice by adding a special section on the effects of the aggression because it considered this factor to be a critical determinant of the economy's performance.[78]

Perhaps the greatest effect at the national level has been the massive diversion of human, material, and financial resources from productive activities, capital investments, and social welfare to national defense requirements. Defense allocations climbed from 15 percent of the budget in 1982, to 20 percent in 1983 (the year that the war escalated dramatically), to 30 percent in 1984 and nearly 50 percent in 1985.[79] In that year, defense needs accounted for 25 percent of the Gross Domestic Product, 40 percent of internal production, and employed almost 20 percent of the economically active population (including combat activities and defense-related economic activity.)[80] One in every five male adults (age eighteen and over) was mobilized into defense, pulling them out of productive activity (or preparation for productive activity), distorting the structure of the labor market, and intensifying labor shortages.

By 1985 the reorientation of the nation's resources to defense had forced a total freeze in the health and education budgets. The rate of state investment in development projects was drastically curtailed, which has meant abandoning or postponing numerous long-term projects that are central to the process of capital formation and accumulation on a national scale.

The countryside has borne the brunt of the direct effects of the war. By 1984, the war had brought the rural economy in major stretches of the war zones virtually to a state of collapse, as over a quarter of a million peasants ceased to be producers and became internal refugees, forced to relocate due to the counterrevolutionary terror. The accumulated effect of this massive displacement, the destruction of the rural infrastructure, including transportation and storage systems, resulted in the virtual disintegration of rural trading and market networks. In many areas the merchants and state agencies that distribute credit, purchase and transport crops, and provide manufactured goods for peasant production and consumption had to abandon their activities. This led thousands of peasant families to revert to subsistence production.

The disruption of the peasant economy in the northern region, traditionally the country's breadbasket, is a prime cause of the food shortages and long lines in the urban centers (which the Western press is so fond of depicting). According to the Finance Ministry, by 1984 the dislocations had resulted in the loss of 50 percent of the basic grains produced in these zones. Thus, military aggression in the countryside leads to shortages and discontent in the cities, contributes to rural labor shortages, and makes export-crop production difficult. The massive migration to the cities has led to a burgeoning informal sector, distorting pricing and distribution policies and taxing the urban infrastructure to the breaking point.

Education and health have been hit particularly hard. Between 1981 and 1985, the contras razed 14 schools, forced another 359 to close, and murdered 149 teachers; 25,680 primary and 10,095 secondary school students were thrown out of classes. Thousands more adults lost access to education as 840 adult education centers were closed. Similarly, 50 health centers in the war zones, all constructed after 1979 and including a complete hospital, were either destroyed or had to be abandoned. More than a quarter of a million people lost access to health care as a result. The war has impeded the extension of health services and sanitation. Malaria and polio—completely eliminated by 1982 thanks to massive vaccination campaigns—reappeared in 1984.[81] The destruction of housing, energy, transportation, and communications systems has also contributed to deteriorating living standards.

While those in the countryside have felt the *direct* destruction hardest, the urban and semi-urban populations have been stung by its indirect effects. The deterioration of social services, shortages of basic goods, and spiralling inflation triggered by the war were the principal reasons for the dramatic 20 percent reduction in urban per capita consumption and the 50 percent drop in the urban workers' *real* wages between 1982 and 1985. The impact is worsened because of the tremendous achievements made between 1979 and 1982. The precipitous drop in the living standards of the working classes followed a sharp rise in the first few years of the revolution as a result of immediate measures to redistribute wealth and expand social programs. People's raised expectations are thus open to manipulation by the counterrevolution.

It is hard for those who have not lived in Nicaragua to imagine the daily frustrations imposed by wartime conditions. For a typical Managua family, a trip to the market or to work is a daily odyssey. At certain times, up to half of the (already deteriorated) public transportation vehicles have been out of service for lack of spare parts and the need to use them in defense-related activities. Family vehicles often sit abandoned for months on end for lack of a spark plug or tire. Prolonged shortages of food and household items (such as toilet paper) are compounded by endless lines and cutthroat scrambles to get the few items a family needs.

One particularly unpleasant problem during 1984 and 1985 was the occasional shortage of butane and propane gas for cooking. In early 1984, the FDN began sabotaging the trucks that come from Guatemala carrying propane and butane. From January to June, nine of these giant trucks were either partially or totally destroyed by contra commandos, who placed time bombs on them as they passed through customs at the Honduran border. By the summer of that year, the inevitable shortages of cooking gas began, creating all kinds of difficulties for families that depended on it.

While the most aware citizens may be able to make the connection between these problems and the war, this cannot be expected always to be the case, particularly when mass frustration is exploited by the counterrevolution. Managua's reactionary daily *La Prensa*, for example, suddenly "discovered" the gas shortages, publishing front-page pictures of lines and interviews with angry housewives—but the contra sabotage of the trucks went unreported.

The U.S. strategy is to create a climate of malaise and even anarchy, to project the Sandinistas as incompetent administrators, and to discredit the government's economic policies. For instance, a May 1985 NSC memorandum justified the embargo by claiming that "depressed economic conditions in Nicaragua were, of course, due to disastrous economic policies adopted by the Sandinistas and not to any actions by the United States."[82] Reactionary elements inside the country use demagogy to inculcate these images in the population, and these are then magnified abroad by the U.S. propaganda machine. The shortages and lines at Managua's markets were favorite stories in the Western press at the same time that same press "discovered" the "secret war" that was causing these shortages and lines: the connection itself was not discovered. When the government established a quota system to guarantee equitable distribution of scarce supplies, they were accused of "Communist rationing."

The complex chain that links together military, economic, psychological-ideological, and informational aggression, so easy to see in this situation, is nothing less than the workings of "total war at the grassroots level." Every man, woman, and child in Nicaragua feels the pressures of the U.S. war. The socioeconomic effects of the aggression are a tremendous war tax imposed on the Nicaraguan people by the United States. The war means postponing socioeconomic development, sacrificing future prosperity for survival in the present. It ultimately means setting back the hopes and aspirations of the Nicaraguan people for years, perhaps decades. And this is precisely its intention.

6
Casting Long Shadows: The Conflict Environment

Low-intensity conflict involves a wide range of conflictual contingencies, including: coercive diplomacy, propaganda and psychological operations, special intelligence operations, terrorism and counterterrorism, security assistance projects in relatively benign and varying degress of hostile environments, insurgency and counterinsurgency, military and paramiliarty deployments with limited goals. *This concept posits a larger conflict environment that casts long shadows over seemingly localized political, political-military, and military strife.*

—"Low-Intensity Conflict:
The Strategic Challenge"[1]

The crisis of hegemony the United States faces in Central America is regional, and thus U.S. strategy is regional from conceptualization to implementation. A key aspect of the type of warfare Washington is waging is that it takes place in a much broader area than that of the military battlefields in conventional warfare. Pentagon strategists refer to this area as the "conflict environment." This environment runs from Mexico to Colombia, and each tactical initiative the United States takes in any part of the area is ultimately tied into the long-term goals for the entire region. Many initiatives, however, take place in the context of the war against Nicaragua. A look at Honduras and Costa Rica shows the extent of the United States' activity in the conflict environment, and particularly how these activities beyond Nicaragua's borders are linked to what the Reagan administration is trying to achieve *inside* Nicaragua.

Honduras: The Maneuvers Program

Resources have been mobilized and coordinated in the conflict environment through ongoing programs of military "exercises," principally in Honduras, but also in Panama, Costa Rica, the Caribbean, and the Pacific. The United States has been conducting "joint" exercises with the Honduran armed forces since 1965, but two months after the Reagan administration took office the Joint Chiefs of Staff (JCS) approved a five-year program to beef up the maneuvers, in accordance with Reagan's incipient Central American policy.

Then, in mid-1983, the administration decided to expand vastly the scope and duration of these maneuvers. They were now to continue virtually uninterrupted, allowing for constant troop mobilization and the establishment of a permanent U.S. military presence in the region. The original JCS scheme was part of a strategy for winning rapid military victories and of possible direct U.S. interventions in Central America; the 1983 changes were made to suit the needs of low-intensity warfare. Between October 1981, when Falcon View, the first of the "new maneuvers," was held, until the Terencio Sierra '86 exercises in early 1986, there were over thirty-five exercises of varying size and duration, with some ninety thousand U.S. troops participating.

One key objective of the maneuvers is on-the-ground training of U.S. forces involved in the Central American war. Leading LIW proponent and counterinsurgency expert Col. John D. Waghelstein emphasized the importance of immersing these forces in the conflict environment. "We've got to understand that classroom training is just not the way a soldier learns this stuff [LIW]," he argued. "He needs a laboratory that duplicates real world experience, and I don't mean on the military reservations."[2]

The seven SOF branches have been the most extensively involved in the maneuvers, followed by those detachments from the four services that are the most appropriate back-up and support units for low-intensity operations. Through the exercises, these forces have gained practical experience in a wide range of defensive and offensive land, sea, and air tactics. Virtually every possible wartime contingency has been tested on the Honduran game field.

Readying U.S. forces for direct operations, however, is only a secondary purpose of the "laboratory." The key aim is to transfer the traditional role of intervention to local forces, with the Pentagon doing the training, command, and back-up. The maneuvers, along with the physical infrastructure installed through them, have allowed the U.S. military to reorganize and train the Salvadoran, Honduran, Costa Rican, and contra armies in counterrevolutionary warfare. "For the U.S. and its allies to succeed . . . there must be greater emphasis on the development of [SOF] irregular warfare units," stated the Heritage Foundation's 1984 publication *Mandate for Leadership II*. "These can project U.S. power effectively into areas of low intensity conflicts. . . . *Even more important is irregular warfare training for Central American forces*."[3]

A 1985 General Accounting Office (GAO) report on the maneuvers described the "force multiplier" effect that U.S. troops have on indigenous armies.[4] This "force multiplier" effect facilitates the transformation of indigenous forces, through a process of osmosis, into operatives in low-intensity warfare. The U.S. detachments act as a centrifugal nucleus around which local forces throughout the region can be reorganized and guided. The Honduran "laboratory" provides the conditions for the U.S. forces to insert themselves into the conflict environment and direct the Central American counterrevolution.

The maneuvers are also indispensable for reinforcing the armed counterrevolution against Nicaragua. As FDN chief Adolfo Calero put it: "The maneuvers provide a shield for stepped-up [FDN] activity." Each time a maneuver is held, said Calero, "there is a stage being set up for some spectacular [contra] moves."[5] In many of the exercises the contras participate alongside U.S. and Honduran troops, receiving training in, and exposure to, advanced military equipment, forms of organization, and tactical maneuvers.[6]

In addition, the maneuvers provide a powerful psychological stimulus for the contras. They provide the ground troops in this U.S. war with what some U.S. military analysts have called the "mantle of inevitable success," giving them psychological strength, even where that does not correspond with their actual battlefield capacity. Even when the mantle was "tattered," as it was following battlefield setbacks in 1983, "the Reagan administration's commitment of more than 4,000 troops to large-scale exercises here and the arrival of the U.S. flotilla off the Central American coast are seen by the rebels as having done much to stitch it up."[7]

The Contra Supply and Intelligence Systems

Since the massive use of conventional arms tends to lead to generalized—as opposed to selective—repression, and can generate anti-intervention sentiment among the population, these are generally avoided in a low-intensity campaign. Instead, there is heavy reliance on intelligence, logistics, supply and command, which permits a high level of direct, yet practically invisible, U.S. participation. The low-profile nature of such sophisticated assistance gives it a minimal political cost, yet it is crucial to the regional counterrevolution's continued operation.

In the war against Nicaragua, this strategy has meant supplying the contras with an extremely sophisticated supply system on the one hand, and with timely intelligence on the other. No less than fourteen Honduran airfields—several of which are capable of handling the most advanced U.S. aircraft—have been installed or upgraded during the maneuvers and serve as transit points for the delivery of tons of weapons and material to the contras inside Nicaragua.[8] During every maneuver, teams of U.S. Army engineers open up the jungle, construct roads, and build bridges. This resulting network of roads is used for transporting weapons and supplies to the war fronts inside Nicaragua. At least three port facilities have also been constructed or upgraded.

By 1985, this network of land, sea, and air routes included at least ten bases in Honduras, El Salvador, and Costa Rica, twenty-eight land and water infiltration routes, and no less than five air corridors.[9] The FDN's supply network centered around four bases in Honduras: Palmerola, which serves as the command center for the U.S. occupation forces; El Aguacate, constructed by U.S. Army engineers during the 1983 Big Pine II maneuvers and later turned over to the CIA, the SOF units working with the contras, and the FDN high command; Jamastrán, constructed during the April 1984 Granadero I maneuvers; and Birahuas, built in 1985 and made into the FDN's own air base.

Weapons and supplies for the contra forces arrive at these bases through various channels. Some are brought from Howard Air Force Base in the Panama Canal Zone, others from stockpiles on the U.S. mainland, still others from the Honduran Armed Forces Logistical Supply Center (CALFA), where, since 1983, huge reserves have been stored for use throughout the region. The Honduran armed forces act as the logistical bridge for the land-based movement of supplies, while the airdrops are the responsibility of U.S. SOF units, the Honduran air force, and the handful of FDN pilots.

Land-based way stations in the supply network are run directly by the FDN, and include six centers, called "Logistic Resupply Centers," which run the length of the border. From there, deliveries into Nicaragua are made over at least twenty-nine land routes.

For their part, the MISURA bands operating on the Atlantic Coast have direct supply lines from airfields set up on both sides of the border, as well as through a fleet of *pirañas,* which depart from the southeastern tip of Honduras and make their way into Zelaya over the hundreds of rivers that run through the dense jungle. MISURA was a subordinate Miskito detachment of the FDN, and its supply route therefore depends on the Somocistas.

The ARDE's supply network began at the Ilopango military base in El Salvador. From there, supplies were airdropped to the ARDE's principal base, La Penca, until it was captured by the Sandinistas in mid-1985. Supplies also went by air to the properties of John Hull in northern Costa Rica; from there they were sent overland to ARDE units inside Nicaragua, using at least four major routes, or were flown in by helicopter. The ARDE was also given a fleet of *pirañas* to use in shipping supplies from Costa Rica's Atlantic Coast into southeastern Nicaragua.

The infrastructure of the conflict environment has also made it possible to erect around Nicaragua an immensely sophisticated electronic surveillance "fence": it captures, 24-hours-a-day, every telephone and radio communication, every land, air, and sea movement inside Nicaragua's territorial limits.

As part of this "fence," at least six radar stations, as well as two huge electronic tracking stations commanded and operated by U.S. Air Force personnel, have been installed in Honduras. One of the tracking stations is located on Tigre Island in the Gulf of Fonseca and uses "the best technology we've got," according to a congressional source.[10] The other sits atop the country's second highest mountain, thirty miles south of Tegucigalpa. Known locally as "Carrot Top," this super-secret espionage installation is surrounded by minefields and endless coils of barbed wire. It is capable of simultaneously linking up with ground-based electronic listening devices, surveillance aircraft, satellites, and portable satellite-linked radios carried by combat troops (including the contras) on the ground. The center's personnel, with an array of electronic intelligence at their fingertips and using a new process that fuses tactical intelligence data from various sources into one picture, can literally "watch" the border skirmishes between the contras and the EPS on their screens. This is facilitated by data received from ground-based listening devices installed along the Honduran-Nicaraguan border.[11]

Satellite-surveillance and radar and other installations in the Panama Canal Zone, combined with continuous spy flights over Nicaraguan territory, give the DOD a flight-monitoring capability that extends from Mexico to Colombia. Between 1981 and 1985, the Nicaraguan Defense Ministry detected 2,809 spy flights over the country. Both the satellite and the aerial surveillance plug into diverse and extremely sophisticated apparatus deployed by the United States. For example, sonic buoys placed in Nicaraguan ports by *piraña* speedboats transmit coded data on maritime movements to overflying reconnaissance aircraft, to land-based installations, and to satellites.[12]

The raw data gathered by the electronic "fence" is processed and churned out as intelligence flows to the contras. Employing advanced, fully computerized photoanalysis techniques, the DOD has the capacity to process and deliver spy flight and satellite photographs in a matter of hours, a process that took between two and three days during the Vietnam war.[13] Using the modern field radios that have been supplied to each FDN task force, the contras inside Nicaragua are constantly informed on Sandinista troop movements by the U.S. advisers in Honduras, boosting many times over their operational and logistical capacities.

In addition, since at least early 1983, the U.S. Navy has maintained a minimum of one frigate or destroyer off Nicaragua's coasts, rotating them in four- to six-week tours of duty, to monitor communications, particularly EPS radio communication.[14] This naval presence is another essential part of the contra rearguard, not just for gathering intelligence but also for providing a platform from which to launch direct attacks, primarily on the Pacific Coast. From serving as the support-base for the mining of the harbors and the sabotage at Puerto Sandino and Corinto, to the "softening-up" activities off San Juan del Norte during Pastora's April 1984 siege of that town, the naval-based back-up has given the contras a decisive edge in several engagements.

Direct Combat Support by Special Operations Units

The "low-key intervention" carried out by traditional naval, air, and intelligence units is complemented by the activities of several top-secret units inside Nicaragua, including the U.S. Army's Intelligence Support Activity (ISA), the 160th Task Force, and the Delta Force.[15] Of the various activities in which these units engage, one important one is helicopter missions, for which dozens of landing pads have been carved out of the jungles in the frontier region during various military exercises.[16]

The U.S. commandos, drawn from the 160th Task Force of the 101st Airborne Division (stationed at Fort Campbell, Kentucky)—perhaps the most secretive of all SOF units—specialize in helicopter logistics and back-up operations behind enemy lines. Although the Pentagon has refused to reveal the numbers involved, much less confirm the veracity of the charges, at least sixteen members of the "Night Stalkers," as they call themselves, were killed in action during 1983 alone. When family members were interviewed in 1984, all repeated the same story: They understood that the unit's members were carrying out top-secret, high-risk missions in Central America, or simply in the "south." Each soldier had been given thousands of dollars in "bribe" money, to be used to pay his way out of enemy territory if captured, and was told to carry a major credit card with at least a $1,000 line of credit. He was instructed to conceal any official connection to the U.S. government if captured, and to wear only civilian clothes. The army had worked out cover-up stories to be released in the event of a SOF operative's death. "If I ever die in an accident, don't ever believe I wasn't working for the army," David Jordan, a member of the unit, told his wife Brenda.[17]

Many of the helicopter missions in Nicaragua apparently involved shuttling contra units across the border to carry out sabotage operations, and pulling them out hours later. "Don told us he flew a bunch of trips into Nicaragua" before his death in March 1983, said the father of 160th Task Force member Donald R. Alvey. "He was kind of vague about the missions. He'd go somewhere and pick up a group of people in a jungle clearing—armed troops, speaking Spanish—and take them to another clearing in the jungle somewhere," he said. "His job was to fly them in, put them down, be gone six or eight hours, then put in the chopper again and take them back out. Don said one time you could tell damn well they had been in a fight because a lot of them were wounded."[18]

Other relatives recalled that their sons or husbands had spoken of ferrying troops into Nicaragua from container ships standing offshore. Still others quoted the men as saying that they were trained to throw out decoy flares to confound the heat-seeking missiles used by Sandinista air-defense. To deceive the Sandinistas into thinking that they had hit and disabled a Night Stalker chopper, the crews sent up artificial smoke and rolled their craft as though they were about to crash. And on more than one occasion, EPS commanders have reported hitting unidentified helicopters that had penetrated Nicaragua from Honduras and were able to go back across the border under clouds of smoke.

Using cover-ups for those killed is not a new technique. During the Vietnam war, deaths of military personnel on secret assignments were also laundered to conceal the missions, according to one Pentagon official, who called the process "bodywashing." "If a guy was killed on a mission, and if it was sensitive politically, we'd ship the body back home and have a jeep roll over on him, or we'd arrange a chopper crash or wait until one happened and insert a body or two into the wreckage later. It's not that difficult."[19]

Donald Alvey's family was told that he had died in a helicopter crash off the coast of Norfolk, Virginia. Judy Scharpman was told that her cousin, Richard J. Thompson, was killed in a crash in the Panama Canal Zone. Brenda Jordan was told that her husband David died when his chopper's fuel system failed during a maintenance flight at Fort Campbell.

The Night Stalkers operation is but the exposed tip of extensive SOF involvement *inside* Nicaragua. Another was a 160th Task Force mission to ferry the Delta Force into action.[20] In this case, small commandos from the Delta Force were sent into Nicaragua for quick-strike, clandestine attacks behind enemy lines, and then extracted by the Night Stalkers. The Nicaraguan Defense Ministry believes that at least six of the contras killed in battle in 1985 were U.S. citizens. EPS and militia columns have clashed with enemy units whose members were light-skinned and spoke English.

Perception Management: The Invasion Scare Scenario

> Military deception is an aspect of strategy and tactics that is often used but seldom acknowledged. . . . deception is the deliberate misrepresentation of reality done to gain a competitive advantage. . . . [the terms lying and deception] are often used interchangeably.
>
> —U.S. Army, *Field Manual FM 33-5: Psychological Operations, Techniques and Procedures*[21]

Millions of U.S. citizens were glued to their televisions on election evening, 6 November 1984, when a "news" item interrupted the voting returns: "intelligence sources" had announced that Soviet freighters believed to be carrying advanced MiG-21 jet fighters were approaching Nicaragua. White House officials warned that the United States would "not tolerate the delivery of such planes" to Nicaragua, and threatened direct action—possibly "surgical strikes"—to prevent their delivery. The "artificial MiGs crisis" had begun.[22]

Since early October, U.S. warships had been patrolling Nicaragua's Atlantic and Pacific coasts, and aircraft from these ships had been carrying out flights along the coasts. On the morning of 7 November, at least three separate military exercises began in Honduras, and another four began during the following week. Thousands of U.S. troops were mobilized in land, sea, and air maneuvers; leave was canceled for army units at Fort Bragg and other bases in the continental United States that housed SOF and Rapid Deployment Forces, and all these, along with the Panama Canal Zone, were placed on alert.

In Washington, the threats mounted as officials reported that "reprisals" against Nicaragua were in the works. Once again, a direct U.S. invasion appeared imminent. On 3 November, one day before national elections were to be held in Nicaragua, people had been jolted out of their beds by a deafening boom. For the first time, the Pentagon had deployed a supersonic SR-71 Blackbird reconnaissance jet over Nicaragua. Flying at an altitude of 12 miles and a speed of over 2,000 miles per hour, the SR-71 is one of the most sophisticated reconnaissance aircraft in the world and has been used only on rare occasions and with extreme discretion. The aircraft flew over virtually all of Nicaragua's strategic military and economic installations. This initial overflight was followed by six additional flights; each created a deafening sonic boom that could be heard throughout the country. Under the circumstances, at each boom people wondered if the invasion had begun.

"The situation facing Nicaragua can be described as the most critical moment that the Revolution has confronted since the triumph in July 1979," President-elect Daniel Ortega told journalists in Managua on 10 November. "We Nicaraguans," he said, "are not going to be caught off guard."

In the midst of incredible tension, the entire nation began a round-the-clock mobilization. On the morning of 12 November, the Defense Ministry issued "Emergency Communiqué Number One," ordering all permanent land, sea, and air combat units into a state of alert. The communiqué also instructed all armored and mechanized units in Managua to take up positions in front of the principal production centers and other strategic targets in the capital. At the same time, the Civil Defense National High Command called on the population to activate the defense system that had been established the previous November. Air raid shelters were reconditioned, firefighting, first aid, and rubble-clearing brigades assembled, and emergency meetings were held in every work center and neighborhood.

On the evening of 12 November, we toured the capital. In *barrio* after *barrio*, residents took turns mounting the tanks and armored vehicles—

or any other available platform—to urge each other on in their preparations. Tens of thousands of MPS members slept in their uniforms during those nights, with their weapons by their beds and their radios left on in expectation of further instructions from the Defense Ministry.

The invasion never took place, of course, and there were no MiGs aboard the Soviet vessels. The crisis had been prefabricated and executed with precision. This was a classic *invasion scare,* a powerful and sophisticated psychological operation.

From the U.S. point of view, it was brilliantly planned and coordinated. At the very moment that the Reagan administration was being reelected to office in a "landslide" victory, alleged intelligence reports about the Soviet planes were leaked to the press—a clear message from President Reagan to Nicaragua: "Welcome to four more years, and I have a popular mandate in my country to back me." Nicaraguans had just participated in the first free and democratic elections ever to be held in their country's history. The elections were a serious blow to U.S. efforts at delegitimizing the Sandinista government, and the artificial MiGs crisis was in part aimed at turning attention away from the fact that the Nicaraguan government had a popular mandate which, statistically, was greater than that of the Reagan administration.

State Department officials have admitted that periodic invasion scares that are aimed at terrorizing the Nicaraguan people are a "cornerstone" of the military maneuvers program.[23] "Let them worry," said Gen. Vernon Walters, a retired career officer who was then roving ambassador to Latin America, when asked by a reporter back in 1982 if Nicaragua would be invaded. "We have found that constructive ambiguity is a very powerful political weapon in American foreign policy."[24] The United States wants the Nicaraguan people to live in a state of permanent tension, fear, and insecurity. By creating a national war psychosis, the Reagan administration hopes that the people will either tire of permanent emergency mobilizations and states of alert and let down their guard, or will begin to doubt their own leaders. In either case, an opening is created for counterrevolutionary ideological manipulation. The image of an all-powerful enemy looming overhead will, it is hoped, increase the population's susceptibility to the military, economic, and political pressure. According to the Reagan administration's vision, the anxiety and deprivation will not be associated with the U.S. warmakers, but with the Sandinista government and, in the long run, with the very existence of a revolutionary alternative itself. In this equation, revolution equals interminable anxiety, and the counterrevolution is therefore a way to end the anxiety.

To a certain extent this has worked. It has, for instance, accelerated the defection of people who, in the absence of such psychological pressure, might have accepted the revolutionary alternative. One early defection was that of Arturo Cruz, once a member of the National Reconstruction Government Junta and later Nicaragua's ambassador to Washington. In early 1982, he resigned his ambassadorial post and went on to become an important leader of the counterrevolution. After his resignation he revealed the forces that had tipped the scale: "The U.S. will never allow a government in Nicaragua or anywhere in Central America or the Caribbean to be economically or politically independent. So it's useless to try, and I'm certainly not going to stick to the losers."[25] The heightened tension is also intended to provoke divisions within the Sandinista leadership over how best to respond to the threat. The United States hopes this will lead to a Grenada-style crisis within the FSLN, which could be decisive at a later stage in the war.

More immediately, provoking invasion scares is an integral element of the strategy of socioeconomic attrition. Heightened levels of military mobilization draw resources out of productive activities and social welfare and into defense, exacerbating economic problems and social discontent. There is no more graphic example of such provocation than the artificial MiGs crisis.

Each harvest season, thousands of Nicaraguan students volunteer to spend their vacation time helping gather coffee in the northern mountains, compensating for the rural labor shortage. On 8 November 1984 twenty thousand students had assembled in Managua's Plaza of the Revolution for a rally celebrating their impending departure for the countryside. Instead, Agriculture Minister Jaime Wheelock announced that "in the face of the danger that is currently hovering over our country . . . the first thing we have to defend is the center of Nicaragua, Managua. . . . We would rather see the coffee fall than see the homeland fall."[26] The students were organized into urban militia units, and although there were other volunteers for the coffee picking, the economy still suffered.

In addition, the constant possibility of a direct U.S. intervention forces Nicaragua to maintain a conventional army, prepared for troop landings and attacks against the cities and major installations. Such an urban-oriented defense system, as we saw in Chapter 5, was not an appropriate response to the irregular warfare conducted by the contras. Thus, the United States was able to mobilize resources outside of Nicaragua's borders in order to advance its proxy forces inside the country. An important aspect of low-intensity warfare is that its effectiveness often depends on the paradoxical perception that what is really being waged is *conventional warfare*.

The U.S. diplomatic strategy is also linked to the invasion-scare, military-maneuver schema. The Nicaraguan mobilization creates the proverbial "cry wolf" dilemma: each time a threat fails to materialize into a real invasion, Nicaragua loses credibility with the international community. The United States wants Nicaragua to lock its diplomatic strategy into fighting a direct intervention, while escalating intervention at every other level.

The massing of U.S. resources is also a way to pressure the Nicaraguans into making concessions. "Every time there is an invasion alarm, [the Sandinistas] make some concessions," said one State Department source.[27] Thus, the artificial MiGs crisis unilaterally imposed a limit on the defensive weapons that Nicaragua could "legitimately" acquire. The United States expects that each invasion scare will further modify international opinion in its favor. This is, as Defense Minister Ortega put it, "the strategy of negotiations on the brink of a direct intervention."[28]

The Sandinistas were initially thrown off balance by the military maneuvers and invasion scares, but gradually they began to understand the connection between the operational fronts of the U.S. war. They were then better able to respond. For instance, rather than simply constructing a conventional army, the Sandinista government reorganized its defense capacity, resurrecting the guerrilla expertise acquired during the long years of struggle against the dictatorship and mobilizing for irregular warfare. Similarly, the Nicaraguans demonstrated that the United States had underestimated both their capacity to carry out political and ideological work among the population, and the ability of the Nicaraguan people to adapt to wartime conditions. The threat of intervention produced fear and anxiety, but over time, as we shall see, the permanent mobilization, combined with political work, created a sense of strength and purpose that helped neutralize the U.S. efforts at psychological attrition.

Radio Propaganda: Low-Cost Ideological Penetration

The [Reagan] administration developed . . . and strengthened the Voice of America (VOA), which had received inadequate backing from the Carter administration. Reagan recognized that the VOA is an important and cost-effective asset in U.S. public

> diplomacy and that the U.S. must use it extensively
> in the war of ideas.
>
> —*Mandate for Leadership II*[29]

In addition to contra incursions, maneuvers, electronic encirclement, and diplomatic aggression, Nicaragua faces an invasion of another type, one that has a potentially more powerful effect on the war for the minds of the people. This is the invasion of the airwaves.

The Committee of Santa Fe's *New Inter-American Policy* noted the need to devote more resources to transmitting pro-U.S. ideology around the globe. The Heritage Foundation's *Mandate for Leadership II* expanded on this theme, making explicit reference to radio broadcasting as the most "cost-effective" means of waging the "war of ideas." In 1981 President Reagan gave increased priority to the United States Information Agency (USIA), the official government propaganda apparatus, and appointed his personal friend, conservative millionaire Charles Z. Wick, as its head. Wick targeted Voice of America (VOA), run by the USIA, for expansion. His plan was to spend some $2 billion over five or six years to improve VOA's transmission capacity, modernizing existing facilities and constructing new relay stations.

Central America was accorded particular importance. In early 1985, the USIA began to transmit on Radio Martí, its anti-Cuban station in southern Florida. In the same year, construction began on an extremely powerful short-wave, AM, and FM relay station, with nine separate transmission installations, in Cabo Rojo, Puerto Rico. With a capacity of half a million watts, the station allows VOA to saturate the entire Caribbean Basin.

Nicaragua, of course, was the primary target of these USIA projects. Here the United States pursued a three-pronged offensive: expanding those VOA installations capable of penetrating Nicaragua; setting up radio stations for the contras; and influencing the broadcasting on local private and public radio stations.

The "mildest" level of radio warfare is made up of "low-key" broadcasts that penetrate Nicaragua with a consistent anti-Sandinista and pro-counterrevolutionary line. Typical of these stations is Radio Valle, which transmits from Choluteca, Honduras, within twenty miles of the Nicaraguan border. Commercials are interspersed with musical programs and news spots that "report" on "totalitarian Nicaragua" and the benevolent activities of the United States in Central America. Advertisements include everything from aspirin that will "alleviate daily tension" to new cars that will "solve your transportation problems" and household goods that will make "chores easier." It is no coincidence that the broadcasts are more easily picked up in the war-torn zones of northern Nicaragua than in nearby Honduras. They are intended to impress those Nicaraguans suffering most intensely from the social and economic effects of the war with the idea that life is better outside.

Similarly, the Costa Rica-based Radio Colombia, which is run by a consortium of private businessmen, broadcasts commentaries aimed as much at the thousands of Nicaraguans whose radios pick up Radio Colombia as they are at Costa Ricans:

> Costa Rica is a free, independent, and sovereign country. Costa Ricans do not know what this means, because they enjoy it day to day. One doesn't fear persecution or unjust jailing. Because *you*, Costa Rican, are a civilian of a free country—Costa Rican democracy is an example for the world.

The armed counterrevolution also has its own stations, the most powerful of which is the FDN's Radio 15 de Septiembre, which was installed by the CIA (with the assistance of the USIA) early in the war. The station is run from the Honduran armed forces' general headquarters in Tegucigalpa, and its programming is produced in the USIA compound across the street from the U.S. embassy. Its 50,000-watt transmissions reach the Nicaraguan population from Managua to the Atlantic Coast with such FDN messages as: "This is the voice of the Christian freedom commandos," "The Sandino-Communists will be destroyed," "When the FDN triumphs, there'll be no shortages," "The Pope is with us in the struggle against the godless Sandinistas," etc. Captured Sandinista soldiers and abducted civilians are often tortured into giving testimony over the radio about "Communist atrocities," or forced to urge their countrymen to defect from the revolution.[30]

In San José, Radio Impacto, owned by the right-wing business community, has been effectively turned over to the ARDE, whose spokespeople determine the content of its broadcasts. Reactionary elements from the opposition inside Nicaragua are regularly "interviewed" live by telephone about the "repression" they are suffering at the hands of the Sandinistas, while several *La Prensa* journalists are also "correspondents" for Radio Impacto. In addition, Pastora has his own radio station, closer to the border, and MISURA has been given Radio Miskut in southeastern Honduras, across the border from the Nicaraguan Miskito communities.

Overshadowing all of these are the VOA's own installations. In addition to those in Honduras, El Salvador, Belize, Puerto Rico, and on the U.S. mainland—all of which are easily picked up in Nicaragua—the USIA has constructed a $3.2 million VOA installation outside the northern Costa Rican town of Quezada.[31] Construction began in September 1984; transmission began in early 1985. The four towers are capable of beaming their message as far north as Honduras. USIA radio programming is carefully designed by the army's psyops specialists and includes hours of anti-Sandinista programming (shipped in from the United States) in both Spanish and Miskitu.

By 1985, at least seventy-six foreign stations were capable of penetrating Nicaragua on AM and FM bands;[32] of these, twenty-six were operating out of Honduras and eighteen out of Costa Rica. Tiny Nicaragua, with no communications technology of its own, is outgunned five to one: Nicaragua has forty-seven radio stations, but thirty-two are in private hands—mostly of the right-wing internal opposition. The other fifteen, previously owned by Somoza and nationalized in 1979, have been organized into the publicly owned People's Radio Corporation (CORADEP). "In a world linked together by instantaneous electronic and radio communications," commented one analyst, "Nicaragua has been forced into a radio war with foreign forces that possess superior transmission resources and are striving to conquer the hearts and minds of the Nicaraguan population."[33] Most Nicaraguans, especially those in the countryside, do not own television sets, while newspapers are generally restricted to the formally educated. But few of the 3 million Nicaraguans do not have radios, which thus become direct transmission belts for the incessant influx of counterrevolutionary ideology. The thousands of Nicaraguans who turn on their radios every day, particularly in the rural areas, are more likely to hear VOA or contra stations than domestic broadcasts. How many U.S. citizens pick up the Voice of Nicaragua when they turn on their radios each morning?

Beginning in 1984, Nicaragua took the offensive in its attempt to recapture its national airwaves. Plans were drawn up to increase the number of CORADEP stations to twenty, while relay stations were erected in isolated mountain zones in order to reach areas that had previously been penetrated only by the contra stations. In addition, CORADEP has diversified away from the strictly Spanish-language programming inherited from the Somoza era, and now includes Miskitu and English-language programs for the Atlantic Coast. It has also started special programs for peasants, giving information on the weather, farming advice, and other issues of special interest to the rural population. These have attracted many peasants, who now have a reason for tuning into their own stations. Yet it is still difficult for the Nicaraguans to overcome the technical advantages gained by superior resources in this crucial battlefield.

Disinformation in the Conflict Environment

The creation and mass reproduction of disinformation is an elaborate and sophisticated process. The "news" reported by the CIA's paid journalists in Costa Rica and Honduras, for example, often serves as the source for State Department "White Papers" on the Nicaraguan "military threat," on its "aid to Salvadoran insurgents," its "internal repression," etc. The USIA then circulates this material around the world, while the U.S. press reproduces it at home.[34]

Penetrating the Costa Rican and Honduran press has been a particularly successful way to manipulate the population (and governments) of these countries. CIA director William Casey has admitted that the agency relies heavily on journalists in Central America as paid intelligence agents, and uses them in tasks ranging from recruiting local collaborators to blocking information unfavorable to the U.S. government.[35] And former FDN leader Edgar Chamorro has testified that while he was working for the CIA in Honduras, he had at his disposal fourteen Honduran journalists paid by the agency. Chamorro has also said that his CIA bosses told him there are many more journalists on the agency's payroll in Costa Rica than the fourteen that were made available to him in Honduras.[36]

During the war of liberation, the Costa Rican press maintained an anti-Somoza stance, in accordance with the position taken by its own government and local mass sentiment. But by 1982, the shift to an anti-Sandinista stance was well under way. By 1983, hardly a day passed without the pages of the major newspapers being full of stories about the "Sandinista threat" to Costa Rican sovereignty and the "consolidation of totalitarianism" inside Nicaragua; entire pages were dedicated to statements by ARDE spokespeople or by reactionary elements inside Nicaragua.

Leading the propaganda campaign in Costa Rica were the country's two principal dailies, *La Nación* and *La República*, both of which are monopolized by far-right sectors of the business community. *La Nación*, for instance, publishes the ARDE's weekly propaganda bulletin in its entirety as a special weekly supplement. According to some sources, the owners and editors of these newspapers meet weekly with U.S. embassy personnel to coordinate information, with the overall aim of creating a nationalistic anti-Nicaraguan atmosphere advantageous to U.S. designs in the region.[37]

A typical tactic is to use the Costa Rican media to tarnish the image of any prominent citizen who opposes those designs. One such target was the venerable José Figueres, long-time leader of the ruling PLN and perhaps the country's most prominent politician. Ironically, Figueres had himself been an employee of the CIA; but in the 1980s he had come out firmly behind the neutrality position, seeing it as necessary for the preservation of internal stability.

In late 1985, *La Nación* and *La República* published a letter they had "obtained," supposedly written by Nicaraguan Ambassador to Costa Rica Leonor Argüello and addressed to Figueres.[38] The letter thanked Figueres for his participation in Nicaraguan propaganda campaigns inside Costa Rica, aimed at improving the Sandinistas' image. The wire services immediately transmitted the story around the world, and the Costa Rican right-wing exploited the letter in their struggle to gain the upper hand against the Costa Rican left and other advocates of neutrality. Virtually ignored was the fact that both Figueres and Ambassador Argüello vehemently denied the letter's authenticity. The Nicaraguan embassy decided to bring charges against both papers. Two months later the Costa Rican Judicial Police (investigative branch) confirmed that the letter had been forged.[39]

Such manipulation has also been used to provoke confusion inside Nicaragua and within the ranks of the FSLN. In August 1984, in the midst of the election campaign, full-page advertisements appeared in newspapers in Costa Rica, Venezuela, and Panama, signed by the "Friends of Tomás Borge." The advertisements read "Not Cruz, not Ortega. Borge for President," and went on to promote the Nicaraguan Interior Minister as "the last true Sandinista revolutionary, the only one that can force through the promises of the 1979 revolution."[40]

Several days earlier, the Nicaraguan government had charged that the CIA was planning such tricks as part of its campaign to split the FSLN leadership—perhaps combined with an assassination that would look like the result of an internal power struggle. For months, in fact, both the United States and reactionary elements inside Nicaragua had tried to conjure up an internal FSLN struggle over who was to be the presidential candidate. According to the propaganda, Daniel Ortega represented the so-called moderate faction and Tomás Borge the "hard line." Of course, such efforts to fabricate faction fights and sow suspicions are the bread-and-butter work of intelligence agencies.

Chemical and Biological Warfare

Biological or bacteriological warfare is the use of infectious microorganisms (living substances) against people, livestock, and plants for the purpose of producing disability or death. International conventions to which the United States is a signatory prohibit both biological and chemical warfare. Nevertheless, as one congressional report stated as early as 1969, "Biological weapons are extremely adequate for covert use. They function through delayed reaction, are difficult to detect and only small amounts are needed; in addition, biological agents are invisible, odorless and without flavor, and since they don't normally produce immediate physiological damage, their early detection would be almost impossible."[41] In short, they are ideal weapons for low-intensity campaigns.

While there is as yet no conclusive proof, there is accumulated evidence that the United States has employed both types of weapons in the war against Nicaragua. For instance, in April 1984 peasants in the far northern town of Yali reported that during a raid the contras warned them to leave the area because they were going to detonate bombs that produce "poisonous fumes."[42] Just days earlier, doctors in a San José hospital had reported that two ARDE members were treated for burns caused by white phosphorus, the use of which is expressly prohibited by international conventions. The ARDE said that the two were injured inside Nicaragua when explosives they were carrying accidentally detonated.[43]

The most suspicious events came a year later. In early 1985, an outbreak of dengue fever hit Nicaragua, and by fall it had reached epidemic proportions. The sickness, which produces intense muscular, bone, and joint pains, high fever, eye irritation, and splitting headaches, was first reported in the southwestern port of San Juan del Sur, where it was treated initially as a local health problem. By September, *la quebradora* (the crusher) had affected half the population of Managua—some 500,000 people. The government declared a "state of epidemiological emergency," and the Health Ministry launched a massive anti-dengue fever campaign.[44] President Ortega, meeting with health workers on 28 September, warned that "we can't rule out the presence· of the enemy's hand."

The dengue virus is transmitted by one of the most common species of tropical mosquito, *Aedes aegypti,* whose rapid reproduction makes it possible to spark epidemics in densely populated areas by introducing a relatively small number of virus-carrying insects. (Each mosquito produces about three thousand eggs during its five- to six-week lifespan.) Deliberate application of the virus is very difficult to prove, however, both technically and juridically. The virus-carrying mosquito can be introduced by overflying aircraft, sea-based vessels, land infiltration, or even by U.S. agents inside the country, using such simple but sophisticated methods as releasing the shutter of a camera which triggers the ejection of the virus.[45]

The 500,000 dengue victims in Managua comprised a veritable "time bomb," since there are two different categories of the virus, benign and hemorrhagle. The first produces intense suffering but is not likely to be fatal; it usually requires a week's rest (there is no vaccination). The second, however, causes internal hemorrhaging, which provokes shock and convulsions that can lead to death. The benign variant can develop into the hemorrhagle variant if not treated in time.

A major human catastrophe was avoided by a timely government effort that had massive participation. The Health Ministry mobilized twenty thousand *brigadistas* in Managua alone to lead neighborhood fumigation and sanitation campaigns (*Aedes aegypti* thrives in stagnant water and in garbage dumps). The government sent out fumigation aircraft and mobile pumps to drain puddles. Hospitals and health clinics set up special round-the-clock "dengue windows." By October, the epidemic was under control and the benign virus had not become hemorrhagle at a generalized level. Ten people had died, however, and the nation's scant resources had been further drained: the fumigation alone cost $6.5 million, and millions of work and school hours were lost.

The outrage in Nicaragua over the dengue epidemic had barely quieted when there were reports of U.S. experiments with chemical warfare in Honduras. In late December, residents of the northwestern municipalities of Villaneuva and San Manuel in northwestern Honduras, claimed that mysterious aircraft had come in at night, flying low and spraying "yellow rain." "When we heard the noise of the planes that night [25 December], we ran out to the patio and a yellow liquid drenched us," recounted one Villaneuva resident. According to local reports, the flights continued, once every six nights, until late January of 1986. By the new year, people were flocking into the health centers, complaining of all kinds of disorders, including skin rashes, fevers, digestive and respiratory difficulties. The health disorders were almost identical to those produced by Agent Orange, the toxic defoliant used extensively by the United States in Vietnam.[46] By February, the "yellow rain" was creating general panic in the northern zones. The National Industrial and Construction Workers Union (STINCAH) charged that the U.S. forces in the country were experimenting with lethal chemicals on Honduran civilians, planning their future use in Nicaragua and other parts of Central America.

The U.S. embassy in Tegucigalpa, however, denied that U.S. forces had anything to do with the "yellow rain," and, incredibly, claimed that "We have never used chemical weapons against Vietnam."[47]

Nation Building and Militarization

The foundation of a strong hemispheric coalition is
built on stable, democratic nations and, therefore,
much of U.S. SOUTHCOM's mission evolves to
the business of nation building. Two aspects of
nation building critical to success are internal defense and internal development. Internal defense
provides the necessary security to protect society
and the economy from insurgent actions in order
that internal development can progress unhindered. They are inseparable and must be approached in a coherent and coordinated fashion.

—Lt. Col. David L. Caldon,
USMC, U.S. Southern Command[48]

In addition to its immediate aims in the war against Nicaragua, the
United States seeks to shape the internal political system of each
country in the conflict environment. The United State conceives of this
activity as *nation building:* the process of politically and ideologically
legitimizing a counterrevolutionary project in the eyes of the country's
population and the world community, and consolidating those national
institutions which form the girders of the project. The long-term
objective of nation building is to create an externally linked economy
that will be part of a project of regional capitalist development and that
will further integrate the Caribbean Basin into the process of U.S.
capital accumulation.

Nation building involves two interrelated processes. The dominant
one is what the Pentagon calls "internal defense." Here the United
States penetrates the military and security apparatus of the target
country, reorganizing it and inserting it into every aspect of national
life. This apparatus is also articulated with, and subordinated to, its
U.S. military counterpart, which is installed in the conflict environment. The second aspect of naton building is "internal development"—
economic aid, civic action, development programs—whose immediate
goal is to win over the "hearts and minds" of the population. The
relation between internal defense and internal development is complex
and symbiotic: nation building is effected through the coordinated
efforts of U.S. military, paramilitary, and civilian institutions, including
the Pentagon and the CIA, the AID, the USIA, the Peace Corps,
congressional foreign aid programs, and a host of right-wing private
organizations.

The vehicle used to carry out the nation-building project in Central America is *militarization,* which ties internal defense to internal development. One SOUTHCOM official has described this fusion as "security development."[49] Militarizaton has become an important aspect of nation building in Central America, because "counterrevolution building" simultaneously requires a major effort at "revolution destroying," given the advanced stage of development of revolutionary forces.

Militarization should not be confused with *militarism.* The latter refers to the traditional build-up of local military forces, and the replacement of a country's civilian groups and institutions by its armed forces, which then assume control of the state apparatus. Traditional Latin American militarism, most recently expressed in the military dictatorships and strongman regimes that constituted the dominant political order in the Southern Cone and Central America during the 1970s, was a response to the U.S. strategy that preceded LIW, in which the United States relied on brute military dictatorships to repress revolutionary forces and safeguard imperial interests. As one Costa Rican analyst has put it:

> Militarism in Central America is a specific type of political system, in which the armed security forces occupy the preeminent role in the political and economic functions of the state, and in which the authoritarian methods of social control over the society's political relations predominate. In contrast, militarization is a countertendency to the organic crisis of political and economic relations that imperialism faces in the region, whose ideological underpinning is the new Northamerican counterinsurgency doctrine, and its principal political force is U.S. [activity] in the region. The militarization of social life is induced by a subject "external" to the national society.[50]

It is important to distinguish carefully between four concepts: nation building, militarization, internal defense, and internal development. Internal defense and internal development are effected *through* militarization, which is the process whereby the U.S. seeks to engage in nation building. Through militarization, the military organs of the society concerned (which are connected with and subordinated to U.S. military and civilian institutions) actually penetrate deeper into every aspect of social, economic, and political life.

The militarization process can be seen most clearly in El Salvador and Guatemala. In Guatemala, with the resettlement schemes and civil defense patrols, the military has become the paramount authority throughout the country: the military buys up peasant crops, brings consumer goods to the peasantry, integrates civilians into the military patrols, and generally exercises total control at the grassroots level. At the same time, there is a "civilian government" in power and the military tries its hardest to promote social and economic development among the peasants.

Militarization is not a prerequisite of nation building. In Central America, however, the presence of an advanced armed revolutionary challenge requires the militarization process, since internal development cannot be effected without destroying the revolutionary forces. Combining the creation and stabilization of political, social, and economic institutions with a parallel effort to crush the revolutionary challenge is achieved through militarization.

The process of militarization in Central America is expressed through an *offensive against the regional rearguards* of the revolutionary forces, and the construction and consolidation of the *regional rearguards* of the counterrevolutionary forces. (In this context, rearguards must be conceived as socioeconomic, political and military). In both El Salvador and Guatemala, militarization has been the process through which the United States seeks to *destroy the rearguards* of the FMLN and the URNG. In Honduras and Costa Rica, on the other hand, the aim is to transform the civilian-military institutions in order to *construct and deepen* the counterrevolution's own rearguard. In Honduras, for example, the civic action programs that accompany every maneuver are part of the effort to build a human rearguard for the counterrevolution. During the Big Pine II maneuvers, for instance, such projects included examining over 47,000 medical patients and 7,000 dental patients, administering over 200,000 immunizations, donating 30,000 pounds of food and 101 metric tons of medicine and clothing, repairing and constructing schools and repairing Red Cross ambulances.[51] Besides gaining support for the government, these "humanitarian" gestures were meant to place the U.S. penetration of Honduras in a benevolent light. Photographs of Marines vaccinating Honduran children are printed in Honduran newspapers and flashed around the world.

A more comprehensive concept of "civic action" has been developed by the Pentagon and called "humanitarian assistance," or the application of human and material resources to projects whose explicit purpose is to win hearts and minds. "Humanitarian assistance [is] a fundamental Department of Defense mission in low intensity warfare," Gen. Gorman said in 1984. It is "an integral part of military operations."[52]

It is in this context that we must look at the June 1985 congressional vote for $27 million in "humanitarian aid" to the contras. While this was seen by some as a respectable alternative to direct military aid, this view both ignores the military foundation of "humanitarian assistance" and obscures the central role of nonmilitary activities in a war whose very essence is political. But if some liberals fell for the benevolent pretenses, the DOD was quite clear about its aims: "War is about how people live, not about how they die; therefore, strange as it might sound, an ounce of pesticide may well be worth a 500-pound bomb."[53]

Constructing the human rearguard involves more, however, than massive civic action programs. It involves such diverse U.S. agencies as the AID and the Peace Corps, and U.S. penetration of such key institutions as the education system and the mass media. "Whoever controls the educational system determines the past . . . as well as the future. . . . We must provide the ideal behind the instrument of foreign policy through educational programs designed to win the minds of mankind," states the Committee of Santa Fe's *New Inter-American Policy* document.[54] The Kissinger Commission recommended a "dramatic expansion" of scholarship programs for Central Americans who want to study in the United States, as well as direct assistance in developing the region's educational systems. By 1985, the commission's recommendations were being implemented in Honduras, and about thirty prominent teachers from high schools around the country were invited to the United States for an eighteen-month course; their posts were filled by Peace Corps "volunteers."[55]

Winning hearts and minds is the preferred method of building a human rearguard, but outright repression is also important. One frequently used method for turning the Honduran population against the Sandinistas and toward the contras is orchestrating attacks by Honduran soldiers disguised as EPS troops. Peasants in the border region have reported that Honduran soldiers dressed in EPS uniforms enter their villages demanding provisions. Later, the same soldiers return, dressed in Honduran army attire, singling out those among the peasants who most readily handed over goods or showed sympathy for the Sandinistas. These peasants are then arrested, accused of collaborating with a foreign force, interrogated and jailed for long periods, or killed.[56] In this way the human rearguard is "cleansed" of those who are considered the most difficult to influence through noncoercive means.

The Struggle over Neutrality: The Case of Costa Rica

The militarization process in Honduras presented few major difficulties for the United States, but the task in Costa Rica has been more difficult because popular support for neutrality and entrenched social-democratic political traditions present serious obstacles to U.S. control.[57] By 1985, however, the United States, particularly by penetrating the Ministry of Security, had managed to construct a substantial Costa Rican military-security apparatus linked to the U.S. military and the Costa Rican state.

Through the militarization process, Costa Rica's relative internal equilibrium has been altered, and internal struggles and contradictions have surfaced that the United States has as yet (by 1986) been unable to resolve. In effect, the positions of social and political forces in the country have been defined on the basis of attitudes toward militarization.[58] The United States has been able to exploit these differences in order to reconfigure Costa Rican politics and create a more stable internal ally. This job was made easier by the strong pro-U.S., anticommunist ideology that pervades the country, and by a neutrality resting on an ambiguous mass sentiment toward "staying clear" of the war situation in the rest of the isthmus rather than on anti-imperialist beliefs. This left Washington ample opportunity for political manipulation.

Relying heavily on the Costa Rican media, the United States first attempted to whip up an anti-Sandinista sentiment. It was a crude form of perception management, portraying the image of the Sandinistas as a "totalitarian, militarist dictatorship." Nevertheless, the U.S. psychological warfare hawks used it to convert a gut antimilitary feeling into a gut anti-Sandinista feeling. This would then be transformed into support for militarization and for the anti-Sandinista campaign.

This strategy first began in 1982 and 1983, and proved difficult to realize. In that period, the neutrality forces maintained the initiative.

The issue seemed cut and dried—since the U.S. plan for the region was leading toward direct intervention, aligning with the United States would mean dragging Costa Rica into a massive military conflict. The combination of anti-Sandinismo and antimilitarization became a powerful mass-based movement in support of Costa Rican neutrality. This movement not only involved the popular classes, but also important sectors of the ruling PLN and other elite groups. A public outcry followed Jeane Kirkpatrick's suggestion, during a February 1982 trip to San José, that an army be reinstituted: a poll taken after the visit found that 83 percent of Costa Ricans opposed such a move.[59]

The struggle first came to a head in November 1983, soon after the Grenada invasion. The neutrality forces exerted sufficient pressure to secure the resignation of Foreign Minister Fernando Volio, a key promoter of the U.S. government's designs on the country.[60] Ambassador Winsor publicly bemoaned the resignation as "a loss to the West, since [Volio] was closely identified with the U.S. line."[61]

Three days later, under heavy popular pressure, President Monge proclaimed the country's "active, permanent, and unarmed neutrality." The Neutrality Statue committed Costa Rica to "abstaining from all hostilities and all support for the parties in conflict, to impeding the transport of troops, munitions, or supply columns through our territory," and "to [making] every effort possible to impede Costa Rican territory from being used as an operating base for parties involved in the war."

If put into practice, the statute would have meant an end to the contra rearguard in Costa Rica. The United States wasted no time in launching a counterattack. Over the next few months, it moved to bolster pro-U.S. elements in Costa Rica, conspired against the pro-neutrality forces, and forced a redefinition of "neutrality" which made it meaningless in practice. Resorting again to economic blackmail, the Reagan administration suspended—just days after the proclamation of neutrality—previously contracted loans with AID and the U.S.-controlled IMF.[62] To demonstrate that, regardless of the Neutrality Statute, the Nicaraguan counterrevolution would proceed, the United States also ordered ARDE forces to launch an attack against Nicaragua from Costa Rican territory. Before daybreak on 18 November, literally hours after Monge had announced the statute, three hundred Costa Rican-based contras laid siege to the southern Nicaraguan town of Cardenas while another one thousand massed on the Costa Rican side of the border at Peñas Blancas.

Meanwhile, the U.S. Embassy in San José set about gathering the scattered pro-U.S. forces together to make a stable and reliable ally. Most dependable was the right-wing business community, which had come out forcefully against neutrality. With this pole of support established, the United States sought to broaden its base by bringing in factions and groups inside the political parties that would go along with the U.S. project. These included the right wing of the PLN and much of the Social Christian Unity party (PUSC—the Christian Democrats), the principal opposition among the elite. It also continued its economic blackmail and the contra provocations. Throughout the first half of 1984, as part of the "General Offensive" launched in February, contra activity escalated. In April, a State Department memorandum asserted that tensions between Costa Rica and Nicaragua "provide us with the possibility of helping to tilt the political balance [in Costa Rica] in our favor."[63]

The United States conspired even further with its local allies in an attempt to remove pro-neutrality officials who occupied key government positions.[64] At the top of the list was Edmundo Solano, the progressive minister of public security, who had continuously kept the Civil Guard, which his ministry controlled, out of the militarization process. On more than one occasion, the Civil Guard had dismantled ARDE camps and arrested roving contras. The newspapers set the stage for the U.S. move by splashing unsubstantiated charges of corruption in Solano's ministry across their pages, and by depicting him as a "Sandinista crony."

Throughout the first six months of 1984, the right was on the offensive. The second showdown erupted in mid-July, when the "rightist amalgamation"—as the pro-U.S. grouping was called—gave the Monge administration thirty days in which to meet a series of demands, threatening a nationwide managerial strike if it did not. The demands included removing Solano and his supporters from the government, cracking down on "Communist elements" (the rightists' label for pro-neutrality popular forces), supporting "foreign political groups" (the euphemism for the contras), and accepting military assistance from "friendly countries" in order to "improve our national security and defense system." Within days, rumors of a right-wing coup were rampant, probably a deliberate part of the agitation. Right-wing paramilitary groups threatened to take action in support of the managerial strike. The mass media encouraged an atmosphere of political instability and then attributed it to the "weakness of the current government" and its "softness on the Nicaraguan Communists."[65]

In the midst of this turmoil, the U.S. battleship USS *Iowa*, with 1,400 Marines aboard, illegally entered Costa Rican waters and fired its guns into the ocean, in an exhibition described by Ambassador Winsor as a demonstration of U.S. support for Costa Rica's "defense and independence."[66]

As tensions mounted, Monge caved in. In a tactical move, he requested the resignation of most of his cabinet, and Solano was dismissed, along with Minister of the Presidency Fernando Berrocal, Solano's closest ally. The U.S. ambassador then moved quickly, meeting with key government representatives, the business community, and the media. Benjamín Piza, a West Point graduate and a founder of the Movement for a Free Costa Rica (MCRL), a neo-fascist organization formed by Nazi sympathizers in the 1940s, was named minister of public security. With this ploy, the United States and its internal allies had captured the most important institution for the militarization process.

This was a turning point in the "covert operation" against neutrality. Piza made total penetration of the ministry—and, therefore, of the Civil Guard—possible. From the moment he took office on 1 September, the Civil Guard stopped interfering in contra activity.[67]

The original dichotomy between neutrality and counterrevolution was clearly giving way to a more diversified stance. Ever since his trip to Washington in June 1982, Monge had clearly favored the right-wing position, although he often seemed to straddle the fence between the two sides, and he was now redefining neutrality in practice while maintaining it as a principle in word. This came to be known as the "Monge Doctrine": relative military neutrality, together with active alignment with the United States on the political, diplomatic, and ideological fronts. This was a far cry from the Costa Rican tradition of popular support for neutrality, which called for national independence and nonpartisanship in the Central American conflict.

During this period, U.S. strategy toward Central America had moved from direct interventionism to low-intensity warfare. But, while in the first period any type of Costa Rican neutrality was unacceptable to the United States, in the second period Monge's redefined version of neutrality was not only acceptable but could be used further to weaken popular support for neutrality.

Having gained control of both the key ministries in San José and strategic territory in the northern zone, the United States was able to proceed with militarization *despite* internal opposition and still have the government "officially" serve its interests in the nonmilitary theaters of the war.

New factors, however, were constantly cropping up that revitalized the neutrality forces: the United States had to remain vigilant. On several occasions it repeated the tactic of fabricating border incidents between Costa Rica and Nicaragua in order to "neutralize" neutrality. These incidents not only kept the neutrality forces on the defensive, but also facilitated the militarization process.

The Militarization of Costa Rica

The large-scale development of military, paramilitary, and security units in Costa Rica since 1981 has been the most visible aspect of the political, ideological, and economic changes brought about by militarization and nation building. Costa Rica's police structures had consisted of the Civil Guard and the Rural Guard, whose combined membership was less than eight thousand. The Civil Guard, attached to the Ministry of Public Security, was founded during the 1948 civil war as the country's principal national police force, while the Rural Guard was created in 1969. The state's intelligence and security organs, led by the Judicial Police, barely totaled some five to six hundred staff members.

The United States began the militarization process with a low-key program to create an officer corps within the Civil Guard which could serve as the nucleus for the military apparatus. In 1981 the United States sent a few high-ranking Costa Rican officers to the Panama Canal Zone and the U.S. mainland for basic training courses and indoctrination into U.S. military tactics and strategy. The trickle soon became a stream and then a flood. Beginning in 1983, U.S. mobile training teams periodically arrived in Costa Rica to teach communications techniques, the handling of light artillery, methods of patrolling, and counterinsurgency tactics. In early 1985, some four hundred Civil Guardsmen were sent to the Regional Military Training Center (RMTC), the U.S. training base in the northern Honduran port city of Puerto Castilla.

Between 1982 and 1984, Civil Guard and Rural Guard membership almost doubled to nearly fifteen thousand, and special units were set up within the two organizations, including mobile commandos and the crack Chorotega company (permanently stationed along the northern border). The Judicial Police was expanded, professionalized, and converted into a sophisticated internal intelligence agency.

At the same time, paramilitary forces linked to the state mushroomed, led by the Organización Para las Emergencias Nacionales (OPEN), which was created by presidential decree in 1982. Its stated purpose is to reinforce the Civil Guard, but its ten to fifteen thousand members, who also hold civilian jobs, provide links—through family, neighborhood, and work centers—to the population at large, playing the ideological role of reinforcing pro-U.S. sentiment. Only people with "proven democratic ideology" are permitted to join.[68] In March 1985, the OPEN was converted, by decree, into the official "reserve" for the permanent military bodies. Other paramilitary groups, linked to neofascist groups financed by the right-wing business community, engage in mafia-style dealings, ranging from drug trafficking to running an illegal arms market. Led by the military wing of the MCRL, these groups worked hand in hand with the counterrevolution in the field and served as intermediaries between the contras and the "official" state security organs.

By 1985, Costa Rica had some forty thousand nationals under arms. When the ARDE and FDN contras and U.S. military and intelligence advisers are added in, this is a formidable presence for a country supposedly "at peace" and without an army.

The United States has also set about arming the Costa Rican forces with modern military hardware. The first shipments, in 1981 and 1982, were described as "non-lethal" military assistance, but nevertheless caused a local scandal. Yet within a few years, such shipments had become routine, and included thousands of M-16 rifles, 50-caliber machine guns, 81 mm. mortars, 90 mm. recoilless rifles, M-60 machine guns, helicopters, and observation and transport aircraft, as well as ground and river transport vehicles. U.S. "security assistance" jumped from $358,000 in 1981 to over $15 million for the first quarter of 1985.[69]

All this was dwarfed by the plans for Costa Rica's northern border zone, which was to become a strategic rearguard for the Nicaraguan counterrevolution. Installing the contras in that region was achieved through a semi-secret "Northern Zone Infrastructure Development" project, financed by the United States and carried out under the supervision of U.S. military engineers.[70] Its objectives were to build a physical infrastructure—from roads to communications networks to airstrips—for ARDE and to settle the sparsely populated northern zone with landless peasants from other regions. Through development projects, civic action, and indoctrination, this population was to constitute a human rearguard for the counterrevolution and a secure social base for nation building. The project's culmination was the installation of the El Murciélago U.S. military base in May 1985. Once completed, the northern zone became a slice of denationalized territory, incorporated into the counterrevolutionary rearguard and under the effective control of the United States.

Ironically, El Murciélago was built just a few miles from the Nicaraguan border on a large property that had once belonged to Anastasio Somoza.[71] Almost overnight, working in secret, teams of U.S. Army engineers leveled the ground, erected electrically charged barbed-wire fences around the complex, and set up signposts: "Zone Off Limits to Civilian Population." Twenty buildings were constructed for the training squads, while two mansions used by Somoza for wild weekend orgies were turned into command headquarters for the new base. Soon the locals were calling it Costa Rica's EEBI, a sardonic reference to the Somoza National Guard training school, which had been established by the United States in the 1970s.

The arrival of SOF training squads was again protested. The May inauguration of El Murciélago as the headquarters for the SOF contingent signaled the "death of unarmed neutrality," as an editorial in the

San José weekly *Tico Times* put it. The government tried to quell the protests by stressing that there were "only" forty Green Berets at El Murciélago, but—as with the issue of the fifty-five U.S. advisers in El Salvador—numbers were in any case not important: all that the United States needed was a solid core of SOF specialists who could begin the "multiplier force" effect.

The political attention that was focused on the northern zone led the authorities in San José to crack down on armed "foreigners." In an attempt to save face, on 25 April five mercenaries—two Britons, two Americans, and one Frenchman—who were operating with the contras out of John Hull's farms were arrested and locked up in San José's Reforma Prison. They were told that this was a temporary measure to reduce public criticism and that they would be released shortly. In early June, the five, still incarcerated, were told that they would be tried for "violating the country's neutrality." Angry at having been made scapegoats, they decided to tell their story to the press.[72] Robert Thompson and Steve Carr, the two U.S. citizens, reported that they had left Ft. Lauderdale, Florida, along with seven U.S. Air Force members, in a U.S. Army cargo plane loaded with military equipment. The equipment was unloaded at El Salvador's Ilopango military base, to be airlifted to northern Costa Rica. The two mercenaries continued on to San José.

The other three told how they had been recruited in Europe through a network set up by CIA agents and Pentagon officials. John Hull and Bruce Jones came to Miami to escort them to Costa Rica, where they were rushed through customs, weapons and all, and brought to the northern zone in a Civil Guard vehicle.

"This neutrality that we supposedly violated never existed," a furious Carr told reporters from prison. The five told of how the Civil Guard regularly supplied them with "precise information, including maps and diagrams of the [Nicaraguan border] guard posts, the routes taken by the Nicaraguan patrols and the routes that we should take [into Nicaragua] to avoid them and achieve the effect of surprise." They even reported seeing Green Berets in civilian clothes training contras and checking bridges on Hull's farms in order "to determine their weight load" and decide what vehicles could cross.

By 1985, the northern area had been so transformed that it was no longer recognizable to those who had known it even four years earlier. A modern eighty-mile highway—sardonically described as a "three-lane freeway to nowhere"—ran the length of the border strip. "A traveler on the road is struck not only at how it dwarfs the surrounding countryside," said one visitor, "but how it links critical support points for the contra war against the Sandinistas."[73] The highway is strong enough to support heavy land-based vehicles and wide enough to be used as a landing strip. Some forty prefabricated barracks, built in the period 1982–83 for the Rural Guard and the Civil Guard, have been upgraded into well-equipped military bases. The United States has also installed high-technology communications and surveillance equipment, which serve the same function as the "electronic fence" in Honduras.

The civic action component has been integrated into the militarization process. U.S. and local forces have evacuated peasants from areas surrounding the most sensitive installations and have created new settlements in areas set aside for civilian development. AID has bought and distributed thousands of parcels of land to the peasants and has provided loans and other assistance to the larger ranchers and farmers. Hundreds of other families have found employment opportunities in construction and development projects. According to one report, "Those jobs, along with other monies AID is pouring into the area, have reinforced political loyalties here—most locals are strongly pro-United States and anti-Sandinista."[74]

An Announced Ambush

By mid-1985, however, the national debate inside Costa Rica was once again turning in favor of neutrality. This sentiment became particularly widespread following the arrival of the Green Berets, and increased on 25 May, when student groups, trade unions, factions of the ruling PLN, and others convened the Patriotic Forum for the Peace and Sovereignty of Costa Rica, which was designed to provide an institutional channel through which to resist militarization.

The United States decided this was the right time to provoke another border incident. On 30 May a Civil Guard patrol was ambushed on the Costa Rican side of the border; two guardsmen died and another nine were wounded. Within hours, and with no substantiation, the Costa Rican government accused the EPS of carrying out the attack. Monge ordered yet another chill in diplomatic relations, while Foreign Minister José Gutierrez went so far as to warn that Costa Rica was ready to invoke the Rio Treaty and invite U.S. forces to "protect" Costa Rican "sovereignty." The Costa Rican press unleashed the most vociferous attack on the Sandinistas to date, exhorting the population to take up arms and "march to the border." Right-wing business organizations demanded that diplomatic relations with Managua be cut immediately and a "state of national defense" declared.[75] The Costa Rican Security Council called an emergency meeting, which was presided over by Vicepresident Armando Arauz and the U.S. ambassador to Costa Rica.[76]

The campaign was coordinated with the mobilization of the Costa Rican fascist right, which decided that this was a good time to test its strength within the government. On 8 June Nicaraguan diplomats warned Costa Rica that the MCRL was planning to attack the Nicaraguan embassy in San José. The government ignored the warning, and members of the MCRL and the ARDE then launched the attack, burning the Nicaraguan flag and inflicting serious damage on the building. Despite repeated calls by embassy personnel who were trapped inside to the Civil Guard headquarters just 300 meters away, no help arrived until an hour after the assault began.

Evidence had meanwhile surfaced that confirmed the Sandinista position that the ambush of the Civil Guard patrol had been carried out by ARDE members, and that the Costa Rican government, with the U.S. ambassador's help, had orchestrated the entire incident.[77] Nicaragua had insisted that a joint border commission, which had been set up the year before, be convened in order to ease tensions, and had proposed a demilitarized border zone; Monge rejected both suggestions, and instead asked for OAS intervention. To his fury, the OAS sent the case to the Contadora Group for investigation. One month later, the group reported that there was no conclusive evidence that the EPS had carried out the attack.

In the interim, however, the growing demand for neutrality had been stifled. The national war hysteria had not only strengthened the hand of the pro-U.S. forces, but it had provided a smokescreen behind which El Murciélago could be established and operations begun. More importantly, the Ministry of Security could decree that the Civil Guard be the first permanent force in the Costa Rican "army"—in one fell swoop undermining the thirty-six-year-old constitutional ban on a standing army.

The popular neutrality forces, while they could no longer forestall militarization, nevertheless continued to exist, as was clear in the February 1986 presidential election. The country's relationship to Nicaragua and the regional war was the dominant issue throughout the campaign. Of the two candidates—Oscar Arias for the PLN and Rafael Calderón Fournier for the Christian Democratic opposition—the latter was favored by the United States. Although Arias was even more anti-Sandinista than Monge, he nevertheless campaigned on a Monge-type neutrality platform, while Calderón called for total involvement in the counterrevolution. The race was close, reflecting the stalemate between the two sides, until Calderón publicly declared he would be prepared to go to war with Nicaragua if Costa Rica were "threatened." From that point on, Arias was the favorite.

The problem of opposition to U.S. plans for the region continues. In February 1986, 187 more U.S. military engineers arrived. Their mission, ironically called "Operation Peace Bridge," was to link the modern roads in the north to a major highway running straight down to the Panama Canal Zone. This would facilitate the rapid movement of men and equipment from SOUTHCOM to the Nicaraguan border. On the day they arrived, officials from the outgoing Monge and incoming Arias administrations were meeting with their Nicaraguan counterparts to discuss ways to improve bilateral relations. Yet by this point the militarization process had gone so far that it was doubtful it could be controlled by the Costa Rican state.

Militarization in Nicaragua?

> Costa Rica, Honduras and El Salvador are being threatened by a Soviet-bloc and Cuban-supported Sandinista army and security force in Nicaragua. . . . The infrastructure for a formidable air force is developing rapidly in Nicaragua . . . [the] Marxist-leaning state has received more firepower by far than all her neighbors in the region combined.
>
> —Reagan administration "Background Paper"
> on the "Nicaraguan military buildup"[78]

The militarization of Central America is expected to continue into the 1990s, yet the United States continues to charge that there is a "military buildup" in Nicaragua. The U.S. public is periodically treated to televised White House press conferences on the topic, full of the latest "intelligence findings," aerial photographs, and maps. "Cuban-style" bunkers, "Soviet-style" obstacle courses, and "Czechoslovakian-style" military tents all represent a "serious threat to Central America" and the "national security of the United States."[79] In addition to providing a public-relations smokescreen behind which to continue the U.S. build-up, this barrage hides the real issue: Nicaragua is the only country in the region being subjected to an attack by a major foreign power, and its acquisition of weapons and defense systems is more than justifiable. The Sandinista government would in fact be betraying its own people if it failed to provide them with the means to defend themselves against such foreign aggression. The defense build-up has been forced upon Nicaragua by the United States, and then portrayed as an offensive build-up to be used against its neighbors. And even given that it is necessary, it is still untrue that Nicaragua's build-up outstrips that of its neighbors, and the real facts and figures demonstrate the eminently defensive character of Managua's armaments. In FY 1980 the United States supplied $10 million in military assistance to El Salvador, Honduras, Guatemala, and Costa Rica. By FY 1986, this figure had skyrocketed to $233.8 million. The total for the entire period surpasses $1 billion.[80] Even the State Department's own claim that "Soviet-bloc" military assistance to Nicaragua for the period 1980–84 totaled $350 million belies the U.S. assertion that Nicaragua has received more firepower than all its neighbors in the region combined.

Similarly, the facts on military aircraft in Central America put El Salvador, not Nicaragua, in first place with 163 military aircraft—followed by Honduras with 115, Guatemala with 102, and finally Nicaragua, with no more than 31. Costa Rica had 14 before new aircraft arrived in early 1985.[81] More importantly, the *composition* of the region's air forces tells more about their capacity than the actual number of aircraft. Nicaragua does not possess a single advanced fighter-bomber or attack plane—that is, an aircraft capable of launching offensive operations against its neighbors—while Honduras had at least 23 such planes. Similarly, the United States has gone to great lengths to project the FAS's MI-24 Soviet helicopters as a threat to the region. And indeed, these *are* offensive weapons, but they have been used against the contras *inside* Nicaraguan territory; they are in any case not capable of long-range operations. Both Honduras and El Salvador have comparable helicopter gunship fleets.

In early 1985, the United States whipped up a new scandal over the construction of the Punta Huete airfield just north of Managua. But the airfield had been under construction since 1977, when it was begun by Somoza in order to provide the Nicaraguan air force with a separate military airfield. The DOD claims that "when Punta Huete becomes operational, it will be able to accommodate any aircraft of the Soviet-bloc inventory."[82] Yet the Palmerola airfield in Honduras is *already* operational, is being used to wage war against Nicaragua, and is capable of accommodating any aircraft of the U.S.-bloc inventory.

The only numerical advantage Nicaragua enjoys over its neighbors is in the area of tanks and armored vehicles, which the Sandinistas have acquired as part of preparations to confront a direct U.S. intervention. But Central America's mountainous terrain, especially the steep and jagged ranges on the northern borders, makes it impossible to use these vehicles as an offensive force outside the country. As one U.S. military expert put it, "This is not tank country. The Honduran Air Force . . . would have a field day against the slow-moving main column of Sandinista tanks."[83]

Ironically, all of the Reagan administration's charges of "Nicaraguan militarization" have been rebutted in reports compiled by former U.S. military personnel.[84] As one such analyst concluded: "In terms of capital expenditures, the Soviet-bloc stake in Nicaragua for the construction of military infrastructure and in military assistance is small in comparison to U.S. investment for the same purposes in El Salvador and Honduras."[85] And one internal DOD report concluded that "the general increase [in Nicaragua's armaments] is in its majority oriented toward defense, and [Managua] has dedicated its efforts to improving its capacity to respond to an [internal] insurrection."[86] Nevertheless, the U.S. fury over Nicaragua's "build-up" is to a certain extent sincere: the acquisition of defense systems is allowing the revolution to defeat the armed contras, and preparing it to resist other forms of U.S. military aggression, including a direct invasion.

But numerical and tactical comparisons are not the real point. As noted earlier, a key aim of the U.S. strategy is to create, and then exploit, the perception of an "offensive militarization" in order to force the Nicaraguans into unilateral disarmament, thus weakening their ability to defend themselves. The United States has promised "surgical strikes" if MiGs are brought into Nicaragua, laying down a tacit "limit" to the weaponry Nicaragua can acquire. Yet when the Pentagon decided, in late 1985, to supply the Hondurans with U.S.-made F-5 combat jets—comparable to the Soviet MiGs that never arrived—Managua did not threaten "retaliation" against either Honduras or the United States.

An Invasion?

Everything that we're doing [in Central America] we'd also be doing if the aim were to [invade] and overthrow the Nicaraguan government.

—Reagan administration official[87]

Is an invasion of Nicaragua possible, or is the threat of one a calculated bluff on the part of the United States? What we have argued in this chapter might be interpreted as ruling out the possibility of an invasion. On the contrary, a direct invasion could take place, and what concerns us here is the nature and character of such an event, its contextualization and its conceptualization. An invasion must be reexamined in the context of low-intensity warfare, and once this is done, the seeming contradiction disappears between the argument that the logic of the U.S. war against Nicaragua runs contrary to the invasionist strategy on the one hand, and the assertion that an invasion may take place, on the other.

It is first necessary to distinguish between an *event* and a *strategy*—that is, to distinguish between means and ends. The objective of the war against Nicaragua is to separate the Nicaraguan people from the revolutionary project and the leadership, and to win them over to the U.S. counterrevolution. The tactics are varied, but the strategy is the same. In the classic invasionist interpretation, invasion is the strategy, and the tactics are to create the conditions for an invasion. In the framework of low-intensity warfare, however, the invasion is reduced to being a *tactical instrument*, a means to achieve the objective. Thus, if the United States believes that a direct invasion *can* achieve the objective of destroying the revolution and stabilizing the counterrevolutionary alternative, such an invasion may indeed take place. The scenarios are many. Perhaps the National Security Council will reach the conclusion—whether or not it corresponds to reality—that mass discontent bred by the war of attrition is sufficient to provide a social base for a counterrevolutionary project put in place through an invasion. In this scenario, however, the purpose of the invasion is *not* to defeat the revolution. If a majority of Nicaraguans support the counterrevolutionary project, then the revolution will already have been defeated. The invasion will merely consolidate the victory.

In this framework the destruction of the Sandinista revolution and the overthrow of the Nicaraguan government are not synonomous. A revolution cannot be reduced to a government whose functionaries are revolutionaries. The purpose of an invasion in low-intensity warfare against Nicaragua would serve the tactical objective of removing the Sandinista government on the heels of an already-attained strategic objective of destroying the revolution.

In Grenada, the revolution was defeated before the U.S. invaders ever set foot on the island. The extent to which U.S. pressure on that Caribbean nation fomented divisions within the leadership is a question that may never be answered. Nevertheless, the invasion itself merely transferred state power to the counterrevolutionaries. The Grenadan people—the raw material of the revolution—were already divorced from the highest institutional expression of the revolution, the government. And, of course, if the United States believed that its troops were going to face massive and prolonged resistance, Grenada might never have been invaded.

In this context, all the activities in the conflict environment—particularly the massive infrastructure built up through the maneuvers program—serve the dual purpose of advancing the strategic objective of destroying the Sandinista revolution and of laying the groundwork for possible direct action, including an invasion. In this sense, as contradictory as it might seem, the maneuvers in Honduras *are* "pre-invasions"—dry runs for an invasion that remains a live *tactical* option. Similarly, low-intensity warfare may be abandoned as a strategy at some point down the line because of political shifts in Washington, world events which redefine global objectives, or whatever. In the meantime, the Nicaraguan people are preparing to resist a direct U.S. invasion, not only because this is a real possibility, but also because such preparations simultaneously further the defeat of the counterrevolution and consolidate the revolution.

7
The Internal Front: 1979–1984

The Sandinista Revolution is a revolution betrayed, a revolution that has left in its wake a trail of broken promises, broken hearts and broken dreams. Tragically, there is less personal freedom, far more repression in Nicaragua today than there was five years ago. [The Nicaraguan people] are trapped in a totalitarian dungeon.

—President Ronald Reagan, 19 July 1984

We must see this war in its real context, in its entirety. It spans all realms, from the guns which assassinate and the slander and dirty lies which poison, to the war which is fought out in the minds of men. It is *this* aspect of the war which worries us most.

—Tomás Borge, 5 August 1985[1]

On the morning of 20 June 1984, a Catholic priest named Amado Peña left his parish in a suburban neighborhood of Managua, briefcase in hand. A few blocks down the palm-lined street, a young man in blue jeans intercepted the priest, identified himself as a State Security agent, and asked Peña to open his briefcase. Visibly shaken, Peña responded: "I'm just carrying bibles and rosaries." The agent then opened the briefcase himself, revealing its contents to a hidden video camera crew: it contained several pounds of C-4 plastic explosive and an assortment of FDN posters, emblems, and publications.

Three days earlier, the authorities had discovered the nucleus of an incipient FDN political-military front in Managua: the priest was the last member to be apprehended. Subsequent testimony by the leader of the cell, Pedro Ernesto "El Pez" Sánchez, revealed that for over three years its members had been establishing contacts with the leaders of the right-wing parties, the newspaper *La Prensa*, the Catholic church, and several trade union and professional organizations aligned with the right in order to secure material and logistical support for military actions in the cities.

The attempt to bring terrorism to the cities, which dates back to the beginning of the war, has escalated immensely since 1984. In that year alone, security forces captured over three hundred weapons from FDN-ARDE members in the cities, including machine guns, automatic rifles, grenade and rocket launchers, and some five hundred pounds of C-4 plastic explosive.[2] The contra effort is often coordinated with the work of social and political groups that operate legally inside the country: it is the latter that we call the "internal front."

Military activity is only a secondary function of this front, however. Its primary function has been to complement external aggression with political and ideological attacks on the revolution from within. It acts as the *internal rearguard* of the counterrevolution. Its principal targets are professionals, the urban working classes, the rural proletariat, and the semi-urbanized peasants who are concentrated around cities of the Pacific Coast.

The 1979 insurrection was concentrated in this developed zone, and it was here that the FSLN first consolidated its authority. The level of political consciousness here means that counterrevolutionary operations must be far more complex and sophisticated than the type of crude manipulation used in the countryside. While it may be possible to convince a peasant on the agricultural frontier that the Sandinistas will come to "eat your children and send your women to Russia," you cannot say this to a resident of Managua. In addition, the psychological operations aspect of the internal front takes on a more sophisticated form than that of the armed contras because it operates without any *direct* link to military operations. The psychological operations of the armed contras, on the other hand, are never separate from the guns in their hands.

La Prensa director Jaime Chamorro candidly described the division of labor between these two fronts during a talk to a group of U.S. citizens visiting Managua in early 1985. "The armed resistance is fundamental to stopping the imposition of a Communist state. The contras are fighting with arms, and we are fighting in another way, together with the political parties and private enterprise, trying to prevent Nicaragua from becoming a Communist state."[3]

After the "quick military victory" approach was abandoned, the internal front took on heightened importance within the larger counter-revolutionary project. At the same time, what had been an affinity of interests and ultimate objectives between the armed contras and the internal front moved quickly toward an organizational fusion of the two. By 1985, the Reagan administration was viewing them as an integral whole: "The internal Nicaraguan opposition, armed and un-armed, represents a genuine political force," according to Secretary of State Shultz.[4]

The internal front operates within the framework laid out in the U.S. Army's *Psychological Operations in Guerrilla Warfare* manual, which defines psychological operations as the "planned use of propaganda and other psychological actions to influence the opinions, emotions, at-titudes, and behavior of hostile foreign groups in such a way as to support the achievement of national [U.S.] objectives."[5] Such opera-tions include a host of sophisticated techniques with which to manipu-late the target population. The subjects receive and assimilate messages that establish associations and spark feelings which lead them to ques-tion their political and moral convictions. This leads them to question the authority and integrity of the leaders and the truth of official information, to withdraw from the political system, and, it is hoped, to plug into an alternative one.

The ideological assaults of the internal front are carefully linked to the assaults of the armed contras. The first grind away at the social and economic fabric of the society in order to undermine the revolution's ability to satisfy the basic material needs of the population and to weaken its ability to defend the nation. The internal front uses psycho-logical manipulation and ideological obfuscation in order to convert hardship into a generalized climate of fear and insecurity. Discontent over material conditions, it is hoped, will be transformed into opposi-tion to the revolution itself—and, ultimately, to support for the counter-revolutionary project. But although the message is essentially a simple one—we were better off before the revolution, and we would be better off with the counterrevolution—it is rarely stated outright. Instead there are subtle assertions, such as "There are long lines for everything now, before there weren't"; "Before we had cornflakes, now we don't"; "Before sugar and gasoline were not rationed, now they are." Lines, rationing, shortages, and so on are portrayed as characteristics of the revolution itself; without it, lines would go away, cornflakes would come back, and rationing would end. This "verbal terrorism" ultimately boils down to one message: we would live better without the Sandinistas. The counterrevolution should triumph.

Background of the Internal Front: A Truncated Bourgeoisie

The key groupings chosen to carry out this ideological aggression inside the political systems of revolutions are generally the overthrown ruling classes. In Nicaragua, the former ruling class was displaced from state power but the majority of its members remained in Nicaragua—a fact that sets the Nicaraguan revolution apart from those where such classes disappeared (Cuba, Vietnam, Ethiopia), had not fully emerged (Angola, Mozambique), or were only partially displaced (Chile, Jamaica). The continued presence of these groupings, which gain legitimacy because of the Sandinista policies of a mixed economy and political pluralism, gives them exceptional leeway to undermine the revolution from within. They have been able to carry out many of their operations *legally* because of the broad liberties accorded them by the government.

The Reagan administration would like the world to believe that the "democratic opposition" inside Nicaragua is made up of a majority of the population which is struggling against an increasingly isolated and totalitarian Sandinista clique. According to the White House, this "democratic opposition" played a major role in overthrowing the Somoza dictatorship but was forced out of the anti-Somoza coalition by an armed minority—the FSLN. In fact, this is far from the truth: from the start, most of the key figures in the internal front were members of the bourgeoisie and did everything possible to *prevent* a revolutionary outcome to the overthrow of Somoza.

For most of the Somoza family's forty-five years in power, the bourgeoisie considered that its interests were adequately represented by the dictatorship and securely protected by the National Guard. It was not until the earthquake in 1972, when the Somoza clique monopolized the process of reconstruction, that minor disputes became fissures. By this time, the popular movement led by the FSLN was becoming a national force. The bourgeoisie suddenly found itself caught between a mass movement that was threatening the entire structure of class domination and the dictatorship, which was no longer capable either of representing its interests or of holding back the popular upsurge.

The Somozas had effectively represented the bourgeoisie politically for most of that class's reign, so the capitalists had concentrated on organizing themselves economically. In 1974 more than a dozen business and employer groups formed the Superior Council of Private Enterprise (COSEP), an umbrella organization of production, trade, and investment associations. In the same year a small, more democratic, sector of the class formed the Democratic Union of Liberation

(UDEL), led by *La Prensa* editor Pedro Joaquín Chamorro. At its convention in 1974, COSEP supported government repression against popular protest as necessary to "insure law and order," but at the same time condemned Somoza's "unfair competition." "The dominant classes," wrote FSLN leader Jaime Wheelock in 1983, "began the task of seeking a substitute, [which] appeared as a struggle against Somocismo when in reality it was an effort to sustain Somocismo without Somoza."[6] But it was not until 1978 that the bourgeoisie seriously turned to the business of organizing itself politically. In April, Robelo and other directors of COSEP formed the Nicaraguan Democratic Movement (MDN).

In October 1977 the FSLN launched its general offensive and it became clear that Somoza's ouster was only a matter of time. What remained in dispute was who would hold the reins of the antidictatorial movement and what would follow the fall of the regime; and this struggle was fought out during 1978.

In February, the bourgeoisie called a general strike. Although it was broadly supported by the workers (managers even paid their wages during the strike) as part of their own anti-Somoza struggle, the strike failed in its objective of forcing the dictatorship to negotiate with the bourgeois opposition. This failure paved the way for the September 1978 insurrection—the decisive point at which the offensive passed fully into the hands of the FSLN. The bourgeois opposition tried desperately to regain the initiative, but ultimately failed. In February 1979 it called another general strike, this time under the banner of the Broad Opposition Front (FAO).[7] The strike failed as an attempt to pressure Somoza to resign, which led to a last-ditch effort to prevent a revolutionary triumph—the formation of the Patriotic Reflection Committee, which was to negotiate with Somoza and the United States over the dictator's departure. Once the final insurrection began in June, however, the Patriotic Reflection Committee collapsed, and most FAO members watched the liberation war from the sidelines—from Miami, Caracas, and other Latin American capitals.

When the leaders of the internal front project themselves as impartial defenders of freedom and democracy and claim that they oppose Sandinista totalitarianism now, just as they opposed Somocista tyranny in the past, they are concealing a major difference. This is that Somoza had become a hinderance to a *part* of their class, whereas the Sandinistas are a hindrance to the *entire* class. With such propaganda, the bourgeoisie also tries to conceal what is in essence a class conflict between the Nicaraguan bourgeoisie and the popular classes represented by the revolutionary state. When these people talk of the revolution being betrayed, they are not referring to a deviation from the FSLN's Historic Program (drawn up in 1969), which is in fact being implemented, but a betrayal of their assumption that they should have inherited state power.

Some—perhaps the majority—would undoubtedly have used that power to reimpose Somocismo without Somoza; others entertained liberal dreams of a more benevolent "third-way" capitalism. With the triumph, however, both these divisions and that between the pro- and anti-Somoza factions quickly dissolved and the entire class—whether its individual members resided in Miami, Tegucigalpa, San José, or Managua—united under the counterrevolutionary banner. Its historic weakness as a class did not allow it to develop its own project, independent of the U.S. counterrevolution. This does not mean that contradictions do not exist within the bourgeoisie, however: rivalries, personal ambition, different political perspectives, strategies, tactics, and programs are there, but they have become secondary in the face of the Sandinista "threat."

Having lost political power, members of the bourgeoisie were then faced with three options: they could participate in the legitimate political opposition, whose bottom line demanded patriotism; they could "retire" from politics but remain in the country, operating within the framework of the guarantees and limits of the mixed economy;[8] or they could join the counterrevolution. While some sectors chose the first two options, the majority of the class chose the counterrevolution.

(Under the Sandinista mixed economy, the state has assumed the role of catalyst for all socioeconomic development, stimulating and supervising the entire productive apparatus. On the other hand, the state has achieved social control over the surplus through a monopoly over the financial system and foreign trade rather than through expropriations— that is, the disappearance of private capital. Within this model, private capital must carry out the "social function" of production and of making a significant contribution to the social surplus, respecting the "logic of the majority," as the Sandinistas put it. Yet, in accordance with Sandinista practice, those sectors of the bourgeoisie which chose to continue producing within the mixed economy also enjoy extensive state support—guaranteed credit, prices, foreign exchange for importing essential production inputs, etc.—to such an extent that they are in fact better protected than they were under Somocista capitalism from the vagaries of the market and from bankruptcy. In sum, the Sandinista project has left open an important space for the bourgeoisie, although it is no longer the ruling class, to play a fruitful role in society.)

Perhaps the development that most upset the bourgeoisie was the establishment of mass organizations aligned with the FSLN, created as national structures through which the people would have a voice, intervene in state policy, and fight for their interests. Most Nicaraguans called this "people's power." For its part, the right called it "state-party confusion." They also began to demand elections, with a view toward erecting bourgeois-democratic structures before this revolutionary democracy could be consolidated. Nonetheless, despite bourgeois warnings of "totalitarian tendencies" and an ongoing propaganda offensive against the Soviet Union and the socialist world, cross-class unity around the initial process of reconstruction prevailed.

By 1980, the class character of the revolution was no longer in doubt and the bourgeoisie, increasingly aware that a reformist project would not materialize, turned to the task of delegitimizing the revolutionary project. Frustration over their loss of control over the economy, the removal of Nicaragua from the U.S. camp, and the assertiveness of the popular classes all crystallized under the banner of "betrayal of the revolution." The bourgeoisie charged that political pluralism, the mixed economy, and nonalignment had been thrown overboard in exchange for a one-party state and subordination to the socialist countries.

In March 1980 COSEP began what was to become an internal-front tradition of spreading rumors of a provocation before it happened, when it warned that Nicaragua was "on the threshold of a crisis." One month later, the crisis came: MDN leader Alfonso Robelo, who had emerged as the leading representative of the bourgeoisie within the government, and Violetta Barrios de Chamorro resigned from the Junta, charging that the revolution was "steering away from its original goals."[8] Their resignation further sharpened divisions among the staff of *La Prensa*, and from that point on the newspaper moved fully into the counterrevolutionary camp. The demand for elections moved to the top of the agenda, no longer because there was any hope for an electoral victory, but as a way to delegitimize the government. Charges of "creeping totalitarianism" and the "erosion of democracy" grew in frequency and intensity.

The bourgeoisie had hoped that Robelo's resignation would spark a major crisis, forcing the Sandinistas to respond to the threats of an end to national unity by accepting concessions that would bring about a realignment of forces in its favor. But the maneuver failed, underscoring the impotence of the bourgeoisie, which now began a strategic redefinition of its position. Just days after Reagan's 1980 electoral victory, the five COSEP representatives to the Council of State—the provisional legislative body—resigned their seats, stating in a communiqué: "The most radical sectors of the FSLN party, overt Marxist-Leninists, are preparing the implementation of a Communist political and economic system in Nicaragua."[9] Their walkout was a clear statement that they were giving up the effort to undermine the revolution from within.

On 17 November 1980 COSEP vice-chairman Jorge Salazar was killed in an exchange of gunfire with a police patrol near Managua. A warrant was out for his arrest on charges of plotting against the security of the state, and six M-16 submachine guns were found in his van. Several other COSEP members were also arrested for involvement in the plot. *La Prensa* and other rightist organizations were loud in their condemnation and indignation, organizing a huge funeral for Salazar and charging that one of their finest representatives had been murdered by the Sandinistas. Then, on 22 November the government released documents about the case and allowed the press to talk with three of the accused—Leonardo Somarriba, vice-president of the COSEP-affiliated Nicaraguan Chamber of Commerce; Mario Hanon, president of COSEP's Association of Rice Planters; and landowner María Lan de Lacayo. It was apparent that Salazar had indeed been busy gathering funds, weapons, and political backing for a coup d'état against the government. The network had been infiltrated by State Security agent Alvaro Baltodano, who revealed the details of the plot, including the names of the former National Guardsmen in Honduras, Miami, and elsewhere who were coordinating it from abroad.[10]

With this incident, the bourgeoisie broke new ground, that of armed adventure, at the same time that the new administration in Washington was formulating the military option for Nicaragua. The advent of Reagan, and the birth of the U.S.-sponsored destabilization program, helped push the Nicaraguan bourgeoisie farther in the direction it was already moving. Once the Salazar network was broken up, the key card in the bourgeoisie's deck—the possibility of an alliance with the National Guard—was revealed. This signaled the beginning of a process of increased linkage with the larger counterrevolution, headquartered in Washington. Perhaps not surprisingly, Salazar's widow is now a member of the FDN's political directorate in Tegucigalpa, while one of the most vicious of the FDN's regional commands is named after Jorge Salazar. While the bourgeoisie's political parties continued to keep one foot in the legal political realm, from this point on the center of the class, represented in COSEP, had made its decision and became the internal front of the counterrevolution.

(Robelo's departure from the country in late 1981 to help form ARDE prompted the first post-triumph exodus of Nicaraguan capitalists into the leadership of the contra organizations. Among those who left with Robelo were the bulk of the MDN directorate, including prominent merchants and industrialists. It was the only right-wing party to literally transfer its structures from the legal opposition to the armed counterrevolution.)

The remaining organizations of the internal reaction came together in October 1981 to form the Nicaraguan Democratic Coordinating Committee (CDN), a coalition of four political parties, two trade union federations, and COSEP—the same list of groups singled out for U.S. assistance by the Heritage Foundation in a 1980 *Backgrounder*.[11]

Nearly five years later, in June 1985, Arturo Cruz acknowledged that the "internal opposition," as the White House was calling it, was to receive part of the U.S. economic assistance for the contras since it was part of the "organized democratic resistance"—and thus exempt from the embargo against Nicaragua imposed in May 1985.[12]

Of the parties, the Social Christian party (PSC), a member of the Christian Democratic International, is the largest. The Nicaraguan Conservative party (PCN) is an outgrowth of the traditional oligarchic Conservative party, which, with the Liberals, alternated in and out of power during most of the nineteenth and early twentieth centuries;[13] the Social Democratic party (PSD) was founded in 1979 by those members of the PCN and MDN associated with the editing of *La Prensa;* and the Liberal Constitutionalist party (PLC) broke with Somoza's Nationalist Liberal party over minor differences in 1967.

The two trade union federations owe their existence to Somoza, whose combination of repression and cooptation only allowed moderate and compliant unions to exist.[14] The Federation of Trade Union Unity (CUS), affiliated with the International Confederation of Free Trade Unions (ICFTU) and the AFL-CIO's American Institute for Free Labor Development (AIFLD), describes itself as social-democratic, while the Nicaraguan Federation of Workers (CTN) is loyal to the Social Christian party. The two together have 4,404 members registered with the Labor Ministry, and represent some 2 percent of the organized workforce.[15] They continue to function because of substantial foreign funds.

COSEP, with thirty-five thousand members, is by far the dominant voice in the CDN and the most effective representative of bourgeois interests. It brings together the remaining large-scale agricultural producers, exporters, and importers, wholesale traders, industrialists, and upper-level professionals who pay their allegiance to the right. Although not a formal political party, COSEP describes itself as the "political guide" of the CDN and wields more influence than all the rightist parties combined. "COSEP is the internal bellwether for our policy," one U.S. Embassy official reported in 1981. "Its survival is key to our role here."[16]

During the first few years after 1979, when the revolution was still weak and unorganized, the political organizations of the right sought to accumulate floating sectors of the middle classes and the most backward sectors of the peasantry to stake out an organizational pole opposed to the FSLN. Despite these efforts, by 1984 the PSC—the strongest party in the CDN—could only boast 2,000—3,000 affiliates, and when, on 10 January 1984—the sixth anniversary of the assassination of Pedro Joaquín Chamorro, Sr.—the most right-wing parties tested their strength in a "freedom march," *La Prensa* ran headlines for days calling on the population to join the event, billed by the international wire services as Nicaragua's "first opposition demonstration" in recent times. Yet at least one-half of the two hundred people who came were journalists, and the CDN leaders subsequently—and very quietly—slipped back into their air-conditioned offices.[17] Tomás Borge would later comment, "How are we to prove to the world that we have political pluralism here when the opposition can hardly muster up a hundred individuals?"

Given this inability to attract a mass base, and their inability to relate to popular assertiveness, the political organizations of the internal front have experienced a steady process of demoralization, reflected in their constant vacillation and visible frustration. By 1985, *La Prensa,* which acts as the public forum through which the various bourgeois political factions can be unified, warned that the growing internal bickering was threatening to lead to total disintegration: "We must overcome our inaction, apathy and divisiveness. The least we can do is remain united, both within each party and in the unity of the Democratic Coordinating Committee. Only by first putting our own house in order can we confront the adversary."[18]

The CDN has managed to compensate in part for its domestic weakness by shifting a major portion of its activity to the international arena, where its influence is not dependent upon a social base, but rather on political alignments that are tied to U.S. policy. Although this "internationalization" responds to the United States' need to legitimize the opposition and isolate the revolutionary government in the international arena, it is also a key platform for the internal front's accumulation of power. When Arturo Cruz arrived in Nicaragua on 23 June 1984, in the heat of that year's electoral campaign, only three hundred people came out to welcome him at the international airport, despite a publicity campaign whose intensity far surpassed that of the 10 January "freedom march." If Cruz's importance was "missed" by the Nicaraguan people, the United States fully understood that its significance lay in its international impact. Washington's propaganda machinery worked hard at building an international image of the banker as a "synthesis of the Nicaraguan democratic opposition." His arrival was front page news throughout the world.

As part of the overlap between the internal front and the international war theater, the U.S. embassy in Managua and the Nicaraguan right have organized an elaborate "interview network" with CDN representatives for journalists, U.S. congressional delegations, and other international visitors. The internal front is presented not only as a "model" opposition, but as *the* political opposition. U.S. strategists then try to hide the authentic political pluralism that exists in practice in Nicaragua. After all, six *additional* political parties oppose the FSLN from both the left and the right,[19] vigorously criticize the Sandinistas publicly, and push their alternative programs throughout the country. What separates these groups from the CDN, however, is that the latter, as Sandinista leader Dora María Téllez has put it, "are not the creators of their own political [program]. Rather, they are mere internal amplifiers of Reagan's program."[20]

La Prensa: "In the Service of Truth and Justice"

Oscar Leonardo Montalbán, one of the FDN's press secretaries, is much sought after by journalists in Tegucigalpa. And when reporters in Costa Rica want a statement from Pastora's faction of ARDE, they look for the group's spokesman, José Dávila. ARDE press communiqués are often written by Mario Alfaro Alvarado. In Washington, D.C., the media crowd can go to Steadman Fagoth's local representative, Adriana Guillén, or to FDN associate Humberto Belli.

These are all experienced journalists. Montalbán was *La Prensa's* star reporter, Dávila its economic columnist, and Guillén one of its talented editorialists. Assistant editor Alfaro reworked their articles under the supervision of Belli, who was the paper's chief editor. Pedro Joaquín Chamorro, Jr., was *La Prensa's* co-director until he left Nicaragua in late 1984 to join the contras.

But while *La Prensa* often serves as liaison between the armed contras and the internal front, its principal field of operations is within the latter. It managed to hold on to a modicum of credibility by capitalizing on its anti-Somoza history, as well as Chamorro, Sr.'s martyrdom.[21]

Fred Landis, a U.S. psychologist and specialist in the scientific manipulation of information, has explained how the CIA goes about taking over a newspaper and putting it to work against people that the U.S. government has defined as adversaries:

> The appropriation of newspapers by the CIA proceeds through certain discrete, identifiable stages. These include: using an international press association, firing many of the staff, modernizing the physical plant, changing the format of the front page, promoting a counter-elite to replace the socialist government, and using divisive propaganda to create artificial conflicts within the society. . . . The propaganda offensive is coordinated with economic sabotage, paramilitary terrorism, and other psychological activities.[22]

The pattern that Landis outlines is strikingly accurate with regard to *La Prensa*. As of March 1980, the direction the paper was going in was no longer in doubt. First, Pedro Joaquín Chamorro, Jr., then the paper's advertising manager, was elected to the board of directors of the Inter-American Press Association (IAPA).[23] Then his uncle, Xavier Chamorro—the one member of the paper's editorial board who opposed its rightward drift—was fired as director and replaced by Pedro himself and by Xavier's brother, Jaime Chamorro. Agitation by *La Prensa* journalists, typesetters, and other workers over Xavier's firing (which the board of directors tried to present as a resignation) led to the resignation of some 85 percent of the workforce, which went on to establish, under Xavier's leadership, a new pro-revolutionary independent newspaper, *El Nuevo Diario*. Before long *La Prensa*'s physical plant was modernized, including a new building, typesetting equipment, and presses.

By mid-1980, the metamorphosis was complete, and the paper set about the task of waging psychological warfare in earnest. There were three distinct aspects of this warfare:

1. *Selection of information. La Prensa* has not only become the mouthpiece of the internal reaction, publishing in bold headlines each proclamation issued by, and activity of, the right, but a large proportion of the pages are devoted to putting across the U.S. worldview.

Alexander Fenell surveyed *La Prensa*'s international coverage for January 1984. The paper published 660 articles on international issues, along with 140 photos, which took up 43 percent of all news space. A full 30 percent of this coverage was on events in the United States or the activities of U.S. politicians. And more than half of *this* news consisted of the direct opinions and statements of the U.S. government. In other words, nearly one-sixth of *La Prensa*'s international news space was taken up with declarations of the Reagan administration. While the U.S. government received 605.8 column inches for its opinions and positions on Central America, the Nicaraguan government only received 40.8 column inches on the same subject.

Almost daily, the paper publishes material from USIA bulletins (which are issued by the U.S. embassy), often without crediting the source so that they appear as "independent" news articles. Fenell asks, "Is there any other paper in the world that dedicates one-sixth of its international news to the official opinions of a government which is militarily attacking the country where the paper is located? What would happen if the *New York Times* had given one-sixth of its coverage to the opinions and positions of the North Vietnamese government during the Indochina war?"[24]

Fennell also found that the contra aggression only took up 2.2 percent of the paper's space. Jaime Chamorro defended this scant coverage as follows: "*La Prensa*'s editorial policy is to not publish abuses committed by the contras, when they bomb and kill some people, some children, or some mothers, for example, since it is impossible to publish the abuses of the government and we don't want to be propagandists for them."[25]

2. *Subliminal propaganda. La Prensa*'s subliminal propaganda literally leaps off the paper's front page. As Landis puts it, "The reason the front page resembles a psychological warfare leaflet is because it *is* a psychological warfare leaflet." The aim is to create feelings of fear, anxiety, and mistrust, and then to identify these feelings with the Sandinistas and their project. The technique is the careful selection and juxtaposition of key words and photographs which invoke recurring images of economic, social, and political chaos and human suffering. The U.S. Army's *Psychological Operations Field Manual 33-1* states, under the heading "Pictorial and Photographic Propaganda," "A photograph or picture can often insinuate a derogatory charge more effectively than words. The combination of words and . . . selected and composite photographs can be extremely effective."[26]

The "news" that constitutes the raw material for these images falls under two headings: on the one hand, bizarre crimes, gruesome accidents, unnatural incidents such as birth mutations and other stomach-churning scenes, and religious events; on the other hand, conventional local and international news, such as Nicaraguan government decisions, U.S. policy pronouncements, or the Middle East conflict. The actual information contained in these stories and photo captions is usually accurate and objective. The images are evoked by associating words and pictures, leaving the reader to draw conclusions without realizing it— the feeling is provoked faster than the mind is able to absorb it through thought. What sticks with the reader is the association between unease and the Sandinistas. A parallel but contrasting association is also projected that associates U.S. officials and local right-wing leaders with feelings of hope and salvation. The socialist countries are portrayed as weak and losing; the United States as all-powerful and invincible.

Some concrete examples will help describe this process.

• 20 March 1984. The headline reads "Concern for Nicaragua." Immediately below are four photographs, the first a raging fire in an industrial complex, the second a number of vehicles and buildings on fire, the third a bombed-out city block, and the fourth a chilling scene of a corpse alongside naked men, women, and children huddled together in smoking rubble. The immediate association is that of a Nicaragua sunk in misery, destruction, and chaos. But it turns out that the headline refers to statements made by Argentine president Raúl Alfonsín, while the photos are of a completely unrelated event—unrelated to Nicaragua *or* Alfonsín—an industrial disaster in Mexico.

• 20 December 1984. The headline reads, "Pope's Message, Don't Be Afraid." Immediately below and to the right is a photograph showing *La Prensa* staff members with their right hands raised. On the left is a picture of the pope, cross in hand, stretching his arm out toward the *La Prensa* workers. Immediately below the pope is another headline: "U.S. Struggles for Peace and Democracy in the Area." Yet the article on the pope has nothing to do with Nicaragua, while the photograph's caption tells of newly elected *La Prensa* trade union representatives being sworn in. Nevertheless, the subliminal message is that the *La Prensa* staff are being blessed by God through his representative on earth, the Pope, who tells them to have no fear; *La Prensa* is protected by the Lord, the United States is on its side.

• 8 November 1984. The headline reads, "U.S. Spy Plane over Nicaragua." Below and to the left is a second story, under the boldface title, "Prelude to Attack." Below the headline and to the right are three photographs: on top, a U.S. Air Force spy plane; below it, what appears to be a laser apparatus shooting a powerful beam to the right, into the third photograph, which is of a wrecked truck. Above the third photograph, boldface letters declare, "Suddenly, the Truck Falls by the Wayside." The combination of words and photographs in sequence is visually frightening; the spy plane is the prelude to a U.S. attack, which takes the form of a powerful force (the beam) leaving the revolution (the truck) in ruins. Upon closer examination, the first and second stories are unrelated: the truck was a cement mixer that tipped over on a construction site outside Managua, and the picture of the laser beam has no caption whatsoever and is never explained. This page was published in the midst of the artificial MiGs crisis. Others of its kind are frequently coordinated with U.S. movements in the conflict environment.

3. *Disinformation*. The CIA defines disinformation as "black propaganda." According to Ralph McGhee, a CIA analyst for twenty-five years, it is employed "where the necessary circumstances or proofs are lacking to support U.S. intervention; the CIA creates the appropriate situations, or else invents them."[27] Among the methods used are forged documents or the complete distortion of facts. Landis cites *La Prensa's* lead story on 16 August 1981, which reported that Foreign Minister Miguel D'Escoto had profaned the church. It turned out that the story originated with an obscure Mexican newspaper which had allegedly sent a reporter to cover D'Escoto in New Delhi six months earlier. The reporter later claimed that his tapes were garbled and he could not reproduce the interview. *La Prensa* had picked up the story from *El Diario de las Americas* in Miami, a paper run by the Cuban exile community, with documented links to the CIA.

La Prensa's use of this technique is sophisticated enough that it is usually impossible to accuse the paper of lying or even to prove that it knowingly used false information. In fact, the paper's power rests on the credibility it maintains through its apparent objectivity: its motto is "in the service of truth and justice." But ideological manipulation is merely the *means* for transforming a determined way of thinking instilled in the reader into a determined way of acting; in this way, *La Prensa* tries to win over the social base of the revolution to the counterrevolution.

There is not doubt, however, of *La Prensa's* direct ties to the counterrevolution. One of the more spectacular revelations of such links came from a *La Prensa* reporter who was also local PSD president for Managua, Luis Mora Sánchez. On 29 April 1984, after repeated warnings by State Security that he cease his moonlighting activities as a correspondent for the Costa Rican-based ARDE radio station Radio Impacto, Mora was arrested. During extensive courtroom testimony, which was aired on national television, Mora admitted that he had been an ARDE agent since 1982, that the ARDE had told him to form a "western front" in Nicaragua's Pacific region, and that the first people he recruited were fellow *La Prensa* journalist Máximo Alonso, photographer Jorge Ortega Rayo, and chauffeur Sergio Meléndez.

In one of his most astounding remarks, Mora claimed that a functionary from the U.S. embassy attended the weekly meeting of *La Prensa's* editorial board, in order to direct and coordinate the paper's strategy, and specifically identified then-U.S. Ambassador Anthony Quainton as the most frequent attender. He also reported that leaders of the right-wing parties, trade unions, and members of the Catholic church hierarchy participated.

The Mora case shows more than press ties with the counterrevolution, however: it also shows how the illegal activities of the internal front are processed by the U.S. propaganda machinery so that they come out as Sandinista repression. Following Mora's arrest, the State Department released a statement "regretting" the suppression of Nicaragua's "independent press," while both the White House and the Inter-American Press Association charged that Mora was being indicted for "carrying out his work as a journalist." In this way, the counterrevolution was able both to feed the anti-Sandinista propaganda campaign and to take the heat off of Mora's damaging revelations.

Chaplains of the Counterrevolution

"The Pope Is With Us," "Christ Is Our Liberator," "With God and Patriotism, We Will Defeat Communism," declare FDN propaganda leaflets and posters. Photographs of the head of the Catholic church in Nicaragua, Archbishop Miguel Obando y Bravo, adorn contra offices and literature.

The effort by the counterrevolution to promote Obando y Bravo's image dates back to the beginning of the war. The Institute for Religion and Democracy (IRD), founded in 1981 and the principal New Right religious organization that has been responsible for promoting and furthering the Right's program in the religious arena, noted that "the Church has become the principal obstacle to the totalitarian transformation of Nicaraguan society because . . . its authority and support are superior to that of all other groups."[28] In late 1981, the IRD invited Obando y Bravo to Washington to receive a special award for his leadership in the "struggle for democracy" in Nicaragua.

The strategy of prolonged antipopular warfare conferred upon Obando y Bravo the leading role in a rewritten script. The turning point came with his April 1985 appointment as cardinal of Central America. As Vice-president Sergio Ramírez put it, the United States "needed to strengthen the political figure of Obando y Bravo as the leader of the internal opposition, given the rightist organizations' weakness, incapacity, and their lack of a prestigious, respected leader."[29] Speaking in the name of the FDN and ARDE, Arturo Cruz was more candid: "With his elevation to cardinal, Obando y Bravo is now our indisputable leader."[30] And the cardinal quickly acknowledged his new role. In

June 1985 he held his first mass as cardinal for the contra community in Miami, and told the gathering of four thousand that "I want to take this opportunity to give all of you Nicaraguans who are outside the country my warmest greetings. I urge you to keep your faith, don't lose hope. The Lord is testing us, but he will give us strength to bear the cross."[31] Calero, Pastora, and the other FDN-ARDE leaders who had organized the event were delighted.

In sharp contrast to the weak bourgeoisie, the Roman Catholic church in Nicaragua has always been a pillar of strength. For five hundred years it has played a key role in shoring up the structures of class exploitation and foreign domination through ideological penetration of the deeply religious Nicaraguan people. As in the rest of Latin America, it not only provided the "moral imperative" for colonial rule, but also accumulated vast wealth and property through the expropriation of indigenous lands and the use of Indian slavery. In 1856 the church supported the intervention of U.S. mercenary William Walker, and in 1912 gave its approval to the occupation by U.S. Marines, which lasted until 1925; in 1927 it welcomed the Marines back again, blessing their weapons as they went off to fight Sandino. Through the rise and fall of countless Nicaraguan strongmen, disputes between the Liberal and Conservative parties, and rivalries between Spain, Britain, and the United States, the church has never stopped defending an exploitative social order.

It was, therefore, no coincidence that after the United States installed Somoza, the church took up its role as defender of the dictatorship, christening the first Somoza "prince of the church." For nearly half a century its support for the dictatorship was demonstrated repeatedly. As late as 1970, Obando y Bravo declared, in a toast to Somoza, that the National Guard and the church had only one difference—"our uniforms."

The church hierarchy now flaunts its opposition to the Somoza dictatorship in its final years as part of its attempt to project itself as being "above politics." But it was only after the bouregoisie had joined the anti-Somoza struggle in the late 1970s that the church finally transferred its allegiance from the dictator's increasingly isolated clique to the rest of that class. In fact, Obando y Bravo had attempted repeatedly, through the UDEL and the FAO, to mediate between Somoza and the opposition bourgeoisie in order to defuse the crisis. On the very day of the triumph, he was in Venezuela making a last-ditch attempt to undermine a Sandinista victory.[32]

Once that victory was assured, the church changed its role in, and relation to, the state: while previously it had legitimized a reactionary ruling class and supported its control over state power, now it began to attack a revolutionary class and the state through which that class exercises its hegemony.[33]

As with *La Prensa*, building up a social base is but the means to bring the population into action against the revolution. The first step is to accuse the government of religious persecution. The next is to call on the people—through religious symbolism and psychological manipulation—to oppose the revolution because it "threatens" their religious beliefs. In the third step, the people are called upon to turn this abstract opposition into direct political confrontation. This call to engage in counterrevolutionary activity, issued from the moral sanctuary of the church, is coupled with the active creation of "church-state" confrontations.

By 1984, the religious sphere had become the main ground on which the domestic reaction was organizing politically, and the church the pivotal institution around which the internal ideological battle was taking place. Here the counterrevolutionary forces seek to make the political contradiction between classes appear as a religious struggle between church and state. This mystification has been candidly described by PSD leader Manuel Matus: "What is going on in Nicaragua is a religion confrontation, since Communism is a religion and not an ideology."[34]

The crude mixture of anticommunism and religious manipulation was an essential ingredient of the counterrevolution from the moment the war began. As part of the standard contra uniform, FDN members are issued small rosaries and crucifixes to wear around their necks.[35] Former FDN leader Edgar Chamorro recalled that "the CIA pulled a lot of 'pranks' with the religious question. They paid for a book, *Christians Under Fire,* written by Humberto Belli, which summarized the supposed persecution of the church in Nicaragua but had nothing to do with what was really going on inside the country. This was all part of our plan to use and take advantage of the power of the church and the beliefs of the people. We also sought to mobilize the people against the Nicaraguan government through their religious beliefs."[36] The idea is instilled in each contra's mind that "communism"—the Sandinistas— and Christianity are deadly enemies, and that the counterrevolution is waging a holy crusade to save Christianity. In this way, murder and pillage become acts of faith. It is worse "to kill the soul than the body," says Nicaraguan Bishop Pablo Antonio Vega.

The contras are given the task of transmitting this message to the peasants. The CIA manual urges each contra to incite "indignation over the lack of freedom of worship, and persecution, of which priests are victims; and over the participation of priests such as D'Escoto and

Education Minister Fernando Cardenal in the Sandinista government, against the explicit orders of his Holiness, the Pope."[37]

The internal front transmits the message in more subtle and complex ways. If *La Prensa* carries out ideological warfare through the manipulation of information, the church does the same with religion. The church's technique of "subliminal discourse" has been analyzed by Mexican researcher Ana María Ezcurra, who defines it as the "coexistence of two apparently opposed subsystems actually articulated to each other as equivalents."[38] In the first, the discourse is strictly spiritual and nonconflictual: the church is located on a superior, autonomous plane that is above conflict, particular interests, and party or class positions; it is exclusively dedicated to the common good of the human being. In this context, the church has a monopoly on "unity," in the face of "division," "hate," and "sectarianism," which exist on inferior planes.

In the second subsystem, the discourse is political; it addresses concrete issues that are taking place in Nicaragua and the world, where the church "is part of and takes part in historical and political conflict."[39] In this subsystem, all the arguments against the revolution are reproduced from the sanctified ground of the church. These two subsystems are combined in a subliminal discourse:

> Concealing the political nature of the struggle is made possible through the spiritualism of the nonconflictual. . . . This spiritualism allows [the discourse] to maintain a specific Christian identity as a neutral arena of action and creates the illusion of a religious opposition: "Christianity, Church vs. Sandinismo, Revolution." This discourse not only conceals the political as such, but in addition veils the political position taken, and its counterrevolutionary character.[40]

The argument made by both the contras and the church hierarchy—that the Sandinista government persecutes religion—is then parroted in Washington and becomes a key international issue. In reality, religious freedom in Nicaragua is greater than in any other country in the region: the FSLN's 1980 document on religion guarantees total freedom of worship and respect for religious beliefs. Seventy-six denominations, involving over 1,600 congregations and 96 percent of the population, operate throughout the country.

"Between Christianity and Revolution, There Is No Contradiction"

The Nicaraguan revolution was fought with the active participation of large numbers of committed Christians. Their massive incorporation into the antidictatorial struggle and the process of socioeconomic and political transformation is a product of the deep religious conviction of the Nicaraguan people, and of the recognition on the part of the FSLN that the objectives of the revolutionary movement and those of liberation theology and the popular church, not only in Nicaragua but throughout Latin America, coincided.

Basing themselves on the humane and egalitarian ideals of the Bible and in the rudimentary class outlook of the oppressed in Latin America, working-class and peasant priests and lay workers had begun, in the mid-1960s, to work in the countryside and in the impoverished urban neighborhoods. Although initially focusing on social and self-help projects, many in the popular church movement soon realized that a narrow social-improvement outlook was insufficient in the face of glaring injustices and entrenched power structures. They had come to recognize the political content inherent in any project of meaningful social change, and to look toward political alternatives.

At the same time, the FSLN recognized the revolutionary potential in the organizing efforts of the popular church, and in the early 1970s the two converged. The highest expression of this fusion was the emergence of the guerrilla-priest and the formation of local Christian Base Communities (CBCs), which became the revolutionary nuclei in many areas. In fact, many Sandinista leaders came out of these CBCs. The tradition of "revolutionary Christianity" as it continues to be practiced in Nicaragua today is captured by the slogan that heads this section: "Between Christianity and Revolution, There Is No Contradiction."

While the division between the church hierarchy and the popular church appears as a religious polarization, it actually corresponds to a growing class polarization: the popular church is a project of the popular classes, and the church hierarchy is a project of the displaced bourgeoisie. Given the multipliticy of classes that belong to it, the Catholic church has inevitably become an institution wracked by the unfolding class struggle in Nicaragua.

The threat of a politicized popular church, not just in Nicaragua but in all of Latin America, was recognized by the Reagan administration in the Committee of Santa Fe document: "U.S. policy in Latin America must begin to counter (not react against) liberation theology as it is used in Latin America. The role of the church in Latin America is vital to the concept of political freedom (founded in) private property and productive capitalism." Anything less than this would be "less Christian than Communist."[41] Since the Nicaraguan popular church is an important protagonist in the revolutionary process, the campaign against it has become the front line of the crusade against liberation theology throughout Latin America.

The United States has worked hand in glove with the Vatican in its campaign against the popular church.[42] Pope John Paul II's 1983 tour through Central America and Haiti marked the beginning of a crusade against liberation theology. During his twelve-hour visit to Nicaragua, he used the opportunity to win support for the Nicaraguan Bishops' Conference and Obando y Bravo in particular, castigate the popular church, and criticize the participation of Christians in the revolution. The pope conducted an open air mass in Managua which was attended by 700,000 people. He was introduced by Obando y Bravo, who made a biblical reference to the Roman Empire—implying that Nicaragua was a prison camp and the pope the liberator of the prisoners. The pope's own message is summed up in this key passage:

> Proof of the unity of the Church is respect for the direction given by the Bishops. Christ has entrusted to the Bishops the very important vocation of unifying the local churches. There are cases in which this unity is possible only when each one is capable of renouncing ideas and commitments from without, for the superior well-being with the Bishops, with the Pope, and with the Church. In effect, the unity of the Church is put into question when, [instead of] obedience to the Bishops and the Pope, unacceptable ideological compromise, temporaral options, and even incorrect conceptions of the Church come into play. A divided Church not constructed around the Bishops; any other Church, conceived as "new," untraditional, alternative, or, in the end, the so-called "popular church," is absurd and dangerous. I want to reaffirm that the Church must stay united in order to counteract these diverse, direct or indirect, forms of materialism.[43]

The mass provided the material for perhaps the greatest single propaganda blitz so far regarding the Sandinistas' alleged religious persecution. The first large-scale contra offensive was just getting under way, and the country was experiencing a traumatic period of adjustment to the reality of war. Only twenty-four hours earlier, thousands had filled the same plaza for a public funeral service for seventeen young Nicaraguan militia members who had been killed in a contra ambush earlier that week. The deaths were fresh in the minds of the people, who expected the pope to support their demands for an end to the aggression.

But during the course of his hour-long homily, it became clear that the pope had no intention of referring to the war. When he then ignored a personal request by the mothers of the seventeen victims to say a prayer for their sons and instead prayed for the imprisoned Somocista guardsmen, the crowd could not suppress its sense of betrayal. Scattered chants of "We want the Pope" ("Queremos al Papa") were gradually transformed into shouts of "We want peace" ("Queremos la Paz"), "There is no contradiction between Christianity and Revolution," and then booming cries of "Popular Power!" and "No Pasarán!" The pope was taken aback when his demands for "silence" went unheeded—with four years of revolution behind them, the people were accustomed to asserting their views. Nevertheless, as the representative of God on earth in the eyes of Catholics, many afterward felt a discomforting mixture of shame and righteousness.

The enemies of the revolution had a heyday twisting these events. The *Washington Post* headline was typical: "Pope Heckled in Managua." Radio Vatican went so far as to accuse the Sandinistas of "electronic piracy" for amplifying the chants of a few "troublemakers" to drown out the pope's voice. Managua's Christian Base Communities saw a different significance in the crowd's reactions, however: "The free people of Nicaragua were able to express the centuries-long irrepressible clamor of the oppressed of our continent, and to be the voice of all those in Latin America who have no voice."[44]

While the pope maintained his distance from the Sandinista leaders during the visit, he had no qualms about embracing Edén Pastora and Alfonso Robelo when he went on to Costa Rica. After the Pope had blessed Pastora—who "apologized" for the Sandinistas' behavior—Robelo declared that it was time to "start a holy war" against the Sandinista revolution.

In a highly revealing secret Vatican document, written as a guideline for the pope's visit to Nicaragua and leaked to a French-Latin American news service (Dial) the following June, the Vatican advisers explain "how the church and Christians can face up to a Marxist government and triumph":

> The fact that the Sandinista regime is an enemy means that a policy of understanding cannot bring success . . . a strategy based on strength, unity, and firmness has much more of a chance. . . . The Sandinistas will give in if they see that the entire Catholic community, and the Vatican in particular, resolutely maintains this line and gives its support to the Nicaraguan Bishops. We must work in close collaboration with Monsignor Obando y Bravo, and those members of the Church who work to weaken his influence must be "neutralized."[45]

The Italian newspaper *Il Manifesto* later obtained further details about the document, which indicated that Humberto Belli, through his contacts in the Latin American Bishops Conference, had heavy input in its writing.[46]

Since then, the attacks on the popular church have taken various forms. One is to transfer priests and church workers from their parishes in poor and working-class *barrios* to more comfortable neighborhoods, where liberation theology falls on deaf ears. Another is to pressure the four priests who occupy government posts to resign.[47] Indeed, the Vatican discharged Education Minister Cardenal from his religious duties as a Jesuit in December 1984.

"I sincerely believe, before God," Cardenal said in expressing his "conscientious objection" to the discharge, "that I would be committing a grave sin if, under the current circumstances, I abandoned my priestly option for the poor, presently realized in Nicaragua through my work in the Sandinista People's Revolution." He went on to state that "Vatican policy toward Nicaragua coincides with that of President Reagan. . . . In Nicaragua, there is no basic religious problem between the Church and the Revolution; there is a political confrontation."[48]

But if there is no contradiction between Christianity and the revolution, the counterrevolution is determined to produce one. It wants to make the people believe that their Christianity is incompatible with support for the revolution—much less participation in it.

The Internal Front's Direct Links to Washington

The ideological organization of the enemy is indeed superior to ours from the structural and technical point of view. . . . The Church is a strong organization [whose] generals, task force chiefs, and best-prepared cadre are exclusively dedicated to the ideological struggle.

—Tomás Borge[49]

The internal front's direct institutional and financial links to the United States have greatly bolstered its ability to wage ideological warfare. During the Carter administration, funds were officially allocated by Congress. The incoming Reagan administration immediately suspended bilateral assistance to the Nicaraguan government, but continued funding the internal front through official channels.

One of the prime vehicles for this assistance has been the AID. In September 1981 the AID donated $1 million to COSEP for "leadership development," according to a U.S. embassy bulletin released in Managua on 30 September.[50] Two months later, the NSC proposed to Reagan that aid for "political moderates" and the "private sector" in Nicaragua, originally begun under Carter, should be increased.[51] In August 1982, the Sandinista government prohibited COSEP and the Managua archdiocese from receiving a $5.1 million grant, approved by the U.S. Congress, which the State Department described as "a symbol of political and moral support for Nicaraguans discontented with the Sandinista regime."[52]

The U.S. Army's 1979 publication *Guide for the Planning of Counterinsurgency* details the function of the AID in counterrevolutionary wars, emphasizing its role in the formation of what it calls "American groups," to assist in achieving the objectives of the counterrevolutionary program. Although the "American groups" are under the direct supervision of the U.S. ambassador, their members are usually nationals of the target country.[53] In official AID terminology, these groups are referred to as "Private Voluntary Organizations" (PVOs). An enormous increase in AID assistance to Nicaragua took place after 1979; in fact, in 1980, more AID funds were channeled to "indigenous PVOs" in Nicaragua than to those in any other Latin American nation.[54]

The Nicaraguan recipients of these funds are the members of the internal front (COSEP, the Catholic church, etc.). Between 1981 and 1983, for instance, the archdiocese of Managua received at least $600,000 from the AID and from Catholic Relief Services (CRS)—a figure that is taken from the scant documentation made public and is probably just the tip of the iceberg.[55] CRS is under the formal auspices of the U.S. Conference of Bishops, but operates autonomously and receives the majority of its funding from the AID. The funds were used to organize programs through the Managua-based Archdiocese Social Programs Commission (COPROSA), a parochial council formed by Obando y Bravo in early 1980.[56]

The objective of these programs is to develop socioeconomic programs in marginalized urban and rural communities through which the church can develop a presence. Through this base, it hopes to recruit and train intermediate level cadres, who are chosen for their position in the community and their leadership abilities. Later, both these cadres and the target communities, having been won over to the counterrevolutionary project, are to be mobilized into direct confrontation with the state.[57] The goal of the initial COPROSA program was to organize and train at least one thousand leaders by 1983, and the program was to have a self-sustaining "multiplier-effect."

Just as the contras turned to private assistance, so too has the church hierarchy, in an effort to continue the counterrevolution leadership and cadre formation programs. According to a 9 May 1984, W. R. Grace and Co. confidential memorandum, leaked to the press in July,[58] Obando y Bravo met in New York with company adviser John Meehan to request material assistance for church projects. Meehan's carefully worded memorandum to company president J. Peter Grace states that Obando y Bravo showed him a "well-worked-out and organized plan [the "development plan"], which he has been promoting for the last four years, and which involves the formation of leadership cadre in his Archdiocese who would oppose the Sandinistas." The Archbishop "has dedicated all his resources and knowledge" to the efforts to oppose the Sandinista government, and his development plan is intended to strengthen the hierarchy as "the most solid and effective opposition to the regime today."

Meehan recommended that Obando y Bravo receive the funds, as well as movie projectors and anticommunist religious films—"effective on earlier occasions—Brazil and Chile—to be used in the church's parochial councils." (These films are produced by the "Family Rosary Crusade," and have regularly accompanied covert CIA operations in Latin America. A spokesman for the Family Rosary Crusade told the ANN news service that the institution had already sent Meehan fifteen films for distribution in Nicaragua.)[59] Furthermore, Meehan recommended that the funds be sent through a "third channel," and that in the event of a counterrevolutionary victory, Obando y Bravo's "well-formed leaders" would carry out the role of "supporting and protecting" the new government.[60]

Shortly after Obando y Bravo's visit to New York, the FDN's "Managua cell," led by Pedro Ernesto Sánchez, was broken up and Sánchez provided his spectacular testimony, large portions of which were about his relationship with Father Amado Peña. In one part of this testimony, Sánchez noted that Peña had centered his work on building up these same parochial councils.

The plot thickened when Peña was himself arrested on 20 June. This provoked a fierce campaign, led by the church hierarchy, which culminated in a march through Managua on 9 July, led by the Nicaraguan bishops.[61] The day after, the government expelled ten foreign priests who it claimed had been interfering in Nicaragua's internal affairs. In fact, Meehan's memorandum recommended that the "Development Plan" use foreign personnel to lead the counterrevolutionary parochial councils rather than Nicaraguans. One of the ten, the Canadian Benito Laplante, was directing COVISAMA, another COPROSA-type parochial council, while others worked with COPROSA itself or in other councils. Their expulsion, combined with the Peña incident, sparked off another uproar over alleged religious persecution.

As the United States envisioned it, the parochial councils were to be a network around the country that would form a stable core of counter-revolutionary cadres and would accumulate around them an ever greater number of citizens, acting under the guise of legitimate religious activities. Parallel to this, the political parties of the CDN organized their own U.S.-supported cadre programs, as did the reactionary trade unions. For example, through the American Institute for Free Labor Development—an AFL-CIO-affiliated organization funded by the AID and with close ties to the CIA, whose express purpose is combating the influence of progressive trade unions in Latin America[62]—the Federation of Trade Union Unity (CUS), a member of the CDN, received at least $850,000 for similar counterrevolutionary cadre-formation programs within the industrial working class.

Yet another private conduit for funding the internal front is the National Endowment for Democracy (NED), created by the Reagan administration in late 1983 for the purpose, according to the president, of "promoting the infrastructure of democracy" throughout the world as part of U.S. "competition with the Soviet Union." The NED's budget—$18 million in that year alone—is provided by Congress, which does not, however, oversee its operations.

According to its statute, the NED cannot provide foreign institutions directly with money; it must therefore go through intermediary organizations that solicit funds on behalf of these foreign groups. In Nicaragua's case, the intermediary was the Friends of the Democratic Center in Central America (PRODEMCA), formed in November 1984 with the participation of Arturo Cruz. Its National Council is filled with figures from the New Right, the Reagan administration, and CIA front organizations—among them J. Peter Grace; AIFLD director William C. Doherty; Penn Kemble, president of the Foundation for a Democratic Education, which has served as a liaison between contra leaders and the U.S. Congress; and Max Singer, president of the Potomac Organization, one of the ideological cornerstones of the war against Nicaragua. Through PRODEMCA, U.S. government funds provided to the NED have been subsidizing a CDN project to create a Center for Democratic Studies, another "American group" to train cadres for the internal front (at least $150,000); the Permanent Commission of Human Rights (at least $50,000), which is aligned with the CDN and is dedicated to denouncing alleged Sandinista human rights abuses to the international community; and *La Prensa* (at least $100,000). The CDN and *La Prensa* initially denied any such funding, but after it was confirmed by NED sources, did an about-face, claiming they needed the money to "finance democracy in Nicaragua."[63] These amounts are the tip of a huge iceberg.[64]

The Internal Front in Action

As we have seen, the internal front's destabilizing activities are centered on the reproduction of counterrevolutionary propaganda. Once the basic lines of this propaganda have been drawn up in Washington, the internal front takes responsibility for its diffusion within Nicaragua, adapting it to the national context. The themes are now well known, having been circulated for the past six years—Vice-president Sergio Ramírez has referred to them as the *ejes clasicos*—"classic axes"—of the ideological attacks on the revolution (its political persecution, totalitarianism, its threat to its neighbors, its excessive military build-up, its being a Soviet-Cuban surrogate, etc.).[65] But the internal front also focuses on themes that are more transitory in nature, launching them at specific points in the war and with specific tactical or strategic objectives in mind.

The internal front's operations include a host of *legal* activities. The Sandinistas, in accordance with their policies of political pluralism and civil liberties, have not stopped these activities, although they do not hesitate to denounce them. But when the internal front moves into criminal activities, as it did with the Jorge Salazar affair, it is prosecuted with the full weight of the law, just as in any other country. In each case, the government's activities are depicted as "political persecution," and the internal front repeatedly tries to provoke the government into validating this claim. In March 1981, the internal front attempted to provoke the first mass confrontation with the revolutionary state. Robelo, who was then generally accepted as the leader of the bourgeois opposition, organized a demonstration in the southern town of Nandaime which he said was intended to put the government's "tolerance for pluralism" to the test. *La Prensa* and the right's radio stations had publicized the event, hinting that a confrontation was possible. Smaller MDN demonstrations had been held around the country, and on 14 March throngs of young Sandinista supporters prevented the Nandaime rally from taking place. The ensuing confusion turned violent. *La Prensa* described the affair as "Nicaragua's return to the law of the jungle, the end to many people's hopes."[66] The FSLN, on the other hand, issued an official communiqué stating that the incident was "the people's first insurrectional effort against the reactionairies."

In January 1982 State Security discovered a plot to blow up Nicaragua's only oil refinery and cement factory. Among the nineteen arrested were several leaders of the CDN parties. This, along with a sharp escalation of contra aggression, the blowing up of two bridges in the north, and the revelation of a $19 million destabilization program, led the government to declare a State of Emergency in March, providing it with the legal instruments to prevent further internal destabilization.

This new law had been preceded by the Social and Economic Emergency Law of September 1981, which prohibited the publication of false and destabilizing news. The new decree instituted *prior* censorship only for false news and news relating to military issues. For instance, *La Prensa* would not be able to repeat its summer 1981 campaign to cause consumer panic. It had published several headline stories claiming that Nicaragua's sugar was being exported to Cuba and that shortages were imminent. Thousands of consumers flocked to the markets, hoarding all the sugar they could find, and, in a self-fulfilling prophecy, created a *real* sugar shortage. Most countries institute such prior censorship with regard to military and security matters during times of war, as the United States did during both the Civil War and World War II. The publication of political positions is not censored, as any cursory reading of *La Prensa*—filled as it is with political denunciations of the Sandinistas—confirms.

In fact, Nicaraguans only won *real* freedom of expression after the revolution. Before 1979, the media was monopolized by the dictatorship and the conservative opposition. Since then, the majority has been able to express its opinions, offer criticisms publicly, and hear a diversity of views and information. The country's most popular radio program, "Contacto 6-20," which airs for several hours each day on the Voice of Nicaragua, is a live call-in show in which people from all over the country raise every imaginable concern, from lambasting state bureaucracy to commenting on national affairs, to demanding improvements in their neighborhoods. Following each call, the station dispatches investigators to report back on the complaint. Similarly, *Barricada, El Nuevo Diario,* and the public television and radio stations each have sections or time reserved for public expression. Each week, high-level government officials, led by the president himself, hold "De Cara al Pueblo" ("Face the People") meetings in remote peasant communities, poor Managua *barrios*, textile factories, or with representatives of the medical profession. At these meetings, broadcast *live* on the radio and later shown on television, the participants express their concerns and criticisms directly to the leadership. Has any U.S. president or cabinet member ever held a public meeting to hear what people have to say about his administration? Yet President Reagan's 16 March 1986, national address on Nicaragua—perhaps the most scathing attack on the Sandinistas to date—was aired on Nicaraguan television and published in its entirety in *Barricada*, under the title "Let the People Judge." Has a major speech by the president of Nicaragua ever been published in a leading U.S. newspaper or aired on U.S. television?

Despite the political costs—the censorship was attacked internationally—the government felt that it was necessary to forestall any attempt to repeat a Chilean-style destabilization through the media. Lt. Nelba Blandón, head of the Interior Ministry's Media Office, recalled the role of *El Mercurio* in the CIA's campaign against the Allende government and explained that "we preferred to assume the cost rather than have to tell the people afterward that we had permitted destabilization and a return to the past."[67]

Meanwhile, a CDN campaign for a major reduction in the Nicaraguan armed forces—such that by 1984 there would only be a police force—marked the beginning of another "classic axis": that the Sandinistas have turned the country into a militarized police state. At the same time, all condemnation of contra aggression disappeared from the internal fronts vocabulary.

Robelo's departure and widespread popular rejection of the anti-armed forces campaign dampened the right's initiative, however, and the church issue became a key component of the destabilization campaign. Dramatic events in the summer of 1982 would thrust religion onto center stage.

The conflict began in June, when Pope John Paul II for the first time took a firm position against the revolution in a letter (dated 29 June) to the Nicaraguan bishops, who decided to defer making it public for reasons that became clear later. On 25 July a FDN band savagely murdered fourteen peasants in the northern town of San Francisco del Norte. While such massacres were from then on commonplace, this was the first and had a chilling effect on the nation. As they left the town, the contras had written on the walls of the peasant houses that their attack was carried out "in the name of God." In the following days, Radio 15 de Septiembre boasted of the massacre in similar terms, at the same time praising Obando y Bravo as being "ever more identified with the struggle for the liberation of Nicaragua." The bishops chose this moment to give the pope's letter to *La Prensa* for publication. The government initially censored its publication, but, under heavy criticism, reversed its decision and the letter was published in all three papers on 10 August. The letter unconditionally supported the bishops and lashed out against the "popular church." This set the stage for the following events.

• On 11 August Obando y Bravo's spokesman and Radio Católica director Father Bismark Carballo was in the house of a female parishioner in an upper-class Managua suburb when gunshots were heard from inside. The Sandinista police, who were accompanying demonstrators marching about an unrelated issue in the same neighborhood, ran into the house and dragged out two men, one a naked Carballo—all in the presence of photographers and reporters who had been covering the demonstration. These photographers were later published in *Barricada* and *El Nuevo Diario*. According to the woman, she and the priest were in bed when her husband came home, discovered them, and took out a pistol and began to shoot. Carballo claimed he was lunching with the woman when an armed man entered forced him to undress, and then began shooting. The incident sparked a national scandal that provided ample material for days of propagandizing by *La Prensa* and the church hierarchy, which claimed that the whole incident had been set up by State Security to embarrass the church.[68]

• On the weekend of 14/15 September, rumors were flying in Managua and Masaya that "the FSLN wants to do away with religion," "the government is going to close down the churches," "the Sandinistas are going to outlaw Catholicism," etc.—such rumors are an important part of the internal front's ammunition. They are begun as leaflets distributed by the CDN, are carried in *La Prensa*, broadcast as comments on right-wing radio stations, and so on. Popularly known as *bolas*, the purpose of such rumors is to create an atmosphere of uncertainty; and, like a barometer, they are almost always followed by some political action or provocation.

• On the morning of 16 September, anti-Sandinista students occupied several Catholic high schools to "demonstrate our solidarity with Father Carballo." In Monimbó, an Indian community in the heart of Masaya, the directors of the Salesian Catholic School ordered classes suspended for twenty-four hours to protest "aggressions suffered by the church." The school was subsequently occupied by youth who claimed to be students supporting the suspension. Ten thousand people from the area then marched to the school to protest the occupation, but as they approached they were fired on by snipers inside; two were killed. Other bands of right-wing youth marched through Monimbo telling the residents that the Sandinistas were coming to commit atrocities, and attacking and burning CDS offices and militia posts. Despite demands by the local population that it be armed and allowed to confront the reactionaries, the FSLN responded with restraint, calling on the people not to be provoked. At the same time, security forces peacefully cleared the school and arrested eighty-one occupants, only nine of whom were from Masaya. (Two years later, Sánchez testified that Father Amado Peña and another contra priest had organized the incident.)

Both in Nicaragua and abroad, Monimbó is a symbol of the Sandinista struggle against the dictatorship: its residents rose up against Somoza three times. Monimbó is considered a stronghold of Sandinista support. The third anniversary of the revolution celebration was held in Monimbo under the slogan "Monimbó *is* Nicaragua." In the same month, the FDN had baptized a newly created task force "Minimbó." The incident was clearly a calculated attempt by the internal front to create a popular uprising against the Sandinistas in what was supposedly an impregnable stronghold.

In June 1983 Sandinista State Security uncovered what was perhaps the most macabre conspiracy yet, involving a bizarre assassination attempt against Foreign Minister Miguel D'Escoto and other Nicaraguan leaders, extensive intelligence gathering on the armed forces, ministries, and government officials, the organization of counterrevolutionary "binary cells" (two-man commando units) throughout the country to carry out sabotage, and the massive recruitment of opposition figures and disgruntled Nicaraguans into the contra fold. The full story of the "Benedictine Plot" was told in Managua on 6 June by now-2d Lt. Marlene Moncada of the Foreign Ministry.[69]

In early 1982, Moncada, who was working as consul secretary at the Nicaraguan embassy in Tegucigalpa, was approached by Somocista guardsmen who attempted to recruit her for the CIA. She was instructed by the Foreign Ministry to "accept and play their game." The double agent was assigned a CIA liaison and given the alias "Mirea." In September 1982, the Foreign Ministry transferred her to Managua, where she was contacted by Ermila Loretta Rodríguez, an agent operating as second secretary of the U.S. embassy in Managua, and was given extensive training in espionage.

Mirea's liaison ordered her to travel to Tegucigalpa on her Easter vacation for a briefing on her first "essential assignment." There she was told by agent "Baby Johnson" that D'Escoto was "one of the biggest problems we have in supporting the struggle for democracy in Nicaragua."[70] Johnson instructed her to find the opportune time to offer him a bottle of "treated wine." "Don't worry, we're experts in this. We don't fail, everything will go perfect," Johnson told her.

But everything did not "go perfect." Back in Managua, Mirea received instructions to pick up a bottle of Benedictine liquor that was hidden in a garbage can outside a Managua restaurant and proceed with the operation. Instead, she turned the bottle over to State Security, which had by this time gathered enough information to crack open the entire network. Laboratory analysis confirmed that the chemical agent in the liquor was thallium, a delayed-reaction poison that begins to take effect some ten days after ingestion, bringing about a slow death. Detection of the poison through autopsy is impossible.

While Rodríguez was the CIA agent entrusted with coordinating the "Benedictine plot," David Noble Greig—the embassy's first secretary—was responsible for overseeing all local CIA operations. One of the activities he supervised was organizing members of the Conservative party into contra "binary cells" to sabotage production and supply centers, conduct espionage, and assassinate Sandinista leaders. Some eighty government officials were reportedly on the "hit list." The key CIA liaison for this mission was the lawyer Carlos Icaza, a well-known adviser to the Conservative party and close associate of Adolfo Calero. Icaza attempted to recruit EPS Lt. Jorge Roustran, but he, like Moncada, reported these efforts to his superiors. Icaza eventually introduced Roustran to Conservative Youth president Mario Castillo, the assigned coordinator of commando activities. Castillo was using Conservative Youth branches to establish bases of support in the high schools.

On 30 May Icaza enthusiastically told Roustran that everything was set for the operation to begin: "Sandinismo will be brought down like a house of cards with the help of the United States," he said. For his part, Castillo testified that he was recruited and brought on to the CIA payroll by Calero and Linda Pfeifel, the embassy's political attaché, whose chief responsibility was to work with the right-wing parties and organizations.[71]

The "Benedictine affair" was not the first attempt to assassinate Sandinista leaders. According to State Security chief Lenin Cerna, over two hundred attempts were discovered and neutralized between 1979 and June 1985. Among the methods contemplated had been poison, remote-control explosives, rifles, and even specially designed CIA pens that shoot a single bullet.[72]

The promulgation of the Patriotic Military Service (SMP) Law in August 1983 provided the internal front with another rallying point. During the debates on the law in the Council of State, most CDN representatives walked out in protest; they then released statements charging that the law was a violation of human rights and had been enacted to force the population to defend the interests of a political party. On 29 August the Nicaraguan Bishops' Conference took up the attack, publishing a pastoral letter on the law, which was printed in full on the front page of *La Prensa* and massively disseminated by the right. The letter declared that the Sandinista state "has imposed its legitimacy by armed force. . . . As the state's armed power, the army has no legitimacy since that same state does not have authentic moral legitimacy." The letter concluded by charging that the law "follows the general lines of all totalitarian laws," and that "those who do not share the ideology of the Sandinista Party" are perfectly justified in opting for "conscientious objection."[73] This gave the green light, from the moral sanctuary of the church, for the internal front to organize its draft-resistance campaigns.

The significance of the bishops' letter and the campaign that followed cannot be overemphasized. Not only does the survival of the revolution depend on its military strength, but it depends on mobilizing the population in its own defense—exactly what the internal front wants to prevent. And since the SMP signifies a huge quantitative and *qualitative* increase in the defense capacity of the country, it is not surprising that it has earned the wrath of the counterrevolution.

The pastoral letter also claimed that the Sandinista state was not legitimate because it was "imposed by armed force," thus negating the legitimacy it had earned by virtue of being installed by a mass insurrection. There was also an attempt to reduce the word "Sandinista" to the FSLN, rather than the much broader struggle over foreign domination. By depicting a national army as the army of a political party, the counterrevolution was attempting to create a division between the interests of the population and the organization which that population had chosen.

The church then took its campaign a step further. In October 1983, during the first round of conscription, marches to registration centers and violent confrontations were organized from the pulpit. On 31 October, two foreign priests from the Salesian High School in Masaya, José María Pacheco from Costa Rica and Luis Corral from Spain, were deported for distributing pamphlets urging resistance to military service. The Bishops' Conference once again charged that the church was being persecuted. Since 1983, the government has broken up numerous networks that are encouraging draft resistance and aiding resisters who want to leave the country.

By 1984, the war of attrition required greater unity between the internal and military fronts. In fact, one of the tasks assigned to Pedro Ernesto Sánchez was to consolidate relations between the FDN and the Catholic church, and by 1983 he had succeeded in developing an extensive contra network in Managua that included Catholic priests José María Pacheco and Amado Peña, leading figures in the right-wing political parties, activists of the CTN and the CUS, and COSEP representatives.[74]

Following a trip to Honduras in late 1983 for training in urban sabotage, Sánchez's plans to activate the internal military front moved into high gear. The two overriding tasks, according to Sánchez, were "to achieve unity in struggle between the FDN and the church and to initiate military actions." Several military training schools were opened, with weapons and explosives infiltrated from Honduras.

The most overwhelming evidence of this activity was a State Security videotape of meetings between Sánchez, Peña, and several others. In the film, Sánchez first reads Peña a letter of encouragement from Enrique Bermúdez, and then shows the priest how to handle arms and explosives. Peña assures Sánchez that the pope can be counted on. Sánchez asks, "What tactics does the church have?" and Peña responds, "I have to say now that we are preaching passive resistance, but when the time comes we know that here there is nothing peaceful."[75]

Peña then explains that the first action must be carried out on 21 June, during a planned march of market vendors who wanted the government to exempt them from recently passed consumer protection laws. "We have to do something, but swiftly," Peña says. "Radio 15 de Septiembre is pressuring us, we have to finish off these sons of bitches." Peña instructs Sánchez and the others to disrupt the demonstration and provoke a police action: "Go to the market, we will be there. God wants these sons of bitches to stop messing with us. The most important thing is that there are deaths, I don't care how. We need to light the fuse here. After the first few deaths, the horror will begin."

The Sandinista authorities arrested only those four involved in the conspiracy against whom *material* evidence existed, and let the rest remain free, including Conservative party leaders Miriam Argüello and Mario Rapaccioli. Nor did they arrest Peña, instead, in a tactical decision, placing him in the custody of the Vatican embassy in Managua. Despite this, Obando y Bravo told journalists that "the whole thing is a tremendous set up. The people who are trying to involve Peña are the same ones who always harass the church. These people are artists who can imitate the voice and also the tapes. We know the methods they use."[76] The following day, the Nicaraguan Bishops' Conference issued a communiqué, published in full by *La Prensa*, repeating this claim.

Throughout 1984, the war of attrition was maturing. The internal front and the armed contras moved toward what the CIA manual referred to as *fusion,* while the larger strategic scheme in which this fusion would take place was developing. Washington's intent was to bring all the war theaters together under a coherent plan of action in order to defeat Sandinismo.

8

The Counterrevolution: The "Thousand Factors" That Did Not Come Together

Events, like fruits, ripen, and we must wait until things ripen here. The strategy for bringing about a political defeat must be varied—from individual discontent, to group discontent, and finally national discontent. This is why we are calling for a national dialogue. There are a thousand things that could happen, a thousand factors that could come together to produce a political defeat. When will this be achieved? Sometimes an event totally removed from the circumstances at hand provokes or unleashes an unforeseeable political situation. Although this political defeat is preferable, it might come down to a military defeat. One way or another, all the factors come together.

—Jaime Bengochea,
COSEP vice-president, 1985[1]

By 1985, the various elements of the counterrevolution were acting together, as part of the new strategy structured by the United States. The counterrevolution had made great strides since the founding of the FDN, the subsequent uniting of the FDN and ARDE, the formation of the CDN, and Obando y Bravo's assumption of the mantle of leadership. Yet the qualitative step from coordinated action on the part of several distinct detachments to unification into a single entity had not been made. Such a step was an essential element of the struggle to undermine the legitimacy of Sandinismo and validate the counterrevolutionary alternative.

But another step was also necessary: developing a coherent political and socioeconomic program, including a plan for organizing a new state apparatus. This was not happening, and the war strategists in Washington were by 1985 profoundly aware of this weakness. "What the administration must do," reported one participant in a strategy session held with NSC members and "privatization" leaders, "is establish a positive image of what the U.S.-backed rebels propose to do once the Marxist Sandinista government is overthrown. We all came to the conclusion that we have to get away from the principle that the [counterrevolution] is only against the Sandinistas. The question is what are they proposing."[2]

With such a program *and* its embodiment in a single organizational structure, the counterrevolution would, U.S. strategists hoped, have a secure platform from which to project a positive image in international forums, in the U.S. Congress, with governments in Latin America and Europe, with the U.S. public, and *most important of all*, in the eyes of the Nicaraguan people. This process was conducted in tandem with the development of a comprehensive plan of action—expressed in the call for *national reconciliation*—and the fusion of the internal and military fronts.

The Electoral Juncture: Fusion and Reconciliation

In December 1983 the Nicaraguan government had announced that the electoral process would officially begin on 31 January 1984, and would culminate by early 1985. The counterrevolution was caught off guard: Washington and the internal front had repeatedly demanded elections, never expecting that they would actually be held. But the FSLN had always intended to fulfill a commitment that dated back to its days in the mountains, and the 1979 program called for elections following a period of national reconstruction, which included the creation of new state institutions and civic and political education. By late 1983, this reconstruction had reached the point where elections could be an authentic exercise in participatory democracy and not a bourgeois raffle for power. The FSLN had already been "elected" through the popular insurrection and its program tested in four years of government; now it was to be tested at the ballot box.[3]

The counterrevolution was in a bind: it would no longer be able to use the absence of elections as part of its campaign to call the government illegitimate and totalitarian, and the renewed international legitimacy thus gained by the Sandinistas would give Nicaragua increased room for maneuver on the diplomatic front. The new government was to be formed from the participating parties, in accordance with votes polled, and the electoral laws further stipulated that abstention meant loss of legal status as a party (although not the right to exist as an organization). This confronted the rightist parties of the CDN with a particular dilemma: they could participate and risk a humiliating defeat, in which case their claims to be representative would be laid to rest, or they could abstain and be shut out of meaningful participation in political life.

The United States and the internal front eventually adopted the abstentionist strategy, determined both to boycott the elections and to mount a domestic and international campaign of sabotage. Since the CDN was supposed to be *the* legitimate opposition, the United States could then claim that its nonparticipation was proof that the elections were a "sham." During the August–October 1984 campaign, the contras stepped up their attacks in an effort to make it impossible to hold the elections at all. According to a Defense Ministry report, issued in October, contra attacks increased by about five times during those three months. An NSC "Background Paper" leaked to the press in early November summarized the U.S. diplomatic efforts to undermine the electoral process, including the publication of a "resource book" for distribution to journalists, the U.S. Congress, and key opinion makers that demonstrated the "non-democratic nature" of the elections and a compilation of statements by the CDN urging U.S. journalists, intellectuals, and labor leaders to speak out against the elections and to lobby their counterparts in Europe and Latin America to do the same.[4]

As the electoral process progressed, the positions and actions taken by the internal front were increasingly synchronized with the larger scheme, directed from Washington. In fact, abstentionism served as the vehicle for consummating its transition from ideological affinity to organic affiliation with the counterrevolution. COSEP led the effort to establish the abstentionist line. Firing the first volley on Christmas Eve 1983, *La Prensa* published a "joint" opposition paper, entitled "Free Elections: A Step Toward Democracy," drafted by COSEP and signed by all the CDN members. The document put forward a series of preconditions for CDN participation in the elections, which were in essence a rehash of the "classic axes": there must be a "state-party" separation, the repeal of laws "violating" human rights, the return of all confiscated property, an end to "religious persecution," etc. If these demands were not met, the document warned, the CDN would boycott the elections, which would then become a farce.[5]

The one new demand was that all contras outside the country (referred to as "opposition members in exile") be pardoned and allowed to return to the country under the banner of "national reconciliation," in order to bring an end to the "civil war." Without the participation of the "opposition's clean-up hitters living abroad," the elections "could not be fair." The right knew full well that the Sandinistas would never agree to a dialogue with the contras and that this would thus provide an excuse for boycotting the elections. In the following months, this demand—marching hand in hand with abstentionism—developed into the key strategic issue for the internal front. The NSC "Background Paper" would later brag that "we have had success in [directing] public and private [attention] on the Nicaraguan elections as the key obstacle for national reconciliation and peace in the region."[6] It was a demand that no member of the internal front would have dared to raise before, for fear of being openly associated with the armed contras, and signaled the extent to which the two fronts were coalescing into one single project. With this transition, the subliminal message that "we would be better off without the Sandinistas" became "the Sandinistas are responsible for the war itself because, with their totalitarianism, etc., they have left the Nicaraguan people with no other recourse but to take up arms." U.S. aggression then becomes the "legitimate assistance" of a Western democracy to a population resisting Soviet-Communist domination.

The demand for "reconciliation" had in fact been an element of U.S. strategy since the creation of the armed counterrevolution. By presenting the externally organized and directed aggression as a "civil war" and demanding the return of the contras, the counterrevolution is legitimized as a representative Nicaraguan force—the first step in presenting it as an alternative to the Sandinistas. The theme of "national reconciliation," raised by Assistant Secretary of State for Inter-American Affairs Thomas Enders during his late 1981 visit to Managua, was further trumpeted by Special Ambassador to Central America Richard Stone during his repeated trips to Nicaragua in 1983, and was reiterated in the Kissinger Commission's report in early 1984.

The demand is always presented as an ultimatum: if the Sandinistas reject the "olive branch" of reconciliation—that is, if they do not surrender and negotiate the dismantling of revolutionary power—then their own intransigence is to blame for any escalation of the aggression that always follows the peace offer. The ultimatum—capitulation or increased aggression—was candidly restated by Reagan himself in early 1985, when he answered a reporter's question as to whether the United

States would continue seeking to overthrow the Sandinistas: "Not if the present government would turn around and say 'uncle' to the Nicaraguan rebels."

The internal front's December 1983 proposal provoked widespread indignation, and the demand for reconciliation fizzled out. Once there was no longer any basis for abstentionism, the parties of the CDN began to express their doubts about the wisdom of the abstentionist strategy. Once again the church stepped in: on Easter Sunday 1984, the Nicaraguan Bishops' Conference released a pastoral letter that repeated virtually verbatim the CDN's call for reconciliation. Now, however, the bishops' letter gave the demand an aura of legitimacy that it had not had before, paving the way for the arrival of the "candidate from Washington," Arturo Cruz. It was Cruz who then pushed reconciliation to the top of the contra agenda.[7]

Ever since the electoral process began, Washington had been promoting Cruz's image at home and abroad. COSEP pushed the idea of his candidacy on the rest of the CDN, even as some parties were considering their own candidates. In the period between his resignation as ambassador to the United States and his arrival in Nicaragua on 23 July to "participate" in the elections, Cruz had maintained broad contacts with all detachments of the counterrevolution, from the White House and Capitol Hill to the FDN, ARDE, and the CDN.[8] Thus, he was the perfect individual to pull together the abstentionist plan—despite sharp divisions within the CDN, which was in virtually permanent session from mid-July onward.

Cruz's role during the next months was to outline the strategy revolving around the reconciliation and abstentionism. Although he had been touted as the CDN's preliminary candidate on his arrival in Nicaragua, just two days before the registration deadline he declared that the counterrevolution was a "civil war" brought about by Sandinista "intransigence," and named Pastora, Calero, and Robelo as important members of the "democratic opposition." He then presented nine "conditions" for the CDN's participation in the elections—a carbon copy of COSEP's December document, with one difference: reconciliation became the synthesis of all the other demands. It "is all that counts," as he put it.[9] The government pointed out that the CDN "demands" were in effect an electoral platform, and suggested that the coalition take part in the elections on this basis, and let the people decide. But that was not the plan; as expected, the government firmly rejected reconciliation as a precondition for the elections, and Cruz then loudly refused to run. The boycott was on.

Cruz was also essential to the project of fusing the internal front and the armed contras. On the same day as he was arguing that reconciliation was "all that counts," FDN and ARDE leaders met in Panama City and announced the formal unification of the two groups. Their communiqué declared the FDN-ARDE's full support for Cruz and thanked the "organizations and citizens inside Nicaragua that support our actions."[10] They presented a seven-point program, whose goal was to overthrow the Sandinista government and "install a transitional government of national reconciliation" in order to "democratize Nicaragua." In Managua, Cruz offered to act as "mediator" for the "national dialogue." He assumed the role of a "great democratic opposition leader" around whom the counterrevolutionary project was moving forward. (It was not until later, as we shall see, that Obando y Bravo assumed this position.)

Abstentionism had wide implications for the balance of forces inside the country. It was the most concrete expression of the class struggle at that time, and the principal battlefield for the ideological struggle. Once the CDN had refused to participate in the elections, and the internal front had become openly identified with the armed contras, it felt no need for subtlety in its attacks on the government. In early August, *La Prensa* published an editorial which set the tone. It argued that the precepts of the Monroe Doctrine were perfectly valid, that it was necessary for Nicaragua to "accept U.S. influence" over the country, and that "the so-called 'U.S. aggression' or 'secret war' is in reality the justified defense of the continent by the United States against Cuba and Russia in Central America."[11]

In the final weeks of the electoral campaign it became clear that the abstention of Cruz and the CDN would not discredit the election in the eyes of key sectors of the international community—the Contadora countries, other Latin American democracies, the Socialist International—although it had succeeded in doing so inside the United States. Before departing from Managua on 14 October, barely two weeks before the vote, Socialist International president Willy Brandt, sent to evaluate the electoral process, declared: "One must not make the mistake of thinking that Cruz's group is the only opposition group that exists in Nicaragua. . . . It is astonishing that Shultz is calling the Nicaraguan elections a sham because a sector of the opposition decided not to run of its own accord." Brandt's opinion predominated in the international community.[12]

In the final days of the campaign, the White House sought to widen the boycott, applying intense pressure to withdraw on those parties to the right of the FSLN. It was widely reported in Managua that the U.S. embassy had offered large sums of money and political favors to the

Independent Liberal (PLI) and Democratic Conservative (PCD) party leaders in exchange for their promise to pull out of the contest.[13] On 21 October, after seven hours of debate at a national convention, PLI representatives, led by the party's presidential candidate, Virgilio Godoy Reyes, voted not to participate. The decision led to an uproar among the party's membership, which overrode Godoy's machinations and continued to campaign. Then, during the PCD national convention on 28 October, a fierce debate between those favoring abstention and those favoring participation was broken up by members of the party's youth wing, who physically attacked the abstentionists and prevented a vote on the issue.

In the end, the elections were held as scheduled, and there was massive popular participation. The final results issued by the Supreme Electoral Council, the independent body set up to run and supervise the elections, gave 69 percent of the votes to the FSLN, 13.2 percent to the PCD, 9 percent to the PLI, 5.2 percent to the Popular Social Christian Party (PPSC), and 3.6 percent to the three left parties combined. Even as the votes were being counted, the United States launched the "artificial MiGs" crisis—which served, as was noted earlier, to remove the election from the center of attention.

Approximately 30 percent of the country's eligible voters either did not vote at all (24.6 percent) or cast null ballots (6.1 percent). Of these, thousands were EPS and militia members in active combat, while contra military activity prevented civilians in many zones from getting to the polls. Moreover, many null ballots were due not to a conscious decision but rather to mistakes (i.e., mistakenly voting for two parties rather than one, smudging ballots, etc.). In all, it was estimated that some 20 percent *of the voting age population* consciously chose to abstain or cast invalid ballots. Many of the abstentions were clearly votes for the CDN project, a rough barometer of the extent to which the counter-revolution had managed to win favor among the population. Others could be considered protest votes against the Sandinistas, but did not necessarily imply support for the counterrevolution.[14]

Given that this was Nicaragua's first real democratic election ever, and that it was held in the midst of a war and during a period of profound social transformation, any interpretation of the results must be limited to generalizations. Nevertheless, the results indicated that abstentionism was higher in the agricultural frontier, where the contras had been building a social base throughout the year. Support for the FSLN, conversely, was more consistent in the urban centers of the Pacific coastal belt, indicating the strength of the Sandinistas' political organization, as well as the internal front's inability to make inroads in this region. Overall, the results confirmed that in late 1984 the FSLN indisputably represented the aspirations of Nicaraguans, and that only a minority had come under the political or ideological sway of the counterrevolution.

Reconciliation: The Next Round

Cruz remained the key character in the next round, which had begun in February 1985 and was coordinated with the Reagan administration's effort to get Congress to renew contra funding. The connection was made clear by Shultz, in a speech at the Commonwealth Club in San Francisco on 22 February: the Sandinistas, he said, "will not negotiate their positions unless there are incentives which force them to do so . . . whether it be through unilateral actions or jointly with the opposition."[15]

Contra and CDN leaders had been meeting—in Washington, Miami, San José, and Tegucigalpa. In Managua, on the same day that Shultz made his remarks in San Francisco, the CDN again called for "dialogue" as a way of averting a "growing civil war." On that same day, according to testimony given three months later by FDN defector Efraín Mondragón, Cruz visited the FDN's Las Vegas camp in southern Honduras, announced that he represented the "internal opposition," and reported that they were seeking the "unity" of all those "struggling for freedom." After Cruz left, Bermúdez told Mondragón that this "democratic leader is very important because [the CDN] is our civic face."[16]

A week later Calero, Robelo, Cruz, Fagoth, Pedro Joaquín Chamorro, Jr.—who had left his position as co-editor of *La Prensa* months earlier to join the armed contras in Costa Rica—and other leading contra figures released a "unity document": the Sandinistas were to initiate dialogue within two months or "the possibilities of a peaceful solution will expire." The contras named the Nicaraguan Bishops' Conference as the mediator in the dialogue, and chose Cruz to go to Managua to present the plan to the CDN and form the "united political-military front."[17]

On 11 March, eleven hitherto unheard of groups in San José, among them the Social Christian party in Exile, the Nicaraguan Conservative party in Exile, Nicaraguan Private Enterprise in Exile, and other organizations bearing the exact names of the internal front groups with the additional qualifier "in Exile," announced the formation of the Nicaraguan Opposition Coordinating Committee (CON). They released a communiqué supporting the CDN's 22 February document and the FDN-ARDE unity document. COSEP Vice-president Ramiro Gurdián confirmed that these groups consisted of members of the CDN organizations "currently living abroad."[18] The "in exile" was added to allow those still in Nicaragua to deny their participation in the counterrevolution. Only two days earlier, top CDN leaders had traveled to Costa Rica to meet with the contras.[19]

On the same day that these "exile" groups released their communiqué, the CDN had planned to receive Cruz in Managua. But the government refused to allow him into the country, and warned CDN leaders that their plan would be considered illegal. The CDN accepted the warning without much protest, and released a press statement declaring that their struggle was "eminently civic" and repeating the call for dialogue. The contras did not hide their disappointment at the CDN's cold feet: Calero expressed his "regret" over its unwillingness to "follow through."

With this failure, leadership of the contra "reconciliation" program passed from Cruz to the church hierarchy. "The hope of national reconciliation in Nicaragua now rests with our leader, Cardinal Miguel Obando y Bravo," who confers "moral authority and competence upon our brothers in the conflict," said Cruz.[20]

President Reagan opened this third round of the reconciliation strategy at an April news conference during which he announced his "peace plan" for Nicaragua:

> Reconciliation is indispensable to peace. The Communists in Nicaragua have turned a cold shoulder to appeals for national reconciliation from the Pope and the Nicaraguan Bishops. . . . We supported national reconciliation before and we support it today . . . and we know that without incentives for dialogue and peace [the Sandinistas] will not change.[21]

The bishops took their cue from this and the following day released a communiqué declaring their willingness to mediate in the dialogue. At the same time, Nicaraguan Bishops' Conference President Pablo Antonio Vega, expressing his "hope" for the success of Reagan's "peace plan," arranged a series of meetings with CDN leaders to "organize the dialogue."

The UNO: Toward a Counterrevolutionary Government

The organizational unification of the counterrevolution took a major step forward on 12 June 1985, with the formation of the United

Nicaraguan Opposition (UNO). U.S. officials and diplomats had been working to consolidate the unification ever since the La Penca bombing. With debates raging in Congress over aid to the contras, these efforts reached a fever pitch as dozens of meetings were held in Washington, Miami, and various Central American capitals. Following congressional approval of $27 million in "humanitarian aid," Adolfo Calero for FDN, Alfonso Robelo for ARDE, and Arturo Cruz "unofficially" representing the internal front (the "internal democratic opposition"), announced the creation of the UNO at a press conference in San Salvador.[22] During the conference, the triumvirate—or the "Triple A," as they became known in Nicaragua and to the international press—reported that MISURA would also be included. "Practically all the opposition groups" are represented in the new "civil mechanism," FDN spokeswoman Marta Zacasa said at the time.[23] The aim is "to give a view toward what the future of the opposition will be."

The UNO's "Declaration" was signed by the three men, as well as by representatives of the different "in exile" organizations of the internal front. What had been phantom organizations only a few months earlier had in the interim consolidated their structures and links to those inside Nicaragua. Even the two trade union federations affiliated to the CDN joined UNO, changing a word or two in their names. Those who signed the document were leading members of the CDN organizations who had left Nicaragua, including the Conservatives' Fernando Aguero, the PSC's Roberto Ferrey, and COSEP's Fuad Farach.

"Last March 1, the Nicaraguan Resistance backed the initiative of the Democratic Coordinating Committee [CDN] to bring the Sandinista Front to a national dialogue convened by the Nicaraguan Bishops' Conference," the declaration began. "Daniel Ortega categorically rejected our peace initiative, reaffirming his regime's intransigence and determination to prolong the civil war. With the deadline expired, we express our firm decision to continue united, struggling on all fronts, with a political solution as the priority. . . . committed to consolidating national unity and strengthening our alliances, we signatories agree to form the UNO to guide the efforts of democratic Nicaraguans on all fronts of struggle."[24]

While the Reagan administration chose the moment of the announcement with an eye on Congress, and while the new organization had responsibility for channeling the $27 million in aid, the project was in fact part of a long-term strategy, orchestrated by the NSC, to create an embryonic "government in exile," around which all the forces opposed to the Sandinistas could gather. These forces were to include far more than just Nicaraguans: if the UNO could win legitimacy, it was hoped that key international groups would soon line up behind it.

The UNO's founding declaration laid out a political program under the headings "National Reconciliation," "Steps Toward Democracy," and "Steps Toward National Reconstruction." The program included the release of all prisoners, including jailed National Guardsmen; the dissolution of virtually the entire state apparatus, including the judicial system, the EPS, and the National Assembly; new elections; and the formation of a "Government of Reconciliation," with a corresponding state apparatus. This government was to return to the bourgeoisie most of the properties expropriated since 1979 ("all those productive, commercial, and service activities that the private sector is capable of carrying out efficiently"), institute a "new social pact," create a national economic development program in which the "workers and peasants are an essential part" but the "businessmen and professionals are the driving force," and reduce the state to the role of regulator of private economic activity. Scattered throughout the document were the habitual demands: respect for property rights, freedom of worship and the press, political liberties, human rights, etc. The one new element was the socioeconomic system: a nation-building effort along similar lines to that pursued in El Salvador and the Caribbean Basin as a whole, based on the "initiative" of private capital and the political domination of the local elite under bourgeois democracy. Calero expanded on the concept of the "new social pact": "A democratic capitalism [in which] the right to private property, the most sacred right of man, stands above all else."[25]

The document not only laid bare the class character of the Nicaraguan counterrevolution, but for the first time it assembled its elements into a single document presented by a unified counterrevolutionary constellation of forces.

The development of such a programmatic alternative was tied to the goal of making the Nicaraguan counterrevolution part of a broader regional dynamic. As far back as early 1984, FDN spokesmen were talking about "solving Nicaragua's problems together with Central America's problems."[26] As the United States began the task of popularizing the UNO program, Shultz declared with satisfaction that "it is a program very much in line with the democratic tendency in the rest of the region, a tendency which the United States government is decidedly promoting."[27] The formation of the UNO was the culmination of four years of efforts to unify the counterrevolution. It was the fruit of counterrevolutionary nation building.

The United States expected the UNO to make possible a qualitative advance in the war. The UNO would enhance the attrition process within Nicaraguan society, and, as pressure mounted against the Sandinistas, it would also gain recognition in the international arena as the legitimate political-military representative of the Nicaraguan people.

The UNO immediately moved into action. It mounted a publicity campaign to project itself as a potent force, setting up offices in Washington, Miami, and various Central American and European capitals. Cruz announced that "we'll initiate an intensification of the internal military struggle and of the political struggle abroad."[28] One U.S. official explained that the UNO would "demand representation" in international forums "just as the Palestine Liberation Organization has."[29] Shortly afterward, the UNO sent officials to seek recognition from the United Nations, the Organization of American States, and the Contadora Group, at the same time as the armed contras launched a new military offensive.

More important, the formation of a "Human Rights Commission," complete with a "code of conduct" to eradicate the systematic abuses committed by the contras, was broadly publicized. In August 1985 FDN directorate member Indalecio Rodríguez announced that the UNO would soon inaugurate broad "extra-military services" programs in those northern zones under FDN influence, as part of a campaign to "humanize the war." These programs were to include handouts of food, medicine, clothing, and agricultural tools, and the establishment of a contra "Red Cross"—the counterrevolution's own effort at civic action. Similarly, twelve special commissions were set up to plan "diverse aspects of the anti-Sandinista struggle, and the future of Nicaragua," including schools and highways, legal and health systems. Each commission was to be a "ministry in exile."

The UNO was thus created to be the international-diplomatic wing of the counterrevolution, while the FDN and ARDE were to be the military wings, and the internal front the political-ideological branch inside Nicaragua. The strategy was to defeat the Sandinistas through an accumulation of pressures from all sides—with UNO being the organization to which they would have to surrender.

Contadora or Contradora?

The United States was determined to give the Contadora Group a role as one of these pressure mechanisms. As the UNO was being formed and the reconciliation strategy taking hold, the United States consolidated the changes it had sought in the September 1984 draft of the Contadora treaty to make it more "broadly consistent with U.S. interests." While the first draft had proscribed military maneuvers and foreign bases in the region, the modified treaty, presented in September 1985, instead established vague "regulations" under which these could continue indefinitely. The reference to foreign military advisers was open to such broad interpretations that U.S. advisers could remain. On the issue of armaments and troop levels, the new treaty replaced the former concept of a "reasonable balance" of armed forces in the Central American states, based on the "geographic and geopolitical situation" of each state—that is, on each country's real security needs—with a mechanical equation determined by GNP and equalized force and troop levels. It would, in effect, unilaterally disarm Nicaragua, the only country in the region facing full-scale and many-sided aggression from a major foreign power. As one Sandinista official put it: "On the one hand, they [the United States] want to have world public opinion believe that the peace efforts are advancing, when in reality what has advanced is the aggression against Nicaragua and the process of making concessions to the United States through the discussions on the Contadora treaty."[30] In addition, the protocols which "extraregional forces" (i.e., the United States and the Soviet Union) would sign were watered down to such a degree that the United States was left with having to make no concrete commitment to end its aggression against Nicaragua.

On the eve of the 11 September 1985 Contadora meeting that was to consider the modified treaty, Assistant Secretary of State for Inter-American Affairs Elliott Abrams convened a special meeting—also in Panama—of all the U.S. ambassadors in Central America, together with officials from the DOD, the CIA, and the NSC (in short, the core of the U.S. Central America policymaking and implementation team) to discuss regional strategy for the coming year. The meeting's working document, entitled "The View from Washington" and labeled "secret," was leaked to the press even before the meeting took place.[31]

"Contadora remains central to our policy and our interests continue to be served by the process," the document stated. It went on to map out a plan for assuring that Nicaragua would be isolated in its response to the new "treaty-ultimatum": "Contadora Group fatigue is an important factor now. . . . We need to develop an active diplomacy now to head off efforts at Latin American solidarity aimed against the U.S. and our allies. . . . We need to find a way to turn pressures they bring to bear on us or our friends to our advantage."

The effort to force Nicaragua unilaterally to disarm and to dismantle the structures of revolutionary power through Contadora was complemented by the effort to gain diplomatic recognition for the UNO in and out of Contadora. On the eve of each Contadora meeting, FDN-ARDE and other contra representatives would travel to the Contadora capitals to present their "proposals," while inside the meetings the Tegucigalpa Bloc (El Salvador, Honduras, and Costa Rica) insisted that these "proposals" be discussed.[32]

Unilateral disarmament was the flip-side of reconciliation, intended not just to weaken Nicaragua's ability to defend itself but also to deny the legitimacy of that self-defense. The objective was to "offer" the Sandinistas the chance to surrender to a "legitimate and representative" group, recognized by Contadora and part of a regional settlement.[33]

A Cardinal for the Counterrevolution: "Comandante Miguel"

On 23 April 1985 the U.S. Congress rejected President Reagan's request for continued funding for the contras, and the Vatican announced that Archbishop Obando y Bravo had been selected for promotion to cardinal. "They thought we suffered a defeat [in Congress]," gloated Adolfo Calero after learning of the news. "But on that same day God blessed us with the appointment of Monsignor Obando y Bravo as Cardinal."[34] In the Honduran contra camps, Enrique Bermúdez reportedly ordered giant fiestas to celebrate the appointment.

The national and international prestige Obando y Bravo would gain as cardinal was essential to the role he was to occupy as the undisputed leader of the counterrevolution. There was widespread suspicion that heavy U.S. pressure was behind his selection.[35] A few months earlier, the NSC had stressed the need to continue joint efforts with the Vatican to push the "Nicaraguan church issue."[36] Nicaraguan Vice-president Sergio Ramírez explained it this way:

> [They need Obando] to sell the idea of reconciliation inside the country; dialogue with the contras is an essential element of the Reagan administration's political scheme, and Obando is sent here with this objective—to go around the country preparing the climate that allows him to speak with force and authority on reconciliation.[37]

Obando y Bravo's Mass in Miami on his way home from his investiture was the symbolic donning of the contra crown. It "was a scene of high emotion, a symbol of unity," wrote one U.S. reporter.[38] It was broadcast live on Radio 15 de Septiembre, and simultaneously transmitted by Radio Católica in Managua. FDN printing presses churned out thousands of posters with a picture of the cardinal and Calero embracing. According to one FDN dissident, the CIA ordered all its stations in Central America to "go big" in their propaganda operations on the new cardinal.[39] From then on the contras would refer to Obando y Bravo as "Comandante Miguel."

The counterrevolution now sought to revitalize the reconciliation issue to provide a new level of internal confrontation. A few days after his return, Obando y Bravo began a whirlwind tour of the country to push reconciliation. Any remaining doubts regarding the new strategy were dispelled on 8 July, during a religious procession in Managua organized by the cardinal's diocese and the CDN. During the march, CDN members passed out leaflets calling for national reconciliation and spray-painted slogans on public buildings, such as "I take my cue from Obando, and I'm ready to die with Calero" and "With the Christian Resurrection, we will defeat the Revolution."

Between June and December, Obando y Bravo left Managua to lead over eighty mass meetings ("religious processions") around the country, an amount of activity unprecedented in the history of the Nicaraguan church.[40] Tens of thousands of people came out for these meetings, demonstrating Obando y Bravo's drawing power, but most were expressing their religious, not necessarily their political, sentiments. Obando y Bravo's task was to convert the religious into the political at a mass level, through reconciliation.

Throughout this period, *La Prensa* dedicated its front page to sensationalist coverage of every move the cardinal made, often publishing the texts of his open-air addresses. Radio Católica broadcast each mass live. The cardinal was made into an almost mythical figure and the theme of reconciliation into a biblical undertaking. The church hierarchy and the CDN printed thousands of posters of Obando y Bravo, with the captions "Cardinal of Peace," "Cardinal of Youth," "Cardinal of Hope," and above all "Cardinal of Reconciliation."

The reconciliation issue was fast becoming the vehicle for building the social base of the counterrevolution. Former CIA agent Philip Agee has noted that a key political goal of U.S. counterrevolutionary campaigns is creating an "emotive cause." "As the 'cause' is established, efforts can be made to foment popular disillusionment with the Revolution."[41] The demand for reconciliation and dialogue, once greeted with outrage, was repeated so often that it began to gain acceptance among certain sectors of the population, which began to wonder why peace could not be achieved in this way. "This war is causing hell for us all; why don't [the Sandinistas] just sit down and talk it out with the contras, even if they are sons of bitches?" a Managua mechanic asked us in September 1985, expressing the exact feeling the United States and the counterrevolution were trying to create. The aim was to channel an authentic yearning for peace after six years of relentless aggression into discontent with the revolution as the "cause" of the war. In this construct, the counterrevolution, with the church hierarchy at its helm, is portrayed as a force for peace and the Sandinistas and their supporters as the warmongers, needlessly subjecting the population to suffering.

In the face of this campaign, the Sandinistas maintained a steadfast position against any surrender disguised as "peace." The FSLN is keenly aware that those who have not learned from history are doomed to repeat it: in 1934 the first Somoza, installed in Managua by U.S. Marines, invited Sandino down from the northern mountains for "negotiations." Once there, he was disarmed and murdered, and his supporters were massacred. "To conduct a dialogue with them," Tomás Borge said, "would mean that we give them a legitimacy they don't have, that we forget who they are and lose sight of their strategic objective: to destroy the Sandinista Revolution and return Nicaragua to a neocolonial status. Accepting dialogue would be the beginning of a series of concessions that in the end would lead us to forsake revolutionary power, the power of the people."

"We will conduct a dialogue with them," Borge concluded, "when the gentlemen of COSEP count all the grains of sand in the ocean, and all the stars in the sky, and the day they finish counting, they'll have to go back and count two times more, and then we'll think it over many times before giving an answer."[42]

The Campaign Heats Up

With Obando y Bravo's tour, the United States sought to "harvest" the progress made in generating mass discontent in the nearly two years of the war of attrition. It was a time for organizing the discontented into conscious identification with the counterrevolution, to test out the counterrevolution's ability to reach and mobilize masses of people and—in the best of cases—turn them against the government in violent confrontation. These activities were described in the CIA manual as "preconditioning campaigns": "These campaigns must be aimed at the political parties, professional organizations, students, laborers, the masses of the unemployed, the ethnic minorities and any other sector of society that is vulnerable . . . [in short] the popular masses."[43] All this activity was concentrated in the urban zones: in a sense, the front line of combat was shifting from the northern mountains to the Pacific Coast cities.

The manual describes the inculcation of the "popular masses" with the counterrevolutionary political message as "awareness building." This message would reach the crowds through Obando y Bravo's own homilies, in which the two subsystems of the church's subliminal discourse (analyzed in Chapter 7) were synthesized into one under the reconciliation banner, the thousands of leaflets passed out with themes ranging from dialogue to draft resistance, and other forms of demagogy. The "movement will be able to receive reports [to determine if] the majority are united in common, greater hostility against the regime." If conditions were considered ripe, "the order to fuse/join will be given."[44] Each of Obando y Bravo's religious-gatherings-cum-political demonstrations provided the mass concentrations described by the manual: "Mass concentrations and meetings are a powerful tool, [and] fusion occurs in tight connection with mass meetings." In this sense, the "order to fuse/join" meant inciting the masses, through the calculated activity of counterrevolutionary cadres in the crowd, violently to confront the government, be it by attacking nearby government installations or simply rampaging and rioting. "Anti-government hostility must be generalized," says the manual in its final section on moving toward an insurrection against the Sandinistas.

The clandestine organizational form for coordinating contra activities during this period was constituted by the "triangles of resistance." Then-FDN field commander René Fernández told us in July 1985: "We're developing the internal command structures, the 'triangles of resistance,' that make propaganda for our struggle and let the people know what to do."[45] According to former FDN commander Efraín Mondragón, the triangles would bring together the internal and armed fronts in decisive actions, and religious manipulation would be central to that process.[46] The triangles of resistance were to be operative at the moment of fusion and mass action.

The plan was to use increasingly confrontational and provocative mass meetings to back the Sandinistas against the wall.

If the government responded with repression, according to the strategy, anything from mass outrage (with or without violence) to pre-insurrectional conditions was possible. In the "best-case" scenario, the triangles of resistance were there to lead street protests, strikes, and civil disobedience, and to spread rumors, conduct sabotage, and create social chaos. Antigovernment sentiment would be directed toward violent confrontation and the demand for surrender ("reconciliation") to the counterrevolution. If the Sandinistas did not respond with repression, then the campaign could still move forward. In either case, went the thinking, the attrition process would be intensified.

Such events as Obando y Bravo's national tour were accompanied by an escalation of contra activity in the zones of military conflict, open destabilizing activities in the urban areas, and increased efforts to mount an internal military front. In July, the FDN launched a new offensive from Honduras. In early August, State Security broke up "Operation Candle," a major effort at urban terrorism. Four hundred kilograms of C-4 explosive, along with rockets, grenades, and automatic weapons, were confiscated in Managua alone. Local elements of the internal front were implicated in the plot, including COSEP president Enrique Bolaños, who had received a letter from Calero asking for his "financial assistance" in establishing the urban units. (Bolaños was not arrested since there was no proof that he had actually given economic aid to the urban units.)[47] FDN commander Julio Zelaya Rojas had admitted a year earlier that urban contra units "receive their [financial] assistance from Nicaraguan businessmen."[48] In the following weeks, several other military cells were broken up.

On 8 September a contra group tossed a bomb into a discotheque in the Segovian city of Ocotal, killing four and injuring eighteen, all civilians. Three months later, on 4 December, another contra group placed a time bomb in the San Pedro Church in the southern Pacific Coast city of Rivas, shortly after a visit by Obando y Bravo. The bomb exploded just as dozens of people were filing into the church in a traditional *Purisima* procession, perhaps the most important religious holiday in Nicaragua. Twelve people were wounded, including two young children. The act was intended to make it appear that the government was against the *Purisima*—for several weeks the internal front had been spreading false rumors that the government planned to prohibit the celebration—but the plan backfired when the government caught the culprits, who identified themselves as FDN members. "This is a despicable, inhuman, and above all anti-Christian act," said the local priest, Fr. José Antonio Quevedo. "The most curious thing is that it happened at the same time as some people were telling us that the government wouldn't let us celebrate the *Purisima*."[49] The church hierarchy, maintaining its silence about contra aggression, refused to condemn the bombing.

Meanwhile Obando y Bravo's archdiocese was busy with its own destabilizing activities. Starting in September, both archdiocese spokesman Bismark Carballo and *La Prensa* began announcing that COPROSA (the AID- and J. Peter Grace-funded organization for the formation of counterrevolutionary ideological combatants) would soon begin publishing a new weekly, *Iglesia*. The government notified Carballo several times that the new publication would have to be registered with the Interior Ministry's press office, in accordance with the laws of the country. Carballo responded that the church was not subject to the laws of the nation. In October, the first issue was ready, and the church began distribution. The tabloid was dedicated to the cardinal's tours, to criticizing "Sandinista repression of the church," and, above all (taking up one-half the issue), to urging young men to evade the military draft. On 12 October the government confiscated the illegal edition of the newspaper.

The draft was a principle target of the "triangles of resistance." On 24 July the contras attacked a busload of mothers going to visit their sons—SMP recruits—in the war zone, killing eight and seriously injuring eighteen others. *La Prensa* editorialized that the government should initiate a "dialogue" with the contras to end the "violence." A few days earlier, an ARDE band had attacked and destroyed a boat transporting civilians down the Río Escondido to Bluefields on the Atlantic Coast. The contras claimed that the boat was attacked because an SMP soldier was aboard, and urged civilians to stay clear of Sandinista soldiers. All these barbaric acts were part of an effort to depict the EPS as not being in the interests of the people, dangerous to be near, and a source of suffering.

Only days before the first issue of *Iglesia* appeared, the diocese in Granada hid seven young men who had been drafted. The government had earlier reached a verbal agreement with the religious authorities that seminary students would be exempt from military service, and the archdiocese immediately claimed that the seven were seminary students—a claim that was proven to be false. (They all attended the public high school in Rivas.) Similar illegal encouragement of draft resistance began taking place in dioceses around the country that were connected to Obando y Bravo's archdiocese.

Then, in November, the government uncovered a sweeping campaign by reactionary sectors of both the Catholic and Protestant churches to boycott the SMP. Among the evidence presented by Omar Cabezas, head of the Interior Ministry's political directorate, at a 28 November press conference were secret documents confiscated from two Protestant lay workers who had recently returned from an IRD conference in Washington. According to the documents, the IRD had given them thousands of dollars and instructions on organizing a boycott campaign. Neither of them denied the plans, and one, Nelson Alvarez Blanco, justified the illegal activity by claiming that "I don't accept any human laws because my master is God."[50] Another lay worker attached to the archdiocese had smuggled a printing press into the country, to be used to produce anti-SMP leaflets and other counterrevolutionary literature.

The connection between this printing press and the U.S. counterrevolution was exposed when Carl Gershman, director of the National Endowment for Democracy, which had earlier channeled hundreds of thousands of dollars to the internal front, admitted that his agency was working to set up clandestine publishing houses inside Nicaragua, in tandem with funding for anti-Sandinista literature published abroad.[51]

Other internal front contingents pursued similar plans in their respective sectors. Workers in several of the country's sugar mills and factories, for instance, denounced the CDN-affiliated trade union, CUS, for plans to provoke work stoppages and paralyze production.[52]

During this period, street gangs appeared in Managua neighborhoods for the first time—bands of youth who went around attacking the houses and property of known FSLN leaders, police stations, and the offices of local government and grassroots organizations. The CIA manual had forecast just such activity: "[Urban groups] will be mobilized toward areas where the hostile and criminal elements of the FSLN, CDS [Sandinista Defense Committees], and others live, armed with clubs, iron rods, placards and if possible, small firearms, which they will carry hidden."[53] Most of the gangs' members could be identified by their expensive imported leather jackets and studded wristbands—they could not possibly have come up with the money for such clothing on their own, and it was widely assumed in Nicaragua that their funding came from the same "businessmen" who funded the FDN's urban operations.

Political Defeat?

According to the scenario played out in 1985, all the elements of the war of attrition should by now have been falling into place. The contras should have worn down the economy and won a social base among the peasantry. On the Atlantic Coast, the Miskitos should have been leading a rebellion for their own liberation. U.S. activities in the conflict environment should have whipped up an atmosphere of fear and tension. In Contadora and other international forums, the armed contra movement, well-entrenched inside Nicaragua, should have forced the Sandinistas to enter into dialogue. All of this should have gained the UNO acceptance as a legitimate alternative. Obando y Bravo, as the figurehead, should have led street confrontations which, along with urban terrorism, should have created such a climate that "individual discontent" would have become group discontent and then national discontent. The EPS should have been weakened by the SMP boycott, and divided from the people. Under such tremendous and manifold pressure, the Sandinistas would be forced to "say uncle." And if a military component was needed to seal a victory, the United States was fully prepared to act, whether through massive threats, "surgical strikes," or a large-scale intervention in which hordes of Nicaraguans would welcome the U.S. forces (or at least not resist them). It must be remembered that the essence of this scenario was a *political battle* for the validation of the counterrevolutionary project.

Obando y Bravo had made significant progress within the framework of the attrition strategy, but the hoped-for "generalized antigovernment hostility" had not materialized. There are many reasons for this. Among the most important are that the Sandinistas did not fall into the trap of repression, which might have triggered mass violence and international condemnation, and that the counterrevolution underestimated the difficulty of transforming religious sentiment into political sentiment, an underestimation rooted in its failure to appreciate the political consciousness that had developed among the masses during six years of revolution. As Comandante Dora María Téllez put it to us, "To the degree that his message became ever more openly political, the Cardinal began to lose influence among the population, which was close [religiously] to the figure of the Cardinal. The people are capable of distinguishing between a religious position and a political one cloaked in religion."[54]

Low-intensity campaigns are nevertheless extremely flexible. The failure of the cardinal's project does not mean that the strategy of the war of attrition had collapsed or was coming to an end, but that it had to push on in new directions, since tactics are configured to the conditions of the moment. As COSEP vice-president Jaime Bengochea pointed out: "There are a thousand things that could happen, a thousand factors that could come together to produce a political defeat. When will this be achieved? Sometimes an event totally removed from the circumstances at hand provides or unleashes an unforeseeable political situation. One way or another, all the factors come together."[55]

But the key point is that the revolution is not a passive object. It is the expression of a conscious and thinking people acting in their own historic interests. And the revolution has its own tactics and strategy. The United States saw Obando y Bravo as a good shepherd who would herd the Nicaraguan "sheep" against the Sandinistas. But the Nicaraguan people are not "sheep"; they are active subjects. This was the one factor that did not enter into Goliath's calculations. We now turn to this factor.

Part 2
The Revolution
Defends Itself

9

Total Defense:
The Military Theater

The United States worked out an integral design which uses all the enemy's resources in order to destroy revolutionary change in Nicaragua. . . . *in the face of their total war, we are waging a war of total defense.*

—Defense Minister Humberto Ortega[1]

For us defense is a *political* process. It is only military in that we are forced to take up arms in order to defend ourselves, but for us the process of defense is essentially political—political conviction, political motivation, political organization.

—Vice-president Sergio Ramírez[2]

From the beginning of its war, the United States tried to force Nicaragua into a position where defending the country and continuing the revolutionary transformation would be incompatible activities. The fact that military aggression was the most pronounced feature of the U.S. campaign concealed the complex psychological and political operations at its core. By concealing their real strategy, the political warriors in Washington hoped to force the FSLN to divorce the process of social transformation from that of defense, leaving the revolutionary project wide open to attrition.

But even as the White House was "burning the midnight oil in order to make its plans," as Tomás Borge put it, the Sandinistas were "kindling their ability to analyze."[3] The counterrevolution's initial inroads gave the Nicaraguan leadership the raw material they needed to learn more precisely how the United States was operating. The Sandinistas quickly found that they could be weakened politically even as they kept the contras in check militarily. In order to survive, Nicaragua had to do more than prevent the contras from advancing on Managua, and more than ward off a direct invasion. The Sandinistas realized that the war did not "boil down to a battle, as for example, the defeat of Napoleon in the battle of Waterloo or the great battles like that of Stalingrad," Humberto Ortega explained. "This war is eminently irregular and therefore the theaters and lines of combat are less easily defined."[4]

The Sandinista revolution is attempting to destroy what remains of the old system of class exploitation and build a new system in its place; the U.S. war, on the other hand, is an attempt to reimpose the old system. This means, therefore, that each step taken in building the new system is *also* a defense against the counterrevolution. "We reached a point in which defense, a military advance, could not continue if there were not also social and economic transformations that meant a deepening of the revolutionary process," Humberto Ortega told us.[5] From this point of view, defending and deepening the revolution are elements of a single process, and these depend in turn on the political mobilization and engagement of the entire population.

To achieve this, every aspect of national life had to be linked to the defense effort, a process that began in 1984 and which was based on a massive mobilization of human and material resources.[6] Actions taken by the Sandinistas in every area—military, political, social, economic, ideological, and diplomatic—had to be part of this effort. Nicaragua had to wage *total defense* against *total war*. At the core of this new defense concept, which by the end of 1984 was ready to be translated into practice, is the articulation of defense into all areas of the ongoing revolutionary transformation.

Total defense means more than simply *resisting* the counterrevolutionary threat; it's objective is the *neutralization* of that threat. The distinction is crucial: resisting an enemy does not necessarily involve undermining the logic of how it functions; neutralizing it does. For Nicaragua, neutralizing the enemy also required moving from the defensive to the offensive—in fact, to a *global* offensive which would put the military at the spearhead, linked to social, economic and political measures. These two factors (from resisting to neutralizing, from the defensive to the offensive) make the strategy of total defense qualitatively different from the strategy that preceded it.

The Strategic Defeat of the Contras

The Evolution of Sandinista Military Doctrine

Sandinista military doctrine has always been based on two key principles. First, the armed forces and weaponry must be defensive in nature:

their purpose is to *defend* Nicaraguan sovereignty from external aggression, not to operate beyond Nicaragua's territorial borders. This is, of course, diametrically opposite to the United States doctrine of defense. Second, defense must be based on the incorporation of the entire population into multi-tiered defense structures, part of the process of creating a people's army.

The Somoza dictatorship was overthrown by a relatively small guerrilla army, backed by a poorly armed but united population which rose up in insurrection. Following the triumph, the FSLN planned to develop a small professional standing army and efficient officers corps, called the Sandinista People's Army (EPS), which would be drawn from the ranks of the former guerrilla combatants. The EPS was to be complemented by the mass-based Sandinista People's Militia (MPS), which would spring from the neighborhood militia units that had been formed during the insurrection. The MPS was officially inaugurated on 24 February 1980, and by the first anniversary of the revolution had a membership of 100,000 volunteers between the ages of sixteen and sixty. The EPS was to be the backbone of the defense effort in the event of large-scale direct intervention, while the militia had two tasks: to protect local installations from small-scale attacks and sabotage, and to serve as the vehicle for bringing the entire population into the resistance in the event of an invasion.

The advent of the Reagan administration made the Sandinistas accelerate preparations for resisting a possible invasion by U.S. or surrogate forces, principally by expanding the MPS. With the initiation of systematic contra activity in 1982, the MPS was sent into action. During this period, the bulk of the military defense was carried out by the Reserve Infantry Battalions (BIRs), special militia units composed mostly of students, workers, and professionals from the cities, mobilized for three- to six-month combat stints in the war zones. The BIRs were complemented by "self-defense communities," which were established in the middle of the contras' first offensive of 1983. These involve stationary militia units, which defend a particular farm or community as well as civil defense programs.

While enthusiasm was high and there was no shortage of volunteers, the MPS units were limited in their effectiveness in the face of the contra aggression. Workers in Managua would be given bolt-action rifles and several weekends of target practice, and then sent to the countryside to guard bridges and economic installations. Their unsophisticated weaponry and brief training period left them unprepared to take on the well-trained, well-armed Somocista units, which were able to seize the initiative because of their superior operational mobility. Similarly, BIR members barely had a chance to become combat-hardened before their tours of duty were over. Given the lack of planning—any and all volunteers were accepted—the ever larger mobilizations were also disrupting production in work centers and undermining the country's medium- and long-term educational-professional organization.

By 1983, it was clear that the small regular army and the large nonprofessional militia were ill-equipped to face what was by then a rapidly expanding war against an enemy army. In less than two years, the Somocistas, thanks to the United States, had moved from scattered roving bands to organized sabotage and terrorist commandos and then to large-scale military units. Although they did not fully assimilate the tactics of the war of attrition until 1984, they had begun adopting irregular tactics in late 1982, putting the MPS at a further disadvantage. When large-scale incursions began in 1983, it was clear that the MPS was insufficient as the principal line of defense.

Behind these shortcomings lay weaknesses in both the military doctrine and structure of the armed forces. Both the permanent army and the militia were organized for urban-oriented defense. This did not mean that armed defense units were confined to urban barracks, but it did mean that protecting urban zones and their peripheries, highways, and major installations was the priority, within a conventional military framework. The character of this urban-oriented system was thus *defensive* and *reactive*, responding to the direct-interventionist strategy that the United States was no longer pursuing, as well as to the permanent threat of invasion. Although it was not believed that invading U.S. troops could be annihilated, it was felt that they could be forced to withdraw if faced with massive resistance. Similarly, contras who assaulted towns and installations were to be resisted, but not necessarily defeated.

The Sandinistas were aware that, in Vietnam, the U.S. invaders were not *militarily* defeated, even though there was virtually no limit to the amount of men, firepower, and resources that the United States was willing to use. The Vietnamese were victorious because the invaders could not pacify the country. If, in Nicaragua, the United States had continued to follow the direct-interventionist line, whose logic leads to the introduction of conventional U.S. forces (as it had in Vietnam), the Sandinista military doctrine and defense structures would have been appropriate. But as the "quick military victory" phase gave way to a period of prolonged antipopular warfare, the contras were no longer the "advance force," part of the strategy of direct invasion. They were now operating as a mercenary force, employing insurgent modalities, and trying to spread across the countryside, win over the peasantry, and wage a grinding war of attrition—in the process acting as the catalyst for the Reagan administration's total war.

In the face of this new situation, the Sandinistas' defensive and reactive military doctrine was clearly inappropriate. Nicaragua could not simply continue preparing to resist direct intervention and waiting for the contras to attack strategic installations. If the revolution merely resisted the contras, it would be bled to death, just as the United States wanted. Survival necessitated defending the revolution on all fronts— the strategy of total defense.

But since a direct U.S. invasion continued—and still continues—to be a real possibility, the Sandinistas could not abandon preparations to resist a massive conventional intervention; instead they had to broaden their military doctrine and structures in order to *also* respond to the war of attrition. "Since late 1984 and early 1985," explained EPS chief of operations Brigadier Commander Javier Carrión, "we've been working hard at defining the most advantageous military doctrine materially and humanly possible, so that our people can triumph over both the mercenary army and a possible U.S. intervention."[7]

An *offensive* and *preemptive/pursuit-oriented* capacity was therefore developed. Without forfeiting the ability to defend cities and installations, the Sandinistas also had to be able to mount offensive pursuit operations and respond to the contras' irregular tactical modalities.* A qualitative reorganization, as well as a quantitative expansion, was now necessary.

The first step was to create an offensive capacity, of an irregular character, and to upgrade existing defense structures, such as the self-defense communities, transforming them from passive into active forces. The reorganization began in mid-1983 with the creation of two new institutions: the Patriotic Military Service (SMP) and the territorial militias.

A mandatory draft was stipulated in Article 24 of the Basic Statute of the Republic, which had been approved by the Junta as the transitional constitution one day after the triumph. It was not until August 1983, however, that the SMP was finally submitted to, and approved by, the

---

*The offensive pursuit of the contras is similar in *form* to traditional U.S. counterinsurgency tactics such as "search and destroy" missions—a term the Sandinistas have used. Nevertheless, in *content* Sandinista and U.S. counterinsurgency are dramatically different. The Sandinista actions are part of a popular project in which the masses are there to defend their own interests. Simply stated, U.S. counterinsurgency seeks to neutralize revolutionary forces, while the Nicaraguans seek to neutralize counterrevolutionary forces.

Council of State (the transitional parliament). Defense Minister Ortega explained:

> By 1983, we were not only ready to create the SMP, but objectively needed this organized force, because defense required stabilizing and better organizing popular participation, and above all improving military preparation and mobilization. . . . How else could we coordinate the massive mobilization of the people to the war fronts and toward the different defense tasks without damaging production levels and throwing the education system, which is the guarantee of our future, off balance?[8]

The introduction of the SMP was perhaps the single most important advance in the nation's defense system, and the cornerstone around which the military was reorganized. The first call-up was in early 1984, and from then on there were two call-ups per year, each involving up to ten thousand youth. The draft solved the quantitative need for full-time professional combatants to reinforce the armed population, and permitted coordinating military defense with socioeconomic life ("defense planning"). The two-year tours of duty made it possible to conduct more rigorous training and to build an accumulation of experience that had not been possible with the BIRs. It also provided the institutional means for carrying through the development of a capacity to conduct irregular warfare. The majority of the draftees were organized into crack battalions, which had previously been confined to a small group of experienced former guerrillas. Named Irregular Combat Battalions (BLIs), these highly trained units were designed to have great operational mobility and tactical flexibility.

Numerous other special units were then created to carry out auxiliary functions and assignments in conjunction with the BLIs, including artillery, armored, commando, intelligence, exploration, border guard, and airborne groups. This reorganization went hand in hand with the introduction of a military technology more suited to fighting an irregular invasion. By late 1984, new communications systems were introduced, as well as artillery and other weapons-support systems tailored for irregular warfare. An airborne capacity was developed, principally through the acquisition of Soviet MI-24 and MI-25 assault and support helicopters, and used in special operations and for the rapid transport of troops and supplies.

The BLIs, the related special units, and the technological innovations constituted the core of the nation's *offensive capacity*. Important as this was, however, it was still dependent upon its being organically linked to the multitiered defense system that was organized within the civilian population, especially in the countryside. This system constituted the nation's *defensive capacity*.

The defense system's first tier is composed of the self-defense communities, and these were expanded throughout the war zones during 1984. The second tier is composed of "territorial militias," which are drawn from the population of a zone and are responsible for defending that zone. Militia members from the Segovias, for example, are organized into several battalions, each one assigned to defend the communities and installations lying within a given set of coordinates. The combatants are thus intimately familiar with the local terrain and are linked with the self-defense communities, from which they come. The Defense Ministry also sharply improved the territorial militia's military capacity: they were given longer training periods, more sophisticated equipment, and so on. This enabled them to move from passive to active defense.

This complex military structure functions as one integrated organism, and provides for broad flexible response. If possible, contra bands are detected by territorial militia patrols before they attack. If they do attack, however, the armed civilian population holds the attackers at bay, while the new communications and transportation systems permit mobile EPS units to arrive rapidly. Fleeing FDN bands are pursued through the synchronized action of all three tiers.

Once the contras are expelled from a zone, the multiple defense units—border patrols, battalions stationed further behind the border, territorial militias, mobile and stationary troops, self-defense militias, and civil defense squads—make it difficult for them to return. "If the contras get through one line, they have to face the next," Carrión explained in 1985:

> We've divided the militia into two parts: one is dedicated to active military operations, pursuing the FDN forces, while the other is responsible for the stationary self-defense of cooperatives, villages, bridges, economic installations, etc. The younger militia members, those who are in better physical shape, carry out offensive military operations, while the older militia members—all those who cannot be mobilized for long periods of time in the countryside—make up the local militias. These two types of militia are complemented by the regular army—the SMP troops who are permanently stationed in one place and the highly mobile BLIs.
>
> This multi-tiered structure operates virtually anywhere there is a population. But there are also zones, principally near the border, which are sparsely populated, where we have to use the BLIs or create border battalions, as we have been doing.
>
> While in general our military doctrine is defensive in nature—in terms of the army, the nation, our government, etc.—and the principal concept flowing from this doctrine is that of territorial defense, this does not mean that we are on the defensive and the FDN on the offensive. On the

contrary, our territorial militias and the BLIs are eminently offensive in nature. They are not used to defend a bridge, a grain silo, or a health center, for example; they are permanently on search-and-destroy missions against FDN bands.[9]

Through these changes, begun in mid-1983 and fully in place by early 1985, the Saninistas regained their tactical maneuverability. The EPS then began to set up units with still greater specialization and more advanced training. By 1986, the first "Special Mobile Units" and "Special Assignment Groups" were operating, allowing a still more flexible response.

In the broader context, all these changes represented the synthesis of pre-triumph popular political-military warfare and post-triumph modern military defense of the revolutionary state and the nation's territorial integrity, a creative new model for young revolutions to follow in resisting the Reagan Doctrine. The developed military doctrine and corresponding forms of organization are the Sandinista revolution's response in the military sphere to the shift to prolonged antipopular warfare; it is *the armed component of total defense*.

The parallel strategy for confronting a direct U.S. intervention also passed through three distinct phases. In the first phase, when defense structures were too new for a frontal resistance to a massive air and seaborne invasion to be possible, the strategy was to concede the major urban centers to the invading forces, with their superior numbers and firepower, and then launch a prolonged resistance through urban and rural guerrilla warfare, which would make it impossible for the aggressors to install a stable puppet government. Reserves of fuel, food, and munitions were deposited around the country. It was expected that the longer the occupation lasted, the higher its international costs would be. These plans were ready in late 1983.

By the time of the artificial MiGs crisis in November 1984, the Nicaraguans had the ability to resist *before* conceding Managua and other urban centers, although they still could not militarily defeat invaders. The strategy at this stage was, therefore, to inflict the highest costs possible, in casualties, military hardware, and economic resources, before withdrawing to the mountains for prolonged resistance. Once again, international and internal pressures would build up on the United States, forcing it to withdraw. Speaking at an FSLN assembly in November 1984, Interior Vice-minister Luis Carrión detailed this strategy:

> Even if the Yankees could send in 100,000 or 200,000 men, for how long could they be kept in Nicaragua, when every day they'd be sending back,

30, 40, 50, or 100 corpses? How long would the U.S. people let Mr.
Reagan keep this up? In Vietnam, the Yankees did not lose their military
capacity, much less their level of organization. But they lost the war
because they were unable to achieve their political objectives, because they
could not smash the resistance of the Vietnamese people, which in turn
sparked the resistance of the U.S. people and eventually forced Mr. Nixon
to withdraw. . . . Imperialism wants to destroy people's power and then
leave the country as soon as possible. The U.S. army's priority is to occupy
the capital in a short time with limited casualties. Then they would have
an important political and moral victory at the national and international
level, because Managua is the symbol of the political power of the Revolution. . . . Thus we must be prepared to make them pay a high price for
every inch of terrain, every block, every house, every tree, every stone of
our city.[10]

The reorganization of the defense structures, the arming of the
civilian population, and the accumulation of combat experience by
hundreds of thousands of citizens all greatly expanded the country's
ability to face a direct invasion. Moreover, in October 1985 the government activated its plan for a national reserve, called the SMP-R. This
organization—membership of which was mandatory to men and voluntary for women—was to incorporate everyone (excepting those women
who did not volunteer) between the ages of twenty-five and forty into
permanent reserve units, organized along territorial lines and available
at short notice. In November, the first twenty thousand Managua
workers and professionals went through an intensive training course
and were assigned to reserve units in the capital, close to where they
worked and lived. They were augmented by those finishing their two-
year tours of active duty, who are immediately assigned to reserve units,
often as officers or instructors. All reserve members receive a 30-day
refresher course each year. This meant that each year, twenty thousand
youth demobilized from active duty are integrated into the reserve—
and each year the number of Nicaraguans who can militarily defend the
nation in the event of direct intervention is increased by at least that
number.

By late 1985, then, Nicaragua had reached the point where it could
both defeat the contras and defeat a direct U.S. invasion, according to
Sandinista assessments. Tomás Borge explained:

Our analysis of Nicaragua's military and active resistance capacity in the
face of a direct intervention has changed in recent months. Before, we
thought that we would be able to neutralize and defeat an intervention
through international solidarity and internal resistance. But now we believe, after a new analysis, that a direct U.S. intervention can be defeated

in military terms. That is, we are not talking about resisting, neutralizing, and in this way defeating an invasion but rather about defeating the military forces that would be introduced into our country.[11]

Only by expanding defense doctrine to include offensive irregular warfare against the armed contras could this point have been reached; the parallel abilities to wage irregular and conventional military defense are thus mutually reinforcing.

From Resisting to Defeating the Contras

It took time for the reorganized defense system to show results, but by late 1984 Ortega was talking of moving to the offensive against the contra forces: "We have made notable advances in the defensive power of the nation, accumulating valuable military experience that will allow us in the following months to greatly increase our troops' actions against the enemy."[12]

This was the belief of U.S. observers as well. In early 1985, following a privately sponsored fact-finding visit, Lt. Edward L. King, a retired U.S. Army officer and former liaison for the chairman of the Joint Chiefs of Staff to both the Inter-American Defense Board and the U.S. delegation to the OAS, observed: "The FDN forces are being out-fought and are not able to accomplish major military objectives. With or without continued U.S. funding, it is very likely that the FDN military forces will be driven from Nicaraguan territory before the end of the year."[13] King commented on the advances Nicaragua had made in reorganizing its military defense structures:

> The Sandinistas used their infantry and crew-served weapons much more effectively than when I had seen them in action in May 1984. In talking with officers and men of the BLI it became apparent that through combat with the FDN forces they are becoming much more proficient. The contras are furnishing them the experience to learn how to be a combat-effective army, something that the Sandinista army was not a year ago. As a result, troop morale in the units of the army I visited was much higher than a year ago. There is now a feeling among many of these Sandinista soldiers that they are winning against the FDN and it is just a matter of time before they will drive them back into Honduras. This was not the general feeling among the ill-trained militia units that were fighting the FDN in 1984.[14]

In his annual year-end analysis of the military situation, Humberto Ortega spoke for the first time of the "decomposition" of the contra forces: "We intend to deepen the strikes that we have been inflicting on the enemy, and we believe that in 1985 we can force them [the enemy] decisively into a more defensive and difficult situation."[15] A few weeks later he expanded on this:

> The war is now in a state of victorious development for the Sandinista People's Revolution over the plans of imperialism. The mercenary forces are currently under permanent pressure from the EPS troops. This situation, assuming it is maintained over the next months, puts the mercenaries on the defensive and [opens up] the possibility of their defeat, thus profoundly weakening this instrument of pressure against Revolution that imperialism has counted on.[16]

Ortega then introduced the concept of the *strategic defeat* of the contras. This meant breaking the initiative the contras had maintained for several years and then eliminating their ability to develop as a political-military force. It did not mean an end to contra activity, much less the annihilation of the Somocistas as a force. In fact, the contras might be able to continue scattered attacks indefinitely. But with their capacity to expand and develop broken, they would no longer be able to act as the catalyst for aggression in the other war theaters. In Ortega's words, the contras would no longer represent a "strategic threat to revolutionary power."[17]

The Sandinista Offensive

The contras massive 1984 General Offensive put FDN and ARDE forces deep in Nicaraguan territory. Despite these gains, a military stalemate lasted for most of 1984. It was during these months of heavy fighting that the newly formed BLIs were getting their first taste of combat, while the specialized units tested out the new military technology and learned how to master the hardware. Slowly the tide was turning, and FSLN leaders mapped out the contours of decisive battles to come.

In November 1984 the Sandinistas broke the stalemate with an all-out EPS offensive that continued uninterrupted until mid-1985. In one operation after another, large-scale FDN units were broken up and dispersed. As they retreated, the EPS mounted pursuit operations that were aimed at cordoning off dispersed bands and then annihilating them. In one highly successful tactic, the militia would form a military cordon around a broad zone where contra units were detected, and then BLIs, backed up by artillery and air support, would move in to destroy the enemy. During this period, Nicaragua saw some of the most high-pitched battles since the war began. Given the intensity of combat, the firepower employed, and the scale of operations, these armed confrontations resembled big-unit warfare in strictly military terms.

In December 1984 and January 1985, the offensive was concentrated in the Nueva Segovia region. By February, most of the contra forces had been driven out or killed. This allowed the redeployment of EPS units into the vast and more sparsely populated zones of Matagalpa and Jinotega (where the bulk of the FDN had dug in), leaving the militias to defend the Segovias. In each place where the contra presence was eradicated, the multi-tiered defense structures were then solidified, and by the second half of 1985 the Segovian population was living in relative security. "We can hand out these land titles because we are victorious," declared one official from the Agriculture Ministry, during a land grant ceremony in December of that year. "The counterrevolutionary presence in our zone is becoming a thing of the past—it is now a zone controlled and defended by our people."[18] One militia member from Jalapa proudly told us: "The childrens' faces are no longer filled with anguish and defeat, but rather with hope."

The EPS offensive in the north peaked in April. According to the Defense Ministry, in twenty-seven battles in the last half of that month alone, the FDN suffered 1,122 casualties, roughly one-third of them fatalities. In May, the EPS captured the FDN's most important base in Nicaraguan territory, deep in Jinotega. The base had been the FDN operational headquarters for most of the north, and had a well-equipped field hospital and an airfield for receiving supplies from Honduras. By the end of that month, the bulk of the Somocista forces had been pushed back into Honduras, while other units had scattered into isolated mountain pockets or moved southward toward the sparsely populated central plateaus of Boaco and Chontales.

With the north more firmly under Sandinista control than at any time since the beginning of the war, the EPS turned to the ARDE troops in the south. The contras in the south had lost the initiative ever since the abortive attempt to take San Juan del Norte a year earlier, but ARDE units had nevertheless maintained a military presence which made it impossible to stabilize the region. They were able to make scattered attacks and to maintain their positions partly because this was an area of isolated, sparsely populated marshland and partly because Sandinista resources had been concentrated in the north.

On 26 May the EPS launched "Operation Sovereignty," a massive military effort to totally expel ARDE forces from Nicaraguan territory. Within days, ARDE's forward bases had been overrun, dozens of contras had been killed, and hundreds more had fled toward Costa Rica. On 11 June Sandinista troops stormed La Penca, ARDE's long-time military headquarters in Nicaraguan territory, and raised the Sandinista flag. Journalists flown into the captured camp some days later landed on the airfield ARDE had built to receive U.S. supplies flown in from El Salvador's Ilopango military airfield. A bulldozer brought in from northern Costa Rica was still in the camp.

The loss of La Penca marked the beginning of the end for ARDE. From June through August, Operation Sovereignty became a mopping-up operation along the banks of the Río San Juan. World attention was focused on this region in July, when ARDE forces on the Costa Rican side of the border kidnapped twenty-eight U.S. pacifists and the twenty journalists who were covering their peace vigil on the river, and held them hostage for twenty-four hours. By August, ARDE had been essentially routed from southern Nicaragua, leaving only a few scattered and hungry members dispersed in isolated areas and without any operational capacity. "The Democratic Revolutionary Alliance is defeated and has no chance of military recuperation," the EPS military commander in the southern region declared confidently.[19]

The contras worked hard to fill this military vacuum. Following Operation Sovereignty, FDN organizers were brought to Costa Rica from Honduras to try and regroup the dispersed ARDE forces. In November, Honduran and U.S. aircraft began shuttle flights to San José and to northern Costa Rica, delivering equipment from FDN bases in Honduras.[20] But these efforts had little impact. By mid-1986, the contras had not been able to launch one single new attack from the south. "The situation has really changed here," reported one Nicaraguan peasant in the border area. "It's rare to find someone who's not integrated into defense, and now when we detect any movements along the border we don't have to be calling the *compañeros* [EPS soldiers]—everyone's ready for defense."[21]

The Political Defeat of the Armed Contras

The Sandinista military offensive was the most visible feature of the strategic defeat. As long as the contras maintained an operational military capacity in large areas of the countryside, the Sandinistas could not advance their project there. There was never any doubt, however, that the heart of the strategic defeat of the contras was their political defeat. Those sectors of the peasantry that had come under contra influence had to be won back and the contra sanctuary destroyed, while the socioeconomic disintegration of the countryside had to be reversed.

Alongside the reorganization of the country's military apparatus, the Sandinistas set in motion mutually reinforcing political, socioeconomic, and ideological initiatives. "By late 1984 we had begun mounting integral plans of action in the zones where the mercenaries operated," Defense Minister Ortega told us. "Our military advances were dependent upon corresponding socioeconomic and political counterparts."[22]

Peasants Manipulated by the Somocistas Are Not "Contras"

The first step in this process was taken when the FSLN recognized that a distinction had to be made between former National Guardsmen and FDN-ARDE members consciously waging counterrevolution, and the thousands of victimized peasants inside the contra ranks. "We should not say that a peasant is a political or ideological enemy of the revolution simply because he has picked up a gun," noted Roberto Calderón, EPS commander in charge of Boaco and Chontales, a region where the FDN had developed its sanctuary. "The majority of the peasants who are with the contra bands have been brutally threatened to make them join. When these peasants suddenly find themselves in battle, they shoot along with the other counterrevolutionaries, firing simply to protect themselves."[23]

In December 1983 the government initiated a series of amnesty programs. The first, which was chiefly directed at the Miskito communities, also included those members of the FDN who were not former National Guardsmen or in leadership positions. From then until the program expired in November 1984, about 1,600 Nicaraguans—the majority Miskito—turned themselves in and were reintegrated into civilian life.

Then, on 22 January 1985, the newly elected National Assembly passed, as its first piece of legislation, an amnesty law that was expanded to include *all* those involved with the counterrevolution, even former National Guardsmen and FDN-ARDE leaders, regardless of whatever crimes they had committed, provided that they turned in their weapons. The measure had a dual purpose: to provide a way for the thousands of peasants forced, physically or through deceit, to participate in the counterrevolution to leave it, and to accelerate the gradual erosion of contra ranks that had begun with the process of strategic defeat. Some observers saw the law as a "concession" to the United States; it was, on the contrary, a defensive and offensive weapon and was a major setback for the counterrevolution.

At first only individuals and small groups of peasants turned themselves in. On 15 February 1985, however, a group of 143 peasants in Estelí collectively laid down their arms and accepted the amnesty. Gradually, the trickle became a stream, and then a flood. There were daily desertions across the country. Efraín Mondragón, who defected in May 1985, was the first high-level FDN leader to cross over, and his defection encouraged several others to follow his example. One after another, these ex-contras told the local and foreign press of their grisly experiences with the FDN-ARDE. And as the news of defections made its way back to the contras ranks, more were encouraged to leave. Soon the Somocistas were trying to work out elaborate schemes to prevent news of the amnesty from reaching their rank and file.

Meanwhile, the amnesty had a major impact on Nicaraguan refugees in Honduras, many of whom were kidnap victims. Most of these people had feared that they would be "punished" if they returned to Nicaragua. UNHCR authorities in Tegucigalpa told us in July 1985 that in the six months after the amnesty was decreed, the number of requests for UNHCR to facilitate refugee repatriation had increased so much that they had to request more staff.

As part of its changed attitude toward the peasants who had been drawn into the counterrevolution, the Sandinista leadership and local FSLN cadres launched a campaign to encourage good relations between the EPS and the peasants. "We have been waging a continuous campaign in our army, teaching our soldiers not to fall into the trap of considering each and every person who lives in a district affected by the counterrevolution a conscious enemy of the Revolution," said Calderón. "We have been able to greatly improve troop-peasant relations. In fact, every one of our soldiers is now also being trained to understand peasant reality and to carry out political and social work with the peasants as part of the military offensive against the counterrevolution."[24] This was an important step in undermining the contra effort to drive a wedge between the revolutionary army and the civilian population.

Reinvigorating the Ideological Struggle in the Countryside

New ideological campaigns were also begun in the countryside aimed at countering contra ideological manipulation and raising the political consciousness of the peasants. From May through November of 1984, the FSLN conducted its "From Pomares to Fonseca" campaign (which was named for Germán Pomares and Carlos Fonseca, two founders of the FSLN who had died in battle, prior to the triumph, in May and November respectively). This involved mainly sending Sandinista cadres throughout the countryside to work directly with the peasants, in order to build a bridge between peasant reality and the broader situation facing Nicaragua, to learn from the peasants, to evaluate FSLN weaknesses in the countryside, and to understand how the counter-revolution had spread its ideological tentacles. These cadres were to bring back the information necessary to draw up and implement the total defense strategy.

On 21 February 1984—the fiftieth anniversary of the murder of General Sandino—over one thousand young people, all senior students in teacher-training colleges, left Managua for four hundred communities in the most isolated regions of the country. These members of the "Fiftieth Anniversay Educational Brigade" were to spend two years teaching basic literacy, as well as Nicaraguan history and politics. The zones they were assigned to were those that, except during the first literacy campaign (in 1980), had remained cut off from the revolution, and had as a result been ideal targets for contra recruitment. The few schools that had been constructed had been destroyed by the contras, and in most of the communities to which the teachers were assigned there were no educational facilities whatsoever. Without this effort, over seventeen thousand children and thousands more adults would have had no access to education. But teaching these peasants had its price: eighteen members of the brigade were murdered by contra bands, and several dozen others kidnapped and taken to Honduras.

The first literacy campaign had been conceived as the first step in an ongoing educational program for the entire population, literacy being a core element of true liberation. Nevertheless, these programs had deteriorated as attention turned to defense, and in the war zones they were virtually abandoned. The Fiftieth Anniversary Educational Brigade was thus the first step in reactivating mass-based educational programs in remote rural communities, even in the midst of war. It was considered an active element of the national defense effort, and an important plank in the ideological struggle against the counterrevolution. It was followed by the government's announcement in early 1986 that grass-roots educational programs would be reinitiated throughout the countryside. "The literacy campaign must be a permanent process," said Dora María Téllez, "because its objective is not simply to teach reading and writing, but to teach people how to interpret and analyze their reality. One of the pillars of the Revolution is that the people understand and know more, just as one of the pillars of exploitation is that the people understand and know less."[25]

Asentamientos and the Plan General Unico

The Sandinistas also sought an integrated solution to the problems faced by the thousands of peasants who had been displaced by the war (internal refugees) and to the existence of the contra sanctuary. In February 1985 the government inaugurated the *asentamientos*, or settlements, program, an ambitious two-year project that involved 135 new communities and about 50,000 families. The project, which grew out of the experience accumulated assisting internal refugees since the early years of the war (particularly in the south), involved relocating two distinct groups of peasants into new communities. The first group included those already displaced by the aggression, while the second included those still living in the war zones, including parts of the contra sanctuary. It was the evacuations necessary for this second group that provided the United States with new fuel for the propaganda furnace. According to Reagan, the Sandinistas are "using Stalin's tactic of gulag relocation for those that do not support their tyrannical regime."[26] But while the U.S. president rambled on with his interpretation of Soviet history and its supposed repetition in Nicaragua, inside the country the relocations were moving ahead to a very different tune. In fact, the *asentamientos* were a long-awaited solution to the predicament faced by thousands of internal refugees. Some had been displaced as early as 1982; others welcomed the possibility of being able to work in peace, free from contra activity. In one community in the north, Quibuto, the terrified survivors of a mid-1984 contra attack demanded that the army move them to a safer area. Although the counterrevolution tried to portray the relocated peasants as a mass of penned-up anti-Sandinistas, the majority were simply victims of the U.S. war. "There in the mountains, the battles were real close," reported one woman who had been relocated to the Portillo *asentamiento* in the Jalapa Valley. "We only want to live and work in peace, and here it looks like we may be able to."[27]

The U.S. image of forced marches to garrisons guarded by troops bore little resemblance to reality. The relocations were organized and carried out by civilians, not the army, which limited itself to setting up defensive cordons around the affected area. Despite initial resentment among some of the evacuated peasants—who, often on short notice, had to leave their small plots of land and their possessions—those who were relocated were soon enjoying the benefits that the *asentamientos* offered.

By concentrating the dispersed communities of remote mountain areas into *asentamientos*, the government was able to introduce social services, technical assistance, and a production infrastructure that would otherwise have been impossible. It was also better able to protect the population from attack. Within a short time, these tangible benefits were creating a climate of confidence and enthusiasm among what the

local press called the "newly born towns." At the same time, the
asentamientos program created "free-fire" zones—now without civilians
who might be caught in the crossfire—where concentrated firepower
could be brought to bear against the enemy. In these zones, the increasingly ineffective contras were rapidly liquidated.

The *asentamientos* program cost over $50 million, which was spent on
installing basic infrastructure, supplying the materials for houses,
building schools, health clinics, day-care centers, and other service
installations, and providing food and clothing until each settlement
could become self-sufficient. Some of the *asentamientos* organized their
land into agricultural cooperatives, while others decided to work it
individually. The government turned over some of the most fertile land
in the country, and provided financing, technical assistance, and equipment for growing both food and export crops.

The reincorporation of thousands of peasants into the productive
process contributed to the nation's ability to resist economic destabilization and freed resources that had been allocated for emergency assistance to internal refugees. At another level, the *asentamientos*
represented a superior form of social organization which, in the long
run, would enhance the efforts to advance the country economically.
Each settlement is to become a pole around which agricultural and
agroindustrial projects are to be developed. In this way, the rural
population is being drawn into the national development strategy, which
in turn gives them the opportunity to improve their living conditions
and cultural level. In 1985, for instance, MIDINRA predicted that once
the *asentamientos* had had several years to consolidate, yields per acre
would be five times greater than in the mountains. Former subsistence
farmers will for the first time produce a major marketable surplus
which will not only yield immediate material benefits for their families
but will make them part of the national economy and strengthen
exchange between the cities and the countryside. This will become the
material basis for strengthening the worker-peasant alliance.

The contact that each *asentamiento* had with the revolution through
its socioeconomic infrastructure was complemented by the democratic
structures set up in each community. Community members elected
their own boards, which were responsible for local decision-making.
Inevitably, those affected by the program increased their identification
with the revolution, thus advancing the ideological struggle.

The *asentamientos* program involved an enormous amount of cooperation between institutions, including the ministries of agriculture, construction, housing, transportation, social welfare, internal commerce,
and health; the army; the Central Bank; and delegates from the presi-

dent's office and from the FSLN at the local and national levels. It was implemented with a speed and precision one would not have thought possible with such a huge undertaking. Its success was in large measure due to the fact that it was the centerpiece of an even more ambitious plan for the political and administrative reorganization of the war zones. Called Plan General Unico, it involved integrating political, socioeconomic, and military decision-making, and then implementing decisions in concert with the local population. Interior Vice-minister Luis Carrión, a member of the FSLN National Directorate, was sent to live and work in the war zones, to put the plan into effect and then oversee its implementation.

"The war is not strictly military, it is also political and social," Carrión said, pointing to the disjointed manner in which policies and projects had previously been carried out. When national priorities had been reoriented toward military defense and the war zones in 1984, dozens of government institutions and hundreds of Managua-based officials had moved into the war zones, but the effort to transfer human and material resources had been hampered by a lack of coordination. For instance, while MIDINRA was giving land to the peasants in one area, the Internal Commerce Ministry was busy setting up distribution outlets in another area—with no knowledge of where MIDINRA was assigning its parcels. At the same time, EPS commanders were proposing to remove people from certain zones without taking into account the plans of the civilian ministries. Popular participation in a number of other programs—be it in the territorial militias, the agrarian reform, or mass organizations—similarly lacked coordination.

Plan General Unico was developed in order to rectify this political-administrative disorder. The first step was to unify the political leadership in each region under one entity, the FSLN Regional Committee. Regional leaders from each ministry, EPS regional commanders, and the political cadres from the FSLN and the mass organizations were all to sit on this body. Branching out below it were similarly structured committees, which were to coordinate political, socioeconomic, and military activities at their levels. "What we have created is a political nerve center that makes the most general and important decisions, which are in turn applied through the multi-tiered structures. . . . This is indispensable if we are to coordinate, down to the grassroots level, all the efforts in defense, so that everyone is acting in one single line, in one single plan, with one single vision," said Carrión. In sum, Plan General Unico was "less bureaucracy, greater ties with the masses, less disjointedness, and more open ears feeling out the positions and opinions of the people."[28]

Reorienting Agrarian Policy

The *asentamientos* program resolved the plight of many internal refugees and permitted the military offensive to move ahead. Yet thousands of other peasant families still faced a myriad of socioeconomic difficulties, resulting from the contra aggression, from weaknesses in the governments' agrarian policy, and from poor administrative structures.

Throughout late 1984 and early 1985, pressure was growing among the peasantry for a deepening of agrarian transformation. Although the first peasant marches began in Masaya, a department on the Pacific Coast, away from military conflict, the agitation soon spread throughout the country. "The time has come for the agrarian reform to move into high gear," said one peasant from San Lorenzo, in Chontales, when Luis Carrión came to speak. "How is it possible that there are some here who have 20,000 acres in a place where thousands of us peasants are without land?" Said another: "We don't want words, we want agrarian reform."[29]

Had it not been for the military advances and the political, administrative, and ideological changes already under way, this agitation might have led the discontented peasants to join the counterrevolution.

As it was, the Sandinistas had already begun a reevaluation of agrarian policy as part of the changes under way to wage total defense. The reevaluation was spurred on by the mushrooming pressure from the peasantry. The National Union of Farmers and Ranchers (UNAG), an organization of principally small- and medium-sized landowners, had been organizing among the peasantry since its founding in 1981. By 1985 it had over 120,000 members. UNAG leaders, along with local FSLN cadres, sensed the peasants agitation and were soon giving it clear political direction. UNAG's charismatic and outspoken president, Daniel Núñez, had been loudly criticizing MIDINRA policies and had won the confidence of many peasants. "Whoever wins over the peasants," Núñez had astutely noted, "will win the war." MIDINRA officials working directly in the field had also been analyzing the weaknesses in agrarian policy. An internal ministry critique, drafted in early 1985, acknowledged that "many of our problems originate from the fact that we have lacked a clear plan of revolutionary alliances in the countryside." The document went on to note that "our forces must work out a plan that reduces the effects of attrition, avoids disorganization and makes possible a sustained defensive effort," and proposed sweeping revisions.[30]

Agrarian Reform Accelerates

Underlying the reevaluation of agrarian policy was the determination to assure that every peasant who needed land would get it. This was not a new policy—in fact, the promise dates back to General Sandino himself and forms one of the most basic planks of the Sandinista program. As we saw earlier, the U.S. war strategists tried in a number of ways to prevent the FSLN from fulfilling this promise. In tandem with exploiting the revolution's objective limitations, the United States attempted to make the Sandinistas perceive defense as, even if momentarily, in contradiction with the land demand. It initially made advances, but the strategy of total defense reversed this contradiction: now defense *necessitated* fulfilling the historic promise of "land to those who work it."

Once the need to reorient agrarian policy was acknowledged, individual properties began to be granted on a massive scale, while the introduction of modern technologies and large-scale production schemes were postponed for the time being. This did not mean abandoning the cooperatives in the long term, but it did mean focusing on the thousands of peasants who, for one reason or another, were not ready for collective production and for whom modern technologies were in any case unrealistic until economic limitations imposed by the war were overcome.

In the first six months of 1985, only about 6,000 acres of land were given out to individuals, but in the second six months, as the new policy was put into practice, this figure grew to over 260,000 acres,[31] or more than double the total amount of land given to individuals between 1981 and the end of 1984. The government also announced that during 1986, another 875,000 acres would be given out, almost all to individuals. This figure is more than the total amount of land turned over to the peasants in all forms (excluding the titles program) from 1981 to the end of 1984. By the end of 1985, a total of 87,000 families had benefited from the reform.

In addition, special attention was paid to those in the agricultural frontier who had been most marginalized and thus most influenced by the Somocistas. In early 1986, for instance, Humberto Ortega announced that in the period 1986–89, over 525,000 acres of land would be given to poor peasants in the central departments of Boaco and Chontales alone, an important region of contra influence.[32]

By late 1985, however, the accelerated agrarian reform program had run up against the limitations of the 1981 Agrarian Reform Law: no more land was available for distribution, yet 50,000 rural families still remained unaffected by the reform. UNAG-led peasant agitation, as well as pressure from FSLN and MIDINRA cadres, culminated in January 1986 with a revision of the law. Where before any "abandoned, idle, deficiently exploited, or rented" land over 1,235 acres in the Pacific Coast region and 2,470 acres elsewhere was subject to confiscation, now *any* land not fully under cultivation and *any* land owned by absentee landlords could be expropriated. In addition, the new law contained an "exception factor," which gave the state the right to declare given zones as areas for agrarian reform if it was "in the public need or social interest." In short, "land belongs to those who work it" remained the guiding principle, while the exceptions were removed. This opened up a vast new pool of land, taken from unproductive state and private properties, and gave the agrarian reform planners new flexibility in solving the land question.

The momentum built up by the peasant movement throughout 1985, combined with changes in agrarian policy and the political and ideological work that accompanied the strategic defeat of the contras, gave thousands of peasant families who had felt cheated by the revolution a newfound confidence that their situation would be solved through organized actions *within* the revolution.

National Unity Takes on a New Character

The changes in the Agrarian Reform Law solved the problem of the legal limitations of the old law, but did not solve the problem of which land should be expropriated. This in turn raised the political question of the state's alliance with the private sector—the issue of national unity. The government decided to distribute both state- and privately owned land. According to Agriculture Minister Jaime Wheelock, the 875,000 acres that are to be distributed in 1986 will be taken in roughly equal amounts from state and private landowners. The state had acquired vast tracts of land with the nationalization of Somoza's properties, including farmland that the state had not had the capacity to utilize well. Where state land was not available, the large private landowners would have to enter into negotiations with the government; if no agreement were reached, the state would have the right to expropriate the land by declaring it to be of strategic importance to the nation. Conservative landowners complained that the agrarian reform tribunals that were set up to arbitrate expropriations were "*exceptional*" and therefore unfair. Luis Carrión could not have been more to the point in his response. "The Revolution, gentlemen, is the great exceptional measure that the people apply against the exploiters," he said. "It is the march of history and cannot be detained."[33]

The ideal was to maintain unity with the private sector *without* sacrificing the interests of the peasantry, but this became increasingly difficult as the majority displaced the old dominant minority. The resulting tensions ultimately had to be resolved in favor of one class or the other. Sandinista leaders continued to walk the tightrope, but made it clear that "when the principle of private property comes into contradiction with the principle of the majority interest, the solution will be in favor of the poor and the workers."[34] Thus, although there was no official change in the concept of national unity, its terms were necessarily being reformulated. "Unity has to respond to the concrete situation of the Revolution, in each place and at each moment," as Dora María Téllez put it.[35] National unity originally meant that virtually any landowner who did not flee the country and join the counterrevolution was considered a "patriotic producer." Gradually, however, national unity was moving, de facto, from a unity based on anti-invasionism to a unity around the concept of revolutionary transformation. "National unity becomes a call for producers to incorporate themselves into the transformation in the countryside," said Wheelock.[36]

Favoring the Peasants and Strengthening
the Worker-Peasant Alliance

The intensification of the agrarian reform program was accompanied by other revisions in agrarian policy. Until 1985, it was the urban sectors that had been the chief beneficiaries of new social programs and economic policies, while the peasantry had suffered most from the war and from the breakdown of the former exploitative system. Now economic priorities were to be reoriented toward the countryside.

In early 1985, the pricing system for agricultural produce was revised: prices paid to the peasants for their produce, and the consumer prices of these goods, were substantially increased, thus transferring a part of the war's economic burden from the countryside to the cities. The government also decided to allocate more of the scant foreign exchange for the importation of consumer goods for the peasantry. Thus, in 1985 some $30 million was allocated exclusively for the importation of peasant consumer goods and production implements. In sharp contrast to 1984, rural distribution outlets were now well-stocked with goods, ranging from machetes, rubber boots, hammers, and nails, to powdered milk and clothing, all at government-controlled prices. In addition, state institutions underwent an administrative reorganization, modeled after the successful Plan General Unico, to permit the efficient coordination of rural services (buying crops, distributing manufactured goods, getting bank credit, etc.). The availability of urban-produced goods in the countryside, together with the new prices and a more responsive state service apparatus, acted as a powerful incentive for the peasants to produce surpluses for marketing in the cities—all of which was made easier as military advances brought relative peace to one zone after another and also allowed thousands of peasants to be reinserted into the national productive process.

As the worker-peasant alliance, rooted in the exchange between peasants and urban workers, was thus bolstered, Sandinista political and ideological work stressed the unity between the two, emphasizing that in the long run improving the productive situation of the peasantry would benefit *both* urban and rural sectors.

The Contra Fish Lose Their Sea

With the material basis for the counterrevolutionary manipulation of the peasantry weakened, the Sandinistas were winning back the confidence of the peasantry and drying up the contras' sanctuary. "Each *manzana* of land we deliver to the peasants," said one MIDINRA official, "is land out of reach of contra influence."[37]

If agrarian policies were inseparable from military advances, the amnesty law was a key link between the two. Peasants tricked or forced into joining the contras were not only offered the opportunity to turn themselves in, but were immediately given land and the means to make a living. "The Revolution defends itself [by advancing] with its own project of transformation. If you find a peasant in the ranks of the mercenary forces, this is because he has been deceived, not because he is defending his own strategic interests," Dora María Téllez explained to us. She continued:

> So what is the best way to show that peasant that the counterrevolutionary project is not in his own interests? By giving land to those who turn themselves in, because it is not the same to *tell* someone he has been fooled; it must be *demonstrated* to him with concrete facts—giving him land and a way to live and produce with his family. This way he understands that the Revolution is *his* project.[38]

While the counterrevolution had to deceive the peasants—disguise itself—in order to win them over, the revolution had to do the exact opposite: it had to *realize itself* in order to win them back. This was vividly demonstrated throughout 1985. As peasants who were under the sway of the contras found that the state apparatus was more responsive to their plight, they began to identify less and less with the contras. Some sought "neutrality"; many others sought incorporation into revolutionary programs. As soon as they did this, however, the Somocistas labeled them "Sandinista" and targeted them for attack. Thousands of peasants soon learned the true nature of the counterrevolution. They also realized that if they wanted to receive land or services from the government, *they would have to defend themselves from the contras.*

By the fall of 1985, peasants all over the country were marching under a new banner: "Land to produce and guns to defend ourselves." At a ceremony in San Marcos, in the war zone, on 11 January 1986, President Daniel Ortega gave each peasant an agrarian reform land title and a rifle to defend his new gain. The ceremony symbolically formalized the reorientation of agrarian policy, the reincorporation of the peasantry into the revolutionary project, and the renewed unity between the peasants and the Sandinistas and against the counterrevolutionary enemy.[39]

One peasant from the interior of Matagalpa who turned himself in under the amnesty program in March 1986 graphically captured the changed balance of forces: The contras, he said, "have lost their social base in the countryside. The Sandinista forces have struck them hard. The same people who used to sell them food are now firing bullets at them, which forces them to move without rest under the fierce persecution of the EPS and the peasant militias. Everything's turned out just the opposite from what they had hoped for. They're thoroughly demoralized."[40]

The Strategic Defeat Deepens

The Failure of Plan Rebelión '85

By June 1985, when the U.S. Congress renewed its assistance to the contras, the FDN could no longer even maintain a presence inside Nicaragua, having been pushed back across the border into its Honduran rearguard. Yet support in the United States for the administration's Nicaraguan policy, as well as the strategy of legitimizing the contras internationally, depended on the FDN maintaing the appearance—if not the reality—of being a belligerent contending force inside Nicaragua. As the FDN poured back across the border into southern Honduras from March to May, they were regrouped in preparation for "Plan Repunte" (Plan Roundup), which was to be the first phase of a larger strategy, dubbed "Plan Rebelión '85." This was the military component of the United States' counterrevolutionary scenario for 1985 and was to be coordinated with Cardinal Obando y Bravo's project for creating chaos in the cities, with an increase in urban terrorism and sabotage, and with the UNO/U.S. diplomatic offensive. Yet Plan Rebelión '85 was also eminently defensive, an attempt to reverse the strategic defeat, to reestablish an FDN presence and regain an operational capacity inside Nicaragua. "The FDN chiefs, the CIA, and Pentagon analysts are keenly aware that the FDN has been losing its political and military ability to challenge the Revolution," explained Javier Carrión. "The simple fact of naming it Plan Rebelión indicates this: the term is related to the attempts to incite a rebellion [with mass] participation. [They know] that if the counterrevolution does not start to develop another type of war, reaching the population in the cities, its war will be lost."[41]

The plan had been meticulously worked out months in advance. According to documents captured by EPS intelligence in July, the supersonic SR-71 Blackbird spy flights, which had terrorized the nation in late 1984, as well as intensive electronic and radar espionage in the first part of 1985, had been used to locate Sandinista military units and to study the movements of EPS forces during its six-month offensive. With this information, the contras planned to introduce new operational tactics based on their analysis of the changes in Sandinista strategy.

Within this framework, Plan Repunte had a dual purpose. The first and most immediate was strictly propagandistic—to capture international attention with spectacular actions. The second was to reinfiltrate thousands of contras into Nicaragua from Honduras, and then to recapture territory lost in the preceding months. FDN troops were now organized into "operational commands," comprising three regional commands and one task force each, and these were to be infiltrated through Jinotega Province into zones where the EPS maintained only a weak presence. The first command would then break through the defensive cordons that had been consolidated in the preceding months and draw EPS units away from large stretches of the fortified border region. This would open an undefended corridor through which a second command could swiftly penetrate into the less protected zones in the center of the country and carry out some spectacular action. This would in turn relieve the pressure on the contra forces that were boxed up in mountainous zones, freeing them up for further operations and making renewed incursions possible.

Plan Repunte was timed to coincide with the revolution's sixth anniversary celebrations. A fleet of U.S. warships was simultaneously dispatched to Nicaragua's coasts, to complement the offensive. The first regional command, baptized "Jeane Kirkpatrick," infiltrated on 19 July, followed by the rest of the operational command. Shortly afterward, the "Jorge Salazar" regional command entered the country, passed over the mountains of Matagalpa, and divided into two groups. One arrived in the central departments of Boaco and Chontales and the other headed westward, toward Estelí. Two other regional commands were used to serve as a supply line for the combatants.

The immediate objectives were to occupy stretches of the strategic Pan-American Highway and to take the city of Estelí. The first target was La Trinidad, a town of eight thousand people directly to the south. In early August, task forces from the Jorge Salazar regional command penetrated La Trinidad, which had previously been untouched by the war. The Somocistas had replaced their traditional blue uniforms with olive green, much like those used by the EPS. After the attack, many La Trinidad residents said they had thought the invaders were Sandinista troops, and for this reason did not activate self-defense structures. The contras did extensive damage to the town before being repelled.

From La Trinidad they then moved on to Estelí, but here they ran up against the city's outermost defensive rings. By this time, permanent EPS units were mounting a counteroffensive. In seven days of heavy fighting, 360 contras died and some 100 were captured.

The attacks were intended to project the image of a vital counterrevolutionary force that was extending the war from the border regions to the center of the country, thanks to popular support. The CIA mounted a major media blitz, bringing in journalists from southern Honduras to accompany the contras. Typical of the media coverage was that of *Time* magazine, whose 12 August headline read: "The Contras' Revived Challenge . . . They Threaten to Expand War."

But in fact it was clearly more a suicide mission. The CIA did not care about the number of contra casualties, since the objective was not military but psychological-propagandistic. The contra rank and file, as always, had been used as cannon fodder. According to José Angel Peralta, a contra captured outside of Estelí, "We approached La Trinidad with confidence, but what the leaders told us in Honduras—that the population would rise up because they hated the Sandinistas, who had made slaves out of the Nicaraguans—did not happen."[42]

Lacking the capacity to sustain the operation, the FDN was rapidly flushed from the region, losing positions as quickly as it took them. EPS pursuit operations inflicted hundreds more casualties. Nevertheless, the FDN continued with Plan Rebelión '85. From August to October they carried out three further major actions: an attack on Cuapa, in the Department of Chontales, and attempts to occupy Pantasma in the north and Santo Domingo in the center of the country. They lost about 120 men at the hands of the local militias and army units in Pantasma and Santo Domingo. The basic flaw in their strategy was a direct result of the United States' myopic focus on the EPS, for by 1985 the armed civilian communities were the defensive backbone of the war. In addition, a new defense structure was quickly created—a "circular urban defense system"—which prevented further attacks such as that on La Trinidad.

By the fall of 1985, the FDN was virtually a spent force in the north, forced to operate in groups of ten to twenty men, roaming in isolated mountain pockets and struggling to elude the EPS and the militias. Most of its men had returned once again to Honduras, but those who remained tried to open up a new operations theater in the politically isolated and historically conservative cattle-ranching region of Chontales and Boaco in the center of the country, and in central Zelaya in the east. But they could not move beyond the sparsely populated center and eastern zones of the department, and in late 1985 the EPS used heavy artillery and air support to isolate the 500–600 FDN members in Boaco and Chontales.

The year ended with another desperate attempt by the United States to reverse the strategic defeat, this time through a technological escalation of the aggression. On the afternoon of 2 December, an FDN column in eastern Matagalpa brought down a MI-24 FAS helicopter as it pulled out of the Mulukuku military base, killing all fourteen Nicaraguan soldiers on board. FDN spokesmen in Tegucigalpa announced that this had been done with SAM-7 surface-to-air missiles. Also known as "Redeye" missiles, the launchers are lightweight and easily carried. The missile itself travels at supersonic speed and uses an infrared heat-seeking system to find its target.

Nearly a year earlier, when the Sandinistas first moved to the offensive, the CIA had announced its intention of vastly improving the contra arsenal: diminished contra *human* resources were to be replaced with greater *technological* resources. The Nicaraguan Defense Ministry reported that U.S. military advisers had been sent to the FDN's Las Vegas camp in January to begin a training program. In May, Honduran newspapers reported that SAM-7 missiles had arrived, and in September FDN spokesman Aristides Sánchez said they were "ready to use the rockets," while the Tegucigalpa daily *El Tiempo* reported that "some 200 [contra] cadre recently graduated from a course given by the United States on the use of the missiles."

The EPS quickly adapted to the new aggression by flying at reduced altitudes, thus placing its choppers out of range of the SAM-7s, which need considerable distance to gather speed and home in on their targets. The FSLN reaction to the missiles was blunt: "Those rockets are worthless because the strategic defeat that we have begun will not stop, and we can assure you that the counterrevolution is over as a strategic project."[43]

The Collapse of the Contras' "Antennas"

One important element of the contra initiative, particularly during 1984, was an elaborate network of *correos*—messengers and guides who made up an FDN intelligence apparatus. The CIA manual referred to this network as the "antennas" of the contra movement.

The *correos* were indispensable to the contras' ability to dodge EPS patrols and attack at the right moment. "Wherever the Sandinistas go, the FDN hears about it almost at once through a vast network of *correos*," wrote one foreign journalist who traveled with the contras in early 1985. "The Sandinistas rarely know where the guerrillas are, and even when they do they rarely catch them, since a *correo* moves twice as fast as a group of armed men. This early warning system was with us every step of the way, drawing a cloak of invisibility around us."[44]

The *correo* network was built up in 1984 and became an essential ingredient of the FDN's conversion into a political guerrilla force. "In low-intensity conflict, there are three important words to remember," counseled leading LIW proponent Waghelstein. "They are intelligence, intelligence, and intelligence."[45] Together with constant U.S. radar and electronic surveillance, the *correo* network constituted the on-the-ground apparatus which provided this flow of intelligence to the contras at the level of local operations.

In contrast to the thousands of peasants who at one time or another collaborated with the contras as an adjunct to their normal activities, the *correos* more often had an ideological and political commitment to the counterrevolution. More aptly described as local representatives of the FDN than as collaborators, the *correos* carried arms, worked full time for the contras, and were paid a salary.

The Sandinista offensive, launched in late 1984, involved the dismemberment of the *correo* apparatus, which accelerated the decline of the FDN's operational capacity. In late February 1986, a month-long

Interior Ministry operation was successfully concluded: forty-nine *correos* were eliminated in armed confrontations and another sixty-five captured. With this, the *correo* network in Matagalpa and Jinotega virtually collapsed: the last waters of the "sea" in which the contra "fish" could move were drying up.

Days after the operation ended, the government held a "De Cara al Pueblo" in Pantasma, in the heart of Jinotega. In late 1983, hundreds of contras had swooped down upon the Pantasma Valley in one of the most brutal massacres of the war. Forty-three civilians were murdered, two cooperatives destroyed, and government installations razed. Now Pantasma was at peace. The crowd included a group of 150 peasants who had been kidnapped by the FDN and had taken advantage of the amnesty. President Ortega, presiding over the event, was visibly moved when sixty-year-old Estaban Vargas took the microphone: "The *correos* are essential to counterrevolutionary activity; it was they who facilitated my abduction by the mercenaries. I suggest," he told the president, "that the government deal as harshly as possible with the *correos*."

Two months later, a similar Sandinista operation, "Plan Llovisna," came to a close in Boaco and Chontales. One hundred and fifty *correos* were captured, lopping off the contras' "antenna" in the heart of the agricultural frontier.

10
Total Defense: The Nonmilitary Theaters

> Nicaragua will remain our major problem and the
> chances for a breakthrough there are limited.
>
> —"The View from Washington,"
> September 1985[1]

> In the political, military, ideological and diplomatic
> terrain we are winning. In the economic terrain, we
> are facing up to the difficulties.
>
> —Alejandro Bendaña, executive secretary
> of the Nicaraguan Foreign Ministry,
> May 1986[2]

The military theater is the catalyst that activates each of the fronts in
Washington's total war against Nicaragua. As long as the contras were
able to maintain an operational capacity, they could play out their
assigned role, while, as we have seen, the United States synchronized
the military element with the other fronts. The strategic defeat of the
contras thus altered the terms of the war. Once the contras lost the
initiative, the counterrevolution began to lose its force in the other
arenas. As Vice-president Sergio Ramírez pointed out:

> To the extent that the armed counterrevolution is weakened, that we
> continue consolidating the strategic defeat, the other U.S. war fronts tend
> to be also weakened. In the diplomatic arena, for example, it is not the
> same to try and impose on us a dialogue with contra forces that are
> controlling territory, that are advancing, as it is with contra forces that are
> being defeated. Nor is it the same for internal counterrevolutionary forces
> to try and destabilize the country when the armed contras are being
> defeated. To the extent that the strategic defeat is consolidated, the forms

of struggle on the different counterrevolutionary fronts are in turn weakened. Thus the entire panorama of the war changes.[3]

Neutralizing the Internal Front

In mid-1985, the internal front had attempted to seize the initiative, but what at first appeared as a potent "insurgency" in reality rested on very shaky ground. Obando y Bravo had returned to the country as cardinal just as the Sandinista offensive was moving into high gear. If the surrender-through-dialogue campaign had been mounted as the contras were expanding their power and influence, it might have gathered enough momentum to pose a serious challenge to the revolution. But the demand for dialogue with an armed opposition on the decline became less and less tenable. "We're doing our part," complained one reactionary in Managua, "[but] the contra is not putting on the pressure."[4] The FSLN let this contradiction play itself out. "The demand for dialogue became weaker and weaker," Sergio Ramírez told us. "Obando's project increasingly sank under the weight of its own contradictions."[5]

As it became clear that church- and contra-led confrontations were not going to escalate around the issue of reconciliation, and that the Sandinistas were not going to be forced into dialogue, the church hierarchy responded by deepening the political overtones of its discourse. And indeed, had the cardinal been able to convert the thousands of people who recognized his religious authority into *political* adherents, then his increasingly open political message might have taken the course the counterrevolution hoped for. But the project was based on two mistaken assumptions: that the Nicaraguan people could not differentiate between a religious and a political discourse, and that they would accept the one disguised as the other. Neither were true, as we saw earlier, and the cardinal began to lose influence among the population.

At the same time, the Sandinistas continued the ideological struggle with the church hierarchy, emphasizing in their own public messages and mass work that it was the counterrevolutionary project that stood behind the figure of the cardinal. The Sandinistas did not ask the people to deny the religious authority of the church, but instead constantly pointed to the facts, which showed that the cardinal's actions were politically motivated.

The FSLN had always countered the church hierarchy's subliminal

discourse with its own brand of "overt discourse," aimed at demystify-
ing the "church-state" issue by bringing it into the political terrain
where it belongs. In his 1984 May Day speech to Nicaraguan workers in
the northwestern city of Chinandega, for instance, Jaime Wheelock
concisely captured the class nature of the issue. He asked the crowd,
"Why is there no contradiction between Christianity and the Revolution? Is this a government of the rich or of the poor?"

The crowd responded: "Of the poor!"

"And who are the ones who could not enter into the Kingdom of
God?"

"The rich!"

"Then who does the Revolution defend?"

"The poor!"

The Sandinistas also reproduced in *Barricada* Somocista posters that
praised Obando y Bravo as their leader, as well as speeches by Reagan
extolling the cardinal as the defender of "democratic" (i.e. U.S.) interests in Nicaragua. All this helped expose the links between the church
and the counterrevolutionary apparatus.

But it was the Nicaraguan popular church itself that went on the
offensive against the hierarchy's manipulation of religion. In early 1986,
tens of thousands of Christians, led by Foreign Minister—and Mary-
knoll priest—Miguel D'Escoto, marched in a procession from Jalapa to
Managua to protest U.S. aggression. "Repent, Miguel Obando y Bravo,
before it's too late," said an orator at one of the dozens of public masses
held along the way. "This is the Lent of definition, and the Lord will
not allow the name of the church to continue being dirtied in order to
massacre a people who are rebelling against an evil empire."[6] The
procession and other religious mobilizations were meant to undercut
the cardinal's attempt to raise the banner of Christianity in the name of
counterrevolution.

As with the church, the Sandinistas let *La Prensa* fade out as a
counterrevolutionary instrument through its own attrition. Although
censorship, as a legal instrument of national defense, allows the government to prevent the publication of *false* information or news on military
or security issues that might jeopardize the nation, it is not aimed at
preventing the publication of the counterrevolution's political positions
and views. But in failing to convert the ideology of the counterrevolution into the ideology of the urban masses, *La Prensa* was left without
any political substance of its own to present to the people. If in 1984, for
example, it could criticize the agrarian reform and argue that the
counterrevolutionary alternative would solve the problem for the peasants, by 1985 it could no longer do this and was reduced to defending

the economic interests of the remaining Nicaraguan capitalists, denouncing land confiscations, and so on. *La Prensa* was reduced to its essence; class defense of the bourgeoisie, and by 1985 the bourgeoisie was talking to itself and not the masses.

But as the newspaper has become a mouthpiece for the United States, it has lost influence among its readership. This is demonstrated by statistics on the circulation of the country's three dailies. In 1979 *La Prensa* was the leading newspaper, selling 180,000 copies a day. By 1983, *Barricada* was selling over 90,000, *Nuevo Diario* 55,000, and *La Prensa* had dropped to some 80,000. By 1986, *Barricada* was over 120,000, *El Nuevo Diario* was at 85,000, and *La Prensa* at less than 70,000.[7]

On 15 October 1985 the government reinstated the National State of Emergency that had been in force since 1982 and was relaxed during the 1984 electoral campaign. The measure was intended to consolidate the military and political gains over the counterrevolution with controls that gave the government greater legal flexibility to confront internal destabilization. The Sandinistas had always made it clear that freedom to conduct political activities did not mean that pluralism could be used for counterrevolutionary activities. "We are flexible, but we know how to exercise our responsibilities," said Jaime Wheelock, "and there is a moment when flexibility begins to undermine the responsibilities we have in defending the interests of the people."[8]

The emergency measure did not prohibit political activities: although it was an important symbolic warning to the internal front, and particularly to the church hierarchy, Obando y Bravo's tour continued unhindered following the decree, and portions of his political homilies were even aired on national television. "The Emergency Law goes into effect only when delinquent activity has been detected," Dora María Téllez pointed out. It did, however, allow the government to bypass normal juridical procedures in breaking up a series of urban contra cells that were preparing to carry out terrorist actions.[9] "The political space is not closed off by the law; it is neutralized by raising the people's political consciousness, exposing the intentions behind the internal front, and, above all, bringing the masses themselves into political-ideological struggle, in defense of their own revolutionary project," she said.[10]

As the internal front lost momentum inside the country, it began to shift its activities to the international sphere. In early 1986, Obando y Bravo was the first of what would become a steady flow of internal front leaders who came to the United States to help the Reagan administration win support in Congress and among the U.S. public for that year's contra aid request. During his two-week visit, the cardinal hand-delivered a letter to UN Secretary General Javier Pérez de Cuéllar in New York, asking him to aid in the church's efforts at "reconciliation" in Nicaragua, and denouncing "intimidation, threats, and pressures" by the Sandinistas against Nicaraguan Christians.[11] He then delivered a harsh anti-Sandinista speech before the OAS in Washington, and spent the rest of his visit lobbying on Capitol Hill for the $100 million in aid. But while the publicity he received in the U.S. media may have helped the Reagan administration, it further weakened his image inside Nicaragua.

As Obando y Bravo arrived back in Managua, COSEP leaders were packing their bags to continue the campaign in Washington. They were still there when Bishop Pablo Antonio Vega followed in the cardinal's footsteps and, in an equally well-publicized trip (financed by the Heritage Foundation), continued the Washington lobbying.[12] Days later, Obando himself was back in Washington, this time invited by the New Right organization Society of the Americas. No sooner had he left than *La Prensa* director Jaime Chamorro arrived. In early May, the *Washington Post* published an op-ed piece by Obando y Bravo in which he declared that the contras "have every right to seek aid from other countries."[13] Meanwhile, in early June the CIA, through its front organization PRODEMCA, organized another U.S. tour for Vega, Chamorro, COSEP members, and other CDN leaders just prior to the House vote.[14] Behind this endless stream of visits lay an inescapable reality: the internal rearguard of the counterrevolution had been all but neutralized as a political force inside Nicaragua.

Despite this, the internal front is still able to continue its ideological aggression and confuse certain sectors of the population. But just as the armed contras have been halted in their own development as a political-military force, so too has the internal front suffered a strategic defeat, having lost the possibility of bringing the population into the counterrevolution.

The internal front has continued with its anti-SMP campaign, but with equally little success. Where before the internal front could manipulate the fear of dying to encourage draft resistance, the reorganization of the military, better training, increased combat efficiency, the division of military labor into defensive and offensive tasks, and more sophisticated hardware have all sharply reduced casualties. In fact, according to the Defense Ministry, only 1 percent of all those conscripted in 1984 died on the battlefield that year.

The counterrevolution had also been able to manipulate the friction between the parents of conscripted youth and the government, particularly by exploiting the difficulty of guaranteeing communications between young people and their parents, and of providing support services for the families of those mobilized. In December 1984, however, the government set up the National Commission for Support to Combatants, a special nationwide institution to assist those mobilized and their families. The commission improved communications, set up programs for parents to visit their sons at the bases, provided financial assistance, and established other services. All of this helped overcome the friction. Then, in November 1985, the first recruits finished their two-year tours. The demobilization of thousands of draftees in a highly publicized national ceremony undercut the counterrevolution's efforts to instill the fear that those drafted would never return.

Further, many of those who had served for two years developed a consciousness and commitment in the heat of battle that they had not had when living easy city lives. These youth, upon their return, transmit their experiences to their families, neighborhoods, and work centers. The SMP thus has an ideological multiplier effect which reduces the space in which the counterrevolution can manipulate. "As important as the SMP is for our military capacity," one young recruit told us, pointing to his own experience, "I'd say it is the most important thing we have going for us in the ideological battlefield."[15]

Institutionalizing Democracy and Revolutionary Transformation

> In Sandino's Nicaragua, we are building democracy for the first time. For us, democracy is literacy and health for the people. For us, democracy is people organizing themselves, workers' rights, agrarian reform, sovereignty, independence and self-determination. For us, democracy is putting an end to selfishness, greed, and the thirst for gold.
>
> —Daniel Ortega[16]

With the 1984 elections, the process of legally institutionalizing popular democracy and revolutionary transformation moved into high gear. The first task of the National Assembly was to draft a new constitution, which is slated to go into effect in early 1987. "This National Assembly is charged with preserving the continuity of the new revolutionary order," said National Assembly president Carlos Núñez. "This means crystallizing the power of the people in the new constitution."[17] Once the National Assembly completed the first draft, the government began a nationwide popular consultation. In community after community, the National Assembly convened "town hall forums" to hear the suggestions of thousands of people representing different social sectors and interests.

The constitution makes the process of revolutionary transformation part of the legal order of the nation. The preliminary draft guarantees such principles as equality between men and women, worker and peasant access to the mass media, agrarian reform based on the concept of land to those who work it, the right to organize, the right and obligation to defend the nation's sovereignty, autonomy for the Atlantic Coast, anti-imperialism and nonalignment as the pillars of foreign policy, and the right to health, education, and housing. Most importantly, it makes it a constitutional principle to eradicate the exploitation by one human being of another. In other words, the social and economic gains already made by the revolution, as well as the ongoing process of revolutionary transformation, are to become irreversible through law.

Underlying the entire constitutional project is the concept of *participatory* democracy. For the Sandinistas, representative democracy, national elections, and the existence of democratic organs of the state—as important as they are—must be subordinated to a concept of democracy that links state power to popular power, that guarantees, as Comandante Bayardo Arce has said, that the "construction of the new society will be carried out under the leadership of the previously dominated classes."[18]

This in turn means equality, an equality that is won by destroying unjust social and economic structures and constructing new ones. It also means guaranteeing the people the means to defend that very revolutionary project that makes true democracy possible. As the Sandinistas have pointed out, what greater democracy could there be than arming hundreds of thousands of citizens to defend their own popular project?

In fact, the backbone of the total defense strategy is the massive incorporation of the people into defense. Popular democracy and defense are inseparably linked through the revolutionary project. According to the FDN, the strategic defeat of the contras is due to Sandinista military superiority. "The people will not commit themselves unless they see a powerful and well-armed resistance," said Enrique Bermúdez at an early 1986 Heritage Foundation gathering.[19] It would be fitting to ask Bermúdez and his U.S. sponsors why the Nicaraguan people committed themselves to the Sandinistas, against the Somoza dictatorship, when the FSLN was so poorly armed that it often relied on nothing but second-hand revolvers and molotov cocktails. History proves that a "well-armed and powerful resistance" is not what motivates a people to rise up against a government. The popular revolutionary project of the FSLN was the motivation for the 1979 mass insurrection, and is still the motivation for the Nicaraguan people to continue fighting, this time against the U.S. counterrevolution.

Because the constitutional process was cementing the very revolutionary transformation that the counterrevolution was seeking to destroy, it became another target of sabotage. Although the parties and organizations in the CDN, as well as the Catholic church hierarchy, were invited to have an input into the draft and to participate in the town hall assemblies, they chose instead to boycott. They also launched a propaganda campaign that claimed that the government—and therefore its institutionalization in a constitution—was not legitimate. Similarly, the UNO called for the dissolution of the National Assembly and the entire constitution-building process—a demand repeated by U.S. envoy to Central America Harry Schlaudeman, in a personal visit to the Nicaraguan embassy in Washington in October 1985. Two months later, the CDN circulated a petition, making the same demands, in Managua, particularly among the opposition parties that belong to the National Assembly. According to Núñez, three COSEP leaders who had just returned from Washington had received instructions from the NSC to bring the legitimate political parties into the boycott in order to discredit the process internationally. None of the parties signed the document, however (although some individual members did). The counterrevolution lacked the strength to impede the constitutional process, and the town hall assemblies were held as scheduled.

In fact, most of the complaints about the draft constitution were that it was too mild: women objected that the sections dealing with their equality were abstract and did not include concrete rights, such as the right to abortion. Peasants charged that agrarian reform should include anti-*latifundista* clauses. EPS soldiers insisted that *every* citizen should have the right to be armed for national defense.

Autonomy and Peace Talks on the Atlantic Coast

We want this autonomy project to be an archetype, to be a bright light that will wipe out racial discrimination, cruelty, and misguided policies toward eth-

nic groups. We hope this project will begin a
contagious healing process, spearheading the
search for solutions to indigenous problems on this
continent. Autonomy, national unity, and revolution will be three victories in a truly revolutionary
process.

—Tomás Borge, September 1985[20]

The revolution was winning the war on the Pacific Coast, but on the
Atlantic Coast the situation was more complex and difficult to resolve.
If in the Pacific region the spearhead of the victory was the military
defeat of the mercenary forces, on the Atlantic Coast it had to be a
political rapprochement with the indigenous peoples. The offensive
against the counterrevolution on the Atlantic Coast therefore took a
radically different form and grew out of a lengthy examination of the
history, culture, and aspirations of the coastal peoples. The process of
rectifying earlier mistakes began in 1983 and led to the gradual reconceptualization of the Atlantic Coast problem.

At the heart of this process was the recognition that underlying the
crisis on the Atlantic Coast was the *ethnic question*. At first, the Sandinistas had regarded the ethnic question as at best a secondary issue, and
had felt that rapid socioeconomic development would be sufficient to
address the coastal peoples' historic demands. Exploiting this miscon-
ception, the counterrevolution made the ethnic issue a *military* issue.
The Sandinistas responded in kind, militarily: they went from im-
plicitly negating the ethnic issue to addressing it militarily. Given the
siege conditions, defending the nation's territory and revolutionary
project militarily was understandable; the problem lay with a weak
understanding of the relationship between the military and the political
dimensions of the conflict.

Over time it became clear to the Sandinistas that the problem could
not be reduced to the fact that some Miskitos had taken up arms.
Furthermore, not all of those who were fighting could be considered
counterrevolutionaries, since the majority were fighting for just claims,
even if in destructive ways. As it had on the Pacific Coast, the emphasis
of the Sandinista response on the Atlantic Coast shifted from the
military to the political.

By late 1984, the foundation for an overall redefinition of policy
toward the Atlantic Coast had been laid. The basis, announced dramatically in December 1984, was to be autonomy for the Atlantic Coast.
This was to go hand in hand with peace negotiations between the
Sandinistas and members of MISURA and MISURASATA, whom the

FSLN now called "Miskitos in arms" rather than counterrevolution-aries. Peace and autonomy were interdependent: only with the cessation of the military conflict could the autonomy project fully take hold, while the project itself would provide the material basis for negotiations between the Sandinistas and the armed Miskitos.

The counterrevolution attempted to depict the autonomy project as a Sandinista gimmick to placate the "rebellious Miskitos." Yet autonomy came from *within* the revolution, as part of its maturation. "When the autonomy plan was conceived, we thought that it could have an impact on the war situation, and we obviously saw it as a way to achieve Nicaragua's desire for peace," noted Manual Ortega Hegg, an official from the Ministry of the Presidency and member of the National Autonomy Commission. "However, we considered it fundamentally a strategic [rather than tactical] measure to resolve a historic problem."[21]

The autonomy proposal was conceived as an integrated response to the economic, political, and sociocultural aspirations of the Atlantic Coast peoples, and presupposed that sufficient power—both political and economic—would be granted to realize those aspirations. Regional governments will include a regional assembly, elected by popular vote,[22] and will be responsible for local economic planning and budget-ing, for the organization and administration of local enterprises, for the use of property, for investment, for management of natural resources, and so on. It will guarantee that the Atlantic Coast peoples will have a say in the local branches of the ministries of agrarian reform and internal commerce, among others, to assure the application of land distribution and local trade policies in accordance with local par-ticularities. Autonomy provides the vehicle for transforming *popular power*, the heart of the revolution, from an ideal into a reality of the Atlantic Coast.

Following the autonomy announcement, the Sandinistas set up a National Autonomy Commission, made up of some eighty members representing all the groups and communities on the Atlantic Coast. Over the next six months, the commission drafted the guidelines for the project; the report that resulted from the commission's activities was published in July 1985.[23] A grassroots consultation then began throughout the Atlantic Coast, starting in September 1985 and carrying on well into 1986. Hundreds of volunteers were trained to carry out door-to-door, village-to-village discussions, using the guidelines (which had been translated into the native languages) to solicit the views of the Atlantic Coast peoples. This exercise in popular democracy, together with community assemblies and other forums, was designed to ensure that the final statute, which is to be incorporated into the national constitution, represents the authentic aspirations of the population. It assumes that the ethnic groups themselves know the best way to make the revolution work *under their specific conditions and in their own interests*, but still within the framework of national revolutionary principles. The inhabitants of the Atlantic Coast have thus been defining the specific content of their own autonomy.

For example, in the Pacific region the principle of "land to those who work it productively" means handing out individual and cooperative parcels, but for the Sumus of the Atlantic Coast it means guaranteeing collective access to "the forests, mountains, and rivers" that embody their history and constitute the material basis for their survival. Similarly, on the Pacific Coast the principle of "equitable distribution of basic goods" means guaranteeing a minimum allotment of corn flour for tortillas, a daily staple; but for a Creole woman in Bluefields it means a minimal allotment of wheat flour, since bread is her family's daily staple.

According to Ray Hooker, a leader of the Bluefields community, elected member of the National Assembly, and coordinator of the National Autonomy Commission,

> Basically, what we're saying to the people of the region is, look, from the political point of view you're now going to elect your own leaders; in large measure, you're going to govern yourselves. From an economic point of view, you're going to handle your own natural resources. From a cultural point of view, we're saying that your different cultural manifestations are all going to be respected, encouraged, and promoted. The educational process will be carried out in your native language. . . . It's democracy being practiced from the very lowest level to the highest, and for all the ethnic groups.[24]

Autonomy is neither separatism nor decentralization. The central government maintains control over foreign policy, international trade, internal security, and national defense, but autonomy means that equality and cultural-ethnic diversity will be guaranteed. It means, paradoxically, that national unity will be strengthened as Nicaraguan identity is redefined and expanded. Put another way, autonomy is the political expression of the revolutionary alliance between the oppressed peoples of the Atlantic Coast and the popular classes of the Pacific Coast.

The first attempt to come to terms with an armed group was the effort to negotiate with Brooklyn Rivera, head of MISURASATA. In a brief encounter during the September 1984 UN General Assembly session in New York, Daniel Ortega invited the Miskito leader to return to Nicaragua for talks with FSLN leaders and to tour the Atlantic Coast without restrictions. This initial breakthrough was made possible by

Rivera's announcement that his group was no longer seeking the destruction of the revolution but wanted only to secure indigenous rights within it, and that secession from the Nicaraguan nation could not be a solution for the Atlantic Coast peoples.[25]

In October, Rivera made the visit, and after he left he continued to talk with FSLN representatives. Although both sides initially saw the talks as a positive step, it soon became clear that Rivera's CIA advisers, pressures from the counterrevolution, and his own personal ambition were preventing him from continuing discussions in the interests of the Atlantic Coast peoples. During one negotiating session, he actually interrupted the meeting to go outside for "consultations" with his U.S. advisers.[26] "All these guys start out fighting for their people," said one Nicaraguan Miskito in Costa Rica. "But they get a taste of money and power and from then on they only fight for themselves. That's what's happening to Brooklyn."[27]

Rivera's opportunism was evident in the demands he put forward during the talks. He insisted, for instance, that discussions of the autonomy project be confined to the FSLN and MISURASATA, as the authentic representative of the Atlantic Coast peoples—thus denying the legitimacy of the other groups (MISATAN and MISURA), as well as of those who were not represented by any one organization. For the Sandinistas, on the other hand, the nature of autonomy had to be decided through a process in which the wishes of all the Atlantic Coast peoples were taken into consideration, as expressed by the people themselves. Rivera also demanded that the EPS withdraw from the Atlantic Coast, leaving "defense" of the communities to MISURASATA. Besides giving up the nation's sovereignty, this would have left FDN and ARDE forces with a free hand in the region.

In April 1985 the two sides finally agreed to a "cessation of hostilities," but Rivera quickly violated the accord. In the following month he took credit for four of eleven attacks in the region, mostly against civilians and social installations. Shortly afterward, the talks collapsed altogether.

Rivera's problem (and that of his U.S. mentors) was summed up by the head of the Interior Ministry's political directorate, Omar Cabezas: "Brooklyn Rivera politically fears us because *we took away his banner*"—the banner of indigenous liberation.[28] In effect, the "fourth world" ideology was no match for an autonomy project that was part of a popular social revolution. Moreover, peace and autonomy did not depend on Rivera. Autonomy provided the basis for peace talks because it met the demands that many Miskito combatants were fighting for. As the Sandinistas' good faith became increasingly clear to both the armed and civilian population, which in any case wanted peace, dissension over continuing the war grew within the ranks of both MISURA and MISURASATA.

MISATAN, whose politics already successfully combined the ethnic question with the revolution, acted as a go-between in the initial contacts between the government and representatives of the armed groups. These efforts culminated on 17 May 1985, when José Gonzales, the Interior Ministry's representative for Zelaya Norte, met with MISURA Commander Eduardo Pantín in the Miskito community of Yulu, west of Puerto Cabezas. The two agreed on an effective cease-fire, and this meeting became a key turning point in the peace process. "In a few hours of responsible negotiations, we achieved what we were not able to do in five months of dialogue with Rivera," said Gonzales.[29]

The accord signed by Gonzales and Pantín opened the door for Miskito combatants to take part in the autonomy project. Many field commanders in both MISURA and MISURASATA, including Pantín, were tired of fighting, felt the desire for peace among the people, and recognized that the new FSLN efforts—provided they continued—would render armed struggle meaningless. In the meantime, the accords did not demand that either side put down their weapons. Rather, as one Interior Ministry official involved in the negotiations explained, "The Revolution is not asking the indigenous people to put down their rifles. They are instead being asked to aim them at the real enemy."[30]

Following the accord of 17 May, representatives of the government, of the armed Indian groups, and of the indigenous communities set up a peace commission to continue the process of dialogue in Zelaya. Before long, armed MISURA combatants were walking the streets of Puerto Cabezas side by side with EPS soldiers, a scene unimaginable a few months earlier and one that vividly underscored the changing reality of the Atlantic Coast. *La paz armada*—armed peace—was being achieved.

In certain zones, MISURA units took the responsibility for defense against attacks by the FDN and by those sectors of MISURA and MISURASATA that were still pursuing a war policy. In several instances, local Miskito commanders agreed to receive weapons, ammunition, and supplies from the EPS rather than maintain their supply lines with Honduras; this gave them the opportunity to participate in the defense against the contras without falling into the contradictory situation of being dependent on them. In several cases, EPS and Miskito troops conducted joint patrols.

On the basis of the cease-fire, the government decided that the Miskito families evacuated from the Río Coco during Red Christmas could safely return. A tripartite commission was formed—between

MISATAN, those MISURA members involved in the dialogue, and the government—to coordinate the return, and MISURA agreed to provide military protection. The return, an expensive and time-consuming operation, began in mid-July 1985. Three years of jungle growth had to be hacked away, villages had to be reconstructed, and emergency food and other supplies had to be guaranteed until the communities could achieve self-sufficiency. Nevertheless, by early 1986 some eighteen thousand people were once again living along their beloved river, and another important step in the process of gradually rebuilding trust had been taken. The cease-fire also made it possible for Miskito and Sumu refugees in Honduras to return. Starting in May 1985, more than one hundred began coming across the border each month. Those returning reported that many others were afraid to do so because of contra threats. In addition, restrictions on movement and the use of identity cards—both implemented after Red Christmas—were suspended, responding to a key demand of all the Atlantic Coast peoples. From May 1985 until the end of the year, there was relative tranquility on the Atlantic Coast, for the first time in four years. Discussions on autonomy were conducted without major incident, despite scattered FDN attacks.

If FDN and ARDE forces on the Pacific Coast faced massive desertion by the peasants who had been forced into their ranks, on the Atlantic Coast the counterrevolution was facing a "revolutionization" within the very organizations it had created to fight the Sandinistas—the organizations themselves, in a sense, were "deserting" to the revolution. It was an accumulative process, which unleashed a dynamic of its own. This process often left the armed organizations based in Honduras and Costa Rica without leaders, spokespeople, or lines of command inside Nicaragua. New commanders, once they sensed the positive reaction of the people, would then themselves desert. Those outside the country were subjected to FDN and U.S. propaganda and could not see the authenticity of what was happening in Zelaya. "The armed indigenous forces in Honduras have lost contact with the people and are unaware of the gradual but definite transformation in the relationship between the Miskito people and the government," said Miskito leader and National Assembly member Hazel Law. "Those outside believe the situation in Zelaya Norte is the same as it was in 1982." The FDN, not surprisingly, saw it differently: "The Miskitos are a lazy bunch," complained one trainer. "You wouldn't believe how many of them desert after we have finally put a little courage into them."[31]

As the autonomy process developed, the United States became increasingly concerned that the new Sandinista policy was undermining the foundations of its counterrevolutionary project in that area. U.S.

policymakers immediately set about sabotaging the autonomy project, and with it the peace talks. This counteroffensive found support among a sizable grouping of Miskitos who had learned that it was easier to live off the war—through bribes and crime—than to build peace. But as increasing numbers of Miskito combatants reintegrated into the autonomy process, it became easier to see who among the spokespeople for indigenous rights was really interested in the Indians and who was interested in the war. Gradually the latter lost legitimacy as they were exposed as mercenaries depending on U.S. dollars and the suffering of their own people. As the autonomy process deepened, the real enemy was coming into focus; the smokescreen was receding.

Then, on 22 June 1985, Eduardo Pantín was killed in Yulu. Some who claimed to have witnessed the event said that he was accidentally shot when his pistol fell from its holster, but most suspected that Fagoth had ordered his assassination in order to sabotage the peace accords.[32] After Pantín's death, many involved in the dialogue became targets of the contras; some were forced into hiding. When the United States cut off food supplies to those Miskitos who were participating in the peace process inside Nicaragua, the FSLN responded by sending them government food rations.

The U.S. counteroffensive began during the talks with Brooklyn Rivera, who later admitted that ARDE, the FDN, and the United States had all been opposed to his brief flirtation with the idea of negotiations. In mid-1985, as the cease-fire accords were going into effect, Washington was working hard to unite the "hard-line" factions of MISURA and MISURASATA into a new "purified" counterrevolutionary organization—and allocated at least $300,000 of the $27 million in humanitarian aid approved by Congress in June for that purpose.[33]

Days before Pantín's death, the "pro-war" representatives of MISURA and MISURASATA had met in Miami and announced the formation of a provisional commission, called Asla (Miskito for unity), which would coordinate the work of forming the new group.[34] Following the meeting, Rivera announced that within sixty days the "Asla unified command" would meet in Honduras to elect a leader and form a single organization.

At the 31 August–3 September meeting, held at MISURA's principal base of Rus Rus, Asla leaders formed a new contra organization called KISAN (Miskito acronym for Nicaraguan Coast Indian Unity). KISAN immediately aligned with the FDN and began to counter the peace and autonomy processes, both militarily and politically. A minority who opposed the resumption of armed conflict was beaten back by the "hard-liners." Rivera, who was barred from entering Honduras and condemned for having negotiated with the Sandinistas—even if only briefly—regrouped his followers back into MISURASATA. Fagoth, who had been ousted from MISURA a few weeks earlier in reprisal for his heavy-handed domination, was, by the time of the meeting, doing public relations for the FDN in Miami. He was replaced by Wycliff Diego, his long-time right-hand man.

KISAN was headed by an assortment of Miskito mercenaries, FDN members from the Pacific Coast who came in to command, and U.S. advisers who came to oversee. The KISAN leadership made its position clear from the start. One leader, Roger Herman, reported that "KISAN doesn't want a negotiated peace. We want a victorious peace."[35] Another KISAN spokesman added, "We are in agreement with the FDN and ARDE . . . because we're fighting for the same thing."[36] In November KISAN joined the UNO. It still had the power to attract Miskitos from certain communities inside Nicaragua, but principally recruited from the Honduran refugee camps, which KISAN controlled.

In late November, however, only three months after its founding, a faction broke off from KISAN and returned to Nicaragua, where it joined with the Miskitos already involved in dialogue; it adopted the name KISAN for Peace. Some three hundred members of KISAN for Peace established themselves in the communities southwest of Puerto Cabezas, defending their zone from the FDN-KISAN troops, with weapons and supplies from the EPS. "Those of KISAN for War are mercenaries: for them the indigenous struggle is a way to make money," said Reynaldo "Rafaga" Reyes, a one-time confidant of Fagoth and a KISAN for Peace leader. "In my guts, I now regret all the bloodshed, because I understand that there are other roads to peace on the [Atlantic] Coast. In Honduras, I began to realize that the Sandinista government was maturing and that this dialogue can stop the war."[37] Reyes's comrade, Rayli Wilson Fagoth, was more militant: "We want peace and we are facing a common enemy—the FDN and the CIA."[38]

By December 1985, KISAN was ready to resume hostilities. In January 1986 the United States began its "Cabanas '86" military maneuvers in Gracias a Dios. U.S. Army engineers renovated the Rus Rus base and built a new airstrip to facilitate the transfer of weapons and equipment. KISAN columns infiltrated across the border and established a presence in communities along the Río Coco, where those recently returned from Tasba Pri had established themselves. Hundreds of FDN troops were brought from the west of Honduras—so many that the contras bragged that they outnumbered the Miskitos. Such KISAN-FDN infiltration was possible because of the virtual absence of EPS troops—withdrawn at the request of the returning communities.[39]

In March, the counteroffensive began. Attempting to repeat Red Christmas, the contras forced some 2,500 civilians from three towns to cross the border. In early April, another 10,000 were taken across. The 6,000 who remained behind then asked the government for help in bringing back family members who had been taken to Honduras. Others, fearful that KISAN would return, asked to go back to Tasba Pri.

The new "exodus" was intended to bolster the counterrevolution's diminishing social base on the Atlantic Coast, but the best it could hope for was to consolidate the Honduran rearguard into "liberated Miskito territory." Americas Watch, which sent representatives to the Honduran Mosquitia, reported that: "KISAN had sown terror as part of a deliberate plan to evacuate the Miskitos from Nicaragua. . . . In a sense, it is like moving the sea to the fish. It seems that if KISAN cannot obtain military victories in Nicaragua, at least it can maintain a kingdom in the [Honduran] Mosquitia with funds from the United States and support for its civilian base from the international refugee agencies."[40]

Even as KISAN was grinding the axe of war, peace and the autonomy project were moving ahead. On 17 May 1986—the first anniversary of the cease-fire—the Sandinistas announced a pilot project in zonal autonomy in the area defended by KISAN for Peace. In an emotional ceremony in Yulu, Tomás Borge declared: "Enough of talking about autonomy; it must now be applied. We're not going to wait until the law is approved. We are going to test the law before it is passed."[41]

Although the counteroffensive showed that the United States can maintain an indefinitely smoldering conflict on the Atlantic Coast, exploiting the lingering mistrust and bitterness of the past, by mid-1986 the tide was clearly turning in favor of the revolution. The United States is the one factor preventing peace on the Atlantic Coast. "If imperialism withdrew," said one local official, "we believe the conflict could be resolved so quickly that we'd have peace almost overnight, and with it immediate possibilities of development."[42]

Much still needs to be done, but the *Sandinista* revolution has begun on the Atlantic Coast. With or without war, the autonomy project—as the vehicle for the true liberation of the Atlantic Coast peoples in unison with Nicaragua's national liberation—represents a major advance for the revolution. Yet in a war situation it is also a defense against the counterrevolution. Thus, once again, the deepening of the revolution and the defense of the revolution are inseparable.

The International Front

> The international front has been, and will continue
> to be, one of the most important in obstructing the
> various forms of U.S. aggression. The belief that
> the survival of the Sandinistas People's Revolution
> is fundamentally dependent on our own forces nei-
> ther diminishes the importance of the international
> struggle nor negates the fact that the existence of
> our revolution is possible only in the context of an
> existing correlation of world forces.
>
> —FSLN statement, May 1984[43]

Contadora

As we saw in earlier chapters, in addition to trying to isolate Nicaragua internationally, the Reagan administration has used its warfare
diplomacy to try to force Nicaragua to enter into a "dialogue" with the
counterrevolution—i.e., to surrender—and to disarm the country unilaterally.

Diplomatic muscle is attained by real power relations. The United
States was for a time able to advance its diplomacy because it enjoyed
the initiative—the result of the gains the contras made in 1984, Obando
y Bravo's offensive, and so on. But as the revolution consolidated and
the internal front virtually collapsed, Nicaragua's ability to reject "reconciliation" with the contras—in Contadora and other international
forums—was strengthened. The Reagan administration gradually
shifted its focus—without abandoning the reconciliation platform altogether—toward "unilateral disarmament."

In late 1985, the Sandinistas moved to put an end to Washington's
diplomatic game. When the modified Contadora treaty, which would
force Nicaragua to disarm unilaterally, was presented in September
1985, it became clear that Contadora had reached a point where a
"peace treaty" would be used to sanction the U.S. war. The Sandinistas
refused to keep quiet about this farce any longer. "There are some who
have been confused by our good will, believing that by pressuring
Nicaragua they can wring so many concessions from us that all the
wishes and desires of the U.S. government are satisfied," said one high-
level FSLN official. "Obviously this is a serious error, which has led to
the deterioration of the negotiating process and its Latinamericanist
positions."[44]

Then, on 11 November 1985, Daniel Ortega presented the government's new position. Nicaragua would not sign the treaty because it completely ignored the U.S. aggression, which was the principal factor in the Central American crisis: "The absolute, immediate, and categorical prohibition of international military maneuvers, of any kind," stated the communiqué read by Ortega, "is an irrevocable position of principle." In addition, any treaty would have to be accompanied by a special protocol signed solely by the United States, which would commit it to "the cessation of all forms of aggression against Nicaragua, including covert assistance delivered through private organizations and individuals." The communiqué continued:

> For Nicaragua, the level of arms necessary for the defense of our sovereignty is determined by our ability to resist U.S. aggression. . . . The Nicaraguan people have the right to a level of armaments and of military and paramilitary forces capable of putting them in a position to defend their sovereignty with dignity.[45]

No further unilateral concessions would be wrung from Nicaragua. The Contadora nations had to begin pressuring the United States or abandon the project altogether. "To mediate this conflict means to confront the U.S. government one way or another," said one FSLN official.[46]

At the same time, conscious that Latin America had an objective interest in challenging U.S. policy in Central America, the Sandinistas appealed to Bolivarian nationalism, calling on the eight nations of the Contadora and Lima groups to "say clearly to the United States that it is making a mistake with Nicaragua and, thereby, a mistake with Latin America." By underscoring the United States' disregard for national sovereignty in Latin America while defending its own with dignity, Nicaragua touched Latin America's "soft spot." If the Latin American negotiating group did not take a firmer position against the United States it would fold, and all of Latin America—both popular and bourgeois democratic interests—would be weakened in the face of the United States' application of the Monroe Doctrine to the 1980s. "This is a challenge not just for Nicaragua, but for all of Latin America, because the contradiction between U.S. imperial interests and Latin America's interest in its own sovereignty and independence is playing itself out today in a dramatic and cruel way in Nicaragua," said Sergio Ramírez. "Nicaragua, a small piece of Latin America, is defending the entire continent's frontiers."[47]

The U.S. response was that nothing would be allowed to stand in the way of the war effort. "Our commitment to the contras is indefinite," declared Shultz in late 1985. "We are simply going to continue forward with the war."[48]

With Washington and Managua both having thrown down the gauntlet, the Contadora nations were thrown off balance. In order to allow the Contadora process to regain momentum, Nicaragua proposed a five-month suspension of the negotiations. This was accepted. In the interim, the Nicaraguans called on the Contadora nations to negotiate directly with the United States on ending the aggression against Nicaragua.

The Sandinista initiative triggered a rapid-fire series of diplomatic moves that put the United States on the defensive. In January 1986 the eight Contadora and Lima Group nations (representing 90 percent of Latin America's population) met in Caraballeda, Venezuela, to find a way to break the impasse. The resulting Caraballeda Declaration called for direct talks between the United States and Nicaragua (thus acknowledging that these are the two parties to the conflict, not Nicaragua and the contras), an end to any foreign military presence in Central America—including maneuvers, advisers, and bases—and an end to any support for irregular forces in the region.

A few days later, the Reagan administration began a campaign for congressional approval of a further $100 million in funding for the contras. Latin American indignation was such that the Contadora and Lima nations' foreign ministers traveled to Washington to meet personally with Shultz and demand that the administration cancel the funding request and respect the Caraballeda Declaration. Shultz was unmoved, demanding instead that the Nicaraguans cease all military activity against the contras and open a church-mediated dialogue with them. The foreign ministers were outraged. "The Caraballeda Declaration expresses the opinion of almost all of Latin America," said the Argentine foreign minister following the meeting, "and the United States will pay a high price for ignoring it."[49] Peru's foreign minister was even more forceful, declaring that the Contadora countries should break diplomatic relations with the United States if it continued its present course.[50]

As its position deteriorated, the Reagan administration dispatched a string of high-level officials to the Contadora countries. When these envoys made little headway, the Reagan administration's announcements became increasingly bizarre. At a December meeting of the OAS, Shultz declared that the Sandinistas had supplied arms to the M-19 guerrillas who had seized Colombia's supreme court a month earlier. The Colombian foreign ministry rejected the charge as unsubstantiated.[51] A few months later, Reagan announced that the Nicaraguans had trained and armed a team of Brazilian guerrillas. Brazilian Foreign Minister Robert de Abreu Sodre flatly rejected the claim, adding, "The extremist position of Reagan makes the search for peace in Central America difficult."[52] In late March, Reagan announced that the FSLN was setting up "guerrilla *focos*" in Argentina and Uruguay—accusations immediately rejected by both those countries.[53]

Just before the Contadora negotiations were to be resumed, Daniel Ortega strongly reiterated the Sandinista position:

> Nicaragua will *never* disarm its people. Not one single rifle will be taken away from Nicaragua in *any* negotiations. We're not disarming the people, we're not disarming the Revolution; this is final. The Contadora peace treaty *cannot take away* the security of the Nicaraguan people, it cannot become an instrument of U.S. aggression, and it is on this premise that we are going to discuss [the treaty] in the following days.[54]

When the foreign ministers of the Contadora and other Latin American nations met again on 6–7 June in Panama City, a new section to the draft treaty took virtually all of the Nicaraguans' security concerns into account. This section specified that there be no support for irregular forces or for the use of one country's territory in attacks against another, that military blocs or alliances that jeopardize the security of any Central American country be prohibited, that international military maneuvers and foreign advisers be *proscribed* (rather than just *regulated*), that the United States sign a protocol binding it to these commitments, and that there be a return to the concept of a reasonable balance of forces in the region based on security needs. This was in effect a new treaty: a document "broadly consistent with U.S. interests" had become one that was broadly inimical to imperial designs. "The United States is not going to like this," said one diplomat in Panama, after the new draft was announced.[55]

And indeed, the United States had already made it clear, in a leaked "secret" document, that the "collapse [of Contadora] is better than a bad agreement."[56] The document noted that Contadora "group fatigue" could be used to facilitate the two-track approach of molding the negotiations to suit U.S. needs or, failing that, of neutralizing the peace group through attrition and diplomatic sabotage until it eventually folded, unable to fulfill its mission. And within a week of the Panama summit, the Honduran, Salvadoran, and Costa Rican foreign ministers met in San José and suggested that they were ready to throw in the towel on Contadora. "We are going to put aside the fraternal tutelage of friendly countries [Contadora] and instead look to our own options," declared the Salvadoran foreign minister. It appeared likely that the United States and its allies would jettison Contadora altogether.[57]

The U.S. Failure to Isolate Nicaragua

The Sandinistas' ability to perceive the convergence of interests between Nicaragua and diverse international forces, and then mobilize these forces against U.S. policy, has been most vividly demonstrated in Latin America. The degree to which the U.S. effort to isolate Nicaragua from the other Latin American nations, as the prelude to general international isolation, has failed was demonstrated in February 1986, when the Nicaraguans convened the Conference of Latin American and Caribbean Political Parties for Peace and Non-Intervention. Delegates represented 115 parties and political organizations from 33 countries across the continent, spanning virtually the entire spectrum of social-democratic, social Christian, liberal, Communist, and progressive forces—including some from almost all of the political parties in power at the time—as well as observers from the international wings of these tendencies. It was an outpouring of Latin American unity around anti-interventionism—and one that took place despite obvious and manifold political differences among delegates. Latin America had come a long way from the time when the United States had been able to isolate Cuba following its revolution.

In their effort to mobilize international opinion, the Nicaraguans focused on the United States' flagrant disregard for the international legal order, warning that this precedent jeopardized not just Central America, but the very foundations of international peace and stability. In April 1984 Nicaragua initiated a lawsuit against the United States in the International Court of Justice, accusing the United States of violating, by its aggression, the UN Charter, the OAS Charter, the Treaty of Friendship, Commerce, and Navigation between Nicaragua and the United States (which the United States unilaterally suspended with its economic embargo in 1985), customary law, and other international juridical commitments.

In May, the court handed down a preliminary finding and ordered the United States to cease all aggression. The Reagan administration responded that the court had no legal authority to consider the Nicaraguan claims and that its order was therefore invalid. This position was rejected by the court six months later. Finally, in June 1986, after two years spent collecting evidence—during which time the United States boycotted the proceedings—the court declared the United States the aggressor country, ruled that it was violating international law, and ordered the cessation of U.S. aggression and reparations for damages.

Although Nicaragua did not expect that the United States would end its war simply because it was found illegal—and the World Court is not invested with any power to enforce its rulings—as Alejandro Bendaña, executive secretary of the Foreign Ministry, put it, the ruling "is a reaffirmation that justice is on our side, and one more element that makes it more difficult for the Reagan administration to justify its aggression."[58]

The international front has been a disappointing one for the United States, which has been unable to secure support or resources from the international community (beyond from its Central American allies and from various right-wing client regimes around the world). Most U.S. allies in Western Europe hold the Latin American position that the conflagration in Central America is more inimical to their interests than is coexistence with Nicaragua (although some groups, such as the Socialist International, have their own strategies for discouraging deeper revolutionary transformation in Nicaragua). Moreover, Western Europe and Japan have been expanding their trade ties with Latin America, competing with the United States for economic control. The active solidarity of the Non-Aligned Movement, and particularly the political and economic support of the socialist nations, have also been important factors in preventing the United States from gaining international acceptance of its war.

Broad international solidarity has also played a key role in Nicaragua's defense. Between 1979 and 1985, over 500,000 people visited Nicaragua, among them tens of thousands of U.S. citizens. Hundreds of voluntary "brigades" come to Nicaragua every year to help build schools, houses, and health clinics, to harvest coffee and cotton, to assist in emergency relief programs for war victims, and to provide technical aid in industrial, educational, and agricultural facilities. The majority of these brigades bring with them thousands of dollars worth of tools and materials, bought with money raised by solidarity organizations all over the world. Hundreds of tons of donated food and medical, agricultural, and other supplies have been sent to Nicaragua as the result of grassroots campaigns, thus helping replenish what the U.S. war has destroyed. All of this activity raises political consciousness about U.S. intervention against nations seeking independence and sovereignty.

The political and economic support of friendly countries around the world, combined with the solidarity and anti-interventionism shown by the international community, constitute the critical *external rearguard* for the revolution, an indispensable aspect of the struggle of the Nicaraguan people to gain control of their own destiny.

The Economic Front: Survival and Transformation

The strategic defeat of the contras meant that the spearhead for carrying out socioeconomic attrition was losing its effectiveness. This provided the revolution with greater room to confront the long-term implications of attrition on the economic front. The success of the 1985–86 "coffee battle" underscored the relation between the strategic defeat and the economy.

In late 1984, we traveled through the northern coffee-growing departments of Jinotega, Matagalpa, and Estelí. It was just two days after the El Pericón massacre, in which nearly thirty civilians on their way to the harvest had been gunned down and burned alive by an FDN commando unit, and we could see the coffee battle in progress: dozens of *brigadistas* (volunteer harvesters) were hitchhiking along the highway in full gear, hoping to get a quick lift to the farms that had been assigned to them; trucks were going back and forth, transporting sacks of coffee to regional warehouses, soldiers riding on top to protect against attack; special EPS units were heading off to remote areas where contra movements had been reported.

We visited the Asunción Loaisiga state farm, which had been confiscated from Somoza in 1979. Students from Jinotega, to the north, were sharing the tasks of harvesting and "vigilance." Wiping the sweat from his forehead and putting down his shovel for a moment to speak with us, a young man named Gustavo Ruiz explained his feeling about being there at that time: "Rather than intimidating us, that act of barbarity [the El Pericón massacre] has strengthened our determination. We swear by the blood of those fallen *compañeros* that we will redouble our efforts until the coffee battle is won."[59] Ruiz and his eight friends were digging a trench at the top of a steep hill that overlooked the farm, the last part of an elaborate "circular defense system" that was designed to protect the farm from contra attack. Further off, militia and EPS units had formed a huge military cordon around the coffee farms.

In that harvest, over 10 percent of the country's coffee farms had had to be abandoned because of FDN activity, the coffee beans left to rot on their branches. Another 10 percent had been destroyed by the Somocistas, who laid siege to 57 peasant cooperatives and 32 state farms. All told, 25 percent of the crop had been lost due to the war. Four hundred and fifteen coffee pickers and small producers had been killed by the contras. But the determination of people like Ruíz, multiplied throughout the nation, provided the raw material necessary for the stunning advances that would be made in the battle against the contras in the following year. When we returned for the 1985–86 harvest, mobilization was no less intense but roads too dangerous the year before were now open and flowing with traffic. Hundreds of workers and volunteers were again picking beans on once-abandoned farms. Others were reconstructing the installations that had been razed by the contras. The contra threat still existed, and in the most dangerous areas militia members were doing all the harvesting—rifles on their shoulders and coffee sacks in their hands. In the 1985–86 harvest not one life was lost, every attempt the contras made to attack the farms failed, and all production goals were met.

Coffee production—in other countries simply another agricultural activity—has in Nicaragua become one more part of "total defense," as political, economic, military, and ideological aspects of defense are brought together. Each harvest season sees a massive military deployment to protect the pickers. And the thousands of urban youth and workers who labor side by side with peasants under wartime conditions undergo an experience that sharpens revolutionary consciousness and commitment. Once back in the cities, these "coffee combatants" pass their experiences on to those who stayed behind—in their homes, neighborhoods, schools, and work centers.

By 1986, Nicaragua had all but overcome the initial impact of the economic embargo. It ultimately forced the acceleration of agroindustrial advances and stimulated national production of intermediate and capital goods, as well as the emergence of an indigenous technology. For example, according to officials from the Industry Ministry, one long-term project—the installation of a steel smelter—plans for which were to be drawn up in 1986, was advanced so that construction could begin by the end of the year. The steel will be used for the production of agricultural implements, industrial spare parts, and as the basis for a machine tool industry. This will constitute the first links between existing light industry and heavy industry, and the first step that will articulate the different branches of industry with other sectors.

In response to the embargo, the government expanded state support for the "innovators' movement." This movement had begun spontaneously among industrial workers following the 1979 insurrection, in plants that had been paralyzed for lack of spare parts and machinery. The workers took it upon themselves to make missing parts and invent entirely new components with the resources at hand, often achieving the seemingly impossible. "Thousands of rural and urban workers depend on the innovators," explained Daniel Ortega. "One innovator can activate the entire productive force of an economic enterprise."[60] Similarly, some peasants began developing their own pesticides, which were as effective as the industrial versions. These undertakings were the beginning of an indigenous technology, and in fact demonstrate how U.S. economic aggression, aimed at retarding development, paradoxically forces the acceleration of processes essential to the long-term development of the country.

As with the attempt to isolate Nicaragua diplomatically, no other country joined the U.S. embargo. The relative ease with which Nicaragua weathered the embargo shows that the world of the 1980s is too complex and multipolar for U.S. imperialism to cut one country off—again, a far cry from the days of the Cuban embargo, when that country's economy was thrown into chaos overnight.

Meanwhile, the Sandinista leadership has been severely self-critical for promoting the belief that an early improvement in the standard of living could be sustained. This cultivated a false consciousness among portions of the population that the essence of the revolution was immediate material benefits—and thus that the revolution was failing if it did not come up with the goods (which the counterrevolution made impossible). Similarly, it led to a paternalistic image of the state as the "great provider," which in turn retarded popular creativity and collective self-reliance.[61]

"If we had to point to our principal economic error, it would be that we tried to do more than was really possible with our limited material resources. . . . We're no longer going to make such promises or encourage false hopes," the FSLN declared in a 1985 message to the nation explaining the need for austerity.[62] The revolutionary leadership stressed that the *true* achievement to be defended was the seizure of political power by the poor majority.[63] It launched broad campaigns to bring home the fact that only with an end to the war could economic problems be solved, and that the prosperity that would be made possible by revolutionary transformation would be enjoyed only by future generations.[64] "We have twenty hard years ahead of us," explained Tomás Borge.[65] The deeper the political consciousness of the difference between immediate conditions and historic interests became, the less the counterrevolution could manipulate the economic crisis.

In the meantime, the government continued its efforts to confront the economic crisis and improve economic performance. In early 1985, it launched a sweeping new economic program aimed at constructing a *war economy*, described as an "economy of survival." The key would be the efficiency with which the population could organize its limited resources. Production and distribution were reorganized and priorities redefined. The objective was, first and foremost, to meet defense requirements, as well as to guarantee the essential needs of the population and correct macroeconomic distortions generated by the war. The *economy of survival* meant just that: economic activity would be for defense and the basic needs of the people, the two requirements for the survival of the nation. Assemblies were held across the country to discuss the economic crisis, and programs were hammered out at each work center and *barrio*. Under the slogan "Everything for the Combatants, Everything for the War Fronts," worker-management councils and farming communities, in coordination with the Defense Ministry, earmarked part of their production for the war effort and part for civilian consumption. Expanding mass participation in production and distribution decisions came to be referred to as the economic "insurrection."[66]

To bring this about, the state stepped up its intervention in circulation in order to guarantee the equitable distribution of essential goods. With the participation of trade unions and mass organizations, it cracked down on hoarding and speculation within the private commercial sector. A new pricing policy in the productive sector tied prices to real production costs and adjusted salaries accordingly (for rural and urban workers and professionals), and created special state distribution outlets exclusively for these sectors. Agrarian reform measures, combined with new price policies for agricultural produce, were aimed at stabilizing rural production and strengthening exchange between countryside and city. Productive labor was to be rewarded and those in the burgeoning informal sector penalized; price, wage, and distribution policies were to direct resources away from commerce and nonessential consumption and into production. In other words, what resources the country did have would be channeled to production, and to the producers, in order to reestablish the productive potential of a nation whose economic life had been disrupted by foreign aggression.[67]

There were no illusions that the economic crisis could be overcome as long as the war persisted; hardships would continue, and even worsen. But with the new policies the crisis could be controlled and the further deterioration of living standards arrested. Social services—so greatly expanded in the first years of the revolution—were to be maintained. Mass vaccination campaigns against polio, measles, chicken pox, and other diseases were to continue. In 1983 door-to-door campaigns for preventive medicine and improved hygiene were reactivated. Family and communal gardens sprouted up in the urban areas, to supplement rural production. Such activities do not need extensive material resources but rather efficient organization. In late 1985, UNICEF praised Nicaragua's continued tremendous health achievements despite the war, noting that this was possible because of the massive participation of the population in their own health affairs.[68]

In effect, the survival economy meant the synthesis of economic defense and socioeconomic transformation. The deepening of socioeconomic transformation cannot in this case be measured by immediately improved living standards or greater material production. Rather, its essence is the reorganization of production, combined with the greater control by the producers over their conditions of production and the social product. The war economy in Nicaragua means that the country's productive process is thoroughly subordinated to the fundamental interests of the popular classes: defense against the counterrevolution and preservation of revolutionary power, and greater control by the motor force of the revolution—the working majority—over the economic process.

The construction of the war economy has involved liberating the creative potential of the people, as exemplified in the innovators' movement, and deepening mass consciousness of the economic crisis. Discontent over economic conditions is thus transformed into a popular search for solutions. This helps remove the "social" element from socioeconomic attrition. As Sergio Ramírez put it:

> It is necessary to distinguish between what economic attrition and all its consequences represents for a country living at a decisive moment in its history waging a decisive war, and what a crisis, or social attrition, represents. [There will be no social crisis] so long as the war intensifies popular unity, which in turn generates the creative energies necessary for facing the war, winning it, and carrying forward the Revolution at the same time. The empire seeks the strategic attrition of the motor forces of the Revolution, an impossible task because the Revolution would have to stop being popular in order for these forces to fatally exhaust themselves.[69]

The United States had counted on imposing a war psychosis and exhausting the population through permanent threats, the need for massive defense mobilization, economic hardship and sacrifice—all important psychological components of the overall attrition process. Paradoxically, however, the prolonged antipopular warfare is having a very different effect on much of the population: the deeper political consciousness that grows out of the revolutionary process and out of the experience of defense itself provides more than a buffer against psychological attrition; it helps neutralize it. Rather than break down resistance, aggression stiffens it. "The aggression has helped us develop our awareness as workers," one Managua brewery worker reported. "Our struggles have instilled confidence in our own capacity to organize, resist, and survive no matter what our enemy does."

11
Crisis
in the Counterrevolution

The shift in favor of the revolution was triggered by a number of political, socioeconomic, and military initiatives, which were predicated on an understanding of the U.S. strategy. These "push" factors fed into a series of "pull" factors, such as the corruption and infighting endemic to the counterrevolutionary apparatus, which intensified as the armed contras increasingly failed to wage the political and military struggle. The two sets of factors were thus mutually reinforcing, and by 1985 a profound demoralization had set in within the counterrevolution, eroding its ability to maintain cohesion.

The War of Images: Myth vs. Reality

Despite its degeneration as a political-military force, the armed counterrevolution has continued to maintain the illusion that it will provide the spark for an insurrection against the Nicaraguan government. In early 1983, for instance, the FDN claimed it would be in Managua by July, "or by the end of the year at the latest." In January 1984 Adolfo Calero told the press that "our armed struggle and internal difficulties will provoke a collapse of the Sandinista system in the coming months."[1] Five months later, the "collapse" had still not come, and Edgar Chamorro declared that "the total war against the Sandinista regime will now be launched, culminating with an insurrection in the fall."[2]

Far from rising up in insurrection, however, the Nicaraguan population rose up to participate in the country's first democratic elections, in which a clear majority endorsed the Sandinista government. The Somocistas had to rewrite the script once again. In February 1985 Calero announced that "we will resolve the crisis in Nicaragua this year." On 13 June the FDN announced in a press release that "within 45 days, the general collapse of the Sandinista regime will commence, with the execution of the $27 million non-lethal aid plan approved by the United States."[3] Forty-five days later, when the collapse did not come, Calero tried again. "The days of the Sandino-Communists are numbered. July 19, 1985, was the last celebration for the FSLN."[4]

There are no doubt many Somocistas who still dream of the day when they will once again rule Nicaragua. But Calero, Bermúdez, and the other leaders know better: their statements are part of the *war of images* aimed at influencing U.S. and international public opinion—with an image of contra belligerency—and at convincing the Nicaraguans that the counterrevolution is advancing. Above all, the triumphalism seeks to counter the profound demoralization that has set in within the contra ranks. But as the gap grows between the promises of victory and the reality of one battlefield defeat after another, the contra rank and file is becoming increasingly embittered by the realization that they are being manipulated. Desertions multiply, infighting escalates, and the FDN commanders resort to dreaded "disciplinary" measures to keep the foot soldiers in line.

Contra Recruitment: Tactics in the Face of Diminishing Supply

The strategic defeat of the contras is numerically expressed in the steadily increasing numbers of contra casualties. According to Defense Ministry figures, there were 40 contra deaths in 1981, 337 in 1982, 1,853 in 1983, 3,017 in 1984, and 4,608 in 1985. In addition, over 2,500 contras suffered serious injury during the period 1981–85, while some 1,500 were captured. All told, then, 14,000 contras were forced out of action by Sandinista forces in this period—over 60 percent of these in 1984–85 alone.[5] These figures are even more significant when it is remembered that the total number of contra combatants at any given time never exceeded 20,000 (and according to many sources that figure is inflated).

In the first few years of the war the contra army was not only able to replace its casualties with new recruits, but also to expand its overall numbers. But the process of strategic defeat undermined this recruitment ability, and with the launching of the EPS offensive in late 1984, the casualty rate began to overtake the recruitment rate. This was accelerated by the amnesty and the drying up of the contra sanctuary.

As the Sandinistas extended their control over one zone after another, the peasants were less susceptible to contra manipulation and more secure in resisting intimidation. The contras were forced to turn more and more to mass kidnapping, and by 1985 the FDN had created specialized units, called Tactical Operational Commandos (COTs), specifically for kidnapping. One captured contra, Gonzalo Acuña Casco, told how he was incorporated into one of these units. He first spent several months as a prisoner in the Honduran camps, along with some 1,500 fellow peasants who had been brought across the border by force. Like so many others, he finally succumbed to threats and agreed to join the FDN. In the Las Vegas camp, he recounted, "I received military training from four U.S. advisers," including a "course in psychological warfare and the tactics of kidnapping. After the course, I was integrated into a COT." He then spent several months in action inside Nicaragua, and was eventually appointed head of his unit. "Our only missions," he said, "were to bring abducted peasants to Honduras and integrate them into our task forces."[6]

Another, more gruesome, recruitment tactic was also revealed in mid-1985, when a group of 150 peasants turned themselves in. Among them were dozens of children as young as six years old. The most susceptible of all groups to contra terror are those too young to comprehend the reality of war, much less the complex national and international factors that affect their personal situation. Children between the ages of eight and fourteen have been captured in battle; they often confess that they did not have the slightest idea why they were carrying guns and taking orders from the Somocistas.

By this time, refugees in the Honduran camps run by international aid agencies had also become targets for recruitment. Relief workers sensed a generalized desire among the refugees to take advantage of the amnesty and return to Nicaragua, but by July 1985, when we visited the camps, there was a growing climate of agitation. UNHCR and Red Cross officials in Tegucigalpa expressed their concern to us in private about being able to keep the lid on what they described as a potentially explosive situation in the camps, which the FDN were attempting to take over in order to prevent repatriation.

Less than a year later, UNHCR officials went public with their concern. In a Tegucigalpa press conference in June 1986 they denounced the FDN for "threatening to start a war" against the Nicaraguan refugees in order to make them leave the camps and join the contra ranks. They reported that the contras were forcibly entering the camps and forcing the refugees to join at gunpoint, and called on the Honduran armed forces to assist in maintaining security.[7]

Meanwhile, the loss of operational maneuverability inside Nicaragua forced the FDN to rethink its most basic military tactics. As long as it maintained the initiative, it had attempted to remove its wounded from the battlefield, to recover in Honduras and eventually return to battle. But being on the defensive meant that FDN troops were permanently on the run, without areas in which to rest and regroup. Carrying injured contras slowed down a retreat, and the evacuation of the wounded became too great a burden. At the same time, it was too risky to let the wounded remain alive, since they could provide information to Sandinista forces.

In 1985, therefore, the U.S. advisers ordered modifications to these tactics; wounded contras were to be killed on the spot and their bodies left behind. Repeating a story that was soon heard repeatedly, one FDN peasant recruit who had turned himself in claimed that "the U.S. advisers train these special forces in the Las Vegas camp, teaching them how to remove the wounded to places where they can be completely eliminated."[8] "When I was injured," the same peasant reported, "I had to pretend I was dead, since when one of us is wounded, [units of] the more experienced Guardsmen come in to finish us off, so that information can't be given to the EPS." As the word got out among FDN foot soldiers, the tactic of feigning death and later turning themselves in became a widespread means for peasant recruits to save their own lives—ironically, not from the Sandinistas but from their own field commanders.

Corruption, Orgies, and Corpses

By 1985, corruption and internal power struggles among the Somocista leadership were spiralling out of control, at the expense of their military-political efforts. The picture that had emerged was that of a veritable mafia-style contra underworld. The CIA had to reorganize the FDN high command no fewer than seven times between 1981 and 1986. "The leaders of the FDN could care less about the struggle. They're more concerned about having a big house in Miami and accumulating more and more individual prestige and stashed-away bankrolls," then-FDN field commander René Fernández told us in July 1985 in Tegucigalpa. "The FDN can't win. The leaders are scared of dying and dedicate themselves to living the good life in their fancy cars and ritzy restaurants in Tegucigalpa and Miami. They've turned the organization into a business with which to get rich quick."

Typical was Fernández's story of the "video scandal." After being appointed political chief of his division, the Nicarao regional command, Fernández was given the task of filming FDN activities inside Nicaragua for a film to drum up support for the FDN in the United States and Europe. Thousands of dollars in video equipment and film were shipped down from Washington. Fernández delivered the videos to his superior, José Benito Bravo Centeno, known as "Comandante Mack," a former National Guard officer well-known inside Nicaragua for engineering brutal massacres of civilians. "And what happened?" he asked. "Benito Bravo sold them to a foreign journalist for $1500 and used the money to make payments on his house in Miami."

Such behavior by the top leaders sets the tone for all those with any control over resources or decisions. "It's not necessary to go as high as the FDN directorate," Fernández said. "Even the field leaders of regional commands receive thousands of dollars in funds for logistics and supplies which they just stick in their pockets."

Fernández claimed that the majority of FDN members share his disillusionment. "Inside the organization, everyone talks about the outrages committed by the leadership; they're fed up. Many are dying in Nicaragua and no one wants to continue," he said. He added that few dare to speak out publicly for fear of reprisals. Shortly after we spoke to him, Fernández decided to quit the contras. He applied for a visa at the U.S. embassy in Tegucigalpa, hoping to go to live with some relatives in Miami. But the CIA had made too big an investment in him and his application was rejected. And when the FDN leadership got wind of his testimony to the press, he was put on a blacklist of "traitors" targeted for "elimination." In January 1986 he finally decided to return to Nicaragua under the Sandinista amnesty law, and is now living as a civilian in Managua.

Fernández is not the first to refer to such "reprisals." In May 1985 another former National Guard officer and FDN commander, Efraín Mondragón, who had worked in Somoza's Office of National Security (OSN—secret police), revealed other details of the bloody conflict within the FDN. Mondragón was an important figure in the early years of the counterrevolution: after participating in the blowing-up of the Río Negro bridges in March 1982, he led a regional command in the Segovias. But by 1984 he was becoming seriously perturbed by the FDN policy of executing contra members and kidnap victims who refused to fight or obey orders. He decided to speak directly with Adolfo Calero to see if he could "moderate the situation." "Are you crazy?" Calero reportedly retorted. "Do you want us to lose all our people? If we change our policy, we'd lose 80 percent of our troops and then the war would be lost. Keep your nose out of our business."[9] A few months later, Mondragón's cousin and several friends were killed—according to him, on Calero's direct orders. Believing himself to be on Calero's blacklist, Mondragón then sought asylum in the Mexican embassy in Tegucigalpa. Like Fernández, he eventually took advantage of the amnesty and returned to Nicaragua. In his subsequent testimony, Mondragón gave details not only about the crimes committed by the contras against Nicaraguan civilians, but also about the wholesale assassination of FDN troops who fell out with the leadership.[10] He also reported wild orgies in the Honduran-based contra camps, where peasant girls kidnapped from Nicaragua were swapped and U.S. dollars gambled in midnight card and dice games. As the drinking continued, personal resentments and rivalries often turned these orgies into violent brawls. The bodies of the "losers" were buried the next day.

Mondragón also described the "San Judas" FDN internal security center, at one of its bases in the Honduran Department of Choluteca, which borders on Nicaragua. There, contras who refuse to fight, or who for whatever reason wind up on the bad side of the leadership, are interrogated, tortured, and murdered. A special internal security force, based in San Judas, is given the task of capturing and executing deserters. It is headed by former National Guard Lieutenant Armando "El Policía" López, a member of the FDN high command. "Many are shot, while others are slowly slashed to death with knives," Mondragón said. "How many die like that?" we asked him. "It's hard to calculate. I saw dozens of corpses on one hillside outside the base. Hundreds of skulls are scattered all around there."

Others within the FDN have tried to protest. When we were in Honduras in 1985, Boris Leets Castillo, a former Somoza associate living in Tegucigalpa, showed us an internal memorandum dated 10 January 1984, and signed by several members of the FDN high command and numerous field commanders. It was delivered to "Commander in Chief of the FDN, Señor Adolfo Calero Portacarrero" and it charged that "both in its internal and external aspects, our situation is chaotic . . . we have seen that the leadership has been inoperative and incapable of educating, motivating, and training the troops and that the swindling of budgeted funds has been the cause of hunger and general lack of attention to our troops."[11]

The memorandum sparked perhaps the most notorious scandal to date within the Somocista organization. When Calero and Bermúdez ignored the memorandum, there was an internal rebellion, led by former National Guard captain and FDN high command member Hugo Villagra, a one-time favorite of the Argentine advisers to the

FDN high command. For several months, the Honduran papers carried sensational stories on the "FDN split" and its internal witch-hunts. As each side dug in, there were shoot-outs in FDN "safe houses" in Tegucigalpa and in the camps along the border. The CIA eventually stepped in, squarely backing the Calero-Bermúdez duo and its inner circle—what one specialist on the FDN called the "most totalitarian faction."[12]

Bermúdez then ordered the wholesale "elimination" of the rebel leaders. Former National Guard Lt. Col. Ricardo "El Chino" Lau—the FDN intelligence chief, Bermúdez's right-hand man, and perhaps the most dreaded Somocista in the organization—was given this task. "Tito" and other high command members, together with such top field commanders as "El Suicida," "Krill," and "Cara de Malo"—all by then well-known to the U.S. press as the flamboyant "rebel leaders" inside Nicaragua—were captured and summarily executed, while their supporters were massacred in the camps. High command member "Abel" had a more agonizing death: Lau's men injected him with air while he lay in a dentist's chair. Villagra escaped to Florida, where he wound up as night watchman in a condominium complex in Key Biscayne. Others "repented" and pledged their loyalty to Bermúdez and Calero.[13]

Following the failed rebellion, Bermúdez restaffed the high command with his most loyal friends and made El Chino second in command. "When I'm absent, El Chino will give all the orders," he warned the new high command.[14] A year later, it was learned that it was El Chino who had assassinated Archbishop Oscar Arnulfo Romero in San Salvador in 1980.[15]

Somoza's business cronies used to shrug off criticism that the dictator pillaged the country—"He steals but he lets others steal too." In fact, the Somozas were able to forge the National Guard into a virtual family army through the cultivation of loyalties and by allowing each one to swindle in accordance with his degree of power within the guard. Following the suppression of the internal FDN rebellion, the Somocista morality of "rob and let rob" reigned undisputed once again. The ability to extort depended on each individual's quota of power, and internal struggles were reduced to scrambling for higher positions of influence with which to pilfer.

Contra corruption has spilled over into the realm of international drug and arms dealings. In December 1985 the Associated Press reported an elaborate contra network—complete with links to the CIA and the White House—of continental drug trafficking.[16] Drugs were being purchased in South America, shipped to Costa Rica, and delivered to Miami and other U.S. cities. "Virtually every contra faction" is involved in these operations, one U.S. Drug Enforcement Agency investigation concluded.[17]

In early 1986, U.S. West Coast newspapers revealed the workings of a contra drug operation in California. This story began in 1983, when federal drug enforcement agencies captured two Somocistas who were trafficking cocaine for the FDN—one, Julio Zavala, had already raised $500,000 for the contras. Federal agents confiscated 172 kilograms of cocaine, the largest bust in West Coast history. According to the San Francisco *Examiner*, the U.S. government subsequently returned $36,000 to Zavala, after he presented letters from two FDN leaders indicating that the money was allocated for the "restoration of democracy in Nicaragua."[18] Barbara Boxer, Democratic congresswoman from California, demanded a federal investigation into the affair, charging that the arrangement between the contras and the U.S. government reached up to a high level in the Reagan administration.[19]

Yet, incredibly, even as the latest proof of contra involvement and U.S. government complicity in international narcotics dealing was surfacing, Reagan continued to charge the Sandinistas with doing what his administration and its "freedom fighters" were doing. In his 16 March 1986 national radio address to drum up congressional support for that year's contra funding request, he declared: "I know that every American parent, concerned with the problem of drugs, will be extremely indignant upon learning that high officials of the Nicaraguan government are deeply committed to drug trafficking."[20]

The contras have also been involved in black market arms sales throughout the region. Former National Guard officers have acknowledged that a good portion of the funds and equipment allocated for contra ground troops has not even made it out of Miami. "We send the leftovers to Honduras," said a former senator in Somoza's legislature who now resides in Miami.[21] In early 1986, congressional investigations revealed that at least one-half of the $27 million in "humanitarian assistance" approved a year earlier could not be accounted for.[22]

Once the sordid tip of the contra underworld was exposed, story after story surfaced, each more bizarre than the one before. While the details of the contra narcotics traffic were still coming to light, there were reports in Tegucigalpa of an international traffic in Honduran children. In January 1986 a court for minors brought charges against several U.S. citizens, whom local reporters charged were connected with the CIA, for illegally selling Honduran children to families in the United States. According to the public prosecutor, Norma Coto de Murillo, the U.S. citizens were running a string of "fattening centers" around the country, under the guise of charity programs. Impoverished Honduran mothers were encouraged to enroll their malnourished children in these centers and told that the youngsters would be taken care of free of charge. The children were fattened, given vaccinations, and shipped off to adopters in the United States for up to $25,000 a head. The court discovered the operation when a mother who tried to retrieve her son was told she would have to pay 15 *lempiras* (Honduran currency and equal to about $7.00 at that time) for each day the child had been cared for—an amount far out of the reach of most Honduran workers, let alone an unemployed single mother. The profits from this "enterprise" not only went into the pockets of the "child merchants" and their collaborators, but were channeled to the paramilitary activities of the Honduran armed forces and to contras along the border with Nicaragua, as well as to the contra "refugee" centers.[23]

UNO: The Failure of Counterrevolutionary Nation Building

As we saw in Chapter 8, the United Nicaraguan Opposition (UNO) was the culmination of four years of efforts to consolidate a counterrevolutionary alternative. Yet the maturation of this project took hold at the same time that the balance was shifting in favor of the revolution: counterrevolutionary nation building, in effect, was stillborn.

The U.S. advisers were well aware of the military incapacity of the contras and the problems caused by the corruption and infighting. Throughout 1985, the U.S. embassy in Honduras had sent signals to Washington of its growing concern over the counterrevolution's dismal performance, and recommended a thoroughgoing reorganization.[24] The formation of the UNO, in fact, responded as much to increasingly desperate attempts by the United States to salvage the counterrevolutionary project from the profound deterioration described above as it did to the nation-building effort. It was intended to solve many of the problems that were plaguing the counterrevolution, including the multiplicity and heterogeneity of armed and unarmed groups, rivalries and infighting, the inability of the armed contras to act as effective political guerrillas, and the tenacity of the bloody Somocista image. The formation of the "Human Rights Commission" allegedly to eradicate systematic human rights abuses committed by the contras was as much aimed at improving their bloodstained image as at making them a popular fighting force that could regain the peasantry's support and confidence. These two objectives (one external and one internal) went hand in hand with the effort to achieve diplomatic legitimacy for the UNO. "The armed Nicaraguan resistance must understand the absolute necessity of fighting a 'clean' war," counseled U.S. officials working with the contras.[25] How could the "democrat" Arturo Cruz ask European governments to recognize his organization when FDN troops were murdering Nicaraguan civilians in cold blood? How could the U.S. advisers in Honduras recapture a peasant sanctuary for the contras when they were reverting further into indiscriminate terror tactics?

The UNO did receive considerable press attention, but the inevitable contradictions undercut its efforts before it could get off the ground. Even as U.S. officials were bragging that the "rebel movement" was developing "a greater sense of cohesiveness," press reports confirmed that the "UNO leaders have been unable to agree on a coordinated political and military strategy."[26] Friction centered around appointments to key positions, with each of the "Triple A" trying to place those loyal to him in top posts. In the end, Calero was clearly the winner: one U.S. congressional source stated that the Reagan administration, despite the political importance it attached to Robelo and Cruz, would not drop its firm backing for Calero. The bottom line was the Calero-Bermúdez duo. Thus they remained the real power brokers in the Nicaraguan counterrevolution, directly representing its Somocista core.

Similarly, the new Human Rights Commission quickly floundered. Its first head was Nicaraguan lawyer Carlos Icaza, who had left Nicaragua for Miami in mid-1983, following his involvement in the CIA plot to poison Nicaraguan Foreign Minister Miguel D'Escoto and mount urban terrorist actions. Icaza's first act was to claim that most of the contra atrocities were really the work of "Sandinistas dressed up as rebels." Before long, the United States was forced to replace him with a more astute contra, Alvaro Baldizón Aviles.[27]

The "serious diplomatic efforts" the UNO launched at the UN, in Contadora, and elsewhere to break the counterrevolution's chronic isolation, discussed in Chapter 8, made little headway, since its diplomatic recognition was ultimately dependent on its material capacity to wage war inside Nicaragua. In January 1986 Calero lamented that the UNO still had not declared a "provisional government in exile [for] lack of conditions, since we would first have to install ourselves in Nicaraguan territory."[28] Inside Nicaragua, the FDN is all but a spent political-military force: eight months after Plan Repunte was foiled, the Somocistas had still not been able to mount so much as one spectacular action, while thousands of contras were sitting it out on the sidelines in Honduras and Costa Rica, laden with uniforms and supplies, but unable and unwilling to face the Sandinista defense system.

The Somocista civic action programs, also announced as part of the UNO effort, required exercising control over zones inside Nicaragua that the FDN had lost in 1985. Following its formation, the UNO had set up twelve special commissions to "plan diverse aspects of the anti-Sandinista struggle and the future of Nicaragua," operating as ministries in exile—a government that merely had to be installed inside Nicaragua. But most commissions never got beyond the planning stages, while others rapidly folded. The commissions program "was an enormous disaster," admitted Cruz.[29]

Despite all the efforts to change the content of the counterrevolution, its real essence has always remained Somocista and the United States, unable to build a popular base of support for its project, has found itself in the trap of falling back on Somocismo even when this is counterproductive. Cruz, Robelo, the actors of the internal front, and all those who associate with the counterrevolution, despite their pasts, are inevitably sucked into Somocismo. Even when new contra recruits with no previous ties to the Somoza dictatorship hook up with the counterrevolution, they are indoctrinated with the ways and outlook of Somocismo. As Commander Hugo Torres of the EPS put it:

> The counterrevolution is criminal by its nature. This can't be changed by simply establishing a "code of conduct." Their criminal nature is something ingrained by the very way in which the Somocista Guardsmen were educated and in which they have been educating the new contra recruits all these years. Their rampages, their criminality, is a daily part of their lives; their gouging out eyes and sinking bayonets into bodies is to them a natural action.[30]

The Impossibility of Selective Repression

While the U.S. advisers talk of the need to fight a "clean war," defeat makes the Somocista increasingly desperate and they inevitably resort to the only practice they really ever mastered: naked repression devoid of any political component or coherent program. Thus as the Reagan administration moved at the diplomatic level, presenting the UNO as a legitimate political movement representing all Nicaraguans, the distance between this image and the actual behavior of the counterrevolution's ground troops continued to grow.

It was only a month after the creation of the Human Rights Commission that *Newsweek* published a photographic sequence of the brutal contra murder of a captured Nicaraguan peasant believed to have been a

Sandinista sympathizer. The peasant was shown being forced to dig his own grave and lie down in it, then a contra climbed on top of him, ignoring his cries for mercy, and plunged a U.S. army knife into his throat.[31]

Faced with military defeat, contra troops abandoned psychological operations and civic action to win over the population in favor of outright terrorism. One example among many was the FDN attack on the town of Cuapa, in the central Department of Chontales, in early August 1985. This traditionally conservative town was in fact an anti-Sandinista stronghold. "There are people here who are neither friendly nor fraternal with those of us who work with the Revolution," said one local official.[32] "Many here, disaffected and confused by our enemies, have been listening to their preachings of hatred and anticommunism and, with the well-known methods of manipulation, have gone so far as outright collaboration with the counterrevolution." Yet when the contras entered the town, they immediately burned its social service installations, murdered the first few civilians they found in the streets, and grabbed several others, forcing them at gunpoint to identify those in the town who were working with the government—a crude attempt to follow the guidelines of the CIA manual.

But by this point nearby EPS units had been notified. The contras hastily gathered the residents in the town square, pulled out those they suspected of sympathizing with the government, and shot them. The residents, pro- and anti-Sandinista alike, were terrified. As the EPS moved in and local militia members reached for their weapons, the attackers indiscriminately took sixteen civilians hostage and fled into the hills. Eleven of the hostages were killed as they were being dragged along, while the others managed to escape in the turmoil.

The following Sunday, the town's priest, Fr. Domingo Gatti—not known for his sympathies to the Sandinistas—told his parishioners: "People from Managua used to come and tell me I didn't know who were really the bad guys. Today, in 1985, the truth has been revealed before our eyes." Within weeks, Cuapa residents were eagerly setting up their own self-defense structures. The contras might still have been able to dig up supporters in Cuapa, but the area as a whole had unequivocally been won over to the revolution.[33] "There has been an understanding on the part of the population of what the contras are all about," said Roberto Calderón, EPS military commander for the region. "The townspeople of Cuapa have seen that the contras kidnap in cold blood; they saw for themselves that those captured had their throats slit. In the face of this situation, numerous sectors have become conscious of the need to defend their own lives, family, and property against counterrevolutionary activity."[34]

The events in Cuapa were repeated in zone after zone. In another town, also in a zone of FDN influence, fifteen people were kidnapped by the FDN and taken into the hills for forced recruitment. Eleven made it back. As one resident put it, "Before the kidnapping incident, some of us wanted to take up arms [in self-defense structures], and some didn't. But after we saw what the contras were like, everyone agreed. Now we're defending ourselves."[35]

In neighboring El Salvador, the Salvadoran army and its U.S. advisers developed the concept of the "civilian population" and the "masses" as part of the counterrevolutionary strategy there. According to this concept, the "masses" are those civilians who have been judged irredeemably won over to the revolutionary forces, while the "civilian population" constitutes the rest of the population, be they "neutral," supportive of the government, or moderately influenced by the revolutionary movement.[36] In the U.S. war against El Salvador, winning over the "hearts and minds" of the population is the strategic underpinning of the war effort. Thus, the strategy has a dual approach: exterminate the "masses" and apply civic action, psychological operations, etc., to the "civilian population."

In Nicaragua, the U.S. war strategists have applied a similar strategy. The "masses" are those civilians who identify with Sandinismo and the rest are the "civilian population," the strategic target of the war. By 1985, however, the revolutionary base in Nicaragua had consolidated to the point that the "masses" were becoming the vast majority of the country's 3 million people, and the "civilian population" an ever smaller minority. In August 1985 the FDN announced that members of the Sandinista Defense Committees (CDSs), the Association of Nicaraguan Women (AMNLAE), and UNAG, as well as other social organizations, would be considered "legitimate military targets." UNAG brings together over 120,000 small and medium-sized producers, the CDS membership approaches 500,000, and tens of thousands of Nicaraguan women belong to AMNLAE. In other words, "just" targeting individuals identified with the revolution means targeting over half of Nicaragua's adult population. Applying the U.S. tactics of selective repression only against Sandinistas and their sympathizers was therefore becoming a contradiction in terms: targeting only the Sandinistas meant generalized repression against the civilian population, precisely because the revolution enjoyed a deepening mass base.

The U.S. advisers had organized another type of specialized contra unit in 1984, called the Special Operations Commandos (COEs), elite troops with advanced training and military capacity. Commanded by some of the top field officers of the overthrown dictatorship, the COEs are the post-triumph version of the EEBI. Their sole function was to kill anyone identified with Sandinismo. And in fact the COEs, introduced into one of the two peasant war zones, in conjunction with the forging of contra sanctuaries there, were soon unleashing blind terror against the civilian population. It was not the revolution but the counterrevolution turning against itself.

The problem the United States faces is historic. The complexity of low-intensity warfare cannot be grafted on to Somocismo. To overcome the Somocista contradiction, imperialism must *destroy* Somocismo; it is not reformable. Yet neither can imperialism abandon Somocismo, since it is the historic embodiment of all that is opposed to revolution in Nicaragua and the literal foundation upon which the post-triumph counterrevolution developed. As the counterrevolutionary nation-building effort dragged on, with little result, Washington became increasingly frustrated; this Somocista contradiction inevitably disoriented U.S. decisionmakers, who did not know how to procede with the counterrevolutionary project. "Rebel officials complain of receiving conflicting signals from the CIA, the National Security Council, the State Department and the White House," UNO representatives told the *New York Times*.[37]

Every attempt by the U.S. advisers to have the Somocistas absorb an advanced political vision ran up against a brick wall. Bermúdez, Calero, and the FDN high command were obsessed with the desire to return to the days of undisputed privilege. Among the Somocista elite in Miami, Calero—one-time owner of the Nicaraguan Coca Cola franchise—is jokingly referred to as the "new Somoza." "The FDN is a military organization under the command of Bermúdez, whose sole interest is reviving the National Guard, his 'glorious' National Guard," laments Edgar Chamorro. "They have no political alternatives, no democratic program. [Their triumph] would mean a rightist dictatorship. They only want to recover what they lost—their properties and privileges. They are programmed to kill, to destroy Sandinismo, with the sole mentality of annihilating anything associated with it."[38] Chamorro underscored the inescapable contradiction for the United States: "It would be like returning to one of the worst chapters in Nicaraguan history," he said. For all the efforts of the UNO and its U.S. mentor, and regardless of the programs that are drawn up on paper, the association of the contras with "one of the worst chapters in Nicaraguan history" cannot be erased from the minds of the Nicaraguan people. *The counterrevolution cannot be legitimized.* Yet the Reagan administration keeps trying. In early 1986, the administration initiated new efforts to bolster the UNO and transform the counterrevolution. First, it tried to revive the political fortunes of Edén Pastora and his handful of followers. In early March, in the midst of that year's campaign for congressional funding, Assistant Secretary of State for Inter-American Affairs Elliott Abrams brought the "Triple A," along with Pastora and Brooklyn Rivera, to the White House, hoping to incorporate the latter two into the UNO and release an updated "declaration of principles" that would inject new life into the counterrevolutionary project.

Ever since the La Penca bombing, Pastora—the renegade "revolutionary"—had drifted around South America, particularly Panama and Venezuela. His troops had long since disbanded and were being incorporated into the FDN's Southern Front. In late 1984, along with Alfredo César, one-time Conservative party leader and Central Bank director, and other political associates, Pastora had created the Bloque Opositor del Sur (BOS), a political grouping dedicated to seeking financial support in South America and attracting U.S. attention. For his part, Rivera had maintained his ties with Pastora. But the meeting fell apart when the "Triple A" started bickering over the UNO's structures. Pastora insisted that the resurrected Southern Front be under his command, and Rivera complained that his followers' incorporation into the UNO would give the "wrong impression."[39]

Two months later, Washington called UNO leaders to Miami to try again to resolve the infighting. In the preceding weeks, Cruz and Robelo had threatened to resign if they were not given the same amount of power that the Calero-Bermúdez duo enjoyed. The lid was kept—at least temporarily—on the simmering crisis, but local reports warned that the facade could collapse at any moment.[40] At the same time, a group of former National Guardsmen in Miami, mostly FDN dissidents who had participated in the early 1984 rebellion against Bermúdez, formed the Nicaraguan Coalition of Opposition to the Regime (CONDOR), and demanded that John Singlaub investigate Bermúdez's corruption.

Just as the Miami UNO meeting was ending, Pastora, still unable—after nearly four years of intense efforts—to get his quota of power, called another ostentatious San José press conference, during which he declared that the "struggle is useless" and that he was quitting once and for all. He then turned himself in to the Costa Rican authorities. Days earlier, his six top assistants in BOS had been given $5,000 each by the CIA to leave Pastora and join the UNO.[41] Fernando Chamorro was appointed military commander of the dormant ARDE forces, in the hopes that the Southern Front could be reactivated.

The United States was coming around to the fact that, faithful as

Bermúdez and Calero were, they were becoming more of a hindrance than an asset and that alternatives had to be explored. Yet the duo could not be directly challenged—with decades as CIA confidants behind them, they knew too many delicate secrets. Some analysts saw CONDOR as a means to pressure the duo and achieve their replacement without overt CIA participation.[42]

The Contra Republic of "Northern Nicaragua"

As their sanctuary inside Nicaragua dried up, the FDN turned to attempting to secure total domination of southern Honduras, the only territory it has ever really "liberated." Since 1983, Honduran and contra forces had been evacuating the local civilian population from the entire Honduran side of the border—by force, terror, or persuasion. By 1986, some twenty thousand Hondurans had abandoned their homes and farms in the area, while no less than forty villages had been completely occuiped by the contras.[43] The Honduran government—without consulting the Honduran people—had relinquished all sovereignty over the zone, which had become a militarized area of U.S.-constructed military installations, contra bases, supply centers, airstrips, roads, and "refugee" centers. When Calero, Bermúdez, and other FDN leaders are photographed in contra camps inside "liberated Nicaraguan territory," they are in this piece of Honduras, which might be more accurately described as "northern Nicaragua."

Many of the contras in this area, restless and frustrated by the lack of action, turned to banditry and terror tactics against the civilian population. "The Somocistas run around armed as if this were their personal fiefdom," complained one local trader in the Honduran border department of El Paraíso. Many Honduran civilians have been killed in the crossfire as rival contra bands shoot it out, while farm vehicles and cattle have been blown up by contra mines. "Ronald Reagan is supporting us. We can do whatever we want!" is a typical contra response to any local peasant who complains about such outrages.[44]

In January 1986 Honduran coffee producers from the border region sent an angry delegation to the U.S. embassy in Tegucigalpa to demand that measures be taken against wandering contra bands that were paralyzing production. "We [supported the contras] at first, but later they lost all respect for us and our sovereignty. They don't respect anyone anymore," they declared. The embassy responded by promising loans from AID.[45] Meanwhile, the Honduran Human Rights Commission told journalists that Somocista bands were responsible for a rising wave of "delinquencies, robberies, assaults, kidnappings, and other violent incidents," not only in the south, but in the capital as well. The commission denounced a Somocista band for assaulting an armored vehicle from the Merchants Bank of Honduras in late December 1985, killing two people and making off with some $50,000 in cash.[46] Then, on 20 March, two Somocistas brutally murdered William Arsenault, a Canadian priest, in Samorano, thirty miles to the east of the capital. Arsenault had lived in Honduras for twenty years, directed various youth and social service programs, and was well liked among the poor with whom he worked. During his homily the following Sunday, Honduran Bishop Luis Alfonso Santos lashed out against the murder of the Canadian priest and against the government's support for the Nicaraguan counterrevolution. Father Arsenault, the Bishop said, "was not killed by Hondurans, but his death is our responsibility because we have tolerated these people [the contras] in our territory."[47]

The wave of contra delinquency was generating an anti-contra backlash among the Honduran population. Some Honduran military leaders tried to blame the contra crimes on "leftist armed movements," but many in the government and military were beginning to have reservations about Honduras' role as the principal contra rearguard. "If the people trying to overthrow the regime in Managua don't achieve their objective soon, they'll have to look for somewhere else to go and, naturally, they'll come to Honduras," warned leading Honduran conservative Ubordoro Arriaga. "If the contras take refuge in our territory in the face of an imminent defeat, they'll cause us a lot of serious problems."[48]

Eventually, the United States will have to decide what to do with a mercenary force that can no longer fight inside Nicaragua. In the meantime, it has not been averse to using the contra army to serve its local interests. In December 1985, for instance, the Federation of Honduran Workers reported that the U.S.-based fruit multinational Castle & Cooke had employed a contra group to assault striking workers, forcing them back to work at gunpoint. And contra commanders have also established ties with the Honduran ultra-right, drawing up plans to carry out joint actions against leaders of the trade unions, popular movements, and progressive intellectuals, with the tacit support of the most reactionary elements of the military hierarchy.[49] The Canadian priest Arsenault, who had angered some in the government and military by criticizing the detention of several church workers, may have been the first victim of these contra death squads. On 11 May Honduran trade union leader Cristobal Pérez Díaz was found murdered in Tegucigalpa; many said he was the second.

Crisis in the Honduran Rearguard

In addition to the growing outrage over contra activities in Honduras, there has been a growing resentment against the U.S. military presence there. Several times each year U.S. personnel—often drunk and on weekend leaves—have run over and killed Honduran civilians. Accorded diplomatic status, the soldiers are generally immune from prosecution, and a few hundred dollars is simply paid to the victims' families in "adequate compensation." In September 1985 one drunken Vietnam veteran, Joseph John Ryan, a martial arts expert, gratuitously attacked a Honduran university student in the northern city of San Pedro Sula, killing the young man instantly. The population demanded justice, and Ryan was sentenced to a lengthy prison term. Six months later, the U.S. embassy secured his release, and he was reportedly sent to the United States for "psychiatric treatment."[50]

Local anger has also been fueled by the proliferation of prostitution around the U.S. bases and the introduction of previously unknown venereal diseases—among them "Vietnam Flower" and others that are resistant to treatment. In March 1986, following an outbreak of Acquired Immune Deficiency Syndrome (AIDS) among soldiers at the Palmerola base and prostitutes in the city of Comayagua, outside the base, there were anti-Yankee street demonstrations in Comayagua and elsewhere.

Then a new scandal surfaced when a local elementary school teacher found four of her pupils semiconscious in a garbage dump on the outskirts of the city, their faces and hair stained with semen. In the following days, other youngsters were found in Comayagua drugged with narcotics given to them by the Marines. Further investigation revealed that such practices were widespread around the base. Local Christian organizations, the teachers' union, worker and neighborhood committees, supported by the municipal mayor, held meetings and sent protests to the government.[51] On 17 March the National Congress debated expelling the U.S. soldiers.[52]

Added to this local discontent were developing forces within the military and civilian elite against continued collaboration with the U.S. regional project. In late 1984 and early 1985, Maj. Ricardo Zúñiga Morazán, Jr., the son of a prominent Honduran politician, testified behind closed doors to a U.S. Senate intelligence committee on growing human rights abuses on the part of the FDN and Honduran intelligence officials working with the contras inside Honduras and denounced FDN smuggling of arms and narcotics. He claimed that CIA and U.S. embassy officials opposed efforts by nationalist-minded military officers to curb these activities.[53]

Following his return to Honduras, Zúñiga continued to discuss his concerns with other military officers. In September, his decomposed body, which showed signs of mutilation, was found on a farm in El Paraíso. Despite the official cover-up story—that a local Cuban-born businessman had killed Zúñiga for refusing to pay a debt—few doubted what local residents in Daní reported: FDN elements had interrogated, tortured, and then murdered Zúñiga in order to shut him up and to send a warning to all those questioning the Honduran role in the Nicaraguan counterrevolution.

Zúñiga was part of a group of young officers who had been involved in the ouster of General Gustavo Alvarez in 1984 and who were indentifed with Honduran armed forces commander Walter López Reyes. His murder further antagonized those sectors of the military whose reservations over the U.S. project were by now a source of growing concern in the U.S. embassy. As irony would have it, the very sectors that had ousted Alvarez (with U.S. help) were now turning against U.S. schemes. According to one informed source, embassy personnel had drawn up a list of twenty-one Honduran officers they wanted to force into retirement, including Zúñiga.[54]

Less than a month after Zúñiga's murder, journalists from ABC television boarded a Honduran-bound flight carrying the first installment of Congress's $27 million in "humanitarian assistance" for the FDN. U.S. cameramen were the first to greet the plane when it landed in Tegucigalpa, filming Honduran officials unloading the FDN equipment. An embarrassed Honduran government confiscated the shipment and sent the plane back to the United States, and the government publicly protested that the United States was "trying to involve" it in the "Nicaraguan conflict."

This was the first time that Honduras had questioned the U.S. use of Honduran territory for the war against Nicaragua,[55] and although it was largely a public relations ploy, it was a hint of real fissures to come. A few weeks later, the Honduran military closed down La Quinta Escuela, the FDN high command's operational center, located in a closely guarded area of Honduran and U.S. military installations across from the Toncontín airport in Tegucigalpa; it had recently been expanded by U.S. Army engineers to provide space for supplies. The United States was incensed and quickly moved to reassert its authority.[56] In the following weeks, NSC officials shuttled back and forth between Tegucigalpa and Washington,[57] and, as in Costa Rica, they soon turned to economic blackmail, freezing the disbursement of the final $67 million of an AID loan package approved earlier that year.

When it became clear that economic pressure was not enough, the United States turned to a purge of the military. On 30 January, just three days after the inauguration of newly elected President José Azcona, General López shocked the nation by announcing his resignation—due, in his own words, to "extreme exhaustion." Despite the efforts of trade unions, peasant organizations, the Catholic church, opposition parties, and even business sectors, all of which publicly urged López to reconsider, U.S. diplomatic pressure could not be overcome and his resignation became final on 1 February.[58] The AID then announced an end to the freeze on the loan, the embassy got its "list of 21" removed, and the newly installed military command released a communiqué charging "systematic Sandinista aggression against Honduras" and affirming that the government would reopen its territory for supplying the contras. The United States appeared to have gotten what it wanted.

But it had failed to read the writing on the wall: the nation-building project was in deeper trouble than could be resolved by one more military reshuffle. The crisis in the military was not a simple division between pro- and anti-U.S./contra forces. *Everyone* was pro-U.S. and anti-Sandinista; their differences were over tactical questions of how to handle U.S. military and economic aid, power stuggles over control of key posts in the military, and over the level of repression needed for social control. And these divisions were paling alongside the issue of whether or not *both* aid to the contras *and* stability could be maintained. All the shuffle had done was to lop off those sectors that were furthest advanced in their understanding of the consequences of continuing the rearguard role.

Then, in mid-March, as broad sectors of the Honduran population and the government were debating the possibility of expelling U.S. soldiers and contras, and as the word "neutrality" entered the national vocabulary for the first time, several thousand contras attempted to invade Nicaraguan territory. Fierce fighting erupted along the border. The Nicaraguans, deciding to deny the contras the ability to retreat back across the border, destroyed several contra camps, across the border, in what is juridically Honduran territory, including their principal training and supply center. By the week's end, 350 contras had been killed and another 250 wounded; several military vehicles, a helicopter, and stockpiles of "non-lethal" artillery and automatic weapons had been destroyed.

After returning to Washington from a brief tour through Central America, Elliott Abrams announced at a press conference that the Sandinistas had "invaded" Honduras. The United States then launched several weeks of intense propaganda about the Sandinista "invasion" of Honduras—all at a time when Reagan was requesting additional funding for the contras. The Hondurans immediately rejected the U.S.

version of events, however. Honduran presidential spokesman Lisandro Quezada, in an official communiqué, stated that the incident "forms part of the campaign to get congressional approval for aid to the counterrevolutionaries. . . . We have no knowledge of this [invasion]."[59] The Hondurans wanted no part of a U.S. campaign that could only intensify their own problems. "The Azcona government knows that the EPS target is the contras and not Honduran sovereignty," said another government official, tacitly confirming that clashes were going on at the border. For his part, President Daniel Ortega explained: "Very simply, we haven't done anything more than defend ourselves, mounting defensive operations that we have been mounting ever since the counterrevolution began. And we are going to continue there, in the border zone, to prevent the mercenary forces from advancing so much as a single inch into our territory."[60]

Following the release of the Honduran communiqué, Abrams and other officials contacted Honduran authorities. "We [told the Hondurans] that we thought the incursion threatened Honduran sovereignty and its national security, and we suggested that they recognize it internationally," said one official.[61] But Tegucigalpa did not back down, and the United States stepped up the blackmail: "If you don't admit to the problem at the border, then maybe you also don't need our aid and money," the same official told the Honduran president.[62] With that, Azcona promptly "denounced" the incursion, and within hours the United States had sent $20 million in "emergency military aid," at least $12 million of which went directly to the contras.[63]

But having bowed to U.S. pressure only intensified the problems facing the Azcona government. Enraged military and civilian officials publicly condemned U.S. control of Honduran foreign policy. Like Monge in Costa Rica, the new Honduran president suddenly found himself walking a tightrope, pressured internally by the anti-contra sectors and externally by the United States.

One high-ranking military officer explained the growing resistance to the rearguard role: "We helped the contras with the hope that, with North American backing, they would quickly win the war. But this didn't happen, and by late last year [1985], thousands of contras were once again retreating into our borders. We no longer want to continue [with the contras] but North American pressures are very intense."[64]

Central American Nation-Building
vs. the Nicaraguan Counterrevolution

We have the impression that the United States does not know what to do because it is not damaging the

Sandinistas but is doing much damage to its Honduran and Costa Rican allies.

—Editorial, *Washington Post*, 4 April 1986[65]

Through painstaking surgery and costly transfusions, Washington rekindled Somocismo, moribund after its defeat in 1979. Again a spent force inside Nicaragua, this haywire monster, like Frankenstein's, threatened to erode the efforts of its creator.

The Honduran armed forces and polity had been carefully molded to serve the twin needs of internal nation-building and regional counter-revolution, particularly against Nicaragua. These two projects were conceived as mutually reinforcing, but the strategic defeat inside Nicaragua triggered an antagonism between them. As Sergio Ramírez pointed out:

> The difficulties [for the U.S.] begin when the leasing of Honduran and Costa Rican territory is not a question of weeks or months but years; after six years the only thing the contras continue to occupy are those countries' territories. The perspective is that they will remain there, and this is one of the biggest factors of destabilization [for those countries]. The Honduran government and army see that this is something they cannot control or influence, and this presence begins to turn against them. This destabilization factor is organic; it becomes military, political, social.[66]

Nicaragua's advances inside its own borders, as we have seen, are unleashing a dynamic that threatens the Honduran rulers' ability to maintain internal social order, a tendency that will heighten as long as Tegucigalpa continues to accept its rearguard role. If the Sandinistas had not managed to beat back the contras, this contradiction might not have materialized; yet, to the extent that it intensifies, it will tend to create pressures that push Tegucigalpa away from the U.S. strategy, and in this way it will become a factor gradually altering the regional balance away from Washington. The strategic defeat of the contras thus had profound effects at the regional level.

This phenomenon may take a long time to mature, and new factors could crop up to change the equation. So long as Washington itself sees the two projects as necessarily symbiotic, it will have the strength to impose its will on the elite. It will particularly throw its weight behind those factions in the military closest to the contras.

By 1985, the contras and certain factions of the Honduran military-intelligence apparatus more closely resembled one army with two wings than two separate armies. The armed counterrevolution had increasingly *fused* with significant sectors of the Honduran military, particularly the intelligence apparatus, the special "counterinsurgency" units trained by the United States during maneuvers, the battalions stationed in the south (involved in numerous direct and combined operations against Nicaragua), and the semi-militarized immigration authorities.

At the same time, certain Somocistas who had fled Nicaragua in 1979 had penetrated the Honduran economy, buying up shares in local companies and setting up commercial establishments—including restaurant chains, shares in the Mas X Menos and other supermarket chains, importing and exporting houses and clothing stores. Some had branched out into chemical processing, shoe manufacturing, liquor distilling, a trucking company, and fishing enterprises. Others had even penetrated financing houses, such as the Banco Atlantida.[67] This activity may have antagonized certain sectors of the local business community, but it also wed the Somocistas to other sectors—whose shared economic interests were expressed politically in their common cause with the Nicaraguan counterrevolution. In many instances, this economic activity has served to finance contra military activity, but equally frequently U.S.-supplied money and materials are "extorted" into Somocista capitalism, with little connection to the war.

Parallel to such "legitimate" Somocista enterprises, arms and "humanitarian" aid are increasingly channeled into contraband activities, again in close collaboration with the Honduran army, particularly in the south. One journalist who traveled through the southern departments of El Paraíso and Olancho in early 1986 reported how endless stocks of canned foods, clothing, sleeping bags, jungle gear, and other items sent to the contras cannot be found anywhere in the FDN base camps, but flood the shelves of shops throughout the southern part of the country. Honduran authorities, including immigration agents, tax collectors, local administrators, and the military earn lucrative bonuses for their participation in this trade. "Many officers in the army don't like the FDN," reported one analyst in Tegucigalpa, "but they don't oppose them because, with the aid of the United States, the FDN has become a good business for the Honduran army."[68]

What emerges is a complex and thoroughly corrupt web of Honduran-Somocista military, political, and business interests whose common denominator is their mutual dependence on the resources supplied by the United States to the counterrevolution—a new "class" with no ties to production, solely dependent on the "pilfering" of millions of U.S. dollars. This "class" does not share an interest in nation-building with the majority of the country's elite; its sole commitment is to the Nicaraguan counterrevolution. While this is expressed in support for

Honduran participation as the contra rearguard, it is less and less based on a political-ideological opposition to Sandinismo.

This sector, which the United States can count on for full support for Honduras' rearguard role, is moving further apart from the other military and civilian ruling circles as a whole, whose interests lie in the stable, long-term capitalist development of the Honduran economy. Thus, inter-elite strife and deepening disagreement with Washington are forecast. In the short term, the tremendous U.S. pressure on the government, and the influence of those sectors directly tied to the contras, can weigh heavily on the pro-counterrevolution side of the seesaw. Yet the tensions, which bordered on crisis in early 1986, are bound to assert themselves time and again as the Central American conflict plays itself out. Moreover, popular sectors in Honduras cannot be controlled as easily as the elite. On May Day 1986 over 100,000 workers and peasants marched in Tegucigalpa under the banner "Yanquis Basura, Fuera de Honduras" (Yankee Trash Out of Honduras). For its size and militancy, the march was unprecedented in the country.

By 1986, certain sectors of the Central American elite were coming to grips with the fact that their alignment with the Nicaraguan counterrevolution was predicated on its success, and that this was an increasingly remote possibility. As a Nicaraguan foreign ministry official put it:

> To the extent that the war is not a civil war and maintains an international military and political character, to the extent that the contras need Central American territory and external support to exist, they [the Central American elite] face a growing problem which is breaking the original arrangement by which these ruling sectors and classes [participated in] the U.S. intervention.[69]

This phenomenon has introduced a new dynamic into the Central American equation, as sectors of the elite have begun to recognize that they may have to come to terms with the Sandinista government and with the existence of revolution in Nicaragua. Reflecting the emergence of this dynamic, for the first time, not one single Central American government openly supported the Reagan administration's 1986 contra funding request.[70] In May 1986 the five Central American heads of state met in Esquipulas, Guatemala, for a presidential summit, and agreed to form a Central American parliament as a forum for regional political and socioeconomic issues. The fact that this meeting took place without U.S. participation—and to U.S. dismay—made it an unprecedented event. For the first time, the concept of *coexistence* appears on the agenda: accommodation with Nicaragua is preferable to loaning their countries to the counterrevolution. Coexistence is not only in the interest of the Central American majorities, but also of the elite. It opens up the possibility of regional bilateral and multilateral agreements on trade, markets, immigration, and other issues which can contribute to the solution of urgent socioeconomic problems and ease internal social tensions.

As the contras continue to antagonize the people of Honduras and Costa Rica, the greater is the pressure for coexistence. An April 1986 survey in Honduras revealed that 90 percent of the population did not want the contras on Honduran territory.[71] In Costa Rica similar tensions built up throughout 1985 as the defeated ARDE bands turned to roaming about, much like their FDN counterparts in the north, and an early 1986 poll (taken by the ruling PLN) indicated that 91.5 percent opposed the country's collaboration with the counterrevolution.[72]

The United States has demonstrated that it has sufficient power and influence to prevent indefinitely the consolidation of a coexistence position. The push and pull, between confrontation and coexistence, will nevertheless continue to produce periodic crises for the United States and its client regimes. But even as the seesaw bobs, the very existence of the counterrevolution—assuming that it does not regain the initiative—will continue to sharpen contradictions in Honduras and Costa Rica. Seen from a regional perspective, prolongation of the war against Nicaragua is coming full circle: it is once again threatening to become a *liability* for the United States.

Part 3
Conclusion

12
David's Victory

> Our great advantage is that we are mounted on the
> horse of history. And this horse can only march in
> one direction—forward. Sometimes it gets tired. At
> other times it veers slightly off track. But it never
> takes a step backward. The enemy, on the other
> hand, has the great disadvantage of marching
> against the current.
>
> —Tomás Borge[1]

> Andará Nicaragua, su camino a la gloria.
> Porque fue sangre sabia, la que hizo su historia.
>
> —Silvio Rodríguez, Cuban poet and singer

Between writing Chapter 1, in September 1985, and writing this
conclusion, in July 1986, events have only served to confirm our discussion of the Reagan Doctrine and low-intensity warfare. In October 1985
Ronald Reagan himself announced the doctrine to the world community at the UN General Assembly, baptizing those regions where the
United States is fomenting right-wing insurgencies against progressive
governments as zones of "regional conflict." The president called for
"dialogue" between U.S.-sponsored "freedom fighters" and revolutionary governments in Angola, Kampuchea, Afghanistan, and Nicaragua
as a means to achieve "national reconciliation," "power sharing," and
peace, and promised that the United States would continue to back
these counterrevolutions until this end was achieved. Thus, the war
against Nicaragua was to be the prototype for other efforts to force
young revolutionary governments to surrender. Such "regional conflicts" were also at the top of the agenda Reagan brought to the November 1985 summit with Gorbachev in Geneva. By 1986, the United States
was sponsoring an estimated 210,000 "contras" in at least four countries: 150,000 in Afghanistan, 25,000 in Angola, 20,000 in Kampuchea,
and 15,000 in Nicaragua, with an estimated budget of over $600 mil-

lion.[2] As one official put it, the United States is "engaged in a third world war through proxy armies."[3]

In January, over one hundred leaders from the Reagan administration and its "private" wing gathered at Fort McNair in Washington, D.C., for a two-day symposium on low-intensity warfare. The gathering indicated the importance the government has placed on defining and institutionalizing a global strategy of counterrevolution as practiced, above all, through low-intensity warfare. It was followed by the establishment of a secret interagency committee to oversee the entire gamut of U.S.-sponsored counterrevolutions around the globe. This group, named the "208 Committee" for the room in which it meets, determines, according to one report, "which weapons will be shipped, which secret warehouse goods used, which middlemen will deliver them to clandestine airstrips, and sets budgets, goals, and timetables for each operation," answering directly to the NSC.[4] In descending order of importance, in 1986 the committee planned to focus on Central America, the Middle East, Afghanistan, southern Africa, and Southeast Asia.[5]

The first plank of the Reagan Doctrine—turning dictatorships into bourgeois democracies in order to remove the threat posed by their latent instability—has become dramatically more important since Chapter 1 was written. Staying a step ahead of mass popular upsurge, the United States was able to remove Marcos from the Philippines and Duvalier from Haiti, and appears to feel that Pinochet in Chile could be next.[6] As Weinberger put it during the low-intensity warfare symposium, the best way to neutralize a revolutionary challenge is "to diagnose political and geostrategic ills at their incipient stages and to . . . change the leadership" in these countries.[7]

As the key ideological justification for the global crusade against national liberation projects in the third world, "antiterrorism" now eclipses anticommunism, with Libya being portrayed as the lynchpin of a supposed international terrorist "conspiracy." In fact, the U.S. attack against Libya in early 1986 was as much to destabilize the government of Col. Muammar Qaddafi as to back up the rhetoric of antiterrorism with direct action. Not coincidentally, the United States at the same time stepped up its "terrorist" charges against the Sandinistas, claiming that the two countries were operating in concert.

The attacks on Libya demonstrated what Shultz had already noted—that the Reagan Doctrine forecloses no options. "The wide range of challenges we face," Shultz said in October 1985, "requires that we choose from an equally wide range of responses: from economic and security assistance [e.g., El Salvador] to aid for freedom fighters [e.g.,

Nicaragua] to direct military action [e.g., Libya] when necessary. We must discriminate; we must be prudent; we must use all the tools at our disposal and respond in ways appropriate to the challenge."[8] Those executing the Reagan Doctrine view direct military force—be it the invasion of Grenada or the "surgical strikes" against Libya—as a strategy to be used rapidly, overwhelmingly, and with clearly delineated 'objectives.[9] Such naval and airborne forays, with no intention of prolonged military action, are another way to weaken and intimidate opponents, one that might very well be employed against Nicaragua.

The concept of low-intensity warfare has quickly become popularized, and has been interpreted in several distinct ways. Some have argued that it is simply traditional counterinsurgency doctrine in new clothing, while others argue that it is a new way to create conditions for a classic invasion.[10] Both these views obscure the fact that the strategy of low-intensity warfare is a qualitative departure from earlier forms of intervention, and grew out of the lessons learned from those experiences.

In a different vein, some have pointed to the fact that low-intensity warfare has little prospect of success in destroying the Nicaraguan revolution, and that it is therefore not really the strategy that the United States has been following.[11] This is a tautological argument, however, akin to arguing that the United States did not really invade Vietnam since the invasion resulted in failure. Rather, the likelihood that low-intensity warfare cannot achieve U.S. objectives against Nicaragua, as they were initially defined, demonstrates the gap between imperial intent and ability, and indicates the numerous contradictions that the United States faces in trying to hold back history. What is clear is that differences over how the strategy should be implemented are commonplace within the U.S. government.[12]

The sophistication of U.S. strategy worldwide does not mean that its contradictions can be easily overcome. It is not clear, for example, whether the United States can succeed in controlling the Aquino government and can implement a successful campaign against the revolutionary forces in the Philippines. Similarly, the removal of Duvalier has not stabilized the explosive situation in Haiti. In addition, the tremendous military outlay that the Reagan Doctrine requires is exacerbating the already grave fiscal deficit, which could threaten the underpinnings of the doctrine. Nevertheless, such long-term contradictions do not mean that the United States cannot have short-term successes. History has shown that counterrevolution can triumph, if only momentarily—as it did in the Spanish Civil War, Guatemala, Chile, and Grenada.

As we noted in Chapter 1, the Reagan Doctrine is Reagan's in name only, but, from history's point of view, his contribution will be to have consolidated the ideological, political, and institutional changes necessary for its execution for many years to come. Indeed, the administration has attempted to lock U.S. policy into the doctrine for the remainder of this century, to the point where future Republican *or* Democratic administrations will find it difficult to extricate themselves from its general foreign policy thrust.

Central America continues to be the doctrine's cutting edge, and Nicaragua is still its bull's eye. Thus a "failure" in Nicaragua will not mean simply the "loss" of one country; it will inevitably be a setback for the worldwide crusade. The steam generated by the "success" in Grenada has since cooled down, and the political exigencies of the Reagan Doctrine require visible advances. "We must . . . focus on one area we can most easily defend as an important U.S. interest—which ought to be in this hemisphere—and win with whatever it takes to do it," said National Security Adviser Robert McFarlane in April 1986, alluding to the continued importance of Nicaragua. "Then, by dint of making it work in Nicaragua, you will stand a better chance of garnering support in other geostrategic locations. Winning one first is very important."[13] Yet this, the most advanced test case, is in deep trouble.

Twenty Years of War?

> Our commitment [to the counterrevolution] is indefinite. It's just going to go on. I think the message is that . . . we have staying power.
>
> —George Shultz[14]

Evaluating the correlation of forces in a low-intensity conflict requires a different set of measures than in a conventional war. Trends and tendencies are more important than present events. One key measure is the extent to which the target population has coalesced around one or the other of the alternatives competing for its support; another is the extent to which either has gained international legitimacy. The military situation, which is as much determined *by* as it is a determinent *in* the other areas, is thus more a reflection of the underlying correlation of forces than its measure.

In the Nicaraguan case, the strategic defeat of the armed contras, the consolidation of the revolution's peasant base, the neutralization of the internal front, the progress toward autonomy and peace on the Atlantic

Coast, the deepening of revolutionary democracy, and the other developments discussed in this book have begun to alter the correlation of forces in favor of the Sandinista revolution. The ongoing failure of U.S. policy toward Nicaragua has in fact provoked queasiness in New Right circles over the fate of the Reagan Doctrine, as well as divisions over how to proceed with the Nicaraguan project. Some lament that it was an error to have relied so heavily on Nicaragua as the test case: "How is it that Ronald Reagan backed himself into this corner, in which the future of the Reagan Doctrine seems to be in the hands of his Sandinista enemies," two leading New Right commentators complained.[15]

Some observers, noting the difficulty of destroying the revolution, have argued that invasion—that is, the massive introduction of U.S. troops and firepower—is the only alternative remaining to the United States. Such an invasion could take place according to either of two scenarios: it could follow the political defeat of the revolution; or it could come about if low-intensity warfare is abandoned and the United States reverts to a strategy that seeks to defeat the Sandinistas through military superiority.

A U.S. defeat in Nicaragua is nevertheless still a long way off. The counterrevolution's demise can be drawn out over a period of many years, during which time new factors and circumstances may be introduced which could alter the variables.

The fluidity of the U.S. strategy, and the limitless material resources available to it, certainly leaves open the possibility of a reversal in the current tendency in favor of Nicaragua. A revitalization of the counterrevolution that poses it as a desirable alternative could set the stage for a "mopping-up" invasion that transfers state power to it. We believe this unlikely, however, given that the factors responsible for the revolution's advances and the counterrevolution's defeat are too well consolidated for the United States to regain the significant amount of ground that it has already lost. At this point, only a major mistake by the Sandinistas (such as that committed by the New Jewel Movement in Grenada), and not the U.S. campaign, could bring about the political defeat that could usher in an invasion. Nevertheless, even if low-intensity warfare were abandoned as a strategy, the United States would still have to assess the chances of an invasion succeeding in its objectives.

According to a 1984 analysis by U.S. military experts, an invasion in that year would have required at least four divisions (over sixty thousand men), several hundred warplanes, over seven hundred helicopters and miscellaneous tanks, armored personnel carriers, and other equipment. There would have had to have been at least four months of "high-tempo fighting" to gain control over key points, and a five-year occupation period was anticipated for the stabilization of a post-invasion government.[16] The cost over five years was expected to exceed $10 billion, between 2,392 and 4,783 U.S. troops would die, another 9,300 to 18,600 would be wounded, and 208 helicopters and 18 aircraft would be lost. Moreover, the study noted that "this assumes, perhaps unrealistically, that the opposition to the American occupation diminishes dramatically over time," and stresses "how uncertain many of the key assumptions are. . . .In general, these estimates are likely to err on the low side." Even assuming this 1984 assessment was accurate, Nicaragua's resistance capacity has increased many times over since then. By 1986, over 200,000 Nicaraguans had gained extensive combat experience, and hundreds of thousands more had received some training, spent brief periods in combat, or were integrated into the civil defense apparatus.

Even those U.S. rulers who do not favor low-intensity warfare agree that conventional interventions must not be prolonged, as in Vietnam. "With a quick and successful invasion [of Nicaragua], the U.S. might avoid domestic and international condemnation," two DOD consultants wrote in 1984.[17] "The Falkland Islands/Malvinas war, the Israeli invasion of Lebanon and the invasion of Grenada have demonstrated that public support can be created and maintained for short, decisive campaigns." But even the most vociferous proponents of conventional intervention have no illusions that there would be a quick victory in Nicaragua. "Once you put American forces down there against Nicaraguans, the entire country would unify against the Yankees," said Gen. Edward C. Meyer, former head of the Joint Chiefs of Staff. "There would be a lot more resistance than most people expect. As it wore on, I guarantee that the stomach for it would go down not only among the American people, but among any enthusiasts you might currently find in the Army."[18]

The massive deployment of U.S. forces in Nicaragua would also put U.S. readiness in other parts of the world at risk. The United States would face a political crisis of unprecedented proportions in Latin America, and its painstaking regional nation-building effort would be thwarted. Any extended occupation would lead to escalating opposition, both internationally and within the United States itself. The empire simply cannot afford another Vietnam.

But prolonged antipopular warfare is a "long-haul" strategy, and it can last as long as the United States believes it can attain a given set of objectives. To date, the central objective has been the destruction of the Sandinista revolution, but this has been in the context of a strategy for the region. Thus, the United States can decide that the destruction of the Sandinista revolution is out of its grasp, and shelve this objective, at least for the time being, without necessarily ending the war. In this scenario, it would still need the war to pursue broader regional and global objectives. Thus, in mid-1985 Gen. Paul Gorman argued that the counterrevolutionary campaign should continue in order to keep revolutionary forces throughout the region on the defensive: "My Salvadoran colleagues are entirely convinced that were it not for the Sandinista opposition—the freedom fighters," said Gorman, "the Salvadorans would have significantly increased military problems."[19]

Equally as important, the campaign against Nicaragua has an important "demonstration effect." If the United States admits failure in Nicaragua, it could find that the Vietnam Syndrome, which places limitations on conventional intervention, is replaced by a "Nicaragua Syndrome," which would make it difficult to continue to promote right-wing counterrevolution. In fact, the intent of the prolonged campaign, in the first six months of 1986, to secure congressional endorsement for the war was to ensure that the counterrevolution would survive regardless of its realistic chances of victory.

There are already indications that the United States intends to continue antipopular warfare against Nicaragua, but in a framework that *redefines* Nicaragua's position in the regional strategy.[20] The current goal of destroying Sandinismo would be replaced with the goal of isolating and containing the revolution within Nicaragua's borders—while consolidating counterrevolutionary alternatives throughout the rest of Central America.[21]

In mid-1986, the *Miami Herald* interviewed a number of DOD officials and reported that their position could be summarized as follows: the United States should draw a clear line around Nicaragua, maintain permanent aggression against the country, and greatly bolster economic and social development schemes for the rest of Central America. The strategy would be to "partition" the isthmus, making the Nicaraguan alternative of popular socioeconomic transformation a punishing, "no-win" proposition in the eyes of the other Central American peoples. Winning the Nicaraguan population over to the counterrevolution would no longer need to be at the heart of the campaign. "Instead of worrying about throwing out the Sandinistas," counseled former SOUTHCOM commander General Wallace Nutting, "we should be concentrating on developing the hemispheric idea of coalition, building strength through political reform and economic development in the surrounding countries. Maybe if they [the Nicaraguans] see everybody else better off than they are, then perhaps the problem will solve itself."[22]

If U.S. objectives were redefined in this way, we might then see the introduction of a number of hitherto unused tactics, such as direct "surgical strikes" on military and economic installations,[23] pressure on the other Central American countries to break off diplomatic relations with Managua, or a break of relations originating in Washington itself.[24] Urban sabotage and terrorism, with the goal of sowing as much destruction and chaos as possible, could assume renewed importance, providing the internal front with a crucial new role.[25]

If this were to happen, the role of the armed contras would be redefined once again, and they would intentionally revert to being a military strike force with the limited purposes of economic sabotage and social terror. Their inability to win over sectors of the population to their cause or to operate in large numbers would be compensated for by their increased technological capacity. A few highly trained and well-equipped contras may never win over the peasantry, but, using neighboring countries as springboards and relying on greater direct U.S. guidance, they can continue to inflict damage almost indefinitely.

In the first half of 1986, the contras, while unable to carry out a single major attack or reestablish a significant presence inside Nicaragua, nevertheless carried out dozens of acts of sabotage and terrorism, including blowing up a regional electrical substation, destroying schools, kidnapping a group of Germans who were building houses in the countryside,[26] and attacking numerous farming cooperatives and villages. Military brutality in these actions was indiscriminate: the contras had clearly abandoned all pretense of an intention to win local support. Operating in small, scattered units, they slipped in from Honduras and then scurried back to their bases. The only advantage the contras gained from this type of action was that it forced the EPS to operate in hundreds of locations around the country. Despite this, the contras remained permanently on the defensive.[27]

Following House approval of $100 million in contra aid in June 1986, the Reagan administration announced that the contra army would be reorganized into small units of only 100 to 200 fighters, that there would be a dramatic increase in the technological sophistication of the arms to which they would have access (surface-to-air missiles, aircraft, etc.), that they would receive direct U.S. air support, particularly for ferrying contra units, which find it increasingly difficult to infiltrate into Nicaragua over land, and finally, that the contras would be given much greater technical training, on a par with the training U.S. Special Operations Forces receive, to prepare them for these more sophisticated tactics and operations.[28] These plans were meant to consolidate a prolonged contra fighting capacity even when the Somocistas enjoy no social base inside Nicaragua, and indicate that this type of war can escalate even as the United States is being defeated.

Nicaragua has shown its ability rapidly to adjust and respond to each new tactical modification of the U.S. war. Already in mid-1986, urban militia units, until then merely kept on standby in the event of a massive external aggression, began drills for repelling potential assaults and confronting terrorism by contra cells (a task earlier left to State Security). The fact that the diversified tactics the United States can employ are limitless similarly requires that the revolution be prepared to use such instruments as the State of Emergency against local agents of the U.S. counterrevolution.

So long as the U.S. government continues its sponsorship of the armed contras, they will be able to continue military activity. Although the Somocistas have little chance of regaining the strategic initiative, their continued existence *forces Nicaragua to keep its productive process articulated to national defense,* and to maintain nationwide defense mobilization. Until Nicaragua can reorient its productive apparatus to socioeconomic development, the hopes for a brighter future will remain indefinitely postponed.

Contradictions

Should the United States decide to continue the war against Nicaragua, the contradictions that are already evident will gradually heighten. Above all, the incompatibility of the counterrevolutionary project and the nation-building project will intensify. Congressional approval of $302 million for its Central American allies (as part of the 1986 contra aid package) was a recognition of this fact, and of the fact that for any strategy against Nicaragua to succeed, the United States must simultaneously bolster counterrevolutionary projects in the other countries of the region. As Vice-president Sergio Ramírez pointed out:

Accepting that we may be facing aggression for twenty years, the problem for the United States is that in the long run it will have to achieve two things: first, create a type of vacuum and seal off this aggression inside Nicaragua, without also affecting the rest of Central and Latin America socially, politically, or economically. It will be very difficult to achieve long-term stability in Latin America while there is a blazing conflict in Nicaragua. Second, although the United States may manage to create conditions for the continued deterioration of social life in Nicaragua, it will simultaneously have to create proportionally as much prosperity in the rest of Central America. It might try and claim that we live very badly in Nicaragua, that the Revolution only offers poverty and rationing, but they would also have to ensure that the campesinos of Central America have seed, land, tractors, bank credit, that the people have housing, electricity, water, vaccinations for their children, that their daughters are not forced into prostitution, that they have roads, schools, etc. We see this as impossible in historic terms, because imperialism does not exist to bring us prosperity.[29]

The success of the U.S. regional strategy is then dependent on two closely related factors: sufficient socioeconomic development in the region to, at a minimum, meet the most pressing needs of the population; and the neutralization of the revolutionary forces and the popular challenges to U.S. hegemony. The advance of the Salvadoran revolutionaries, the continued survival of the Guatemalan guerrilla movement in the face of brutal repression, and the recurrence of popular organizations and protests in Honduras, Costa Rica, and Panama all attest to the difficulty the United States will face in trying to pacify the isthmus.

As Ramírez notes, it is difficult to imagine how the effort to bring about sustained socioeconomic development can meet with any success. The U.S. strategy for regional development, as expressed in the "economic stabilization and reactivation programs" imposed on most Central American countries through the IMF, the World Bank, and the AID, proposes the restructuring of economies by promoting non-traditional exports, offering broad incentives to the local private sector, dismantling existing state enterprises, further opening local economies to the penetration of foreign capital, and securing overall control of internal economic policies. Economic growth is tied to the expansion of the external market, rather than the internal market. Improved conditions would supposedly result from the creation of jobs in export-oriented agricultural and industrial enterprises, internal accumulation and investment, and some limited financing of social welfare projects. Yet between 1980 and 1985, the GNP in various Central American countries dropped by between 12 and 24 percent,[30] while the combined debt climbed from $6.4 billion to $15.6 billion: interest payments consumed some 18 percent of export earnings in 1985. In this period, the region was a net exporter of capital. In the same period, exports lost nearly 25 percent of their real purchasing power, and the tendency for the terms of trade to continue to deteriorate was clear.[31]

The U.S. model does not involve significant redistribution of wealth, so that anything short of phenomenal growth would have little effect on the impoverished majority. Moreover, IMF-imposed austerity measures (suspension of government subsidies, increased rates for basic social services, an end to price controls, etc.) that have been introduced as part of the economic package have further undercut the welfare of the broad masses. The situation is only worsened by rising military expenditures, which are in most cases combined with a diminishing tax base (as an "incentive" to private enterprise). This results in spiraling fiscal deficits, inflation, and further cuts in social services.

The inability of the United States to ameliorate the desperate plight of the Central American majorities further encourages them to engage in the alternative offered by revolutionary forces. Moreover, the ever-deeper U.S. penetration and domination of all aspects of life in Central America–the thorough *denationalization* of these nations—also further strengthens the desire for national independence.

In order to come anywhere near to creating the necessary levels of development, the U.S. would have to convert Central America into a type of South Korea or Taiwan. But the repetition of such "miracles," which need massive foreign investment and guaranteed markets for exports, is unlikely today: for one thing, the world economy is no longer expanding; for another, there are now visible revolutionary alternatives.

Real socioeconomic development in Central America would require greater integration of the Central American and Caribbean economies, a fundamental redistribution of wealth, a realignment of social priorities, a radical transformation of land tenure arrangements, state intervention in key areas of the economy, diversified trade arrangements with the socialist nations and other third world groups rather than with the U.S. alone—and democratic political structures that would allow for popular participation in social and economic affairs. This is the alternative project that is being offered by the revolutionary movements, and is in fundamental contradiction with the needs of U.S. capital.

Nicaragua's Struggle for Peace and Coexistence

The Nicaraguan people yearn for peace, but they also cherish their hard-won sovereignty. "Peace with dignity," as they put it, is the only *real* peace. The Sandinista government has struggled relentlessly for peaceful coexistence, and has made it clear time and again that it is willing to negotiate *all* legitimate security concerns with the U.S.[32] "It is not we who must draw up the terms of coexistence," explained Alejandro Bendaña. "Our position has always been clearly defined. The question is whether or not the United States can accept the independence of Nicaragua."[33] Currently the United States considers peace and coexistence to be tantamount to "surrender."[34] But for the Sandinistas, coexistence means that the United States accepts the existence of the Sandinista revolution *in practice* and desists from all activity aimed at influencing what goes on inside Nicaragua's borders. The conflict between imperialism and revolution is then reduced to ideological competition, although undoubtedly accompanied by low-key hostilities such as those that Cuba has faced since the triumph of its revolution.

For the Nicaraguans, if the United States is to be forced to accept coexistence, the cost of the war must be raised to the point where the empire stands to lose more than it can gain by continuing its efforts. "The United States is carrying out a war of attrition against us, but we are also waging a war of attrition against them," explained Bendaña. "We are wearing them down, in terms of their global priorities, the political capital they have invested in their Nicaragua and Central America project, all of which has been at the expense of other foreign and domestic policy projects. The time factor is in our favor."

Nevertheless, the time when the United States considers the costs of war to be higher than what it stands to gain is not yet on the horizon. In the meantime, Nicaraguans must continue to defend themselves on all fronts. "Our people must be totally clear that there are no prospects for peace in the short or medium term," said one top-level FSLN official in a somber late-1985 analysis.[35] "The U.S. government will continue to impose its war, and therefore the Nicaraguan people must realize that the most important thing is to keep struggling. This is the only guarantee that we have, and the possibilities of achieving peace are ultimately tied to our victories."

"A War of the Entire People"

The test of a revolution's ability to confront the inevitable counter-revolution is the extent to which it is willing to take all the steps necessary—grounded in its popular base—for its defense. From the autonomy and peace initiative on the Atlantic Coast, to the massive arming of the population, to the October 1985 State of Emergency, the Nicaraguan leadership has shown its determination to take such steps.

The Sandinista victory over the Somoza dynasty was not exclusively a Nicaraguan triumph: it represented the disarticulation of a repressive model of socioeconomic and political domination that had prevailed throughout Central America for a century. Similarly, the ongoing Nicaraguan triumph over the U.S. counterrevolution is not merely a Nicaraguan or even a Central American triumph: it constitutes the initial undermining of a strategy of total and permanent war against people around the globe.

The Nicaraguan national resistance has developed into people's war in the classic sense: a war in which virtually the entire population is integrated into armed and unarmed struggle, and in which every inch of Nicaraguan territory has become a war zone (although not in the conventional, strictly military, sense).

One of the most important factors in determining the ability of the Reagan Doctrine to make gains is the extent to which revolutionary forces can assimilate the changes imperialism is undergoing and respond on this basis, as well as exploit the contradictions in the U.S. project. The Sandinistas have demonstrated that revolution is capable of facing up to imperialism's increasing sophistication and its efforts to impede the march of history.

At the same time, the Sandinistas have charted a course for the Nicaraguan revolution predicated on an extraordinary understanding of Nicaraguan history, the current historic juncture, the country's geopolitical location, and the contours of U.S. strategy. The political line of the FSLN is rooted in the objectives of national independence, self-determination, and the mobilization of the popular masses in effecting social transformation. Practice based on this line has forged a broad front among the popular masses on the grounds of shared historic interests. In short, the FSLN has applied the concept of people's war with remarkable creativity to post-triumph Nicaragua and to the specificity of the U.S. war of attrition. The Sandinistas have named this "La Guerra de Todo el Pueblo" (The War of the Entire People).

The development of political consciousness, with few exceptions, moves down a one-way street. In Nicaragua, the people acted against Somocismo on the basis of an antidictatorial consciousness. The Sandinista leadership was able to broaden this into an anti-imperialist consciousness and then set about the task of deepening this into a more profound historic consciousness, rooted in the struggle of the oppressed classes in Nicaragua and internationally. In a type of warfare whose strategic objective is to win over the population, the degree to which a people becomes conscious of its historic interests is the degree to which it becomes "immune" to the inducements of the war.

The Sandinistas have also understood that revolutions stand little chance of surviving an imperialist siege without broad support from the international community, particularly the socialist and nonaligned countries and the progressive movements and forces around the world.

In addition, the Sandinistas have been able to play off the differences between the United States and its allies, and find common ground with the latter against the United States.

Outside Nicaragua, the extent to which popular forces elsewhere recognize their own potential and exploit the weaknesses of the empire will determine the extent to which democracy, national liberation, and social transformation will gain the upper hand. Continued investigation into the ways in which imperialism is changing to meet new challenges to its hegemony, its strengths and weaknesses, is essential to devising appropriate forms of struggle. The U.S. administration has a better understanding of revolution than it did during its aggression against Vietnam, and forces opposed to the empire must correspondingly deepen their knowledge of the premises upon which imperialism is acting. As one great revolutionary said, "Know your enemy, know yourself."

In this context, it must be remembered that the type of warfare that the U.S. is waging against Nicaragua knows no boundaries. If, for example, solidarity with Nicaragua, or even anti-interventionism, among popular sectors in the United States indicates a convergence of interests between two peoples, it becomes a legitimate target of the U.S. war. The people of the United States cannot forget that they too are protagonists, and that they too have as much to say in the unfolding of history as the Nicaraguan people and U.S. imperialism. The pressure that popular forces inside the United States exert on the government can be a major factor in determining the course of U.S. foreign policy. The people of the United States must take heart from, and follow, the example of, the Nicaraguan people, who have demonstrated that, despite all the death and destruction the empire can inflict on the land of Sandino, nothing will turn them back from the path they have chosen.

Goliath has entered into total war against all those peoples of the world who challenge its reign. The most insidious, if not terrifying, aspect of this conflict is that it knows no distinction between war and peace. War is no longer an exceptional situation, preceded by and prior to peace; it has become a normal state of affairs. In a world of one Goliath and many Davids, Goliath has set for itself the task of neutralizing its opponents "by any means necessary," or as Shultz put it, "active prevention, preemption and retaliation" against every voice that dares to question the order of things.[36]

In May 1985, on the fortieth anniversary of the victory over fascism, the U.S. president laid wreaths on the tombs of Nazi criminals. On that same day, Nicaraguans swore to preserve the continuity of forty years of human struggle against the forces that gave rise to fascism.

"In these last forty years," said Sergio Ramírez, "humanity has broken many barriers, and many poor countries have seized their own destiny in a continuous movement toward progress and freedom. We, a country in revolution, will not surrender before any imperial dictate. We are part of that historic wave of poor and exploited peoples struggling for peace and justice, and we will not cede that place. We affirm this as a pledge before the tombs of millions of men and women who have fallen struggling for the liberation of their peoples in colonial wars, imperialist wars, and wars of liberation, and before those who have died as victims of genocide.

"This is also a struggle that we are continuing and in which we are not alone. Millions of human beings around the world are with us, and the messianic dreams of extermination will not prevail: our dreams will triumph in the end.

"For this we are struggling and for this we will win."

Epilogue

The Chickens Are Coming Home to Roost

If keeping political costs low is one of the key advantages of low-intensity warfare, then this strategy has, in the space of a few short months, proven a dismal and—for the Reagan administration—devastating failure. The quick succession of events since we wrote the preface in September 1986 demonstrates not only the rapidity with which events develop but also how the appearance of unforeseen factors can dramatically alter the overall equation.

The capture of U.S. "flyer of fortune" Eugene Hasenfus in southern Nicaragua in October, followed by the "contragate" scandal (still unravelling as we write), have brought into question the very future of the war. The torrent of revelations that followed Hasenfus's capture and subsequent trial, as well as those still emerging in the "contragate" investigations, confirm what we wrote about the "privatization" process, the contra supply network which stretches around the globe (Chapter 3), and our discussion of the establishment of elaborate, but until now nearly invisible, logistical support structures throughout Central America (and elsewhere), directly administered by the executive apparatus of the U.S. government.

It is still too early to predict how far contragate will go; anything from a mere cut-off of official aid to the contras (a similar cut-off, following the 1984 mining of Nicaragua's harbors, did not seriously affect the war) to a Watergate-type collapse of the Republican administration is possible. Regardless of the outcome, however, it would be foolish to assume that the war will shortly come to an end and that Nicaraguans will therefore be able to enjoy peace. Nevertheless, at this point it is clear that the grandiose plans drawn up by the White House, following the approval by Congress of $100 million in aid to the contras in June, which were aimed at a dynamic revitalization of the counter-revolutionary campaign, have been irreversibly buried.

Without doubt, recent events will accelerate the shift in U.S. policy described in the conclusion, from seeking the destruction of the Sandinista revolution to seeking its containment. In this context, we can expect the accelerated consolidation of the armed contras as a terrorist strike force devoid of any serious political-ideological program but able to punish the Nicaraguans indefinitely. At the same time, the Hasenfus and contragate scandals have highlighted the process we mentioned in Chapter 3, the fusion of private capital with state capital. It is entirely possible that, as a result of contragate, the "state" side will be forced to pull out of the counterrevolutionary project, turning the task of carrying it forward over to the "private" side.

Lost in the spectacular daily headlines surrounding contragate is one simple but precious fact: it is tiny Nicaragua and its five-year-old resistance to an all-out campaign by the most powerful capitalist country in the world that has shattered the credibility of the U.S. government and is shaking the very foundations upon which the Reagan Doctrine was erected. Now more than ever, the image of David and Goliath is appropriate; the slingshot has profoundly wounded the giant.

It is worth pointing out a largely ignored—in the U.S. press—fact which lies behind the contragate scandal. While there is no doubt that the diversion of the profits accrued from the sale of arms to Iran is criminal, it is no less criminal than shedding the blood of thousands of Nicaraguans in five years of war. Yet the countless crimes committed against Nicaragua in these five years did not spark any such scandals. Those congresspeople who are up in arms over contragate are the same men and women who only months earlier had approved the $100 million for the Somocistas. It is ironic that the White House that worked so hard to base the Reagan Doctrine on the "threat of terrorism" had its own dealings with "terrorist" Iran turn against it like a boomerang.

There have been other important developments since September, many of which have been overshadowed by contragate. First of all, the contras' military situation continued to deteriorate in the second half of 1986. Sandinista military sources reported that the FDN suffered at least 6,000 casualties in that year, including 4,000 deaths, and that only 2,000 contras remained inside the country by year end.

Equally important, both the Vatican and the Catholic church hierarchy in Nicaragua itself are now seeking coexistence with the Sandinistas. This is the result of several developments. First, the strategic defeat of the contras, the virtual disintegration of the internal front, the Sandinistas' continued international legitimacy, and the political crises in Washington have shown the church that the counterrevolution has no future. Second, the expulsion of Father Bismark Carballo and Bishop Pablo Antonio Vega, the closing of Radio Catolica and *La Prensa*, and other measures taken in the wake of the approval of the $100 million U.S. aid showed the church that the Sandinistas are prepared to take any step necessary for the country's defense and that hiding behind an ecclesiastic veneer will not guarantee immunity from such measures. Third, the church has steadily lost influence among the masses and has in fact done itself more harm than good by participating in the counter-revolution. And, finally, the Vatican, in a similar vein, has made little headway in its campaign against Liberation Theology throughout Latin America (with Nicaragua being the frontline), and has accordingly recognized that it too stands more to lose than to gain by mounting a head-on campaign against it. In short, the Catholic church has decided that it must come to terms with the Sandinista revolution if it is to have any future in the country.

Following an initial "summit" in September 1986 between Obando y Bravo and Daniel Ortega, three subsequent meetings of a "Church-State Dialogue Commission" were held with a view toward working out an "overall agreement," a modus vivendi in which the church would accept the universal separation of church and state and abide by the laws of the country, while the government would not interfere with the church in organizing and leading the religious life of the Nicaraguan people (it has never interfered with this anyway).

As we predicted, the contradictions in neighboring countries, particularly Honduras, have continued to intensify, spurred on not just by the presence of the contras but by the uncertain political landscape in Washington. The difficulty the contra forces in Honduras are having in their attempt to penetrate Nicaraguan territory has sharply raised tensions between the two countries, whose common border has become the most dangerous flashpoint in all of Central America. In early December over 1,500 contras attempted to invade Nicaragua and, as was expected, were pushed back into Honduras, following a week of heavy fighting. The defeat prompted the United States to ferry thousands of Honduran troops, along with a unit of its own armed forces, to the border region. There clashes between the two armies culminated, on 7 December, in the bombing of military and economic installations inside Nicaragua by planes coming from Honduras—which, Managua charged, might have been piloted by U.S. personnel. At the same time, U.S. press reports (see *Wall Street Journal*, 9 December 1986) revealed that the Honduran government had officially asked the United States to relocate the contra forces from southern Honduras to inside Nicaragua. Despite the fact that the political conditions that would allow for direct U.S. intervention are now more unfavorable than ever, the possibility of a major conflict along the Honduran-Nicaraguan border, as U.S. and Honduran forces try to mount schemes for transferring the contras, is a real danger in the coming period.

All of the tendencies discussed in this book exist today. The late 1986 scenario has simply accelerated a process in motion. Much sooner than could have been foreseen, the chickens are coming home to roost.

Managua, Nicaragua
—December 1986

Notes

1. Inside Goliath

1. Council for Inter-American Security, The Committee of Santa Fe, *A New Inter-American Policy for the Eighties* (Santa Fe: Council for Inter-American Security, 1980). The Committee of Santa Fe was composed of L. Francis Bouchey, Roger Fontaine, David G. Jordan, Lt. Gen. Gordon Sumner, Jr., U.S. Army, ret., and Lewis Tambs. Following the Reagan inauguration, Fontaine was appointed the NSC's Latin American specialist, Sumner was made special adviser to the assistant secretary of state for inter-American affairs, and Tambs was made ambassador to Colombia. Tambs later served as ambassador to Costa Rica, a position of considerable strategic importance within the context of the war in Central America.
2. Maj. Maxwell O. Johnson, "The Role of Maritime Based Strategy," *Marine Corps Gazette* (February 1984).
3. Committee of Santa Fe, *New Inter-American Policy*.
4. John Michael Kelly, deputy assistant secretary of the air force, quoted in Frank Barnet, Richard Shultz, and Hugh Tovas, eds., *Special Operations in U.S. Strategy* (Washington, D.C.: National Defense University Press, 1984).
5. Committee of Santa Fe, *New Inter-American Policy*, p. 5.
6. NSC Memorandum 68, 14 April 1950, quoted in *Naval War College Review* (May/June 1975). The policy was most graphically expressed the following year, in the 1951 Doolittle Report commissioned by President Truman, which stated: "No one should be permitted to stand in the way of the prompt, efficient, and secure accomplishment of this mission. We are facing an implacable enemy. There are no rules in such a game. Hitherto acceptable norms of human conduct do not apply. We must learn to subvert, sabotage and destroy our enemies." See also Warner K. Poelchav, ed., *Whitepaper, Whitewash: Interviews with Philip Agee* (New York: Deep Cover Books, 1981), p. 1.
7. The Carter strategy was essentially "damage control," intended to repair the destruction done to imperialism during the Vietnam era. The human rights policy was a means of regaining the ideological offensive against the Soviet Union, promoting reform in the third world, and undermining revolution. The Carter administration's emphasis on trade and cooperation in international affairs was designed to stabilize the world market and regain opportunities for U.S. capital abroad.
8. These include: Grenada, Nicaragua, Surinam, Mozambique, Angola,

Guinea-Bissau, Ethiopia, Zimbabwe, Iran, South Yemen, Syria, Kampuchea, and Laos.

9. Committee of Santa Fe, *New Inter-American Policy*, pp. 1–2; italics added.

10. The extent to which the New Right coalition gained control of the executive can be seen in the fact that first-term U.S. Ambassador to the United Nations Jeane Kirkpatrick, CIA director William Casey, Undersecretary of Defense Fred C. Iklé, arms control negotiator Eugene Rostow, Secretary of the Navy John F. Lehman, Paul Nitze (who had drafted NSC Memorandum NSC-68), Undersecretary of State for Defense Richard Stillwell, Secretary of State George Shultz, and Ronald Reagan himself, among others, were all members of the Committee on the Present Danger.

11. The administration's base in the citadels of monopoly capital were consolidated shortly after the 1980 elections. Reagan and forty others formed the Business Advisers Committee, which included top executives from some of the largest multinational corporations in the United States. Among these corporations were: Bendix, Sperry, Morgan Stanley & Co., the New York Stock Exchange, Prudential, Metropolitan Life, Goodyear, Pfizer, Merrill Lynch, Fluor, Procter & Gamble, and the Continental Group.

12. The extent to which the Reagan administration is intermeshed with monopoly capital is demonstrated by the business affiliations of its leading members: Secretary of Defense Caspar Weinberger and Secretary of State Shultz are from the Bechtel Corporation; former Secretary of State Alexander Haig represented United Technologies, first-term Attorney General William French Smith was a director of Crocker National Bank, Secretary of the Navy John F. Lehman presided over consulting firms for Northrop, Boeing, and TRW. The financial backers of Reagan's first campaign included beer magnate Joseph Coors, Holmes Tuttle of the Ford Motor Company, founder of Western Geophysical Company Henry Salvatori, heir to the Mellon fortune Richard Scaife, and Union Oil president A. C. Rubel.

13. The military budget for 1986 marked the eighth consecutive year of real growth in military spending, a development without precedent since World War II. The defense budget grew from $138 billion in 1978 to $186.5 billion in 1983 (at constant 1980 prices), which represents a *real* increase of over 34 percent. Moreover, the rate of increase is growing: from a 3.2 percent increase in Fiscal Year (FY) 1980, the budget increased by 11.3 percent in Fiscal Year 1983. For a comprehensive account of how this money has been spent, see *World Armament and Disarmament*, Stockholm International Peace Research Institute (SIPRI) Yearbook, 1984.

14. Quoted in Barnet et al., eds., *Special Operations*. Healy was commanding officer of the U.S. Army's John F. Kennedy Center for Military Assistance.

15. Capt. Mark Cancian, "Future Conflict and the Lessons of Vietnam" *Marine Corps Gazette* (January 1983).

16. Stuart M. Butler, Michael Senera, and W. Bruce Weinrod, eds., *Mandate for Leadership II: Continuing the Conservative Revolution* (Washington,

D.C.: The Heritage Foundation, 1984), p. 287.

17. According to Shultz, "We must heed the cautionary lessons of both Iran and Nicaragua, in which pressures against right-wing regimes were not well thought out and helped lead to even more repressive dictatorships."

18. Vernon Asparturian, quoted in Keith Dunn and William Standenmeir, *Military Strategy in Transition* (Boulder, Co.: Westview Press, 1984).

19. *New York Times*, 25 January 1985.

20. Butler et al., eds., *Mandate for Leadership II*, p. 268.

21. Ibid.; italics added.

22. Some observers claim that, in addition to the differences within the U.S. bourgeoisie as a whole, there are major splits inside the administration itself. But these too are tactical and not strategic. Barbara Epstein, professor of history at the University of California at Santa Cruz, carried out twenty interviews in February and March 1985 with people who have played a part in the formulation of U.S. foreign policy under Reagan, ranging from the "hard-line ideologues" of the think tanks to the "pragmatists" of the State Department. She concluded: "What was especially striking about this [the apparent differences] was that even the sharpest critics did not question the goals of those whom they described as formulating policy on a day-to-day basis; they argued only that the tactics were not adequate to the goals." (Barbara Epstein, unpublished paper provided to the authors, Santa Cruz, California, June 1985.)

23. The U.S. creation of the "contra" army broke post-Vietnam precedent. According to administration officials, "The policy of backing anti-communist insurgents evolved from President Reagan's decision in 1981 to provide funding for Nicaraguan rebels fighting the Sandinista government." See the *Miami Herald*, 4 May 1985.

24. Roger Burbach, "Introduction: Revolution and Reaction," in Roger Burbach and Patricia Flynn, eds., *The Politics of Intervention* (New York: Monthly Review Press, 1984), p. 13.

25. Nicaragua in particular is characterized not by its economic but by its *geopolitical* importance to U.S. imperialism. Direct U.S. investment in Nicaragua is almost insignificant, yet the country has played a key role in the geopolitical equation as a regional gendarme, a potential interoceanic transit point, and a reliable diplomatic pawn in Latin America and international forums. As Nicaraguan Defense Minister Humberto Ortega put it to us: "In Cuba the Yankees left big buildings, hotel chains, factories, highways, and other investments. Here you'll find that they didn't leave anything, because they weren't interested so much in economic exploitation as in basing themselves here as a critical point for regional, Latin American, and world control." Interview with authors, Managua, 8 May 1986.

26. Committee of Santa Fe, *New Inter-American Policy,* pp. 4–5.

27. Ibid., p. ii.

28. Quoted from Reagan's address to a joint session of Congress, 27 April 1983.

29. Cieto Di Giovanni, "U.S. Policy and the Marxist Threat to Central Amer-

ica," *Heritage Foundation Backgrounder,* no. 128 (October 1980). Di Giovanni was an adviser to the State Department in the early days of Reagan's first term.

30. Closing speech by Bayardo Arce to the First Congress of Anti-Imperialist Thought, Managua, 18–20 February 1985.

31. Donald Vought, "American Culture and American Arms: The Case of Vietnam," in Richard A. Hunt and Richard H. Shultz, Jr., eds., *Lessons from an Unconventional War: Reassessing U.S. Strategies for Future Conflicts* (New York: Pergamon Press, n.d.), pp. 180–181. (No date of publication is given in text, but content indicates late 1981/early 1982.)

32. Col. Harry G. Summers, Jr., *On Strategy: The Vietnam War in Context* (Carlisle, PA: U.S. Army War College, Strategic Studies Institute, 1981), p. 1. Summers' book, which is an important critical strategic appraisal of Vietnam from the viewpoint of the empire, maintains that: "One of the most frustrating aspects of the Vietnam War, from the Army's point of view, is that as far as logistics and tactics are concerned, we succeeded in everything we set out to do. On the battlefield itself, the Army was unbeatable. In engagement after engagement, the forces of the Viet Cong and of the North Vietnamese Army were thrown back with terrible losses. Yet, in the end, it was North Vietnam, not the United States, that emerged victorious. How could we have succeeded so well, yet failed so miserably? . . . The answer appears to be that we saw Vietnam as unique rather than in strategic context."

33. More than a few have mistakenly considered LIW to be traditional counterinsurgency with a new name. For example, Richard Alan White writes in his book *The Morass: United States Intevention in Central America* (New York: Harper and Row, 1984), p. 13: "Because of the U.S. public's negative association with the term 'counterinsurgency,' the current military nomenclature is 'low-intensity conflict.' "

34. Col. John D. Waghelstein, "Post-Vietnam Counterinsurgency Doctrine," *Military Review* (May 1985); emphasis in original. Waghelstein is currently strategic research analyst at the U.S. Army War College in Carlisle, Pennsylvania.

35. Col. John D. Waghelstein, "Low Intensity Conflict in the Post-Vietnam Period," address delivered at the American Enterprise Institute, 16 January 1985.

36. The fact that the term "low intensity" is misleading has led some analysts to reject the concept out of hand. For instance, the Managua-based Central American Historical Institute argues in its monthly publication *Envío* (October 1985) that the "concept of [LIW] is problematic [because] the Nicaraguan people do not call 'low intensity' the war that has shattered their dream of finally improving their lives."

37. Dr. Sam Sarkesian, "Low-Intensity Conflict: Concepts, Principles, and Policy Guidelines," *Air University Review* (January–February 1985).

38. Edward N. Luttwak, "Notes on Low Intensity Warfare," *Parameters* (December 1983).

39. Thus was the case of Grenada. Destabilization was carried out for over four

years. To what extent this aggression contributed to the suicide of the revolution has yet to be determined. Nevertheless, the events inside the revolution in October 1983 created the conditions for the full-scale U.S. intervention.

40. Characterizations of apparent differences within the administration over Nicaragua as a conflict between the "hard-liners" advocating an invasion and the "pragmatists" advocating moderation fall short of the mark. Undersecretary of State for Inter-American Affairs Craig Johnson affirmed that "there are divisions, but they are not as described [hard-liners vs. moderates]. No one in a position of power believes in an invasion scenario." (Epstein, unpublished paper. Constantine Menges, the CIA's national intelligence officer for Latin America, special adviser to the president on Central America, and National Security Council member, is a key architect of the war against Nicaragua and is often cited as a "hard-liner" advocating the invasionist line. Nevertheless, Menges wrote as early as 1981: "The military approach alone, *or in excess*, fails to meet the fundamental pressures of the invisible political warfare that is the real challenge [in policy toward Nicaragua]." Constantine Menges, "Coping with Radical Destabilization in the Middle East and Central America/Mexico: Trends, Causes, and Alternatives," *Conflict* 3, no. 1 [1981]; italics added.)

41. *Washington Post*, 16 December 1984. It is not accurate to characterize the threat of an imminent intervention as a "bluff" since, if Nicaragua were to let down its guard and demoblize the defense apparatus, the likelihood of an intervention would be greatly increased since its chances for success would be much greater.

42. Two of the most important works critiquing the errors in the Vietnam war from the viewpoint of the empire are Hunt and Shultz, eds., *Lessons*, and Summers, *On Strategy* (see chap. 1, n. 32). While both these works make similar criticisms, Summers' essential conclusion is that the United States should have waged an all-out conventional effort from the beginning, and that this is what must be done in future conflicts. The contributors to *Lessons*, however, favor LIW, as opposed to conventional warfare, as a means to avoid the errors of Vietnam. Another useful work is Edward N. Luttwak, *The Pentagon and the Art of War* (New York: Simon and Schuster, 1984).

43. The conversation was between Col. Harry G. Summers, Jr., then chief of the Negotiations Division, U.S. delegation, Four Party Joint Military Team, and Colonel Tu, chief, North Vietnamese delegation, the most senior Vietnamese officer on the spot. Quoted in Summers, *On Strategy*, p. 1.

44. For these and other statistics on the extent of U.S. involvement and damage inflicted on Vietnam, see Lawrence G. Grinter, "Requirements of Strategy in Vietnam," in Hunt and Shultz, eds., *Lessons*.

45. There are in fact two contending critiques of Vietnam. The principal one, which is analyzed here, extolled the virtues of pacification and developed into LIW. The opposing critique held that the war was lost because the political leadership refused to let the military fight its war—the armed

forces were "too shackled"—and that a massive escalation very early on, including an invasion of North Vietnam, could have won the war.

46. For a deeper discussion of this issue, see Lawrence E. Grinter, "Requirements of Strategy in Vietnam," in Hunt and Shultz, eds., *Lessons*, p. 124.

47. John Hoyt Williams, "The Real War: Marine Pacification in Vietnam," *The Retired Officer* (August 1983).

48. Ibid., p. 156.

49. For a more detailed discussion by one former DOD official involved in the critique, see Douglas S. Blaufarb, "The Sources of U.S. Frustration in Vietnam," in Hunt and Shultz, eds., *Lessons*, p. 154.

50. Sarkesian, "Low-Intensity Conflict."

51. Even when the Johnson administration attempted to bolster the pacification efforts, starting in 1967, "progress was disappointing, and not merely because the conventional war deprived it of attention and resources. The difficult and cumbersome way in which U.S. agencies were organized to advise and support Vietnamese pacification efforts also hampered progress." Richard A. Hunt, in the introduction to Hunt and Shultz, eds., *Lessons*.

52. Ernest Evans, "Revolutionary Movements in Central America," in Howard J. Wiarda, ed., *Rift and Revolution: The Central American Imbroglio* (Washington, D.C.: American Enterprise Institute, 1984), pp. 186–87.

53. Hunt and Shultz, eds., *Lessons*, p. 151.

54. Quoted in "America's Secret Soldiers: The Buildup of U.S. Special Operations Forces," *Defense Monitor* (Washington, D.C.: Center for Defense Information, 1985), p. 2.

55. These include entities such as the Agency for International Development (AID) and the United States Information Agency (USIA), as well as nongovernmental groups like the American Institute for Free Labor Development (AIFLD) of the AFL-CIO, and a slew of quasi-private organizations tied to corporate, military, and conservative religious circles.

56. Maurice Tugwell and David Charter, special operations specialists from the Center for Conflict Studies, University of New Brunswick, quoted in Barnet et al., eds., *Special Operations*.

57. According to the Pentagon's still-classified (as of 1986) "Defense Guidance Plan," which was signed by Weinberger in 1982, "We must revitalize and enhance special operations to project U.S. power where the use of conventional forces would be premature, inappropriate or infeasible." Parts of the document were leaked to the press in mid-1982. This quote is from the *Guardian*, 6 October 1982. The document, drafted to guide the administration's five-year $1.6 trillion military build-up, constitutes a major statement of policy on the expansion and deployment of Special Operations Forces, as well as on low-intensity warfare. The expansion of SOF includes a 30 percent increase in troop strength from 1981 to 1985, and an additional 60 percent increase by 1990, a 150 percent rise in the budget from Fiscal Year 1980 to Fiscal Year 1985, and a sharp increase in special operations equipment inventory. For these statistics, and for a detailed discussion of the SOF, see Claire I. Pastore, *Anything, Anytime, Anyplace* (Washington,

D.C.: Center for Defense Information, December 1984); The document cites DOD figures.

58. Following three years of revitalization, the Grenada invasion was the debut of the SOF. Nearly all SOF units participated, spearheading the operation. The only non-SOF forces were the U.S. Marines.

59. Luttwak, "Notes on Low-Intensity Warfare."

60. The CIA, however, is open to congressional (and therefore public) scrutiny, and exposures of its sordid behavior in the past have tarnished the "Company's" image. On the other hand, the SOF are not required to report their activities to Congress and can operate in complete secrecy. None other than Principal Deputy Assistant Defense Secretary Noel Koch admitted that "it would not be unusual for things to be done [by the SOF] that I would not know about." (Quoted in *Philadelphia Inquirer*, 16 December 1984.) Koch heads the DOD's Special Planning Directorate, which makes him directly responsible for DOD policy on special operations.

61. *Miami Herald*, 5 June 1983.

62. Members of the NSC are the president, the vice-president, the secretaries of state and defense, the director of the CIA, and the chairman of the Joint Chiefs of Staff. Under Reagan, the NSC has been expanded to include the U.S. ambassador to the UN, the national security adviser, the White House chief of staff, and others.

63. In August 1985 it was "discovered" that the NSC was directing the war against Nicaragua. That this came as a surprise to even informed observers underscores the effectiveness with which the administration had been projecting the war as merely a CIA operation.

64. "This would create a single channel for integrating the appropriate elements involved in low-intensity conflict operations . . . the NSC special group should be supported by a joint center charged with planning and implementing operations. Each of the principal civilian and military elements involved requires a parallel structure to the NSC special group and joint center." *Mandate for Leadership II*, pp. 264–265.

65. Butler et al., eds., *Mandate for Leadership II*, p. 228.

66. Committee of Santa Fe, *New Inter-American Policy*, p. 32.

67. Dr. George K. Tanham of the Rand Corporation, quoted in Hunt et al., eds., *Special Operations*, p. 294.

68. Unnamed administration official quoted in *New York Times*, 29 March 1983.

69. The Office of Public Diplomacy grew in two years from a one-man shop to a staff of twenty and a budget of $1 million.

70. *Miami Herald*, 14 May 1985.

2. The War of the Jackal

1. Carl von Clausewitz, *On War* (Harmondsworth, Middlesex: Penguin Books, 1968), p. 119. The German original was published in 1832.

2. See, for example, the story of "Bill," told in Christopher Dickey, *With the*

Contras: A Reporter in the Wilds of Nicaragua (New York: Simon and Schuster, 1985), pp. 53–55.

3. Information drawn from an unsigned "Dissent Paper" composed by members of the NSC, CIA, and Departments of Defense and State. The paper, which was released in Washington on 6 November 1980 and widely reprinted in the U.S. media, stated that Washington was creating an amorphous "paramilitary strike force" composed of former National Guardsmen and buttressed with exiled Cuban counterrevolutionaries and mercenaries of various stripes. Although the authenticity of the paper has never been ascertained, the information it contains on initial CIA contacts with the National Guard coincides with the general picture that emerged of the first years after the Sandinista victory.

4. Jay Peterzell, *Reagan's Secret Wars* (Washington, D.C.: Center for National Security Studies, 1984), p. 65. Peterzell cites a May 1983 interview with Turner in the *Baltimore Sun*.

5. In 1980 the CIA channeled at least $1 million in covert aid to these groups. See *Los Angeles Times*, 3 March 1985.

6. *Wall Street Journal*, 29 February 1980.

7. Ibid.

8. Philip Agee, "The CIA's Blueprint for Nicaragua", *Covert Action Information Bulletin* (October 1979).

9. Cleto Di Giovanni, Jr., "U.S. Policy and the Marxist Threat to Central America," *Heritage Foundation Backgrounder*, no. 128 (October 1980).

10. Ibid.

11. *Miami Herald*, 5 June 1983.

12. *Dialogo Social* (Panama City), (July 1985).

13. Peterzell, *Reagan's Secret Wars*, p. 75. See also *Washington Post*, 14 February 1982; 10 March 1982; 11 March 1982.

14. The Sandinista government might have supplied the Salvadoran guerrillas with some weapons in 1980 and 1981, but subsequent U.S. charges have all proven false, and several have had an adverse effect on the Reagan administration's position. For further information on this subject, see Orlando Tardencilla, *Sin Tiro de Gracia* (Managua: Editorial El Amanecer, 1985); denunciation by former CIA analyst David McMichael, *New York Times*, 11 June 1984.

15. Lau's role in Romero's assassination was the source of speculation for several years. On 21 March 1985, however, a former Salvadoran military intelligence officer gave details in Washington confirming Lau's involvement, including receipts for Lau's payoff and documents obtained from D'Aubuisson's political party, the Republican National Alliance (ARENA). See AP, UPI, and AFP dispatches datelined Washington, D.C., 21 March 1985.

16. *Los Angeles Times*, 3 March 1985.

17. Ibid.

18. Interview with Julio Ramos in *Barricada Internacional* (June 1984), special supplement entitled "Two Years of Aggression and a Resolute Nation."

19. "Insurgency Activity Increases in Nicaragua", DIA report dated 16 July

1982. The report was obtained by *Counterspy* magazine in mid-1983 and published in its September/November 1983 edition.

20. Senate Arms Control and Foreign Policy Caucus, *Who Are the Contras? An Analysis of the Makeup of the Military Leadership of the Rebel Forces, and the Nature of the Private American Groups Providing them Financial and Material Support*, report prepared by the Arms Control and Foreign Policy Caucus of the U.S. Congress, Washington, D.C., 18 April 1985.

21. *New York Times*, 23 December 1981; 17 January 1982.

22. Francés titled his prepared testimony "The War of Terror Against Nicaragua." It was reprinted as a special supplement to *Barricada* in December 1982.

23. Roberto Bardini, *Conexion en Tegucigalpa (El Somocismo en Honduras)*, (Mexico City: Universidad Autónoma del Puebla, 1982), p. 30.

24. *New York Times*, 5 November 1981.

25. *Miami Herald*, 24 February 1985.

26. *Miami Herald*, 24 February 1985; *Los Angeles Times*, 3 March 1985.

27. Humberto Ortega, interview with authors, Managua, 8 May 1986.

28. *Miami Herald*, 5 June 1983.

29. *Barricada*, 14 May 1985.

30. *Washington Post*, 8 May 1983.

31. Summary Paper presented at a meeting of the NSC planning group for Nicaragua in April 1982. For citation in text, see *New York Times*, 7 April 1983.

32. For a detailed discussion of Red Christmas, see *Trabil Nani* (Managua: CIDCA, n.d.).

33. Quoted in Roxanne Dunbar-Ortiz, "The Miskito Case," *Covert Action Information Bulletin* 18 (Winter 1983).

34. *NACLA Report on the Americas* (January/February 1982); *Envio* (February 1982).

35. Said during a televised interview on WNGT's "The MacNeil/Lehrer News Hour", 14 February 1982; cited in *NACLA Report on the Americas* (January/February 1982). Although accounts of the total number of Nicaraguan Miskitos vary widely, the maximum estimate has never exceeded 180,000, and only 20,000–25,000 live on the Río Coco.

36. *New York Times*, 3 March 1982.

37. Reports cited in Dunbar-Ortiz, "The Miskito Case."

38. Quoted in Roberto Bardini, *Edén Pastora: Un Cero en la Historia* (Mexico City: Universidad Autónoma de Puebla, 1984), p. 96.

39. These two testimonies appear in *Envio* (February 1984).

40. Stockwell gave a press conference—which the authors attended—in Managua in June 1984. The ANN news agency's coverage of the conference was published in *Barricada Internacional*, 18 June 1984.

41. Retranslated from the Spanish. *Barricada* published transcripts of the World Court testimonies during September and October of 1985.

42. Quoted in Gordon Mott, "Honduras," *New York Times Magazine*, 14 October 1984.

43. Quoted from a prepared statement delivered by Buchanan before the

Subcommittee on Inter-American Affairs, Committee on Foreign Affairs, U.S. House of Representatives, on U.S. aid to Honduras, Washington, D.C., 21 September 1982. Buchanan was then director of area studies, Center for Development Policy, and a member of the center's commission on U.S.-Central American relations.

44. *New York Times,* 5 June 1985.
45. The details of the formation of the FDN political directorate, including the quotes, are taken from Edgar Chamorro and Jefferson Morley, "Confessions of a 'Contra' ", *New Republic,* 5 August 1985. Chamorro defected in 1985.
46. *Envío* (February 1984).
47. William I. Robinson, "Nicaragua 'Ready for the Worst,'" APIA News Service, Managua, 20 June 1983.
48. For details on Monge's trip see ACAN-EFE, AFP, AP, and ANN news cables, datelined Washington, D.C., 22–24 June 1982.
49. At that time, the FSLN was still divided into three tendencies: the Prolonged Popular War; the Proletarians; and the *Terceristas*. By 1978, all three tendencies were working together and carrying out coordinated actions.
50. Humberto Ortega, "La Lucha Ideológia y el Caso Pastora," May Day speech to workers in Managua, 1982.
51. For details on these CIA efforts, see Shirley Christian, *Nicaragua: Revolution in the Family* (New York: Random House, 1985), p. 88.
52. Ibid., p. 102.
53. Ibid., p. 105.
54. Quoted in Bardini, *Edén Pastora,* p. 43. Pastora was referring to the siege that month of the Spanish embassy in Guatemala City, and the assassination of Salvadoran Archbishop Oscar Romero, by a Nicaraguan intelligence officer in the pay of Salvadoran fascist Roberto D'Aubuissoin.
55. Ibid, p. 86.
56. *Los Angeles Times,* 3 March 1985.
57. The statement by Pastora's aide is quoted in "Intervention Base is Transferred to Costa Rica," *In These Times,* 19–25 January 1984; quote retranslated from the Spanish.
58. ANN news dispatch, datelined Managua, 4 July 1982.
59. Bruce Jones, quoted in "A CIA Man in Nicaragua," *Life,* February 1985. Jones, a U.S. citizen, is a long-time CIA agent and a farmer in the Costa Rican border province of Guanacaste.
60. Quoted in *NACLA Report on the Americas* (March/April 1984).
61. Oscar Núñez, ANN correspondent in Costa Rica, telephone conversation with authors, 15 May 1983.
62. Quoted in former CIA agent Philip Agee's foreword to *The CIA's Nicaragua Manual, Psychological Operations in Guerrilla Warfare* (New York: Random House, 1985). The Random House volume is a translation (from the original Spanish) and book-form edition of the CIA-devised *Psychological Operations in Guerrilla Warfare* manual, which the agency issued to the

FDN in 1984. (Page references to this work in subsequent notes are for the Random House edition.)

63. *Barricada,* 20 October 1983.
64. *Barricada Internacional,* 24 October 1983.
65. Dickey, *With the Contras,* 259.
66. Richard H. Shultz, Jr., and Alan Ned Zabrosky, "Policy and Strategy for the 1980's: Preparing for Low Intensity Conflicts," in Hunt and Shultz, eds., *Lessons* (see chap. 1, n. 31) 218; emphasis in the original.
67. *Barricada,* 26 October 1983.
68. *Time,* 8 August 1983.
69. Press release of the National Farmers Federation of Costa Rica, dated 10 November, based on testimony given by organization members who had inspected the northern zone following the first reports of "strange movements."
70. *Barricada,* 31 October 1983.
71. ANN news dispatch, datelined Tegucigalpa, 30 October 1983.
72. COHA press release, 18 November 1983.
73. White, *The Morass* (see chap. 1, n. 33), p. 65.
74. On 11 November 1983 the UN General Assembly approved a resolution condemning "outside attacks" against Nicaragua and supporting the Contadora and Nicaraguan peace initiatives. On 17 November the OAS passed a similar resolution (and rejected an alternative resolution against Nicaragua introduced by the United States). The governments of Argentina, Bolivia, Mexico, Venezuela, Peru, and Ecuador released public statements calling for nonintervention in Central America. The Socialist International released a similar statement, and the Christian Democratic Italian government told Sergio Ramírez it would not support a U.S. intervention. For summaries of the international response to the late 1983 invasion threat, see *Barricada International* 21 November 1983; 19 December 1983.
75. *Washington Post,* 20 February 1984.

3. The New Strategy Takes Shape

1. Lewis Tambs and Frank Aker, "Shattering the Vietnam Syndrome: A Scenario for Success in El Salvador," unpublished manuscript, 1983.
2. Humberto Ortega, interview with Joanne Omang of the *Washington Post,* October 1985. The unedited text of the interview, in the original Spanish, was published in *Barricada,* 10 October 1985.
3. For more information on the changing views of DOD officials at this time, see "U.S. Generals Are Leery of Latin Intervention," *New York Times,* 21 June 1983; "Top U.S. Brass Wary on Central America," *Washington Post,* 24 June 1983.
4. For details on Kirkpatrick's trip and her report to officials in Washington, see, *New York Times,* 11 February 1983; *Time,* 8 August 1983.
5. *Miami Herald,* 24 September 1982.

6. Quoted in Alan Nairn, "Endgame," *NACLA Report on the Americas* (May/June 1984).
7. *New York Times*, 28 April 1983.
8. For additional excerpts from the NSC summit's working papers, see *New York Times*, 17 July 1983; *Washington Post*, 7 August 1983.
9. Ibid.; see also *Time*, 8 August 1983.
10. *New York Times*, 4 June 1985.
11. Among Gorman's assignments during his career were: infantry commander in Vietnam and Europe, deputy director of the Pentagon Papers project, staff member at Vietnam peace negotiations in Paris, CIA national intelligence officer in charge of conventional forces, and director of plans and operations for the Joint Chiefs of Staff. For further details, see; *Miami Herald*, 31 May 1984; *Wall Street Journal*, 24 June 1984.
12. National Bipartisan Commission on Central America, *Report of the National Bipartisan Commission on Central America* (New York: MacMillan, 1984). For a detailed analysis of the Kissinger report and four "alternative" proposals which were released around the same time, see Deborah Barry and Jorge Sol Pérez, "El Debate Norteamericano: Cinco Propuestas sobre Centroamerica," in *Cuadernos de Pensamiento Propio*, (Managua: Coordinadora Regional de Investigaciones Económicas y Sociales, 1984).
13. For details on this conference, see Peter Stone, "The Special Forces in 'Covert Action,' " *The Nation*, 7–14 July 1984.
14. Singlaub's thirty-five years of active service ended with his forced retirement in June 1978, as head of U.S. forces in South Korea, following his harsh public criticism of President Jimmy Carter. His career included tours of duty with the Office of Strategic Services, various posts in the CIA (including chief of covert activities in Vietnam, where he was chief architect of the Phoenix Program, in which over twenty thousand Vietnamese were exterminated), and numerous training and command assignments with regular forces. For an interview with Singlaub that includes extensive biographical information, see *The New American*, 11 November 1985.
15. Allan Francovich, interview with authors, New York, 27 September 1985. Francovich produced the award-winning three-hour documentary film *On Company Business*, which exposed many years of CIA covert operations around the world.
16. Richard H. Shultz, Jr., and Alan Ned Zabrosky, "Policy and Strategy for the 1980's: Preparing for Low Intensity Conflicts," in Hunt and Shultz, eds., *Lessons* (see chap. 1, n.31), p. 212.
17. "Months ago, when the Sandinistas showed that they could sustain their final offensive against Somoza's National Guard, an interagency working group was established within the National Security Council to monitor and evaluate developments in Nicaragua," Philip Agee had said in 1979; see Philip Agee, "The CIA's Blueprint for Nicaragua," *Covert Action Information Bulletin* (October 1979).
18. For details on the RIG, the role of the NSC as nerve center and the individuals involved, see the *Los Angeles Times* three-part series on the war

against Nicaragua: *Los Angeles Times,* 3–5 March 1985; see also *Washington Post,* 16 December 1984; *Wall Street Journal* 5–6 March 1985.

19. For instance, FDN spokesmen said that they received some $30 million directly from the CIA in August 1984 which was not authorized by Congress. See Prensa Latina dispatch, datelined San José, 24 August 1984.

20. For a good discussion on the way the contingency funds, transfers, and general budget categories work, see Peter H. Stone, "The Special Forces in 'Covert Action,'" *The Nation,* July 7–14, 1984.

21. *New York Times,* 9 September 1984.

22. These figures are enormous relative to the population being targeted and the amount of destruction it can bring about. Nevertheless, they demonstrate the cost-effectiveness of LIW, considering that the United States was spending $20 billion per annum to wage war against Vietnam.

23. *Miami Herald,* 16 June 1985.

24. Quoted in Barnet et al., eds., *Special Operations* (see chap. 1, n. 4), 34.

25. For interviews with soldiers and residents of Santa Clara, see *Barricada* 2–3 September 1984; see also *New York Times,* 6 September 1984; *Washington Post,* 5–7 September, 1984.

26. *Washington Post,* 7 September 1984.

27. For details on operation "Elephant Herd," see *Washington Post,* 25 September 1984.

28. See, for instance, National Security Adviser Robert McFarlane's comments to the *New York Times,* 8 September 1986.

29. CMA member Bill Johnson, interview with authors, Tegucigalpa, 23 July 1985.

30. For a detailed description of the organizations and individuals involved in privatization, see Senate Arms Control and Foreign Policy Caucus *Who Are the Contras?* (see chap. 2, n.20); see also *Covert Action Information Bulletin* (Fall 1984); "Behind the Supply Lines," *Covert Action Information Bulletin* (Winter 1986).

31. The advertisement was described in *Newsweek,* 4 November 1985. The specific group was not mentioned.

32. *Washington Post,* 17 August 1983.

33. Ibid.

34. For these details, see Senate Arms Control and Foreign Policy Caucus, *Who Are the Contras?;* see also "USA: Privatizar la Guerra," *Pensamiento Propio* (August 1985).

35. Committee of Santa Fe, *New Inter-American Policy* (see chap. 1, n.1), p. 27.

36. CMA member Bill Johnson, interview with authors, Tegucigalpa, 23 July 1985.

37. *Washington Post,* 2 July 1984.

38. *Covert Action Information Bulletin* (Fall 1984).

39. For details of the plan, see *Washington Post,* 8 October 1985. In the summer of 1985, the U.S. press "discovered" that North was a key official on the NSC in the war against Nicaragua. This discovery produced a flurry of investigative reporting, which, while producing valuable information, inac-

curately portrayed the NSC's central role as a "new development." See, for example, *Washington Post*, 8 October 1985; *New York Times*, 8 August 1985.

40. Numerous articles came out in the U.S. press in 1985 on WACL and its operations. For one of the most extensive, see "The Old Right's New Crusade," *Village Voice*, 22 October 1985.

41. See "Behind the Supply Lines," *Covert Action Information Bulletin* (Winter 1986).

42. See *Covert Action Information Bulletin*, (Winter 1986); *Newsweek*, 26 August 1985.

43. *Miami Herald*, 16 June 1985.

44. One 1984 internal administration memorandum stated: "The President stands a good chance of being portrayed in the media as a poor, naive incompetent . . . weak on common sense" if open association were made with Causa and the Unification Church; for more on this subject, see *Washington Post*, 16 August 1984.

45. For details on the Dallas conference, see "Behind the Supply Lines," *Covert Action Information Bulletin* (Winter 1986).

46. See, for instance, *Washington Post*, 27 February 1986, which carried stories on an address by Shultz and a $2.5 million Singlaub program of television and newspaper ads.

47. For example, Canadian journalist Pete Bertle, an FDN sympathizer who spent part of 1984 and 1985 traveling inside Nicaragua with the contras, stressed in his chronicles (published in the *Toronto Sun*) that the task force he accompanied "had successfully avoided contact with the enemy" during its weeks-long trek. Cited in the House of Representatives, Washington D.C., *Congressional Record*, 24 October 1985.

48. Quoted in *Covert Action Information Bulletin* (Fall 1984).

49. See Latin-Reuters dispatch, dateline Tegucigalpa, 5 April 1984.

50. Quoted in *Barricada Internacional*, 5 March 1984.

4. Recasting Tactics

1. Summers, *On Strategy* (see chap. 1, n. 32), p. 67.

2. Dora María Téllez, interview with *Barricada*, 4 July 1984.

3. *Sunday Times* (London), 22 April 1984.

4. Initial reports appeared in the Costa Rican press. For details, see *Barricada Internacional*, 16 April 1984.

5. For the ARDE spokesman citation, see William I. Robinson, "San Juan del Norte—'A Wall of Sandinistas' Evaporates Pastora's Dreams," ANN Special News Service, Managua, 24 April 1984; for information from a classified CIA report confirming that a U.S. warship was responsible for the bombardment, see *Wall Street Journal*, 6 March 1985.

6. ANN dispatch, datelined San Juan del Norte, 13 April 1984.

7. *New York Times*, 1 June 1984.

8. For the Nicaraguan president's initial denunciation, see *Barricada Internacional*, 5 March 1984.

9. *New York Times*, 14 March 1984.

10. For the first U.S. press account of U.S. involvement, see *Wall Street Journal*, 6 April 1984. For colorful accounts of this fiasco, see *Los Angeles Times*, 3–5 March 1985; *Wall Street Journal*, 5–6 March 1985; *Washington Post*, 16–17 December 1984.

11. *Los Angeles Times*, 5 March 1985.

12. See *Barricada Internacional*, 9 April 1984, and the report given by Alfredo Alaniz, Nicaraguan minister of fisheries, to the World Fisheries Conference in Rome on 29 June 1984.

13. *Wall Street Journal*, 6 March 1985.

14. ANN news cable, datelined San José, 4 April 1984.

15. The Honduran Human Rights Commission reported hundreds of cases of political prisoners, deaths, and disappearances since Alvarez had come to power.

16. For a detailed analysis of the coup and its context which supports the thesis that the U.S. had a heavy hand in removing Alvarez, see Gregorio Selser, "Cambios Militares en un País Ocupado." Among other places, his article appeared in *Barricada*, 3 April 1984, and *Pensamiento Propio*, April 1984.

17. The FDN commander was "Pecos Bill," quoted in Dieter Eich and Carlos Rincón, *The Contras: Interviews with Anti-Sandinistas* (San Francisco: Synthesis Publications, 1985), pp. 185–186.

18. *Barricada*, 1 April 1984.

19. *Barricada*, 9–12 May 1984.

20. *Washington Post* weekly national edition, quoted in *Barricada Internacional*, 21 May 1984; italics added.

21. *Barricada*, 5 May 1984.

22. *La Nación* (San José), 5 May 1984.

23. *New York Times*, 11 December 1985.

24. Shultz gave a press conference in Managua to journalists, attended by the authors, before he departed Nicaragua.

25. The document was titled "U.S. Policy in Central America and Cuba through Fiscal Year 1984" and was the summary paper of an NSC meeting held in April 1982; see *New York Times*, 7 April 1983, for reproduction of parts of the document.

26. Said during a press conference in Washington in the second week of December 1985; quoted in ANN dispatch, dateline Washington, 17 December 1985.

27. See "Costa Rica, Seesaw Diplomacy," *NACLA Report on the Americas* (November/December 1983).

28. "Lo Nuestro Es un Proyecto Enredado," interview with Tomás Borge in *Pensamiento Propio*, Managua, June–July 1985.

29. For an overview of Nicaragua's nonaligned foreign policy, see *Envío* (January 1983). On 28 February 1985 President Daniel Ortega presented a "13-point Statement" on the "fundamental policies of the Nicaraguan govern-

ment," which capsulates Managua's policies. The statement was reproduced in *Barricada* and *El Nuevo Diario*, 29 February 1985, and in *Frontline* (Oakland), 1 April 1985.

30. These and other Nicaraguan peace initiatives are summarized in "Nicaragua's Peace Initiatives with the United States," a March 1985 document published by the Nicaraguan embassy in Washington.

31. As late as the annual ordinary session of the OAS in Washington in March 1986, U.S. representatives were still pushing this. See AP, EFE, AFP, and ANN dispatches, datelined Washington, 5 March 1986.

32. Lt. Gen. Gordon Sumner U.S. Army, ret., quoted in "Negotiating with Marxists in Central America," transcription of a conference sponsored by the International Security Council (a CAUSA-affiliated organization) with leading members of the New Right, Washington, D.C., 21 March 1985; emphasis in the original.

33. For a reproduction of the Document of 21 Points, see "U.S.-Nicaragua Talks: Going Through the Motions," an international policy report, Washington, D.C., December 1983, a publication of the Center for International Policy.

34. The full text of the treaty, titled "Act for Peace and Cooperation in Central America," was reproduced by *Pensamiento Propio* as a special supplement to the October/November 1984 issue.

35. For details on the Tegucigalpa Document, see Tom J. Farer, "Contadora: The Hidden Agenda," *Foreign Policy* (Summer 1985).

36. *Washington Post*, 6 November 1984.

37. ANN news cable, datelined Panama City, 1 December 1983.

38. *New York Times*, 31 May 1984.

39. Quoted from copy of Pastora communiqué received by authors.

40. Details of this meeting were reported in an AFP news cable dated 27 May and datelined San José.

41. The information on Costa Rican investigations into the La Penca incident comes from ANN, ACAN-EFE, and AFP dispatches from San José from 30 May to 4 June 1984.

42. The journalists published a comprehensive account of their investigation in *The Nation*, 5 October 1985, under the title "The Carlos Files."

43. As quoted in Leonel Urbano, "Todos Estamos en la Revolución, Menos el Traidor: Dora María Téllez," *El Día* (Mexico), 22 August 1982.

5. Political Warriors and Socioeconomic Attrition

1. *Psychological Operations in Guerrilla Warfare* (see chap. 2, n. 62), p. 39.

2. Conversation with the International Press Club in Managua, 10 November 1984; see *Barricada*, 13 November 1984.

3. The details on the origins of the manual are sprinkled throughout press stories from October to December 1984. See, for instance, *Washington Post*, 20 October, 31 October, 3 December, and 7 December 1984. Also see Philip Agee's foreword, written to accompany the manual's publication.

4. Col. John D. Waghelstein, "Low Intensity Conflict in the Post-Vietnam

Period," address delivered at the American Enterprise Institute, 16 January 1985.

5. The graphic on the manual's cover alternates the words *operaciones sicológicas en guerra de guerrillas*, between rows of people's heads, each head with a large hole in the center, symbolizing the minds of the people as the target (many observers erroneously viewed the holes as bullet holes).

6. *The CIA's Nicaragua Manual* (see chap. 2, n. 62), p. 33.

7. Ibid., pp. 49, 64.

8. Ibid., pp. 62, 63.

9. Ibid., pp. 48, 50.

10. Ibid., p. 47.

11. This and similar testimony was compiled in *Envío* (March 1985).

12. Javier Carrión, interview with ANN, Managua, 17 August 1985.

13. *The CIA's Nicaragua Manual*, p. 38.

14. Javier Carrión, interview with ANN, Managua, 17 August 1985.

15. For a detailed explanation of the Sandinistas' vision of this program, see Jaime Wheelock Román, *El Grán Desafío* (Managua: Editorial Nueva Nicaragua 1983).

16. These statistics are rounded estimations, given by *Dirección General de Reforma Agraria*, MIDINRA. See "Plan Tecnico-Económico 1984-85, 1985-86" for a collection of this data. Our discussion is necessarily simplified because of lack of space. There is also a sizable middle layer of peasants (more than 20,000 families) who own enough property to place them between poor peasants and the *latifundistas*. It must also be remembered that peasant households are large, often including ten or more members, so that peasant families and rural population are two very distinct figures. For a more detailed analysis of the pre- and post-triumph agricultural political economies and the post-triumph agricultural political economies and the evolution of the Sandinista agrarian reform see Jaime Wheelock Román, *Entre la Crisis y la Agresión, la Reforma Agraria Sandinista* (Managua: Editorial Nueva Nicaragua, 1985); Carlos M. Vilas, *The Sandinista Revolution* (New York: Monthly Review Press, 1986); Joseph Collins, *What Difference Could a Revolution Make?* (New York: Grove Press, 1986).

17. For these statistics, see "Plan Tecnico-Económico."

18. *Barricada*, 13 January 1986.

19. Ibid., 4 February 1986.

20. The relation between peasant discontent and the Sandinista agrarian reform was clearly shown in the results of the November 1984 general elections: in those peasant districts where under 10 percent of the population had received land through the agrarian reform, the rightist opposition parties won proportionally more votes than on the national level. See *Envío*, "The Nicaraguan Peasantry Gives New Direction to Agrarian Reform" (September 1985).

21. *The CIA's Nicaragua Manual*, p. 60.

22. There was never any coercion to cooperativize. Moreover, pressure for individual land grants was addressed with the titles program, which the

government erroneously believed would alleviate the problem.

23. For these Sandinista views, see *Barricada Internacional*, 5 December 1985.

24. This quote is taken from an untitled internal MIDINRA document written in early 1985. The document, for circulation among MIDINRA officials and FSLN cadres, was an extremely critical analysis of the Sandinistas' rural policies over the first five years and the ways in which the contras took advantage of them; it included recommendations for reorienting these policies to meet the counterrevolutionary challenge.

25. *The CIA's Nicaragua Manual*, p. 70.

26. *El Nuevo Diario*, 28 August 1984.

27. Internal MIDINRA document.

28. *Congressional Record*, 24 October 1985. The article in which the quote appears, published in the *Toronto Sun* in February 1985, was read to the Congress by Representative Newt Gingrich.

29. *The CIA's Nicaragua Manual*, p. 60.

30. For more detailed information regarding these estimates, see: Center for International Communication, *Nicaragua: The Counterrevolution: Development and Consequences, Basic Information, 1980–1985* (Managua: Center for International Communication, 1985); "La Contrarevolución: Grietas y Corrupción," *Pensamiento Propio* (August 1985); *Barricada*, 10 December 1985.

31. The former FDN commander is Efraín Mondragón, who quit the FDN in mid-1985 and returned to Nicaragua under the government's amnesty program. See his declarations to *El Nuevo Diario*, 15 May 1985.

32. *The CIA's Nicaragua Manual*, pp. 73–74.

33. Ibid., pp. 51–52.

34. Ibid., p. 51.

35. *Barricada*, 7 February 1986.

36. Sergio Ramírez, speech on the occasion of the twenty-fifth anniversary of the foundation of the National School of Journalism; see *Barricada*, 17 May 1985.

37. Blandón told his story to the Nicaraguan press; see *Barricada*, 16 August 1985.

38. Testimony by Efraín Mondragón, *Barricada*, 17 May 1985.

39. Lawrence E. Grinter, "Requirements of Strategy in Vietnam," in Hunt and Shultz, eds., *Lessons* (see chap. 1, n. 31), p. 128; emphasis added.

40. Interview with CMA member Bill Johnson in Tegucigalpa, 23 July 1985.

41. The quote is taken from an "information paper" of the National Defense Council (NDC), a leading New Right privatization group; it is dated 5 December 1984 and signed by Andrew Messing, a well-known Reaganite personality.

42. Interview with FDN field commander René Fernández in Tegucigalpa, 19 July 1985. Shortly after our interview, Fernández quit the FDN.

43. Quoted in *Envío*, March 1985.

44. Various testimonies appear in *Barricada*, 8 February 1986.

45. "U.S. Military Activities in Honduras," a pamphlet prepared by the U.S.

embassy in Tegucigalpa and given to the authors by embassy public relations officer Arthur Skoop.

46. Quoted in Joel Millman, "Town Full of Cheese," *Village Voice* (New York), 24 December 1985.

47. Sister Lisa Fitzgerald, quoted in Dickey, *With the Contras*, p. 161.

48. The FDN member was "Pecos Bill," quoted in Deiter Eich and Carlos Rincón, *The Contras, Interviews With Anti-Sandinistas* (San Francisco: Synthesis Press, 1985), p. 190.

49. Interview with Roxanne Dunbar-Ortiz in Managua in late November 1984. Dunbar-Ortiz gave us the cited statistics following a four-day visit to the Department of Gracias a Dios in southeastern Honduras, where she interviewed Miskito refugees as well as Honduran and MISURA representatives. Similar statistics and testimony on the regular mass kidnappings appeared repeatedly in the Nicaraguan press throughout 1984, and were corroborated by our own research in Zelaya.

50. For a detailed account of the Francia Sirpi kidnapping and propaganda offensive see Ana María Ezcurra, *El Vaticano y la Administración Reagan: Convergencias en Centramerica* (Mexico City: Ediciones Nuevomar, 1984), pp. 54–57.

51. For these specific quotes, see *Barricada*, 22 December 1983; for a comprehensive treatment of collusion between anti-Sandinista Nicaraguan churchmen and U.S. intelligence in the context of the Francia Sirpi incident, see William I. Robinson, "CIA Finds New Moses in Nicaraguan Bishop," ANN Special News Service, Managua, 2 January 1984.

52. Ibid.

53. Ibid.

54. Orlando Wayland, quoted in Eich and Rincón, *The Contras*, pp. 121–22.

55. UNHCR officials, interview with authors, Tegucigalpa, 20 July 1985.

56. Both the FDN and MISURA accuse the UNHCR of being "pro-communist," "paid by the Sandinistas," and dedicated to "brainwashing the refugees with lies, bribes, and pro-Soviet literature." We saw this "pro-Soviet literature" while in Tegucigalpa: educational texts and didactic materials published by UNICEF, UNESCO, and other United Nations organizations. Luise Drake explained that the UNHCR's role is limited to facilitating voluntary repatriation and safeguarding the right of peoples to return to their native lands, in accordance with international law and the United Nations charter.

57. *Miami Herald*, 21 January 1985.

58. "Who Are the Contras?" a report prepared by the Arms Control and Foreign Policy Caucus of the U.S. Congress, 18 April 1985.

59. Among other sources, see the lengthy investigative reports published in the Mexican dailies *El Día* and *Excelsior*, 4 February 1986. A team of Mexican anthropologists spent several years in Mexico, Nicaragua, and the United States studying the Miskito situation and MISURASATA's U.S. connections. Their conclusions were published in the two newspapers, which contain details of the people involved in the ILRC.

60. In October 1983 Nietschmann delivered a report to the OAS detailing alleged human rights violations of the Miskitos. His report attracted considerable attention, and brought independent journalists and researchers from the United States and Europe to Zelaya to investigate its accuracy. Most reported that, although scattered violations had taken place, these were neither generalized nor official Sandinista policy, and that Nietschmann's sweeping accusations were therefore baseless. On 11 June 1985, *Barricada* published a summary of these independent reports. Above all, see the detailed section refuting his report in *Trabil Nani*, a report of the Center for Research and Documentation of the Atlantic Coast (CIDCA), the Managua, 1984. The report is distributed in the United States by the Riverside Church Disarmament Project, 490 Riverside Drive, New York, NY, 10027.

61. Quoted in *Barricada*, 9 February 1986, in reference to 1984 MIS-URUSATA documents.

62. For an analysis of the "fourth world" ideology, see "Sandinismo y el Cuarto Mundo," a report in *Barricada*, 28 February 1986, by researchers Carlos Aleman Ocampo and Gilberto López Rivas.

63. This document was given to the authors during the founding conference of MISATAN.

64. Speech by Sergio Ramírez, "Ultimatum de Reagan: La Nueva Nota Knox," delivered at the National Autonomous University of Nicaragua (UNAN), 12 April 1985, on the occasion of the inauguration of the academic year.

65. Ibid.

66. Quoted in *Heritage Foundation Backgrounder,* October 1980.

67. "Nicaragua: The Challenge of Reconstruction," a report by the International Bank for Reconstruction and Development (IBRD-World Bank), Washington, D.C., 1981.

68. Credits through the bank's normal channels are approved by a system in which votes are in proportion to each country's contribution to the bank's revenues. The U.S. contribution is 35 percent of the total, and the United States can therefore exercise veto power (approvals need a two-thirds majority). Certain loans, however, are channeled through a special "window" in which each member country has one vote and decisions are by simple majority.

69. See E.V.K. Fitzgerald, "Una Evaluación del Costo Económico de la Agresión del Gobierno Estadounidense contra el Pueblo de Nicaragua," a presentation to the Latin American Studies Association, Alburquerque, New Mexico, April 1985. At the time Fitzgerald was an economic adviser to the Nicaraguan government. The report served as the base document for Managua's exposition of the socioeconomic effects of the war before the World Court in September and October 1985, entitled "Evidencias del Gobierno de Nicaragua a la Corte Internacional de Justícia," Nicaraguan Secretariat of Planning and Budget.

70. These figures are rounded approximations, taken from the 1984–85 bulletin of the Ministry of Foreign Commerce.

71. Agro and agro-industrial installations, ranging from slaughterhouses, sugar mills, coffee-processing plants, cotton harvesters, to fumigation airplanes rely nearly completely on U.S. makes and technology. Similarly, most secondary production, including the chemical, textiles, pharmaceutical, metalurgic, plastics, and food-processing industries, as well as petroleum refining, construction, and mining equipment, saw mills, and the country's fishing fleet, are heavily dependent on the United States. Finally, the trade and service sectors suffer similar dependence: sewer and communications systems, for example, were installed by U.S. companies, the country's air fleet was 90 percent American, as was 40 percent of the public bus fleet. These statistics were provided to ANN by the Nicaraguan government's Secretariat of Planning and Budget and the Ministry of Foreign Commerce. See William I. Robinson, "Nicaragua: Embargo Comercial Norteamericano Acelerará Transformación Industrial-Tecnologica del País?" and "El Embargo y el Comercio Exterior: La Producción y los Servicios," ANN Special News Service, June 1985.

72. Within one week of the embargo, the first shipment of Nacaraguan bananas, previously entirely sold to the United States, departed from Corinto for Belgium and other Western European ports. The evening before, Agricultural Minister Jaime Wheelock had announced that new markets for sugar, meat, and seafoods (all formerly exported to the United States) would be opened in the following days. ANN dispatch, Managua, 7 May 1985.

73. See William I. Robinson, "Se Profundiza la Crisis del Comercio Regional," *Pensamiento Propio* (May 1985).

74. The threat was announced by the FDN's Edgar Chamorro on *"Radio 15 de Septiembre"*; see *La Tribuna* (Tegucigalpa), 30 September 1983.

75. The *New York Times* first reported the manual's publication in its 5 June 1983 edition. The manual was later translated into English and published by Grove Press (New York) in 1984.

76. Between 1982 and 1985, the country's export earnings averaged $400 million per annum, according to the Ministry of Foreign Commerce. In 1984, the GDP was calculated at approximately $2.35 billion by the Ministry of Planning.

77. See, for instance, "Costos Directos e Indirectos de la Agresión a Nicaragua, 1980–1984," table compiled by the INIES/CRIES Data Bank, Managua. The Data Bank estimated more than $3 billion in direct and indirect losses.

78. "Notas Para el Estudio Económico de America Latina y el Caribe, 1984, Nicaragua," ECLA, dated 15 July 1985. The section is titled "Effects of the Military Seige on the Nicaraguan Economy."

79. These figures were given by Minister of Industry Emilio Baltodano during a symposium on the country's economic crisis, Managua, 6 March 1985. See William I. Robinson, "Nicaragua: La Defensa, Eje del Programa Económico 1985," ANN Special News Service, March 1985.

80. These figures were given by the Minister of Foreign Cooperation and FSLN National Directorate member Comandante Henry Ruiz to *Barricada*, 13 March 1986.

81. For these statistics, see "48 Meses de Agresión Extranjera," a report by the Nicaraguan Institute for Welfare and Social Security (INSSBI), Managua, December 1984. See also Fitzgerald, "Una Evaluacion."

82. "Nicaraguan Sanctions: Sandinistas' Responsibility for Their Economic Failures," NSC memorandum, 18 May 1985, quoted in *Envío*, "A Survival Economy," October 1985.

6. Casting Long Shadows

1. Robert H. Kupperman and William J. Taylor, Jr., "Low-Intensity Conflict: The Strategic Challenge," in *American Defense Annual 1985–1986* (Lexington, MA. Lexington Books, 1986), pp. 209–210; emphasis in original.

2. Col. John D. Waghelstein, "Low-Intensity Conflict in the Post-Vietnam Period," transcription of a talk delivered to the American Enterprise Institute, 17 January 1985.

3. *Mandate II* (see chap. 1, n. 16), p. 320; emphasis ours.

4. The GAO report was cited in *The National Reporter* (Winter 1985).

5. *Washington Post*, 22 July 1983.

6. See, among others, *Covert Action Information Bulletin* (Fall 1984).

7. *Washington Post*, 31 July 1983.

8. "Military officers who previously participated in training exercises in Europe, South Korea, Southwest Asia and Central America," stated a Government Accounting Office (GAO) report, "told us that the standard practice is to leave nothing behind at the end of an exercise." Parts of the report, including this quote, were reproduced in *The National Reporter* (Winter 1985).

9. Researchers from the Centro de Documentación de Honduras, Tegucigalpa, spent several months investigating this supply network. In June 1985, they released a preliminary report, without title, on their initial findings, complete with a detailed map. The essential aspects of the report were reproduced in *Barricada*, 10 July 1985.

10. *New York Times*, 4 June 1985.

11. For information on "Carrot Top," see Brian Barger, "How the U.S. Spies on Central America," *Mother Jones* (June 1984). Among Barger's sources was an aide to Democratic Senator James Sasser, from Tennessee, who visited the site on a congressional fact-finding mission.

12. In June 1985 the Sandinista Coast Guard discovered and deactivated one of these buoys in the Atlantic Coast port of El Bluff. Other types of espionage equipment have been dropped by aircraft into fields and forests in the interior of the country, according to the Nicaraguan Ministry of Defense.

13. See Alan Nairn, "Endgame," *NACLA Report on the Americas* (May/June 1984), p. 44. See also *Covert Action Information Bulletin* (Winter 1984), "Fort Huachuca Buildup: War Technology in the Desert," for a lengthy, technical description of the advanced technology being developed by the U.S. armed forces and applied in Central America.

14. *Washington Post*, 9 February 1985.

15. *New York Times*, 8 June 1984. For further information, see "America's Secret Soldiers: The Buildup of U.S. Special Operations Forces," *Defense Monitor*, 14, no. 2, and *The Nation*, 7–14 July 1984.

16. The Knight-Ridder syndicated news service first broke the story of these operations in 1984, although they had begun years earlier. The major media networks quickly picked it up and expanded the investigation. "Families: U.S. Unit Has Covert Role," Miami Herald, 16 December 1984.

17. Ibid.

18. Ibid.

19. Ibid. The Pentagon official asked not to be identified.

20. Ibid.

21. U.S. Army, *Psychological Operations Techniques and Procedures*, Field Manual FM 33-5 (Washington, D.C.: Department of the Army, 1966).

22. See *New York Times* and *Washington Post*, 7 and 8 November, for developments at that time.

23. *New York Times*, 30 March 1985.

24. *Miami Herald*, 24 October 1982.

25. Cruz told this to John Gerassi, quoted in "Pluralism vs. Centralism in Nicaragua: The Sandinistas Under Attack," paper presented to the annual meeting of the International Studies Association, Washington D.C., 5–9 March 1985.

26. *Barricada*, 9 November 1984.

27. *New York Times*, 30 March 1985.

28. Interview with the authors, Managua, 8 May 1986.

29. *Mandate II*, page 287.

30. Dickey, *With the Contras*, 167–171.

31. See "Feverish Overthrow Plan Builds Towards Climax," *Covert Action Information Bulletin* (Fall 1984).

32. Much of the data for this section comes from a study by communications specialist Howard Frederic entitled "Radio Warfare Against Nicaragua." Sections of his study were reproduced, along with additional information and commentary, by *Barricada*, 11 November 1985.

33. Frederic, *Barricada*, 11 November 1985.

34. Worldwide disinformation is conducted using methods which range from placing operatives as undercover agents in the established media, to bribing local journalists, to outright ownership of certain media, to employing "friendly assets"—journalists who "lend themselves" to receive "special information" provided by the agency. See "CIA, the Press, and Central America," *Covert Action Information Bulletin* (Spring 1984).

35. See "Profesionales de la Misinformación," ANN Special News Service, Washington, November 1985.

36. Chamorro gave this information in his testimony to the World Court in September 1985. See *Barricada Internacional, 26 September 1985.*

37. See, for instance, reports in *Barricada* by Costa Rican researchers on that country's media, 19 June 1985.

38. *El Nuevo Diario*, 18 January 1986.

39. See AFP, 17 January 1986.
40. See, for instance, *La Nación* and *La Republica* (San José), 7 August 1984.
41. Report prepared by the Senate Special Subcommittee on Work and Social Welfare, May 1969, quoted in Leonel Urbano, "La Guerra Biologica: Otro Crimen Contra Nicaragua?" *Barricada*, 14 October 1985.
42. *Barricada*, 27 April 1984; *El Nuevo Diario*, 27 April 1984.
43. See *Envío* (May 1984).
44. See "Guerra Bacteriológica: ¿Ciencia Ficción?" a study by Heinz Dietrich published in *Pensamiento Propio* (October 1985).
45. Dietrich (in ibid.) notes that in 1966 the CIA experimented in the New York City subways with photographic camera ejection of infectious life forms to determine if such methods provoke suspicion among unknowing civilians. For extensive and startling documented research on CIA and DOD biological and chemical warfare activities, see John Marks, *The Search for the Manchurian Candidate: The CIA and Mind Control* (New York: Times Books, 1979).
46. For details see Hondupress dispatch, 10 February 1986, and ACAN-EFE, 24 February 1986.
47. The 26 February 1986 statement by the U.S. embassy in Tegucigalpa was quoted by AP in a Tegucigalpa dispatch that same day.
48. "The Role of Security Assistance in the Conflict Ongoing in the Caribbean Basin Today: Prevention—Deterrence—Counteraction," internal SOUTHCOM document, Spring 1983. Lieutenant Colonel Caldon is chief of the Policy and Strategy Divisions, Plans, Policy, and Political Military Affairs Directorate (J-5), headquarters, United States Southern Command.
49. For more on this, see Deborah Barry, "Los Conflictos de Baja Intensidad," in *Cuadernos de Pensamiento Propio*, a publication of the Coordinadora Regional de Investigaciones Económicas y Sociales (CRIES) (Managua: January 1986), p. 9.
50. Jorge C. Vargas, "La Militarización y la Reestructuración Nacional en Costa Rica," in *Centroamérica: La Guerra de Baja Intensidad* (Managua: CRIES, 1986), p. 103.
51. These statistics are taken from "U.S. Military Activities in Honduras," a pamphlet produced by the U.S. embassy in Tegucigalpa and given to the authors in July 1985 by embassy spokesman Arthur Skoop.
52. *New York Times*, 1 July 1984.
53. Said by Deputy Assistant Secretary of Defense Noel Koch in *Armed Forces Journal International* (May 1985).
54. The Committee of Santa Fe, Council for Interamerican Security, *A New Inter-American Policy for the Eighties* (New Mexico, 1980), pp. 33 and 52.
55. Created in 1961 by the Kennedy administration, this organization's purpose, according to its current director, Loret Miller Ruppe, is to "utilize volunteers to safeguard United States interests abroad." This was cited in ALASEI Special Service, Tegucigalpa, February 1986.
56. See investigations carried out in the Honduran departments of El Paraíso and Olancho, published in *Excelsior*, 1 April 1986.

57. Vargas, "La Militarización," p. 103. We are indebted to Vargas for his section. In addition, see Jorge Vargas and Miguel Gutiérrez, "Costa Rica es el Nombre del Juego," unpublished manuscript, November 1985.
58. The country's internal economic crisis cannot be downplayed. Within ruling circles, alternative strategies and interests compete on how to resolve this crisis, and the far-reaching effect it has at every level of society. Nevertheless, we assert that the militarization process overrides the issue of the economic crisis, and in fact has come to shape the alternative strategies and positions regarding the latter.
59. *Nacla Report on the Americas* (March/April 1984).
60. During the UN General Assembly debates on the resolution condemning the Grenada invasion, Volio had ordered the diplomatic staff at the United Nations to cast a negative vote. But the staff overrode his orders, voting in favor of the resolution, after getting the go-ahead from Monge. Embarrassed by his defeat, Volio resigned on November 13.
61. "Costa Rican Foreign Policy Crisis Erupts," APIA news service, San José, 22 November 1983.
62. Monge responded by accusing the IMF of "destabilizing Costa Rican democracy." The IMF and AID claimed that Costa Rica had failed to comply with the terms of the loans. For more information on this issue, see *NACLA Report on the Americas* (March/April 1984); White, *The Morass*, p. 224.
63. *Washington Post* (national weekly edition), April 1984.
64. Vargas and Gutiérrez, "Costa Rica," pp. 61–65.
65. See *La Nación* and *La Repulica*, 19 July 1984, for details on the ultimatum.
66. *La Nación*, 20 August 1984.
67. Vargas and Gutierrez, "Costa Rica," p. 78.
68. For more information on the militarization of Costa Rica, see "Costa Rica: Modernizing the Non-Army," *NACLA Report on the Americas* (March/April 1984).
69. Among other sources for the data on the militarization process, see Vargas, "La Militarización," the *NACLA* report on Costa Rica, and "Invasion: A Guide to the U.S. Military Presence in Central America," NARMIC (Philadelphia, May 1985).
70. The program's cost was over $100 million, much of which was financed by the United States. Israel also participated.
71. The story initially surfaced in the *Tico Times*, San José, 26 April. *Tico Times* reporter Kathy McHugh's subsequent reports were reproduced in *Barricada*, 7 and 11 June 1985.
72. See, among others, AP cable, 3 July 1985, datelined San José, for detials on the mercenaries' testimony.
73. "Costa Rica's U.S.-Funded 'Freeway to Nowhere,'" Dean Metcalf, Pacific News Service, 15 January 1986.
74. Ibid.
75. For all of this, see *La Nación* and *La República*, 31 May–15 June, as well as *Barricada* and *El Nuevo Diario* for the same dates.

76. This was reported by the Costa Rican opposition Popular Vanguard party, which published its own investigative report of the incident, reproduced in part in *El Nuevo Diario,* 31 July 1985.

77. Nicaragua made public a radio conversation between Col. Vidal, Civil Guard chief in the northern region, and a Guard member which revealed that Pastora's right-hand man, Ernesto "Tito" Chamorro, had told the Civil Guard on the night of the 30th that an EPS detachment had entered Costa Rican territory. The next morning the ARDE official proceeded to lead the patrol to the zone of Las Crucitas, where it was ambushed. Just a day before the attack, San José security forces had captured five soldiers they claimed were Sandinistas, and then hours later had to explain that there had been a "mix up," and that those under arrest were actually members of ARDE disguised as EPS troops. Later various Civil Guard members admitted that there was no way to know who had fired since the attack came from a concealed area some 800 yards away; others revealed that Colonel Vidal had ordered the patrol to remove emblems from their uniforms identifying them as Costa Rican security forces. For these details, see *La República,* 1 June 1985.

78. Defense and State Department Background Paper, July 1984, cited in the *New York Times,* 10 February 1985.

79. One comprehensive presentation of the U.S. argument is "Background Paper: The Nicaraguan Military Buildup and Its Support for Insurrection in Central America," Departments of Defense and State, July 1984. See also "Background Paper: The Soviet-Cuban Connection," Departments of Defense and State, March 1985.

80. Department of Defense figures, cited in "Invasion: A Guide to the U.S. Military Presence in Central America," NARMIC (Philadelphia, May 1985).

81. See International Institute of Strategic Studies, Stockholm, 1983–84 and 1984–85 reports.

82. Departments of Defense and State, "Background Paper," March 1985.

83. Congressional testimony given on 21 September 1982 by Lt. Col. John H. Buchanan, USMC, ret.

84. One of the most comprehensive studies was done by retired U.S. Army Lt. Col. Edward L. King in April 1985, "Analysis of the Military Situation in Nicaragua." King gathered the material for his report on several visits to Central America, where he went as part of several U.S. congressional fact-finding missions. King had established contacts with many of the region's military leaders during his tenure as liaison officer for the chairman of the Joint Chiefs of Staff and the U.S. delegation to the Inter-American Defense Board of the OAS.

85. Ibid.

86. *Wall Street Journal,* 3 April 1985 (retranslated from the Spanish).

87. Cited in *Washington Post,* 22 July 1983. The official was described as high ranking and had asked to remain anonymous.

7. The Internal Front

1. Tomás Borge, speech on the occasion of the fifth anniversary of the Ministry of the Interior (MINT), *El Nuevo Diario*, 5 August 1985.
2. Interview with State Security chief Lenin Cerna, *Soberanía* (Managua), July 1985.
3. Parts of this recorded talk were published in ANN dispatches, datelined New York and Managua, 19 March 1985.
4. Speech given by Secretary of State George Shultz in Indianapolis, 22 April 1985.
5. Department of the Army, *U.S. Psychological Operations Field Manual, 33-1* (Washington D.C.: Department of the Army, 31 August 1979), p. H-3.
6. Jaime Wheelock, *El Gran Desafío* (Managua: Editorial Nueva Nicaragua, 1983), p. 26.
7. The FAO was formed in April 1978, representing the by-then radicalizing anti-Somocista bourgeoisie. The FSLN kept a foot in the coalition through Sergio Ramírez in order to accelerate this radicalization. But with the formation of the Patriotic National Front (FPN) in early February, a new cross-class national front under FSLN leadership, the Sandinistas withdrew from the FAO and hastened its collapse. The FAO's predecessor was UDEL, formed in 1974 when differences were first emerging with Somoza.
8. Violetta Barrios de Chamorro, the widow of Pedro Joaquín Chamorro, had been appointed along with Robelo as the two bourgeois representatives to the first five-member government junta. She claimed that her resignation was "strictly for health reasons."
9. Cited in *Envío*, September 1984.
10. For various accounts, see *La Prensa, Barricada, El Nuevo Diario*, 17–20 November 1980. See also Sergio Ramírez, "Los Sobrevivientes del Naufragio" (Managua: Nicaraguan Association of Social Scientists, 1982).
11. "U.S. Policy and the Marxist Threat to Central America," Heritage Foundation, *Backgrounder 128*, Washington, D.C., 15 October 1980. It urged "vigorous support for the democratic sectors: The free labor unions, the church, the private sector, the independent political parties, the free press, and those who truly defend human rights."
12. See AP and AFP dispatches, datelined Washington, 14 April 1985, and *La Nación*, 25 August 1985.
13. In 1984, the Conservatives officially split into what is today the PCN and the Democratic Conservative party (PCD), which has distanced itself from the counterrevolutionary program and is currently the second political force in the National Assembly.
14. Militant and revolutionary trade unions did operate, but were subject to permanent repression and were generally forced to organize underground. For a detailed account of Nicaragua's labor history, see Carlos Pérez Bermúdez and Onofre Guevara López, *El Movimiento Obrero en Nicaragua* (Managua: Editorial El Amanecer, 1985).
15. Ministry of Labor, *1983 Report* (Managua: Center for Labor Studies, 1983).

16. Quoted in Roger Burbach, "Central America: End of U.S. Hegemony," *Monthly Review* (January 1982).
17. The authors were present during the "freedom march." See also *Barricada*, 11 January 1984.
18. *La Prensa*, 29 April 1985.
19. These parties are the leftist Popular Action Movement, Socialist, Communist; and the center to rightist Democratic Conservative, Liberal Independent, and Popular Social Christian. The social base of the first three are small sectors of the working class and intelligentsia, while the latter three have staked out bases within the petty bourgeoisie and limited sectors of the peasantry in urban peripheries. Nicaragua's skewed class structure, a product of underdevelopment and foreign dependence, includes a huge informal sector and a large number of small commodity producers (self-employed artisans). The opposition parties to the right of the FSLN are basically expressions of the opposition petty bourgeoisie, led by professionals (lawyers, doctors, middle-level traders), along with a scattering of individual members of the bourgeoisie.
20. Dora María Téllez, interview with authors, Managua, 16 May 1986.
21. Since its founding in 1926, *La Prensa* has been virtually synomonous with its majority owners, the Chamorro family—one of Nicaragua's best-known oligarchic families and the nucleus of the Conservative party opposition to Somoza.
22. "C.I.A. Psychological Warfare Operations: Case Studies in Chile, Jamaica, and Nicaragua," *Science for the People* (January/February 1982).
23. The IAPA is a grouping of North and South American publishing barons, under the influence of the CIA. The anticommunist association has campaigned against revolutionary and progressive movements in Latin America since the Cuban Revolution in 1959.
24. Fenell's study was published in *Barricada*, 21 June 1984.
25. See n.3 above.
26. Department of the Army, *U.S. Psychological Operations Field Manual*, pp. 1–7.
27. Ralph McGhee, "Foreign Policy by Forgery," *Nation*, 11 April 1981.
28. K. Patecek, *Nicaragua: A Revolution Against the Church?* (Washington, D.C.: Institute for Religion and Democracy, 1981).
29. Authors' interview with Sergio Ramírez, Managua, 26 April 1986.
30. AP cable, dateline Madrid, 26 June 1985.
31. *La Prensa*, 14 June 1985.
32. For details of these last-minute efforts, see Shirley Christian, *Nicaragua: Revolution in the Family* (New York, Random House, 1985), pp. 98–118, particularly p. 111 for the efforts in Caracas.
33. Some observers argue that the church hierarchy has its own "independent" interests that merely converge with those of the U.S. counterrevolution. This argument notes, correctly, that for five centuries, the church exercised a paternalistic, ideological authority over the masses from which it derived its influence and special "notch" in Nicaraguan society, and that now it feels this traditional paternalism is threatened by the revolution. But the

character of a social institution with relation to the war is determined not by the individual consciousness of those in it, such as Obando y Bravo, but by the role it objectively plays in the war and the real historic, material circumstances which propel it into that role. The above argument obscures the fact that the *source* for the hierarchy's traditional paternalistic authority is class privilege. In the end the hierarchy's contradiction with the revolution boils down to a *class contradiction,* irrespective of whether individual hierarchy members *consider themselves* FDN members, "spiritual leaders," or "neutral nonpartisans."

34. *Envío* (September 1984).
35. This was reported by the Canadian journalist Pete Bertle, who traveled with the FDN, in the *Toronto Sun,* February 1985, cited in *Congressional Record,* House of Representatives, Washington D.C., 24 October 1985.
36. ANN News Agency telephone interview with Edgar Chamorro in Miami; see dispatch datelined Managua, 29 September 1986.
37. *The CIA's Nicaragua Manual: Psychological Operations in Guerrilla Warfare* (New York: Random House, 1985), p. 62.
38. Ana María Ezcurra, *Agresión Ideológica contra la Revolución Sandinista* (Mexico: Ediciones Nuevomar, 1983), p. 68.
39. Ibid., p. 68.
40. Ibid., p. 69.
41. Committee of Santa Fe, "A New Inter-American Policy for the Eighties," Council for Interamerican Security, Santa Fe, New Mexico, May 1980, p. 20.
42. For an in-depth study of the U.S.-Vatican campaign, see Ana María Ezcurra, *El Vaticano y la Administración Reagan* (Mexico: Ediciones Nuevomar, 1984).
43. See full reproduction of the pope's speech in *La Prensa,* 5 March 1983.
44. *Barricada,* 6 March 1983.
45. This passage was reproduced in *Envío* (December 1983).
46. *Il Manifesto,* 25 November 1984.
47. They are: Foreign Minister Miguel D'Escoto, Minister of Culture Ernesto Cardenal, Minister of Education Fernando Cardenal, and Ambassador to the Organization of American States Edgard Parrales.
48. From "A Letter to My Friends," *Barricada,* 11 December 1984.
49. From the original interview with *Pensamiento Propio,* May 1985, segments of which were published in the July issue of the magazine.
50. This was announced in a 30 September 1981 communiqué released by the U.S. embassy in Managua and signed by AID representative Gerald R. Wein and embassy official Roger Gamble.
51. Jay Peterzell, *Reagan's Secret Wars* (Washington D.C.: Center for National Security Studies, 1984), p. 75.
52. Tom Barry, Beth Wood, and Deb Preusch, *Dollars and Dictators: A Guide to Central America* (Albuquerque: The Resource Center, 1982), p. 90.
53. U.S. Army, *Guide for the Planning of Counterinsurgency* (Washington, D.C.: Department of the Army, 1975), pp. 26–27.
54. Hearings Before a Subcommittee of the Committee on Appropriations,

House of Representatives, Foreign Assistance and Related Programs Appropriations for 1982, part 5, p. 83.

55. The figure comes from Ezcurra, *El Vaticano y la Administracción Reagan*, p. 51, which cites Managua Archdiocese documents, CRS reports, among others.

56. Ibid., p. 51.

57. See Ezcurra, *El Vaticano y la Administración Reagan*, pp. 50–67.

58. The memorandum was simultaneously published in the *National Catholic Reporter* and the Mexican daily *Uno Más Uno* on July 22. The W. R. Grace Company is one of the oldest with operations in the Western hemisphere, with strong interests in the Caribbean Basin region.

59. ANN news cable, dateline New York, 23 July 1984.

60. Not unexpectedly, Obando y Bravo insisted in Managua that the W.R. Grace affair had been concocted by the Sandinistas "to persecute the church." See *La Prensa*, 30 July 1984. J. Peter Grace himself affirmed, at a New York press conference on August 2, the authenticity of the memorandum, and announced that the Archbishop's request had been granted. He said that the donations were "effective arms against communism" in Nicaragua (*Barricada*, 3 August 1984).

61. The IRD launched an anti-Sandinista campaign on that same day "in solidarity with the bishops and in protest over government repression of the Catholic Church." IRD press release, Washington, 6 July 1984.

62. J. Peter Grace was a founder of the AIFLD and led the organization for many years. The AIFLD-CIA connection is well documented. See, for example, William Bollinger, *The AFL-CIO in Latin America: Documents and Analysis on the American Institute for Free Labor Development (AIFLD)* (Los Angeles: Interamerican Research Center, May 1984); and Jack Scott, *Yankee Unions, Go Home! How the AFL Helped the U.S. Build an Empire in Latin America* (Vancouver: New Star Books, 1978).

63. *Barricada*, 21 March 1985.

64. Following Congressional approval of $27 million in humanitarian aid for the contras, Arturo Cruz announced that part of it would be set aside for the CDN.Cruz made this announcement in San José; see *La Nación*, 25 August 1985.

65. See Sergio Ramírez's speech on the occasion of the twenty-fifth anniversary of the Nicaraguan School of Journalism, reprinted in *Barricada*, 17 May 1985.

66. *La Prensa*, 15 March 1981.

67. Quoted in *Barricada Internacional*, 12 March 1984.

68. The finer details and evidence surrounding the case, as well as numerous contradictions in Carballo's own declarations, suggest that the woman's version is the accurate one. See the various accounts in *La Prensa, Barricada*, and *El Nuevo Diario* from 13–16 August 1982. From the fourteenth on, *La Prensa* began a campaign to restore the tarnished image of Carballo, referring to him as "another suffering Christ." The priest would later be invited on a U.S. tour, and in 1983 Obando y Bravo consumated his

resucitation by naming Carballo Episcopal Vicarate and granting him the title of Monsignor.

69. The full text of Moncada's press conference was carried in *Barricada*, 7 June 1983.
70. Ibid.
71. Like a wounded giant lashing out, Washington's response to the cracking open and dismantling of its terror network was not only to deny everything—despite the photographs, films, tape recordings, and numerous other material evidence—but to retaliate by closing the six Nicaraguan consulates in the United States and expelling all twenty-one consular officials and their families. In an effort to make the criminals look like the victims, Reagan charged in Washington that "espionage activities" carried out by the Nicaraguan consulates was "an important factor" in their closing.
72. Interview with Lenin Cerna in *Soberanía* (Managua), July 1985.
73. Nicaraguan Bishops' Conference, Pastoral Letter, 29 August 1983.
74. All of the information in this section comes from Sánchez's four-hour testimony given to journalists on June 19. The authors attended the press conference, large portions of which were reproduced in *El Nuevo Diario* and *Barricada* on 21 June 1984.
75. Ibid.
76. *La Prensa*, 21 June 1984.

8. The Counterrevolution

1. Jaime Bengochea, interview with the authors, Managua, 4 June 1985.
2. *Washington Times*, 9 January 1986.
3. For a comprehensive analysis of the Nicaraguan elections, see William Robinson and Kent Norsworthy, "Nicaragua: Elections and U.S. Intervention," *Latin American Perspectives* 2, no. 45 (Spring 1985).
4. The full text of the *National Security Council Background Paper*, without date but prepared in advance of an 30 October 1984 NSD meeting, was obtained by the authors. The *Washington Post*, 6 November 1984, published the most important excerpts of the document, including the information listed here.
5. *La Prensa*, 26 December 1983.
6. *National Security Council Background Paper*.
7. Cruz, who is a trained economist, spent several years as a Somoza National Guard lieutenant after having graduated from the dictator's military academy. He was expelled from the Guard for participating in an officers' rebellion. He attended Georgetown University and in 1968 began a lengthy career with the Interamerican Development Bank (IDB). The Right hailed him as a prominent member of the opposition to Somoza, invoking his membership in the "Group of 12." When the group's members risked their lives by returning to the country, following the first insurrection in 1978,

Cruz was the only one who stayed behind, claiming in Washington that if he returned he would lose his IDB "retirement benefits."

8. Having lived thirty of his fifty-four years in the United States, Cruz was well known in Washington political circles and his ties to top contra leaders go way back. In 1982, he was instrumental in U.S. efforts to forge the ARDE coalition, acting as "moderator" in the San José meeting in which the contra alliance was created. In 1983 he and several other self-exiled figures formed the "Grupo Rescate" (Rescue Group), one of many fleeting political fronts for the counterrevolution.

9. *La Prensa*, 24 July 1984.

10. Ibid.

11. Ibid., 4 August 1984.

12. See *Barricada*, 15 October 1984. For a summary of reports by international observors to the electoral process and the voting itself, see *Pensamiento Propio* (December 1984).

13. See *El Nuevo Diario*, 26 October 1984, for a summary of denunciations by members of these parties with regard to U.S. embassy pressure.

14. For a detailed analysis of the electoral results, see "The Elections Reagan Would Like to Forget," *Envío* (April 1985). Also see "The Electoral Process in Nicaragua: Domestic and International Influences," report to the Latin American Studies Association (LASA), 19 November 1984. This report was written by a LASA delegation that observed the electoral process inside Nicaragua.

15. U.S. embassy bulletin, Managua, 4 March 1985.

16. *Barricada*, 17 May 1985.

17. Ibid., 11 April 1985.

18. Ramiro Gurdian, interview with authors, March 1985.

19. UPI and AFP wire service cables, datelined San José, 11 March 1985.

20. AP news cable, datelined Madrid, 26 June 1985.

21. Presidential news conference, Washington, D.C., 4 April 1985.

22. The three passed out a press release to journalists during the conference, titled "Declaración de la Unidad Nicaraguense Opositora (UNO)." The citations and information on the UNO program contained in the text are from the press release unless otherwise indicated.

23. Marta Zacasa (speaking from Washington, D.C.) telephone interview with authors, June 1985.

24. "Declaración de la Unidad Nicaraguense Opositora (UNO)."

25. On 3 July 1985 Calero delivered a speech to the Somocista community in Miami elaborating on the UNO program. The speech was reproduced by the FDN as a paid advertisement in the Tegucigalpa daily *El Heraldo*, 20 July 1985.

26. See ACAN-EFE dispatch, datelined Tegucigalpa, 10 February 1984, for interviews with FDN spokesmen on this issue.

27. UPI dispatch, datelined Washington, 29 January 1986; Shultz's statement retranslated from Spanish.

28. AP dispatch, datelined Madrid, 26 June 1985.

29. *New York Times*, 13 August 1985.

30. *Barricada*, interview with Julio Lopez, director of the FSLN's Foreign Relations Department, 5 December 1985.

31. A copy of the working document was attained by the authors. Parts of it were also published in the U.S. press. See *New York Times* and *Washington Post*, 7 and 8 September 1985. Abrams later claimed it was a draft that was not actually used during the session.

32. For example, on the eve of one Contadora meeting in February 1984 in Bogotá, Colombia, the FDN published in that country's largest newspaper, *El Tiempo*, a "peace plan" which basically called for the Sandinistas to set up a provisional government in which power would be shared with the Somocistas. In the meeting, the Tegucigalpa Bloc representatives made similar proposals. See AFP dispatches, datelined Bogotá, 27 February 1984, 28 February 1984.

33. The call for "internal reconciliation," included in the treaty's section on "Commitments Regarding National Reconciliation," was a clear violation of Nicaragua's national sovereignty. Nevertheless, the treaty also stated that national reconciliation should be carried out "in accordance with the laws of each country," which left the "national reconciliation" clause somewhat ambiguous and open to interpretation. Therefore, how it would be translated into practice if the treaty were signed would be determined not so much by the technicalities of the treaty but by real power relations. It was precisely the U.S. intention to build up the counterrevolution's strength so that the treaty would translate into a Sandinista commitment to "reconciliation" with UNO.

34. Statement by Calero read on Radio 15 de Septiembre, 24 April 1985.

35. The selection of Obando y Bravo caused consternation among other Central American archbishops, since several came before him in terms of seniority and qualifications. Moreover, Obando did not appear in the first list of candidates drawn up by the Vatican. See Alfonso Dubois, "El Proyecto Tras el Cardenal," *Pensamiento Propio* (March 1986).

36. *National Security Council Background Paper.*

37. Authors' interview with Vice-president Sergio Ramírez, Managua, 26 April 1986.

38. *Miami Herald*, 16 June 1986.

39. These details were reported by *Barricada* journalist Guillermo Cortes, following an investigative trip to Honduras, where he interviewed numerous FDN members. See *Barricada*, 8 April 1986.

40. The publication *Amanecer*, a religious Managua monthly identified with the "popular church," analyzed Obando y Bravo's whirlwind tours. See "La Gira de Monseñor Obando," in the December 1985 issue.

41. Philip Agee, "The CIA's Blueprint for Nicaragua," *Covert Action Information Bulletin* (October 1979).

42. Speech on the occasion of the fourth anniversary of Revolutionary Vigilance, *Barricada*, 28 April 1985.

43. *The CIA's Nicaragua Manual*, p. 81.

44. Ibid., p. 80.
45. René Fernández, interview with authors, Tegucigalpa, 19 July 1985.
46. *El Nuevo Diario*, 4 July 1985.
47. On 9 August 1985 the Ministry of the Interior presented the captured ringleaders (along with the confiscated weapons and Calero's letter to Bolaños) to journalists in Managua. For a full account of the press conference, see *Barricada*, 10 August 1985.
48. UPI dispatch, datelined Tegucigalpa, 30 April 1984.
49. *Barricada*, 6 December 1985.
50. Ibid., 29 November 1986.
51. *Washington Times*, 10 January 1986.
52. See *Barricada*, 11 January 1986.
53. *The CIA's Nicaragua Manual*, p. 84.
54. Dora María Téllez, interview with authors, Managua, 16 May 1986.
55. Authors' interview, Managua, 4 June 1985.

9. Total Defense: The Military Theater

1. Humberto Ortega, interview with authors, Managua, 8 May 1986.
2. Sergio Ramírez, interview with authors, Managua, 26 April 1986.
3. Tomás Borge, speech on the occasion of the fifth anniversary of the CDS, Managua, 26 April 1985.
4. Humberto Ortega, interview with *Washington Post*. The full text of the interview (in the original Spanish) was published by the Defense Ministry in *Barricada*, 10 October 1985.
5. Humberto Ortega, interview with authors, Managua, 8 May 1986.
6. In 1984 the Nicaraguan government established the Supreme Council for Defense of the Homeland (presided over by President Ortega and including representatives from the Defense Ministry, the Interior Ministry, the Agrarian Reform Ministry, the Health and Education Ministry, and the Foreign Ministry) to coordinate the defense effort at the national level.
7. Javier Carrión, interview with ANN, Managua, 17 August 1985.
8. Humberto Ortega, quoted in "El SMP: Un Deber, Un Compromiso, Una Oportunidad," special *Barricada* publication, 1984.
9. Javier Carrión, *Barricada Internacional* special supplement, "The Strategic Defeat of the Contras," November 1985.
10. Luis Carrión, speech to the Managua Regional Assembly of the FSLN, 20 November 1984.
11. Tomás Borge, interview with the Mexican bimonthly *Panorama*. See *Panorama* (October–November 1985).
12. Humberto Ortega, press conference, Managua, 7 February 1985. The full text of Ortega's presentation was reproduced in *Barricada*, 13 February 1985.
13. Edward L. King, *Analysis of the Military Situation in Nicaragua*, (Boston: Unitarian Universalist Service Committee, 1985).
14. King, *Analysis*.

15. Humberto Ortega, press conference, Managua, 26 December 1984.
16. Humberto Ortega, press conference, Managua, 7 February 1985.
17. *Washington Post* interview with Humberto Ortega. The full text of the interview (in the original Spanish) was published by the Defense Ministry in *Barricada*, 10 October 1985.
18. Ibid., 2 December 1985.
19. ANN news dispatch, datelined Managua, 30 June 1985.
20. *Barricada*, 27 December 1985.
21. Ibid., 7 April 1986.
22. Humberto Ortega, interview with authors, Managua, 8 May 1986.
23. Roberto Calderón, interview with ANN, Managua, 14 August 1985.
24. Ibid.
25. Dora María Téllez, interview with authors, Managua, 16 May 1986.
26. Ronald Reagan, speech to contra leaders, Washington, D.C., 25 March 1985. Cited in *Envío* (June 1985).
27. *Envío* (June 1985).
28. Luis Carrión, quoted in *Barricada*, 10 July 1985.
29. Ibid., 27 February 1986.
30. The document was intended for internal circulation among leaders and cadres of the ministry. It was supplied to the authors by MIDINRA officials.
31. *Dirección General de Reforma Agraria*, MIDINRA report; estimates made in October 1985.
32. This was announced by the defense minister in a 5 April 1986 speech in Chontales. See *Barricada*, 6 April 1986.
33. Luis Carrión, speech delivered at Central American University (UCA), Managua, 5 May 1986.
34. Ibid.
35. Dora María Téllez, interview with authors, Managua, 16 May 1986.
36. Jaime Wheelock, quoted in *Barricada*, 27 April 1986.
37. Anonymous MIDINRA official, interview with authors, Estelí, 15 November 1985.
38. Dora María Téllez, interview with authors, Managua, 16 May 1986.
39. By early 1986 the reincorporation of peasants in the agricultural frontier was so far advanced that these peasants were forming special irregular warfare batallions, called *cazadores* (hunters), made up virtually exclusively of the inhabitants from the heart of the agricultural frontier—people who had earlier collaborated with the contras, and who were intimately familiar with the terrain.
40. *Barricada*, 21 March 1986.
41. Javier Carrión, interview with ANN, Managua, 17 August 1985. Most of the details regarding "Plan Rebelión '85" are taken from this three-hour interview. As chief of operations, Carrión was one of the principal commanders on the EPS General Staff responsible for confronting the offensive.
42. José Angel Peralta, interview with ANN, Managua, 10 August 1985.
43. *Barricada*, 13 December 1985.

44. The journalist was the Canadian Pete Bertle. The article in which the quote appears, published in the *Toronto Sun* in February 1985, was read by Representative Newt Gingrich to the Congress; see *Congressional Record*, Washington, D.C., 24 October 1985.

45. Quoted in "Low-Intensity Conflict in the Post-Vietnam Period," transcript of an informal "conversation with Colonel Waghelstein" held at the American Enterprise Institute on 16 January 1985 and attended by Reagan administration officials and right-wing ideologues.

10. Total Defense: The Nonmilitary Theaters

1. "The View from Washington," a working paper presented for the "Chiefs of Mission Conference" in Panama City, September 8–10, 1985, of top Pentagon, State, NSC and CIA officials, and Central American/Contadora Ambassadors on the course of Central America policy. Stamped "Secret" and dated 4 September 1985, it was obtained by the authors and leaked to the U.S. press later that month. The administration later claimed it was merely a draft and not actually used during the meeting.

2. Alejandro Bendaña, executive secretary of the Nicaraguan Foreign Ministry, interview with authors, Managua, 13 May 1986.

3. Sergio Ramírez interview with authors, Managua, 26 April 1986.

4. *New York Times,* 12 November 1985.

5. Sergio Ramírez, interview with authors, Managua, 26 April 1986.

6. *Barricada,* 28 February 1986.

7. *Barricada* published the statistics for its own circulation. *El Nuevo Diario* foreign editor Mario Fulvio Espinoza gave us the figures for the newspaper, and *La Prensa* staff reporter Enrique García provided us with *La Pensa's* numbers. García's figures, however, are disputed by the government media office, which placed 1985 circulation at around 55,000. García claimed that, without censorship, the paper would sell over 100,000, since it would be more attractive to readers.

8. Jaime Wheelock, speech to Nicaraguan workers, 1 May 1984.

9. For a detailed account of these contra cells and the actions they were planning, see *Barricada,* 19 October 1985.

10. Dora Maria Téllez, interview with authors.

11. IPS dispatch, datelined New York, 21 January 1986.

12. For details of Vega's visit to the United States, see AP, UPI, and AFP, and ANN cables, datelined Washington, 11 March 1986.

13. *Washington Post,* 12 May 1986.

14. This was first reported by ANN, in a dispatch datelined Washington, D.C., 21 May 1986.

15. Germán Castellón, SMP recruit, interview with authors, Managua, 15 January 1986.

16. Daniel Ortega, speech marking the fiftieth anniversary of Sandino's death, Managua, 21 February 1984.

17. *Barricada*, 10 January 1985.
18. *Envío* (November 1985).
19. *Barricada*, 7 March 1986.
20. Tomás Borge, speech delivered at the Fourth Nicaraguan Social Sciences Congress, Managua, September 1985; quoted in *Barricada International*, 26 September 1985.
21. Quoted in "Autonomy: A Promise for All," special supplement to *Barricada Internacional* (October 1985).
22. Representatives elected to the National Assembly (the *national* legislative body) will be drawn from the membership of the regional assemblies in their respective autonomous territories.
23. National Autonomy Commission, *Principles and Policies for the Exercise of the Right to Autonomy by the Indigenous Peoples and Communities of the Atlantic Coast of Nicaragua* (Managua: National Autonomy Commission, 1985).
24. Quoted in *Envío* (March 1985).
25. Rivera's position demonstrated the difficulties imperialism faced in maintaining control over those it had brought into its project, particularly on the Atlantic Coast, where there *were* authentic demands which the counterrevolution had managed to hijack and bring under its banner.
26. *Pensamiento Propio* (June–July 1985).
27. Quoted in "The Atlantic Coast: War or Peace?", *Envío* (October 1985).
28. *Pensamiento Propio* (June–July 1985).
29. Quoted in "Autonomy: A Promise for All," special supplement to *Barricada Internacional* (October 1985).
30. Daniel Martínez, "Se va despejando el camino," *Pensamiento Propio* (April 1986).
31. Eich and Rincón, *The Contras*, 190. Such racism toward Nicaragua's indigenous peoples is typical of the FDN-ARDE and has contributed to Miskito defections from the counterrevolution.
32. For more information on the controversy surrounding Pantín's death, see: *Envío* (October 1985); *Pensamiento Propio* (April 1986).
33. *Guardian* (New York), 2 October 1985.
34. EFE and ANN dispatches, datelined Miami, 21 June 1985.
35. *Guardian* (New York), 2 October 1985.
36. Ibid.
37. Quoted in *Barricada*, 3 April 1986.
38. Quoted in ibid.
39. For more information on these developments, see: ANN dispatch, datelined Puerto Cabezas, 20 March 1986; *Barricada*, 20 March 1986.
40. The report was released in Washington, D.C., 11 April 1986, and portions were published in *Barricada*, 22 April 1986; the citation is retranslated from the Spanish. See: also *Philadelphia Inquirer*, 6 April 1986; *Boston Globe*, 7 April 1985. It should be noted that the counteroffensive was timed to coincide with congressional voting on contra aid.
41. *Barricada*, 19 May 1986.

42. Quoted in H. G. Versi, "El Drama de las Indigenas Miskitas del Atlantico," ANN Special News Service article, Managua (May 1986).
43. *Barricada*, 19 May 1984.
44. Julio Lopez, director of the FSLN's International Relations Department, quoted in *Barricada*, 5 December 1985.
45. Ibid., 12 November 1985.
46. Ibid., 5 December 1985.
47. Ibid., 7 August 1985.
48. *San Francisco Chronicle*, 2 December 1985.
49. For details, see EFE and ANN dispatches, datelined Washington, D.C., 10 February 1986.
50. Ibid.
51. For details of Reagan's charges and the full text of the Colombian government's response, see *La Prensa*, 5 January 1986.
52. *Barricada*, 20 March 1986.
53. *El Nuevo Diario*, 24 March 1986.
54. *Barricada*, 11 May 1986; emphasis in original.
55. Ibid., 8 June 1986.
56. "The View from Washington."
57. For the quote from the Salvadoran foreign minister, see ACAN-EFE dispatch, datelined San José, 11 June 1986; for further comments by Shultz and Tegucigalpa Bloc officials, see same dispatch and ANN dispatch, datelined New York, 11 June 1986.
58. Alejandro Bendaña, interview with authors, Managua, 13 May 1986.
59. Gustavo Ruiz, interview with authors, Jinotega, November 17, 1984.
60. *Barricada*, 11 March 1986.
61. At the same time it is important to note, as Dora María Téllez put it to us, "There are no revolutions without expectations. If the people didn't have expectations of great and dramatic changes in their lives they wouldn't have risen up. Expectations aren't bad; they are part of sustaining the revolution." The Sandinistas' error was in projecting the idea that such expectations could be rapidly satisfied. Téllez tacitly underscored this: "The problem is in the speed of the changes."
62. The "Message to the People," by the FSLN National Directorate was read on national television and radio on 8 February 1985 and published in *Barricada* and *El Nuevo Diario*, 9 February 1985.
63. Again, it is necessary to point out that in the period 1979–81 political power was *not* threatened in the same sense as it was from 1982 onward; on the other hand, immediate economic reactivation and initial reconstruction *was* the principal task. But the Sandinistas had continued from 1982 until 1985 with a mass economic line of unrealistic material achievement.
64. At the same time, the FSLN leadership, as well as mass organization and trade union activists, recognized that bureaucratic problems and mismanagement were aggravating the problems caused by the war, and encouraged popular criticism of these problems.
65. *Barricada*, 28 April 1985.

66. The nation's principal trade union federation, the Central Sandinista de Trabajadores (CST), which includes together over 80 percent of organized workers, was the driving force behind the adoption of the survival economy. The CST designed the various economic policies and pushed them on state authorities, much as UNAG had done with the 1985–86 agrarian policies.

67. For a more comprehensive discussion of the new economic policies see: William I. Robinson, "La Economía Nicaraguense a Seis Años," ANN Special News Service article, Managua (July 1985); "Un Proyecto Monetarista en Nicaragua?", *Pensamiento Propio* (April 1985).

68. For a summary of the late-1985 UNICEF report, see *Barricada*, 7 January 1986.

69. Sergio Ramírez, speech delivered at the National Auutonomous University of Nicaragua, 12 April 1985; published in *Barricada*, 18 April 1985.

11. Crisis in the Counterrevolution

1. ACAN-EFE news cable, datelined Tegucigalpa, 4 January 1984.

2. AP news cable, datelined Tegucigalpa, 22 June 1984.

3. Ibid., 13 June 1985.

4. *Barricada*, 20 January 1986.

5. Nicaraguan Ministry of Defense, *La Contrarevolución: Desarrollo y Consequencias*, (Managua: Centro de Comunicación Internacional, 1985).

6. Testimony given by Gonzalo Acuña Casco after turning himself in to Sandinista forces in August 1985. See *Barricada*, 5 August 1985.

7. For details on the press conference, which was presided over by Waldo Villalpango, UNHCR director in Honduras at that time, see ACAN-EFE and AP dispatches, datelined Tegucigalpa, 4 June 1986.

8. *Barricada*, 5 August 1985.

9. Quoted in ibid., 17 May 1985.

10. Ibid.

11. The document was published in a Tegucigalpa-based contra magazine, *Aca Centroamerica*, given to us by Leets Castillo. Magazine undated but contents suggest publication late 1984/early 1985.

12. For details on the internal FDN rebellion and its aftermath, see Guillermo Cortés, "Radiografia de la Corrupción Somocista," *Barricada*, 12 December 1985. See also *Aca Centroamerica;* Christopher Dickey, *With the Contras*, (New York: Simon & Schuster, 1985), pp. 245–51.

13. Ibid.

14. Ibid.

15. AFP, AP, and UPI dispatches, datelined Washington, D.C., 21 March 1985.

16. AP dispatch, datelined Washington, D.C., 6 December 1985.

17. Ibid.

18. *San Francisco Examiner,* 17 March 1986.
19. *Prensa Latina* dispatch, datelined Washington, D.C., 19 March 1986.
20. Reagan's speech was broadcast in its entirety on Nicaraguan national television on 18 March 1986 and published in *Barricada,* 19 March 1986. The citation is retranslated from the Spanish.
21. *Barricada,* 12 December 1985.
22. *Miami Herald,* 14 April 1986.
23. For details see the Tegucigalpa daily *El Tiempo,* 22 January 1986; ACAN-EFE dispatch, datelined Tegucigalpa, 22 January 1986; and *El Nuevo Diario,* 23 January 1986.
24. This was told to us by then-FDN field commander René Fernández in July 1985 in Tegucigalpa. Fernández had met with embassy officials earlier to express his own concern over FDN incompetence, and was assured that the embassy shared his views and would take action.
25. "The View from Washington."
26. For statements by administration officials, see *New York Times,* 12 November 1985; for reports on disagreements within UNO, see *New York Times,* 4 November 1985.
27. Ibid., 11 November 1985.
28. EFE dispatch, datelined Washington, 31 January 1986.
29. See AFP special report dispatch, datelined Miami, 6 May 1986, for this quote and further details.
30. Quoted in *Barricada,* 10 September 1985.
31. *Newsweek,* 29 April 1985.
32. For details of the Cuapa attack and its aftermath, see *Barricada,* 2–6 August 1985.
33. Ibid.
34. Roberto Calderón, interview with ANN, Managua, 14 August 1985.
35. *Envio* (March 1985).
36. Col. Joseph Stringham, a U.S. adviser in El Salvador, said in April 1984: "It's necessary to distinguish between the masses and the civilian population. . . . The masses are people who live in the zones of guerrilla influence and cannot be considered innocent. . . . Even if they are a defenseless population, the masses do not deserve the qualification of civilian and become military targets." Quoted in the Salvadoran monthly *Revista Centroamericana en la Mira* (May–June 1985).
37. *New York Times,* 4 November 1985.
38. Interview by *Barricada* special correspondent Guillermo Cortés with Edgar Chamorro in Miami; published in *Barricada,* 9 December 1985.
39. AFP dispatch, datelined Washington, D.C., 13 March 1986.
40. See among the numerous reports on the two-week meeting, *Miami Herald,* 1–16 May 1986.
41. This was reported by columnists Roland Evans and Robert Novak, *Washington Post,* 29 May 1986.
42. See *Miami Herald,* 26 June 1986.
43. See special report in *Miami Herald,* 12 June 1986, for these and related statistics on the extent of the Somocista occupation of southern Honduras.

44. *New York Times,* 27 November 1985.
45. See ibid., 27 November 1985, for first story in U.S. press on the plight of the coffee producers. See also *El Tiempo* for a series of reports between November 1985 and April 1986, most notably 29 January and 1 March.
46. See Honduran Human Rights Commission press release, dated 18 January 1986, reproduced by ANN on the same day.
47. AP dispatch, datelined Tegucigalpa, 24 March 1986; ANN dispatch, datelined Tegucigalpa, 25 March 1986.
48. ACAN-EFE, ANN, and DPA dispatches, 16 January 1986.
49. *Excelsior,* 19 March 1986.
50. ACAN-EFE dispatch, datelined San Pedro Sula, 2 April 1986.
51. For details see the special report in *El Tiempo,* 16 March 1986.
52. See ACAN-EFE dispatch, datelined Tegucigalpa, 17 March 1986.
53. This was reported by a U.S. analyst close to the congressmen who spoke with Zúñiga. See "Killing of Honduran Army Officer Linked to Testimony in U.S.," a special report by Denis Volman, *Christian Science Monitor,* 19 November 1985, for this and other details of the Zuñiga affair; see also Allan Frankovich, interview with authors, New York, 27 September 1985.
54. This was reported by Bruce Cameron, who had personally arranged Zúñiga's visit to Washington. He was at the time director of Americans for Democratic Action, a Washington lobbying group. See EFE dispatch, datelined Washington, 19 December 1985.
55. For the ABC mishap and Honduran government protests, see *New York Times,* 23 November 1985.
56. For details on "La Quinta Escuela," see *El Tiempo,* 31 October 1985.
57. See *New York Times,* 23 November 1985.
58. For full details on López's "resignation" and its aftermath, see Rodrigo Díaz, "La Caída del General López Reyes," HONDUPRESS Special Report, datelined Tegucigalpa, 5 February 1986.
59. Government communiqué released in Tegucigalpa, 24 March 1986.
60. Daniel Ortega, press conference, Managua, 28 March 1986.
61. For this quote, see AFP cable, datelined Washington, D.C., 30 March 1986; for further details of events at this time, see *Miami Herald,* 27–30 March 1986.
62. Ibid.
63. This was reported by a high-level Honduran military source to the ALASEI news agency, dispatch datelined Tegucigalpa, 13 April 1986.
64. AFP dispatch, datelined Tegucigalpa, 1 April 1986. The officer asked to remain anonymous.
65. *Washington Post,* 4 April 1986; retranslated from the Spanish.
66. Sergio Ramírez, interview with authors, Managua, 26 April 1986.
67. For one study on the contras' economic activity in Honduras, see the investigations carried out in Tegucigalpa by Guillermo Cortés, "Los Banqueros de la Contra," *Barricada,* 3 April 1986.
68. ANN Special Report, datelined Tegucigalpa, 23 November 1986.
69. Alejandro Bendaña, interview with authors, Managua, 13 May 1986.
70. Azcona opposed it from January to April, but then, following intense U.S.

pressure, caved in and in April traveled to Washington so that the White House could use him in its congressional lobbying.

71. The survey was carried out by the School of Journalism of the National Autonomous University of Honduras (UNAH); see AP dispatch, datelined Tegucigalpa, 18 April 1986.

72. See AFP cable, datelined San José, 17 March 1986.

12. David's Victory

1. Interview with *Pensamiento Propio* (June–July 1985).

2. See *Washington Post,* 9 March 1986, and Robert Cohen, "Estados Unidos en Guerra Mundial Contra Todas las Leyes," ANN Special News Service, Washington, D.C., May 1986.

3. Ibid.

4. See ibid., for details.

5. See ibid., 9 March 1986, and ibid. (national weekly edition), 31 March 1986.

6. By this we do not mean to ignore the struggle of the Philippine masses for democracy as the driving force behind the overthrow of Marcos, or to imply that the installation of the Aquino government was not a major democratic advance for the Philippine people. Rather, the United States was able to abandon its earlier practice of backing right-wing dictatorships even as popular revolutions were overthrowing them, and instead shifted its strategy in order to prevent revolution.

7. Weinberger's address was published as a Department of Defense press release, 14 January 1986.

8. Address before the National Committee on American Foreign Policy, New York City, 2 October 1985.

9. See Weinberger's address for the Pentagon's views on the role of direct U.S. military force in low-intensity conflict.

10. For these and other positions with regard to the debate on low-intensity conflict that began in the United States in 1986, see William Robinson and Kent Norsworthy, "Nicaragua: The Strategy of Counterrevolution," *Monthly Review* (December 1985); Michael Klare, "The New U.S. Strategic Doctrine," *The Nation,* 28 December 1985–4 January 1986; and Sarah Miles, "The Real War: Low-Intensity Conflict in Central America," *NACLA Report on the Americas* (April/May 1986), along with responses in subsequent issues.

11. For instance, this view was expressed to us by one high-level Nicaraguan Foreign Ministry official in May 1986.

12. For instance, see the widespread reports in the U.S. press in May 1986 on infighting within the administration and its private wing over the course of U.S. policy toward Nicaragua. The infighting was clearly not over different strategies, but rather over what tactics and approaches to emphasize, the

relation between diplomatic and military aggression, etc., within the same strategic framework.

13. Quoted in *U.S. News and World Report*, 7 April 1986.
14. *San Francisco Chronicle*, 2 December 1985.
15. The columnists were Rowland Evans and Robert Novak; see the Op-Ed page of the *Washington Post*, 14 May 1986 (retranslated from the Spanish).
16. Theodore H. Moran, "Reaching Beyond El Salvador with an Invasion and Occupation of Nicaragua," in *Central America: Anatomy of a Conflict*, ed. Robert S. Leiken (New York: Pergamon Press, 1984), pp. 166–71. Moran's scenario is drawn from three separate analyses by Pentagon analysts and consultants.
17. Joseph Cirincione and Leslie C. Hunter, "Military Threats to U.S. Security," in *Central America*, p. 181.
18. Quoted in *Miami Herald*, 1 July 1984.
19. Quoted in ibid., 15 April 1986.
20. This does not, however, rule out the possibility that political variables may alter to the point where there is again an effort to destroy the revolution. The United States can reconfigure its tactics and strategy in pursuit of new objectives, but it would without doubt pounce on the opportunity to secure its original objective—should it deem it within grasp.
21. The Reagan administration has invested tremendous political capital in pursuing the goal of obliterating Sandinismo. We therefore doubt that a shift from destroying Sandinismo to containing it could be fully consolidated until a new administration takes office.
22. *New York Times*, 30 June 1985.
23. In mid-1986 administration spokespeople acknowledged that efforts would be made to knock out key economic and military installations in Nicaragua. For details see *Miami Herald*, 27 June 1986.
24. If the United States were to break diplomatic relations with Nicaragua, it might also decide to extend diplomatic recognition to UNO. Some administration officials have proposed that the Nicaraguan model—building the diplomatic legitimacy of a counterrevolution, trying to have it occupy certain territorial zones, and then providing recognition—should be applied to Angola, Afghanistan, and other countries. This was recommended, for instance, by former U.S. Ambassador to Costa Rica Curtin Winsor. See "Saving Central America," *The New American*, 30 September 1985.
25. This development could bring about political realignments inside Nicaragua, whereby members of the internal reaction, believing that alignment with the counterrevolution is a futile undertaking, realize that it is more in their interests to seek an accommodation with the revolution—or throw in the towel and migrate to Miami.
26. The Germans were kidnapped in late May. Pressure from the international community, and finally the West German government, forced the United States to order FDN officers in Tegucigalpa to release the hostages. Shultz tried to claim that the German construction brigade was armed and had

been kidnapped from an EPS military base, a charge that brought ridicule from even the West German Foreign Ministry.

27. *Barricada*, 22 May 1986. According to EPS military intelligence, it was Bermúdez who gave the order, in early 1986, that the contra army should disregard its earlier strategy and focus on sabotage and terrorism against the civilian population.

28. For more details, see *Miami Herald*, 27 June 1986.

29. Sergio Ramírez, interview with authors, Managua, 8 May 1986.

30. See Economic Commission for Latin America (ECLA), *Balance Preliminar de la Economía Latinoamericana 1985*. The figures are: Costa Rica, −13.8 percent; El Salvador, −23.8 percent; Guatemala, −18.5 percent; Honduras, −13 percent; Nicaragua, −11.6 percent.

31. Ibid.

32. These include the removal of foreign bases and advisers; the cessation of international maneuvers on Nicaraguan territory; a commitment, with verification, to stop destabilizing Nicaragua's neighbors, among others.

33. Alejandro Bendaña, interview with authors, Managua, 13 May 1986.

34. Assistant Secretary of State for Inter-American Affairs Elliott Abrams used this term in January 1986 in reference to reaching a negotiated solution with Nicaragua. See *New York Times*, 3 January 1986.

35. The official was Julio López, director of the International Relations Department of the FSLN, in an interview with *Barricada*, 5 December 1985.

36. The phrase comes from a speech entitled "Terrorism and the Modern World," in which Shultz called for a permanent crusade against "terrorism" and justified National Security Decision Directive 138, approved several months earlier, which allowed for "pre-emptive" strikes and reprisals against "terrorists" aboard. See *New York Times*, 26 October 1984.

www.ingramcontent.com/pod-product-compliance
Ingram Content Group UK Ltd.
Pitfield, Milton Keynes, MK11 3LW, UK
UKHW040642280225
455688UK00003B/92